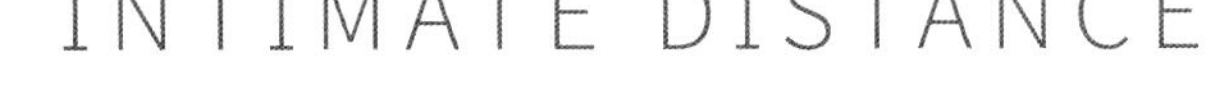
INTIMATE DISTANCE

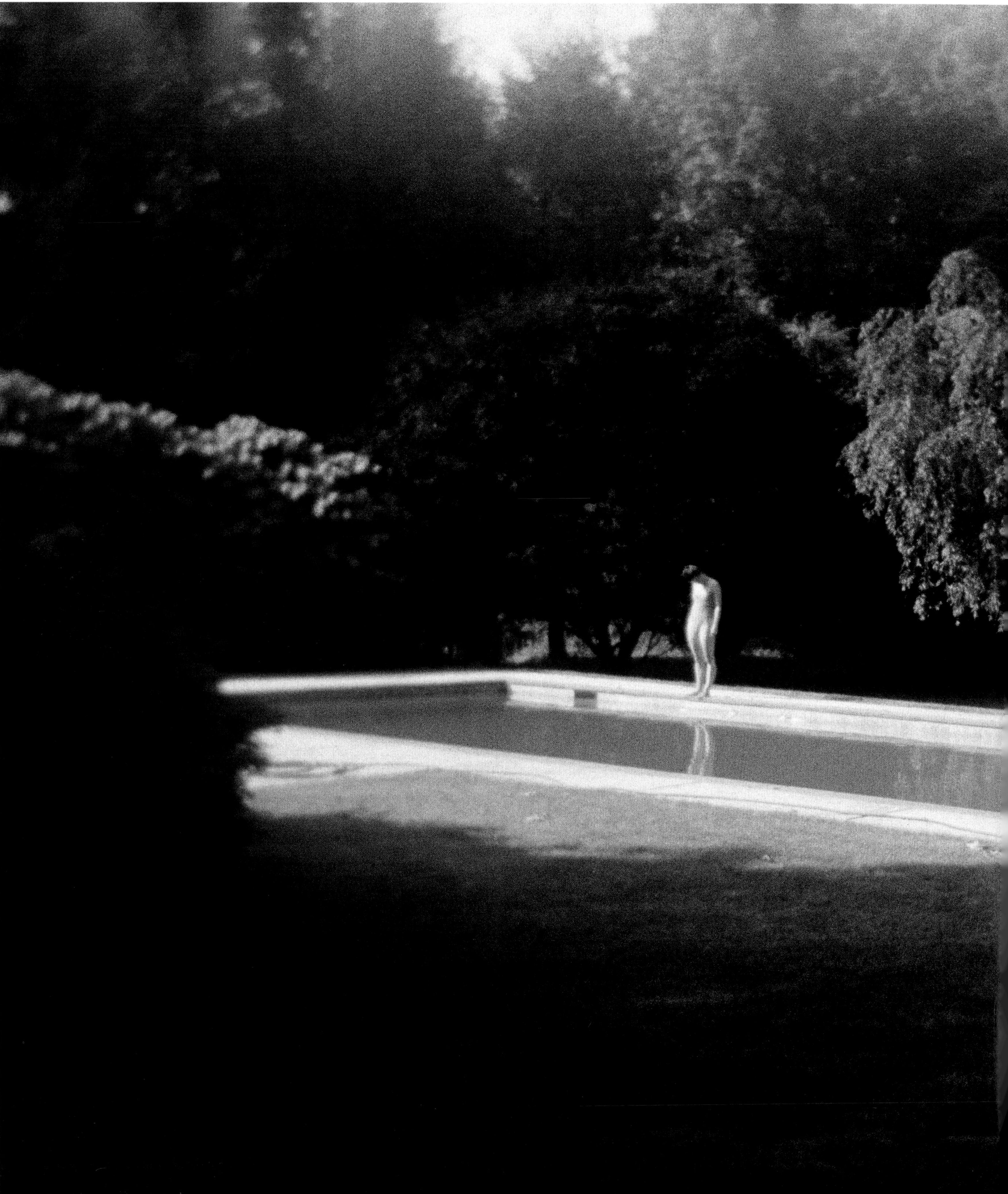

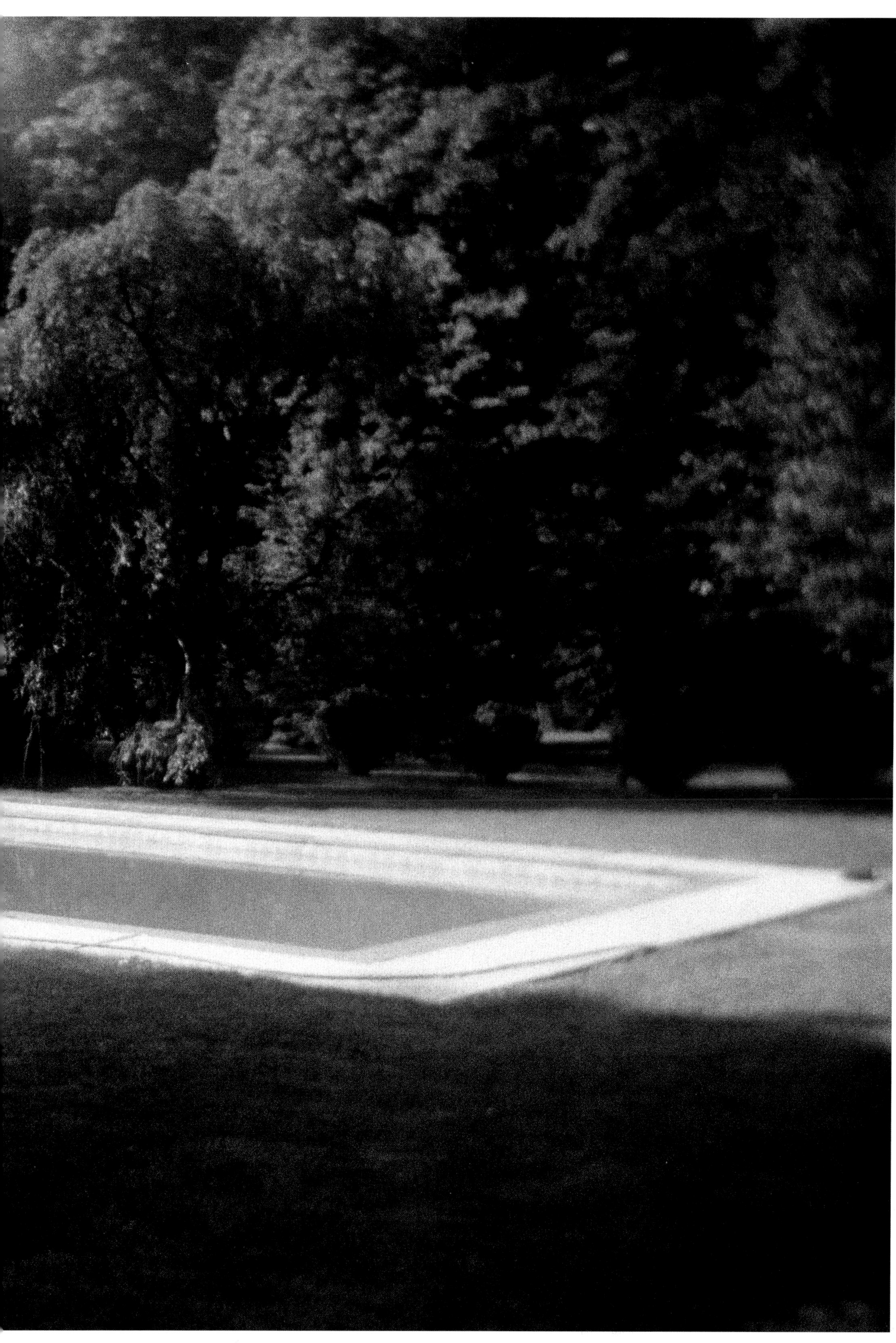

#31 / Westport, CT

1991

#69 / Rockport, MA #176 / Brookline, MA

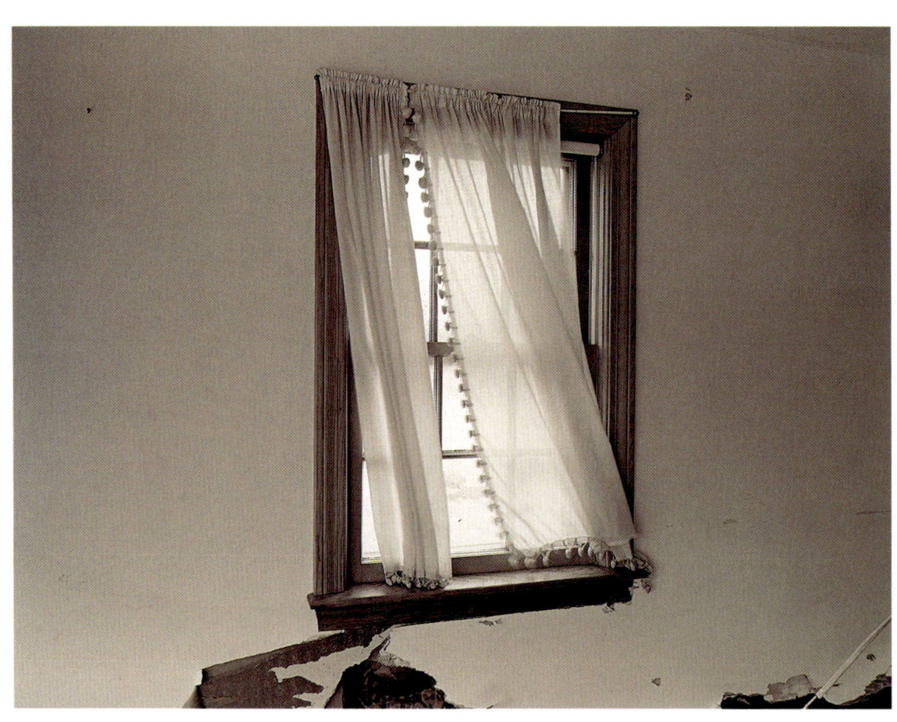

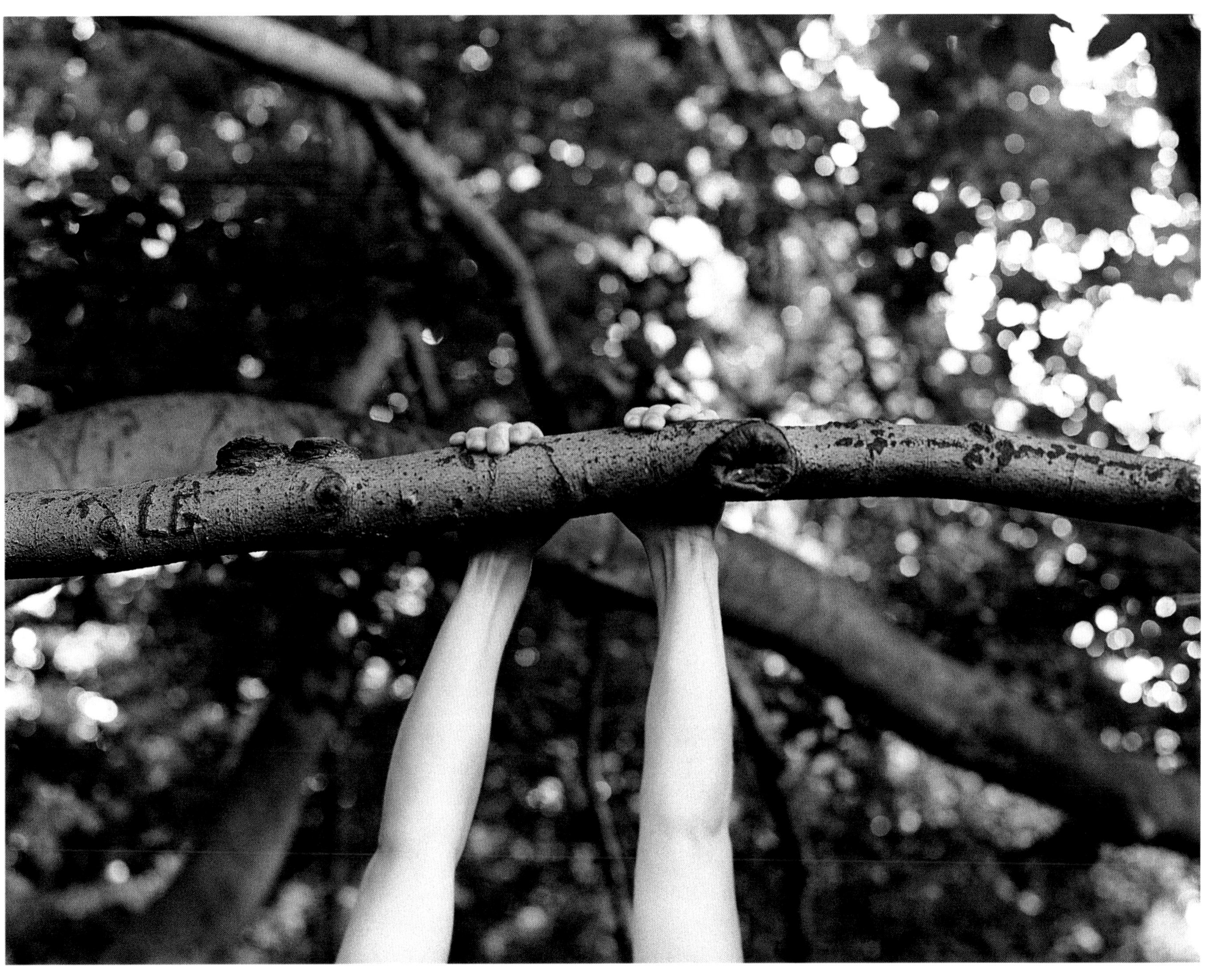

1994

#601 / St. Genevieve, MO

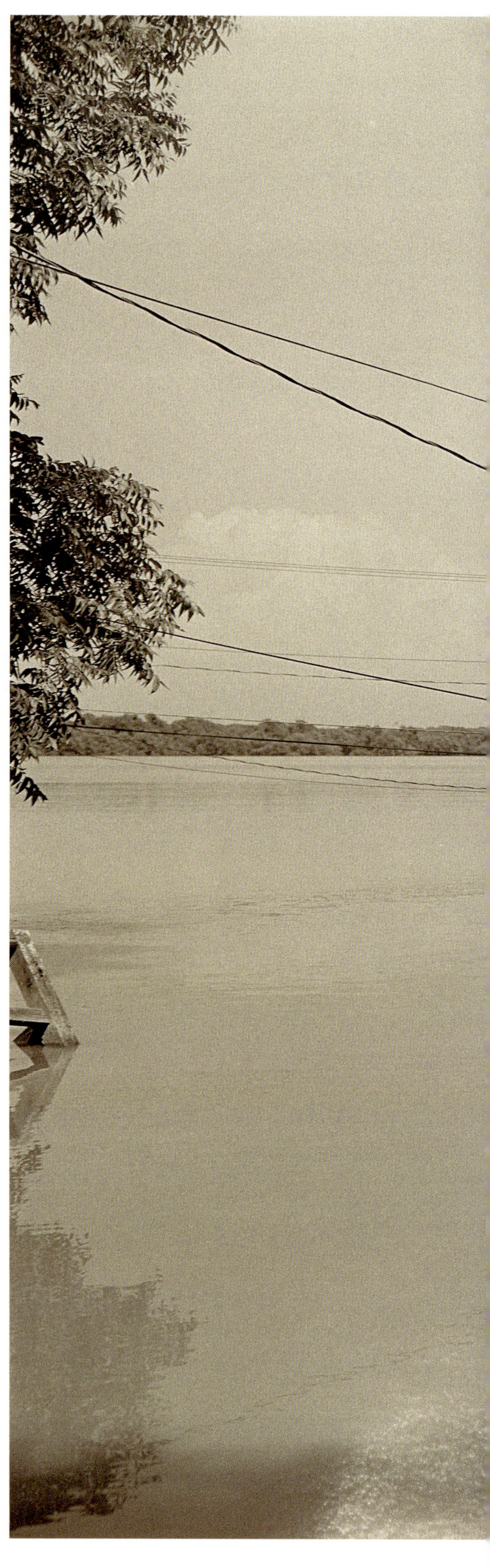

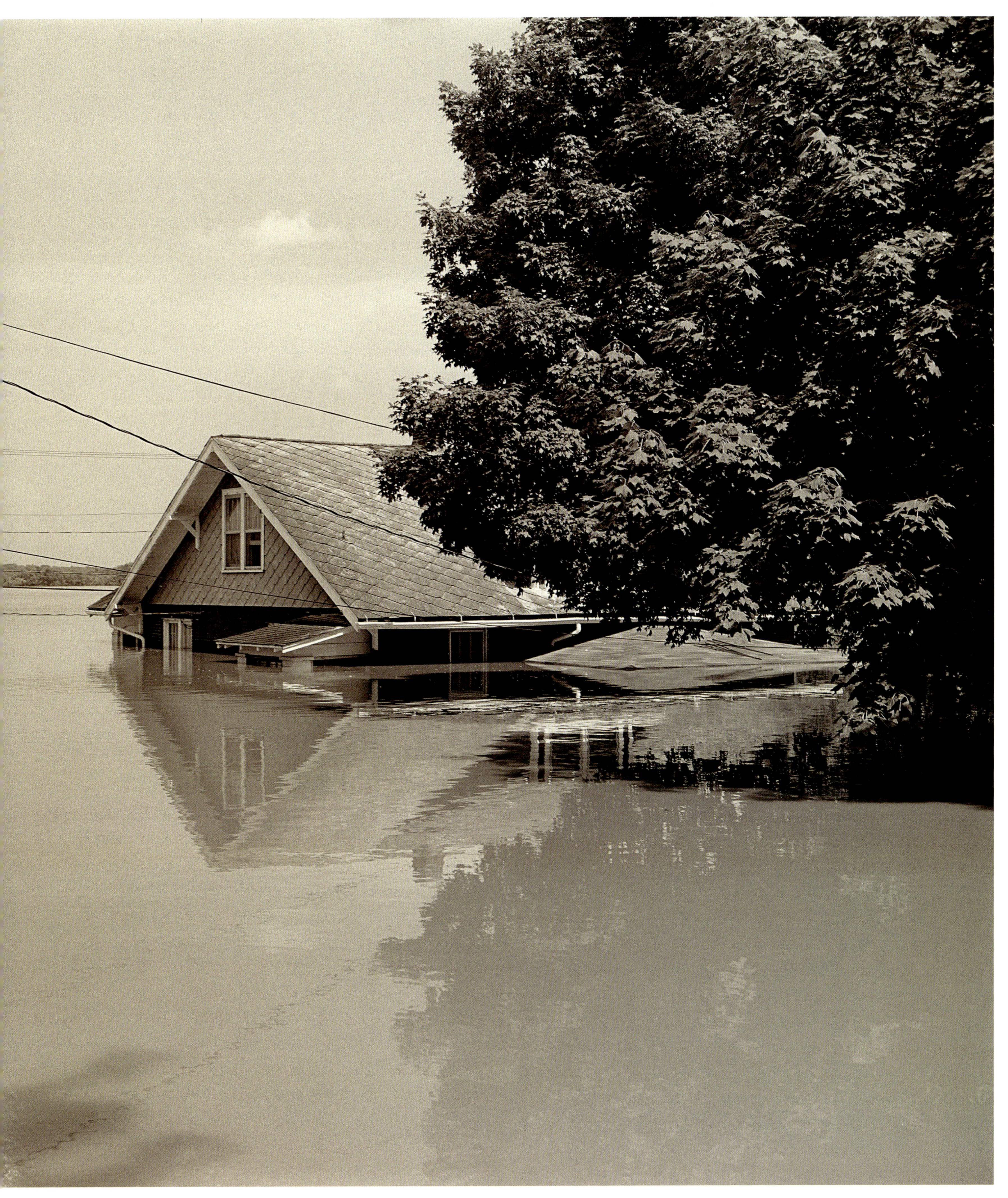

TODD HIDO

INTIMATE DISTANCE

TWENTY-FIVE YEARS OF PHOTOGRAPHS, A CHRONOLOGICAL ALBUM

Essay by David Campany *Texts by* Katya Tylevich

aperture

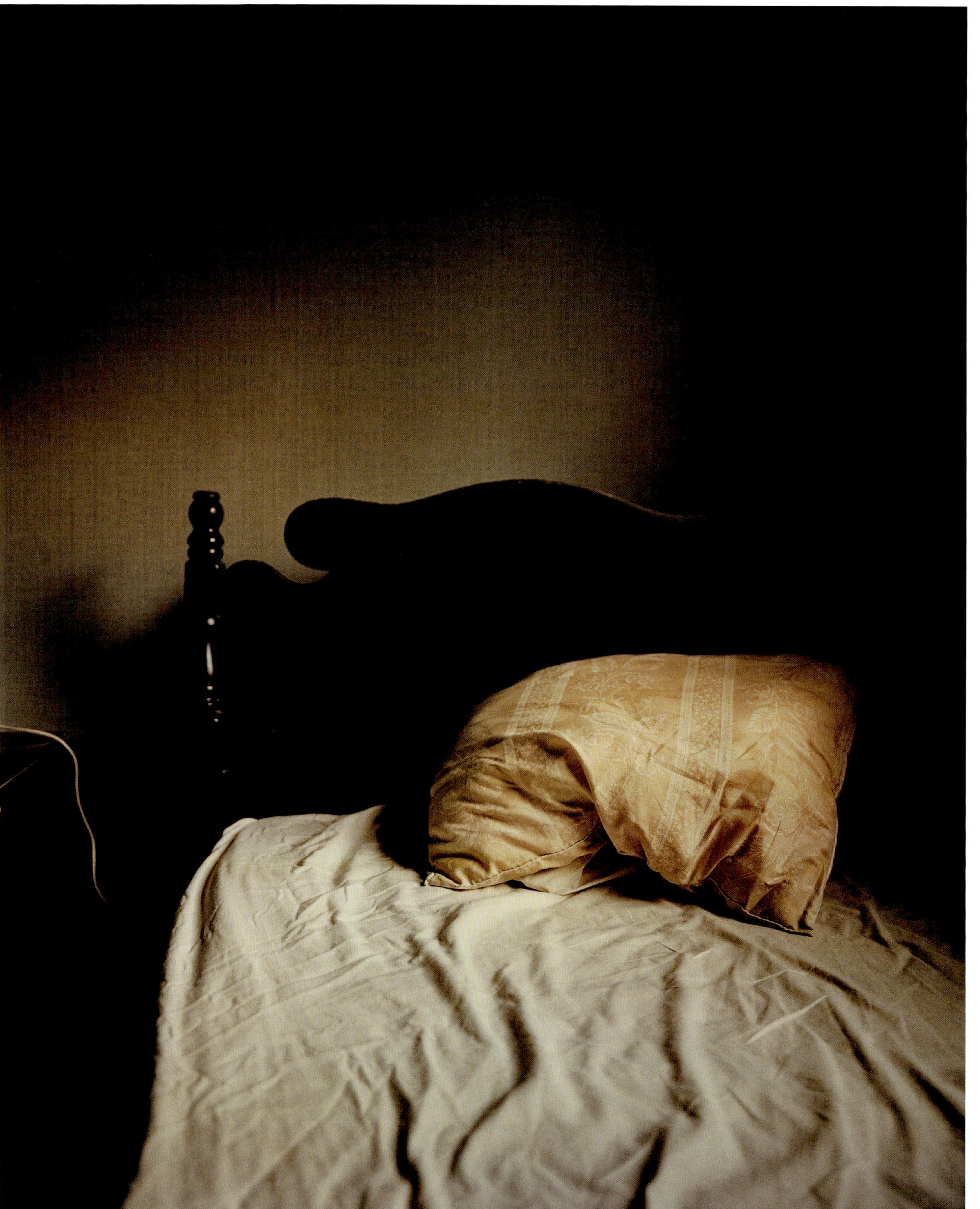

#1447-a / Kent, OH / *House Hunting, Excerpts from Silver Meadows*

CONTENTS

The images in this book appear in the chronological order in which they were taken.

CHRONOLOGY
1968–2001

1968 Born in Kent, Ohio

1989 Moves to Boston to attend the School of the Museum of Fine Arts; works exclusively in traditional darkroom, small-format, black-and-white photography

1991 Sees exhibition *Pleasures and Terrors of Domestic Comfort*, Museum of Modern Art, New York

1992 Attends the Rhode Island School of Design in Providence as an exchange student

1993 Works as assistant to commercial photographer John Goodman

1994 Moves to San Francisco to attend the California College of the Arts and Crafts; studies with Larry Sultan

1995 Begins photographing at night and printing in color

1996 Begins photographing interiors

1996 Begins photographing nudes

1996 Begins working with found photographs

1996 Begins teaching at California College of the Arts and Crafts

1997 Begins photographing in Pacifica and Daly City, California, where he will go on to shoot the majority of the series House Hunting

1997 Group exhibition: the inaugural *Bay Area Now* at Yerba Buena Center for the Arts, San Francisco. Includes seven images from House Hunting

1997 Makes first large-scale print

1998 First solo exhibition: Stephen Wirtz Gallery, San Francisco

1998 San Francisco Museum of Modern Art acquires a grid of nineteen House Hunting images

1998 Begins working with 126 mm Instamatic pictures taken by his own family members

1999 Makes first image through car windshield

2000 Group exhibition: *Immodest Gazes*, Fundación "la Caixa," Barcelona

2001 Nazraeli Press publishes first monograph, *House Hunting*

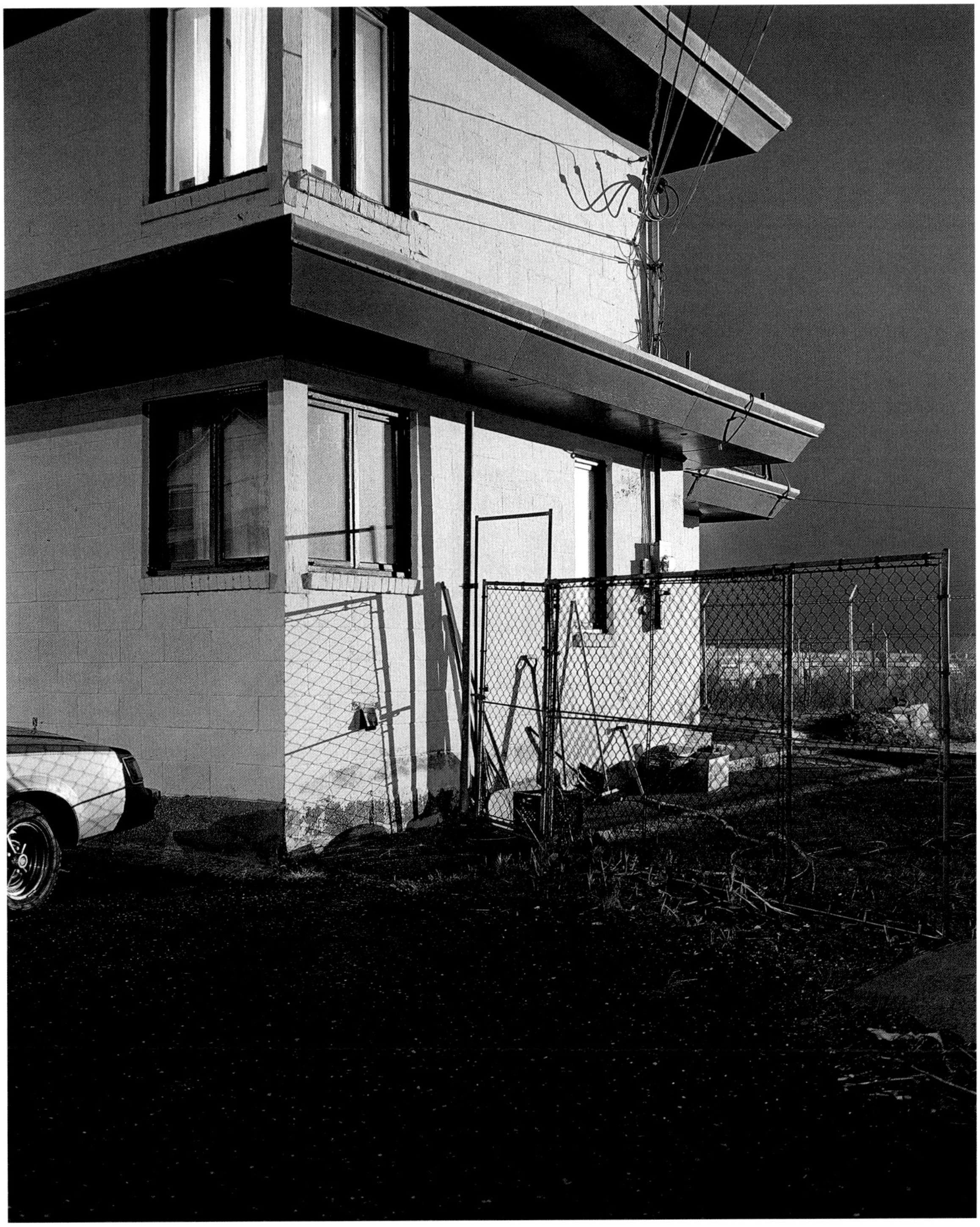

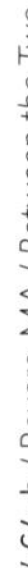
#1464-b / Revere, MA / Between the Two

1995

LIGHT AND DARK CHAMBERS

We all begin in the middle. We are born, and that is the start of something, but becoming an artist happens later, and it happens in relation to what came before. I can tell you that Todd Hido was born in Kent, Ohio, in 1968. I can tell you he came to photography through his love of skateboarding and BMX culture. He'll tell you that too:

> When people skateboard or ride bikes or whatever, they're doing something cool that only happens for a second or two, so they inevitably want to record it—that's the nature of it. You're doing a jump or a trick; you want to record it. What do you record it with? Photography. It's a totally natural progression. You can capture and share what you're doing with people. That's how I got started. I picked up a camera because I wanted to take pictures of my friends.

But it's a hell of a "jump or a trick" from such snapshots to the kinds of photographs that have made Hido one of the most admired and influential photographers of his generation. When a person picks up a camera and starts to feel photography is for them, it is usually for reasons so complex that simple biography will not do. If you suddenly find that a camera really is your means of expression, it is not so much because it gives you the chance of a brave new start, but because it's a way of drawing on the unspoken experience of your life lived so far. Making photographs is so often an act of recognition, conscious or otherwise, that what is before you resonates with things that came before. Those things might be direct experiences. They might be movies, picture books, music, or novels. We can never know for sure. And when we look at the photographs of others we are doing something similar: responding *now* through an elusive *then*. We all begin in the middle.

• • •

Early in the last century, when cinema was very young and photography had not yet found its modern calling, the young artist André Breton and his friend, the writer Jacques Vaché, spent their afternoons in the many movie theaters of the French city of Nantes. They would watch with great intent, but not quite give themselves up to the flickering fantasies. Their hyperactive minds were attuned to the first hint of boredom, that bad turn when a film becomes predictable. Popular cinema being what it is, the moment would sometimes arrive within minutes. Then the pair would rise, fumble to the exit, stroll through daylight to the next movie theater, plunge into the dark, and repeat.

It was a kind of stop-start montage, poetic and even radical. In thrall to chance encounters yet keeping control, Breton and Vaché had no concrete aim beyond the accumulation of mental impressions, which would influence their future work. (The ideas of both men soon shaped the emergence of Surrealism.) They were remaking their own dream world of pictures, in a culture where it was increasingly difficult to distinguish images that were truly one's own from those received from somewhere else. Living in the mind, pictures can never really belong to anyone. The unconscious does not recognize authors, origins, or destinations. What matters for imagery is resonance and restlessness.

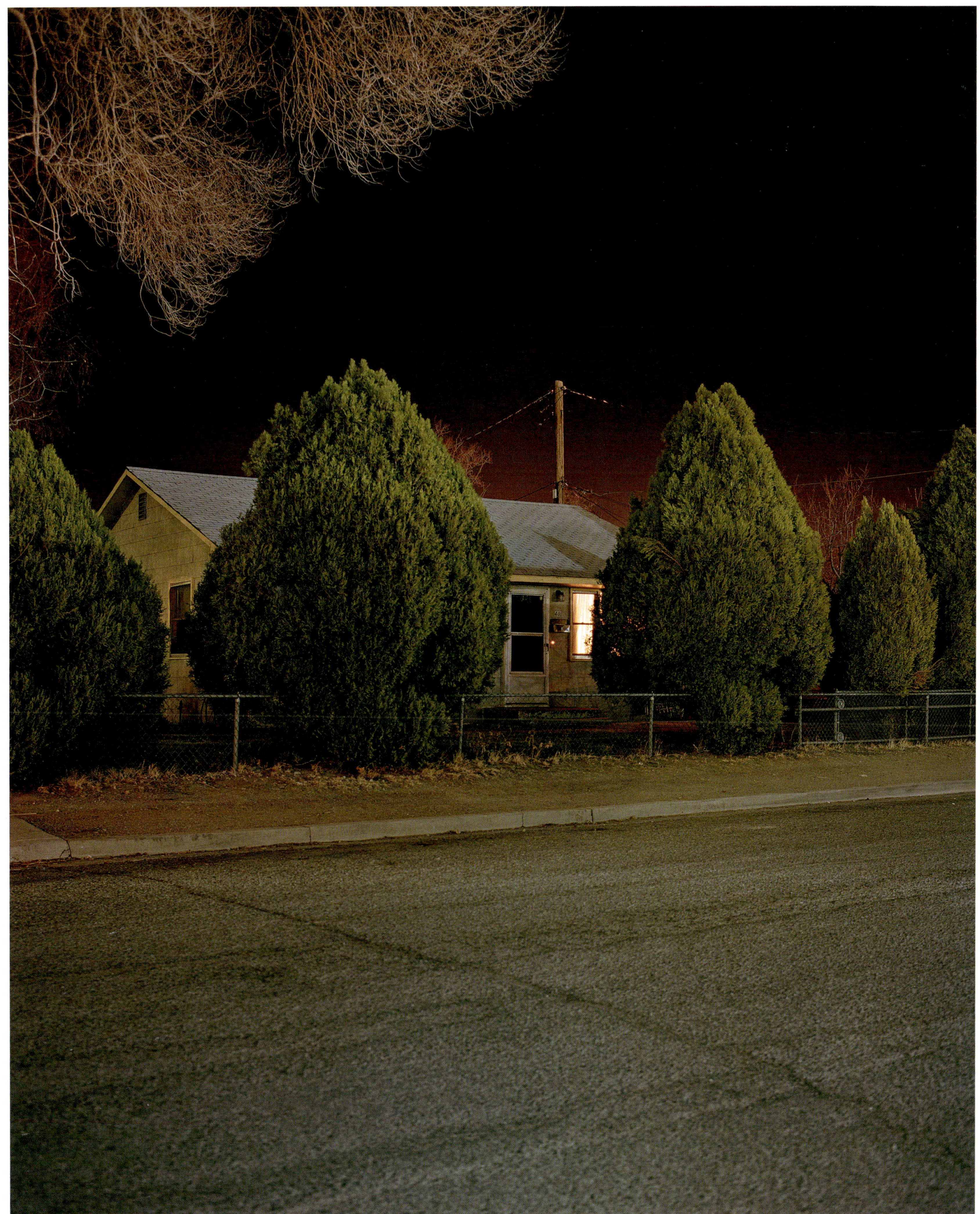

#1536 / Reno, NV / *House Hunting*

#1609-b / Gilroy, CA / *Roaming*

A century on, such a montage can still be poetic, but it barely seems radical. Zapping between channels and clicking through websites are now prosaic activities in an age of distraction. And yet assembling a creative life from fragments, be they one's own or those of others, is more important now than it has ever been. Some say it is the only creative act left.

Perhaps Breton and Vaché were avoiding conclusions. They preferred to start in the middle and defer *The End* forever. As we watch a narrative film, the plot and conclusion dominate our experience, but this is not how we will remember it. What we will recall are unpredictable bits and pieces: short strings of association, lucid scenes, colors, spaces, gestures, textures, vectors. In memory, cinema's images are freed from narrative obligation and resume their essential ambiguity. Narrative is the booster rocket that gets the image pieces into orbit so they can circle the mind, coming around unbidden.

• • •

In 1974, the great photographer Walker Evans gave a lecture to students. Like so many artists of his generation, Evans was a lifelong cinephile, and, when asked if he still watched movies, he mentioned Robert Altman's then-recent films *The Long Goodbye* and *McCabe and Mrs. Miller*. He wondered aloud if they were both shot by the same person (they were—by Vilmos Zsigmond). Evans said he thought them "a marvelous bunch of photography" and something to really learn from.

Influence cannot be confined to one's own medium. It comes from anywhere. A line from Virginia Woolf or Raymond Carver may strike us with a force comparable to that of a snapshot. A musical phrase may dance like a picture. A word may link one ineffable vision to another. A shot from a film can have more vitality as an isolated image than it does in the service of a story.

Still photography has never been too burdened by the weight of narrative. Since its essence lies in the *thingness* of things observed, it has only ever dealt in description and suggestion. Moreover, its muteness and fixity are so different from the noise of the spoken word. Even when sequenced carefully across pages, an arrangement of silent photographs will always feel a little provisional, the concrete particulars of each image finessed by so many open questions. What if this picture is placed alongside this one? What if a turn of the page is a shift from reverie to piqued curiosity, or political urgency? What if a change of scale causes a minor tremor in your attention? What if a smudged view of an unknown landscape resonates with the smudged mascara of an unknown woman?

Good pictures in a book are the "marvelous bunch of photography" that a good movie is in the memory.

• • •

The photographs gathered on these pages were made over the course of the last twenty-five years. During that time, Todd Hido has worked on several substantial groups of pictures, often simultaneously. When each group has come into focus as a project, Hido has published it as a book and exhibited it as a suite of prints. But what we have here is a chronological sequence drawn from the full depth and breadth of his singular oeuvre. It's not exactly a retrospective; instead, like a novelist reviewing his manuscripts or a filmmaker going back to the editing suite, this book hints at its maker's development and working processes. We are invited to see how Hido has spiraled through his motifs and preoccupations. True to the book's title, you will find several kinds of intimacy here. You will also find the ambiguous distances signaled by the titles of some of his previous books: *House Hunting*, *A Road Divided*, *Roaming*, *Between the Two*, *Outskirts*. Wandering through and around, searching and returning.

If these photographs and their arrangement seem narrative, it is because they suggest untold tales and possibility. The suggestions are as much yours as they are Hido's, and as likely to come from cinema and literature as they are from personal experience. Hido is an avid movie lover who says the TV in his house is always on. Impressions sink in and leave their traces, but even he is not sure what they are.

These photographs are made slowly—there are few grabbed shutter instants here—but like so much of the best photography, they seem to have been prompted by flashes of recognition, when the world-as-image corresponded to something half-remembered, unstated but insistent. The images are sumptuous and full of things to look at: landscapes, byways, signs, suburbia, interiors, fabrics,

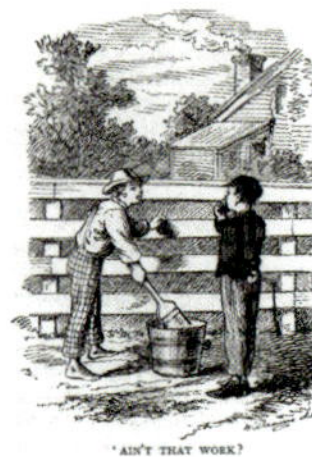

True Williams, illustration for Mark Twain's *The Adventures of Tom Sawyer*, 1876

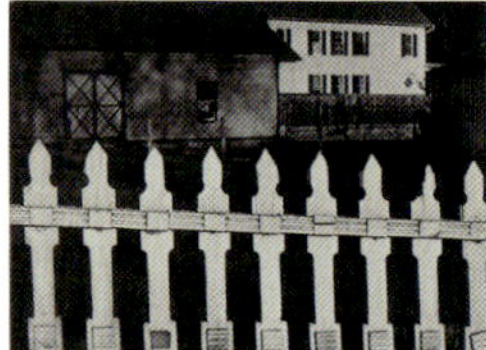

Paul Strand, *White Fence, Port Kent*, 1916

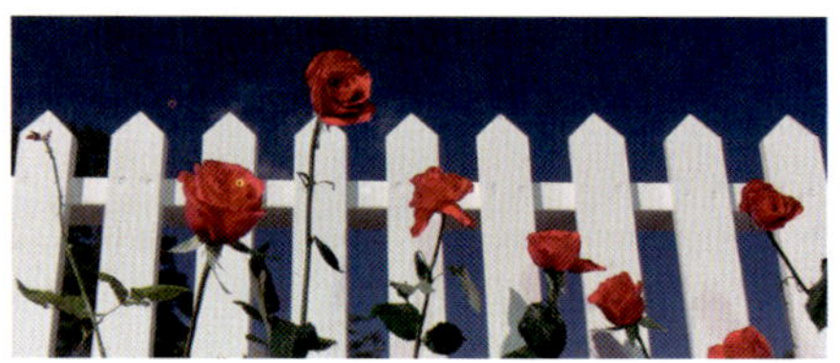

David Lynch, film still from *Blue Velvet*, 1986

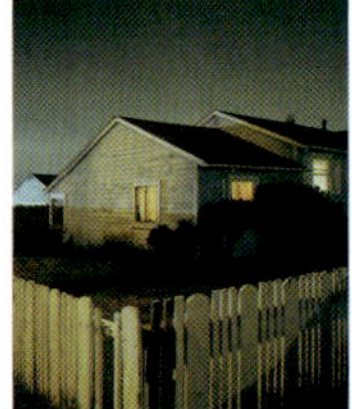

Todd Hido, *#2690*, 2000

and faces. But they give the equally strong impression that this factual-fictional world is less than full. Each image is plenty, yet not quite enough. For all the river of color, for all the thickness of these atmospheres, Hido has the economy of a minimalist.

Can one empty out a photograph? How little would it need? A road trip can be sketched with little more than a horizon and a telephone pole. The anomie of suburbia is all in the paint palette of a real estate brochure washed in sodium light. A door with a number—216—is an unknown motel room, allocated at random. A young woman in such a room is enough to signal hope, fear, loss, or desire. Fill in the gaps as you wish; perhaps your unconscious has already.

• • •

The iconography here is perfectly familiar. Hido is confident enough to inhabit clichés and emerge with something that is his own. His photographs confirm the idea that in much of American culture, motifs matter only because of the inflections they are given. Consider the picket fence: it has been a permanent presence in the nation's literature, cinema, and photography because it is so open to interpretation. Think of the fence at the start of Mark Twain's 1876 novel *The Adventures of Tom Sawyer*: "Tom appeared on the sidewalk with a bucket of whitewash and a long-handled brush. He surveyed the fence, and all gladness left him and a deep melancholy settled down upon his spirit. Thirty yards of board fence nine feet high. Life to him seemed hollow, and existence but a burden."

That picket fence is and isn't the picket fence of Paul Strand's celebrated photograph of 1916, or the one in Frank Capra's *It's a Wonderful Life*, or those in the 1950s TV series *Father Knows Best* and *Beulah*; or the glowing white fence that opens David Lynch's *Blue Velvet*, set against that too-blue sky and lurid roses. All these fences divide home from town, private fear from public life, and are loaded in so many other ways too.

Since appearing on the cover of his 2001 book *House Hunting*, Hido's own interpretation of the picket fence has become something of an emblem for his work as a whole. It is an image that permits the memory of all the fences that have come before. Its composition has the simplicity of a nineteenth-century illustration; the architecture it describes has existed for generations. The colors, seductive and queasy, have the infinite gradation of very mixed emotions. The fence itself, like all American fences, is in need of attention. Behind the house's curtains, something or nothing may be going on: one room has the warmth of a bedside lamp, while another has the cooler light of a TV screen. No drama is represented here. Instead, we have the drama of representation itself, and perhaps the drama of *photography* itself.

A camera is a dark chamber pierced by light. Through a small opening the light passes, falling as an inverted image on a sensitized surface. The light may be too bright or too dim, but adjustments can be made: apertures, shutter speeds, film sensitivities. Such chambers abound in Hido's work. By daytime, the rooms he photographs are darkly sequestered spaces, resisting the sun. At night, houses become glowing chambers.

To move through the pages of this book is to move from one chamber to another, feeling how light itself can be observed, calibrated, and made thinkable. The fall of light can be affectionate or indifferent or even cruel, just like the human life it illuminates. In one photograph, a stained mattress is propped against the window of an exhausted room. Bright sunlight pushes around its edges and seeps into the space. You can see how light is a force. It can be harnessed, or even be created with fire or electricity, but it is a force, with all the beauty of flowing water. Whatever is happening in that room finds its echo in the camera that is there to make an image of it. The room preceded the camera's presence, but without the camera you would never have seen it. Hido entered, exposed the negative that had the potential to become this picture, left the room, and walked out into the light. Everything else that makes the picture what it is—Hido's intentions or yours—is conjecture.

For some of his landscape images Hido has used the chamber of his car. Cruising rural roads, he scrolls through endless vistas in the hope of catching some epiphany of light and form. Many a "road trip" photographer has talked about how their windshield feels like cinema's wide screen—it is a framing device. Hido's windshield is more than that: you can see it in his images, diffusing and refracting the view. The glass also catches Hido's own breath, which condenses into cataracts before him. He stays in the car with his camera, looking out, shooting out, a chamber within a chamber.

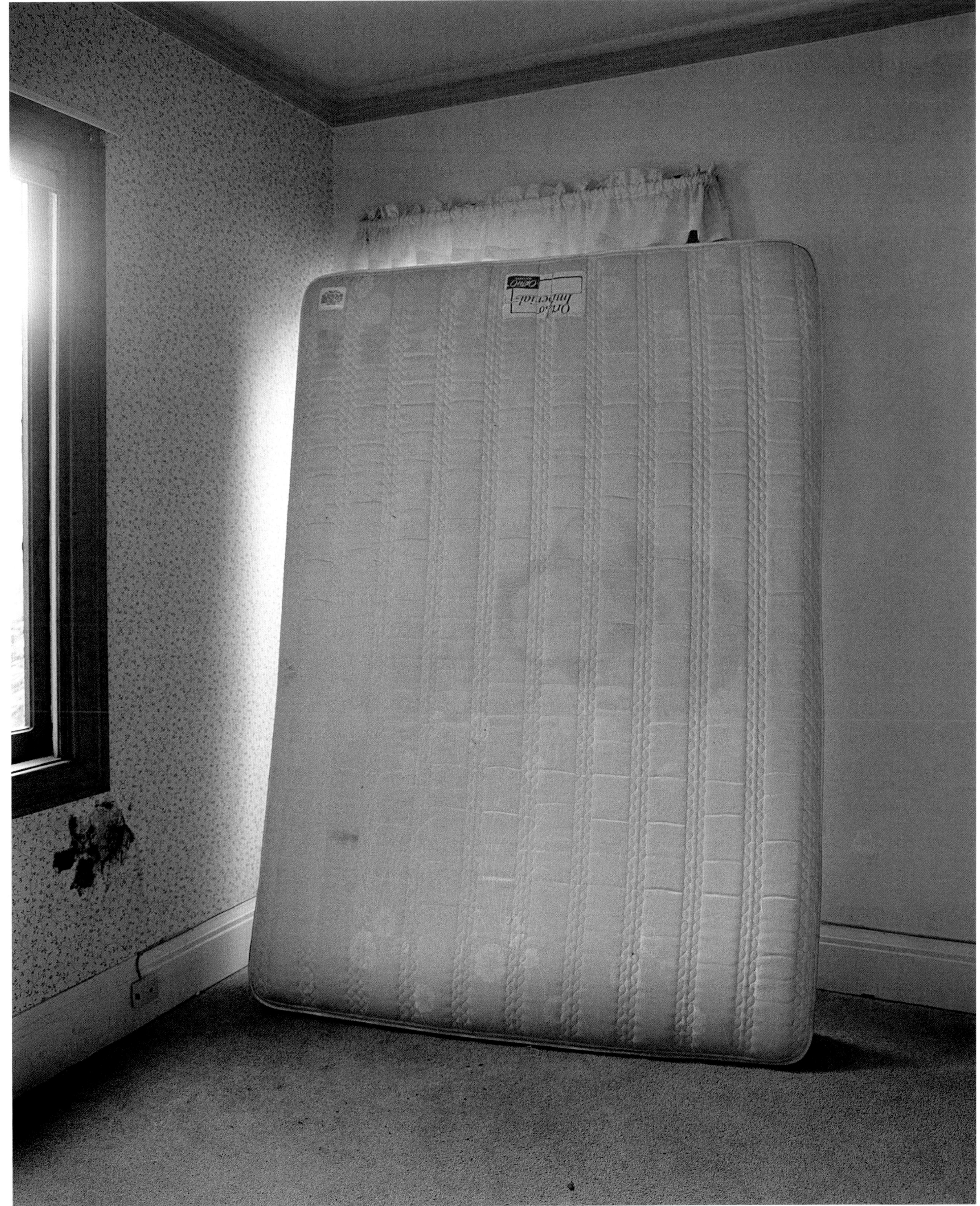

#1637 / Los Angeles, CA / *House Hunting*

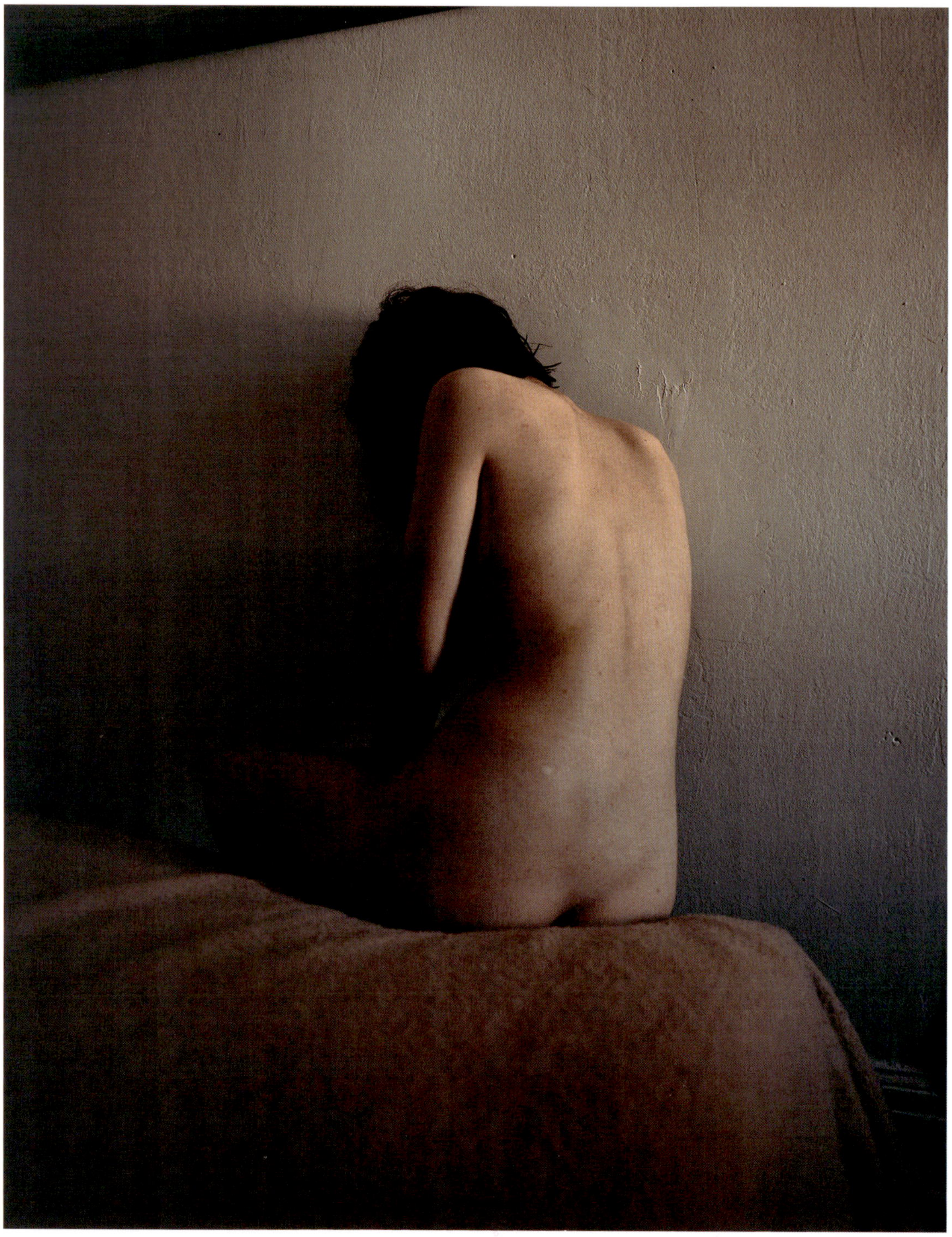

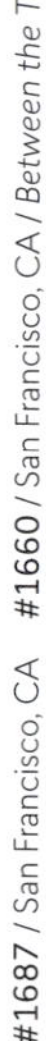

#1687 / San Francisco, CA **#1660** / San Francisco, CA / *Between the Two*

• • •

In 1975 Roland Barthes published a perfect little essay, "En sortant du cinéma" (On leaving the cinema). Its subject is the pleasurable yet strange sensation that comes over us when a film is over. Our body must awaken, "a little numb, a little awkward, chilly," as he puts it, "sloppy, soft, peaceful: limp as a sleeping cat." Our mind must also move from one state, one reality, to another. We need time to adjust. It is a precious feeling, but so transitive that we are rarely encouraged to take it seriously. Barthes does. The sensation of leaving that dark chamber can be quite dramatic. (Maybe this is what Breton and Vaché loved, or feared, prompting them to *choose* their own moments to leave.) Watching a film in a cinema, you are supposed to forget where you are. To enter the illusion, the apparatus must melt away. At the end of the film you mentally reenter your surroundings and once again become aware of the movie theater, only to leave it.

This never really happens with still photography. There is no comparable suspension of disbelief. Yes, a photograph or book of photographs may be immersive, but not in the cinematic sense. The pleasures are very different. Looking at photographs, we never quite "lose ourselves." And in a book, it is in the mental movement from one image to another that meaning is made, without forgetting where you are. Hido's pictures are as immersive as any in contemporary photography, but the pleasures of his sequencing keep churning. One is pulled into the imaginative depths of a picture, only to be lured toward another and another. And unlike a narrative movie, a book allows one to feel what one is feeling—to grasp the pleasure and the churn consciously, as sensations in themselves.

Before a movie is made, the director or location scout goes looking for places to shoot. Usually they will take a still camera. If you have ever seen the pictures made on such reconnaissance trips, you will have sensed their strange status. They are documents, records of places, yet they are also invitations to propose, or suppose, what has not yet happened but could. A good location photograph will leave space for imaginative projection. I think Hido's landscapes and townscapes have this quality. A similar feeling is present in actor portraits made by casting directors, and in the preliminary photos taken of fashion models on go-sees for style magazines. Look at Hido's photographs of solitary women that populate this book. In each case there was an encounter, of which the photograph is the palpable result, but what, or who, was *there*? A player, star or extra, with an unwritten script.

So many of Hido's images hinge on this duality: the retrospective and the prospective. The fact and the wish. The presence and the possibility. His statement that he "photographs like a documentarian but prints like a painter" confirms this, and indicates how the effect is rooted in the very substance of his pictures. It is a constant balancing act, avoiding the sentimentality of "what was" and the cheap melodrama of performed fiction.

But what of the found photos that punctuate the sequence of Hido's own images in this book? They appear to have been rescued from family albums long abandoned, and they also express something of this duality. They come from somewhere undoubtedly specific but unknown to us, and their future is uncertain. For now they have found a resting place amid these porous landscapes and portraits, and the mix is heady. But who knows? It is in the nature of photographs to wander and recombine.

Hido himself has wandered. He has shuffled his deck of photos, spread it out, and made his choices. There is great value in looking back, and risk too. Photographers know this better than most. Can Hido really know who he was when he made an image twenty-five years ago, or even last year? Which is the best moment to be making that call? Now is as good as any. What really matters is the honesty and the intensity of the backward glance, while accepting that one can never know one's own motivations absolutely. In a printed book the choices are definite. The sequence is locked, and the binding is tight. Even so, for all the fixing of appearances, for all the stopping of time and reshaping of history, everything flows onward around a photograph; sooner or later, it gets swept along. As Hido himself once put it: "Whatever I have accomplished, I just keep going." This book is a milestone on that journey.

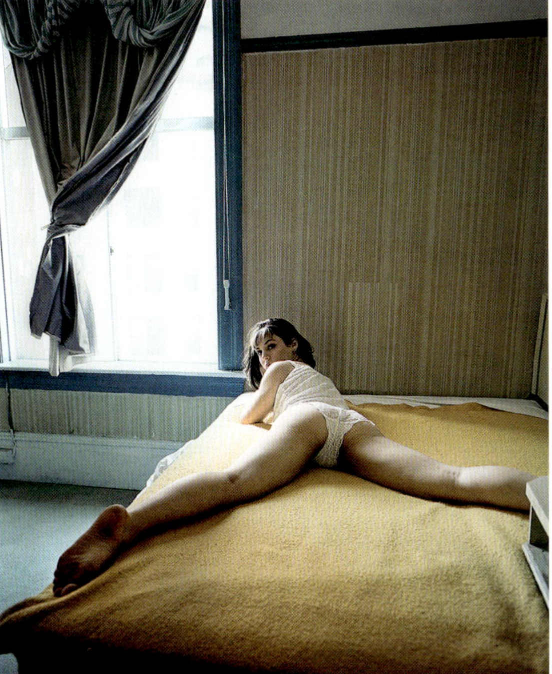

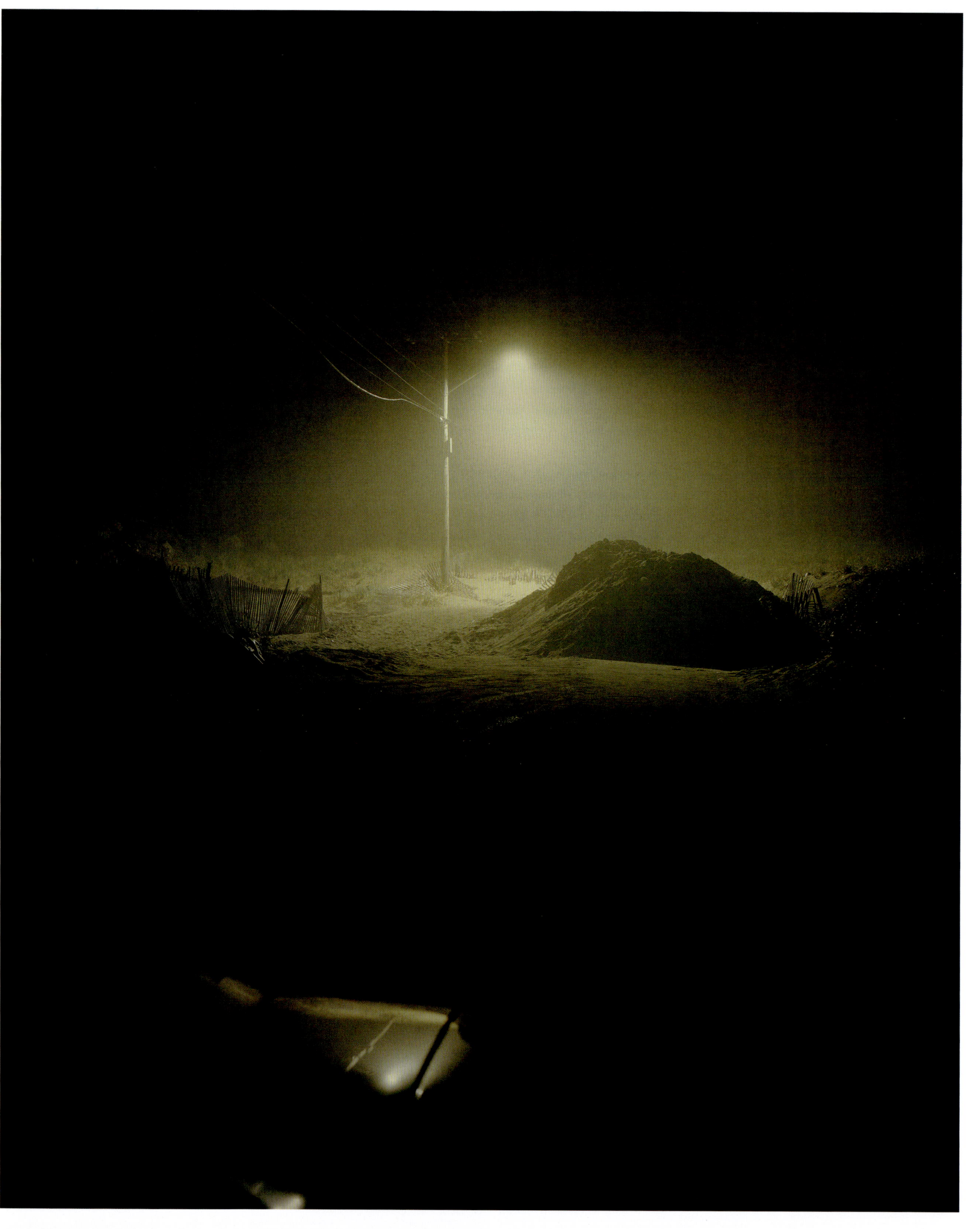

#1726 / Salisbury Beach, MA / *Outskirts* **#1738** / Pacifica, CA / *Roaming*

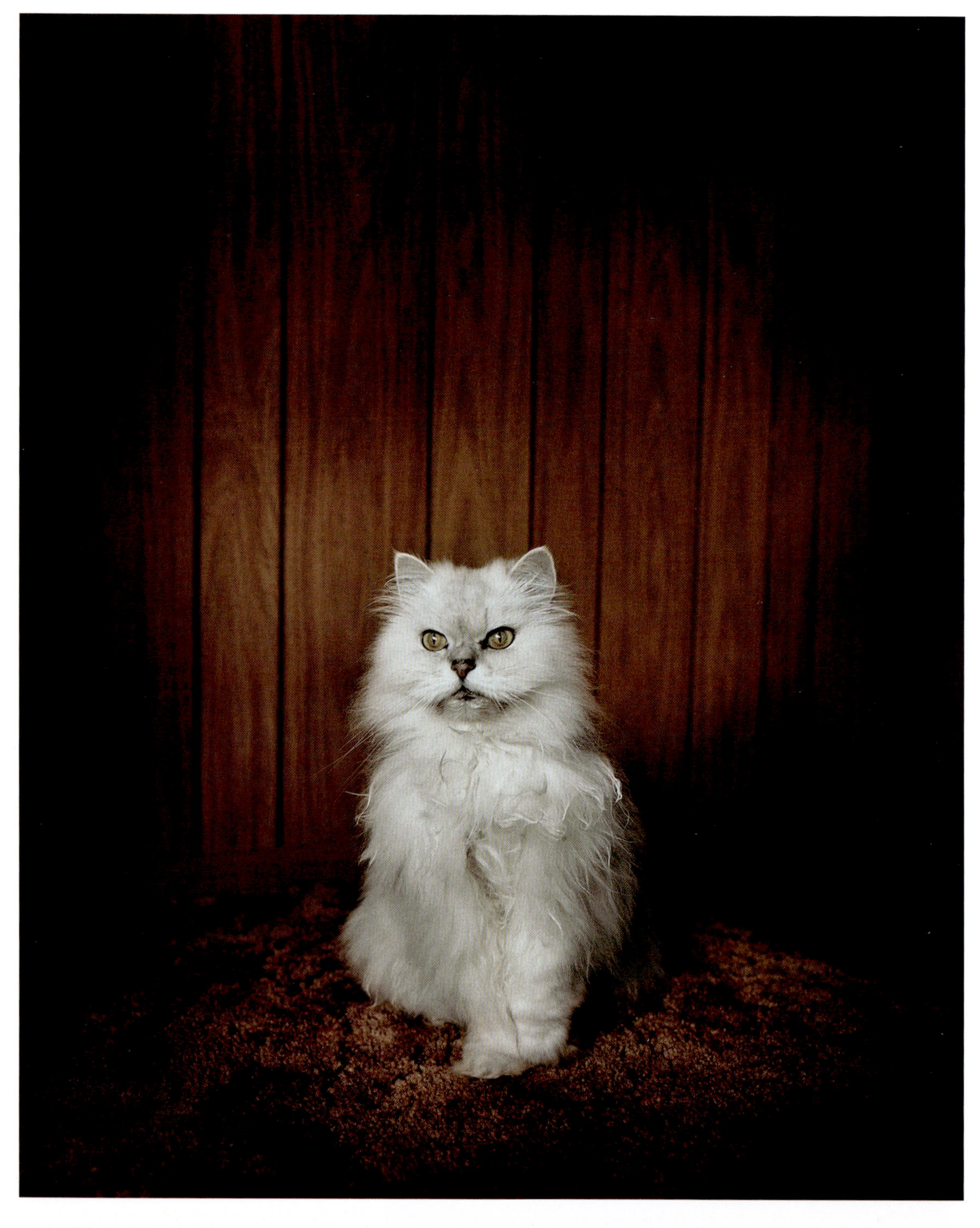

#1843 / Oakland, CA / *Excerpts from Silver Meadows*   **#1765** / San Francisco, CA / *Between the Two*

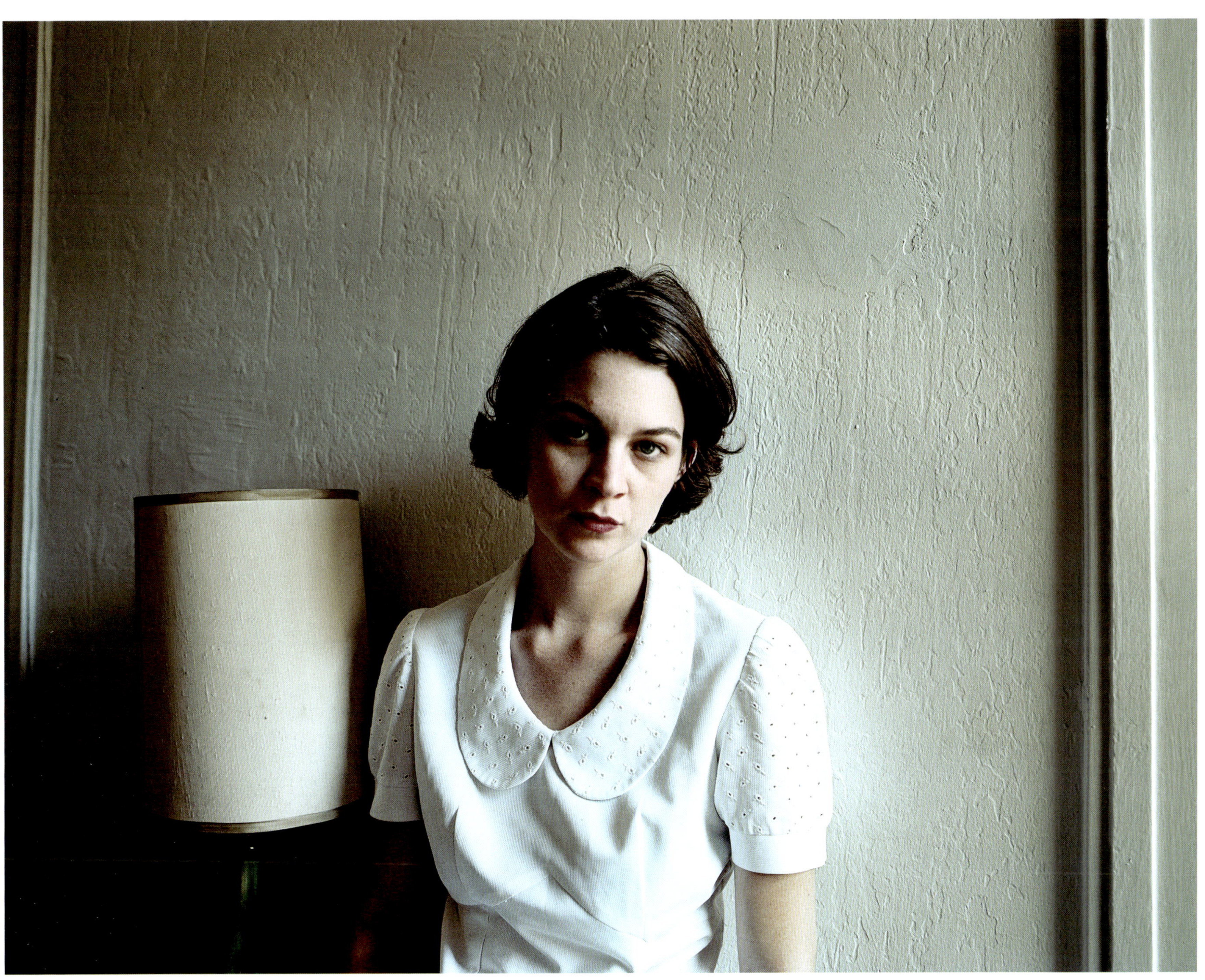

1996

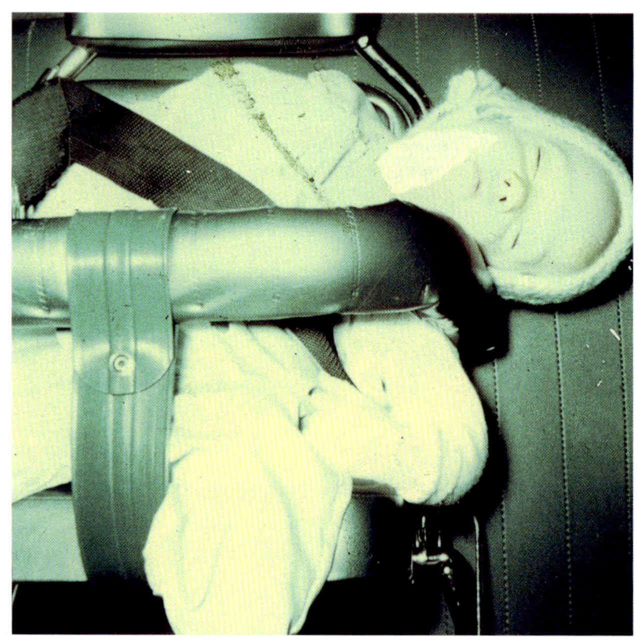

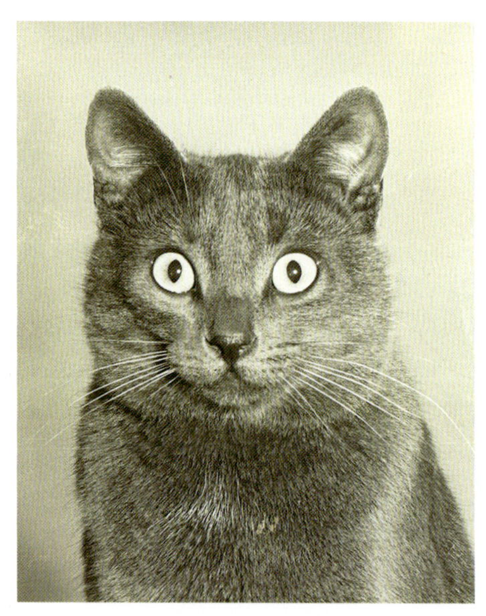

#1859-a / found / *Excerpts from Silver Meadows* **#1741-pussy-cat** / found **#1862** / Daly City, CA / *House Hunting*

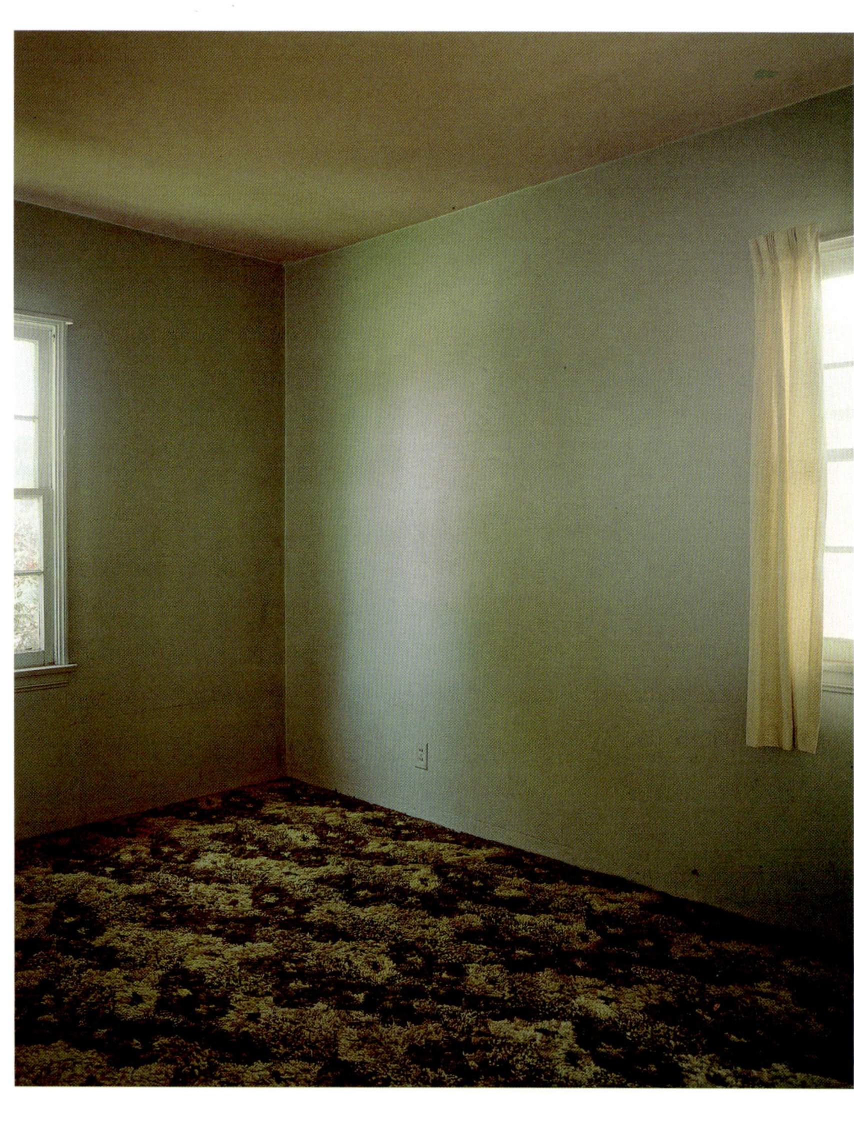

 1996

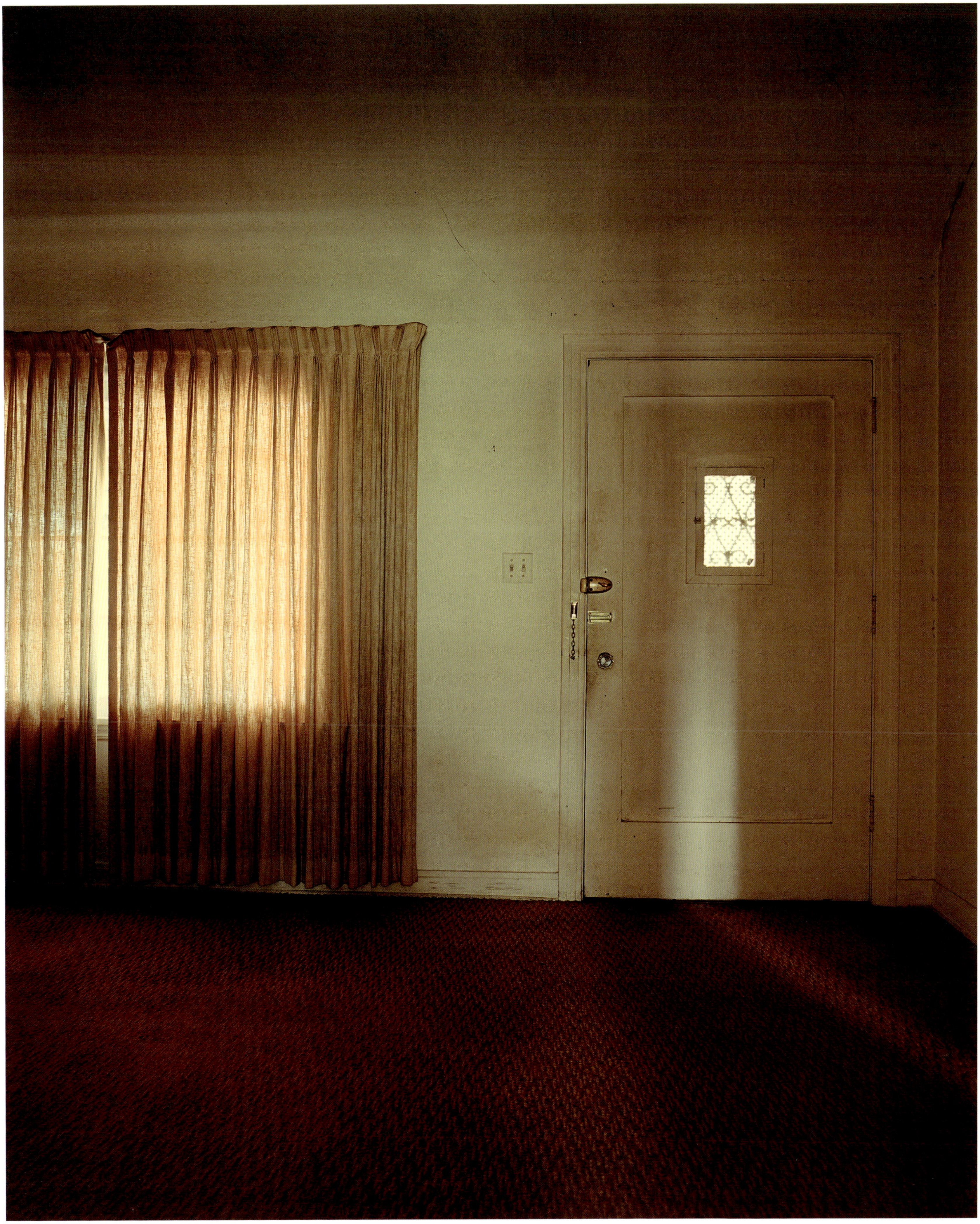

#1922-c / Los Angeles, CA   #1913 / Los Angeles, CA

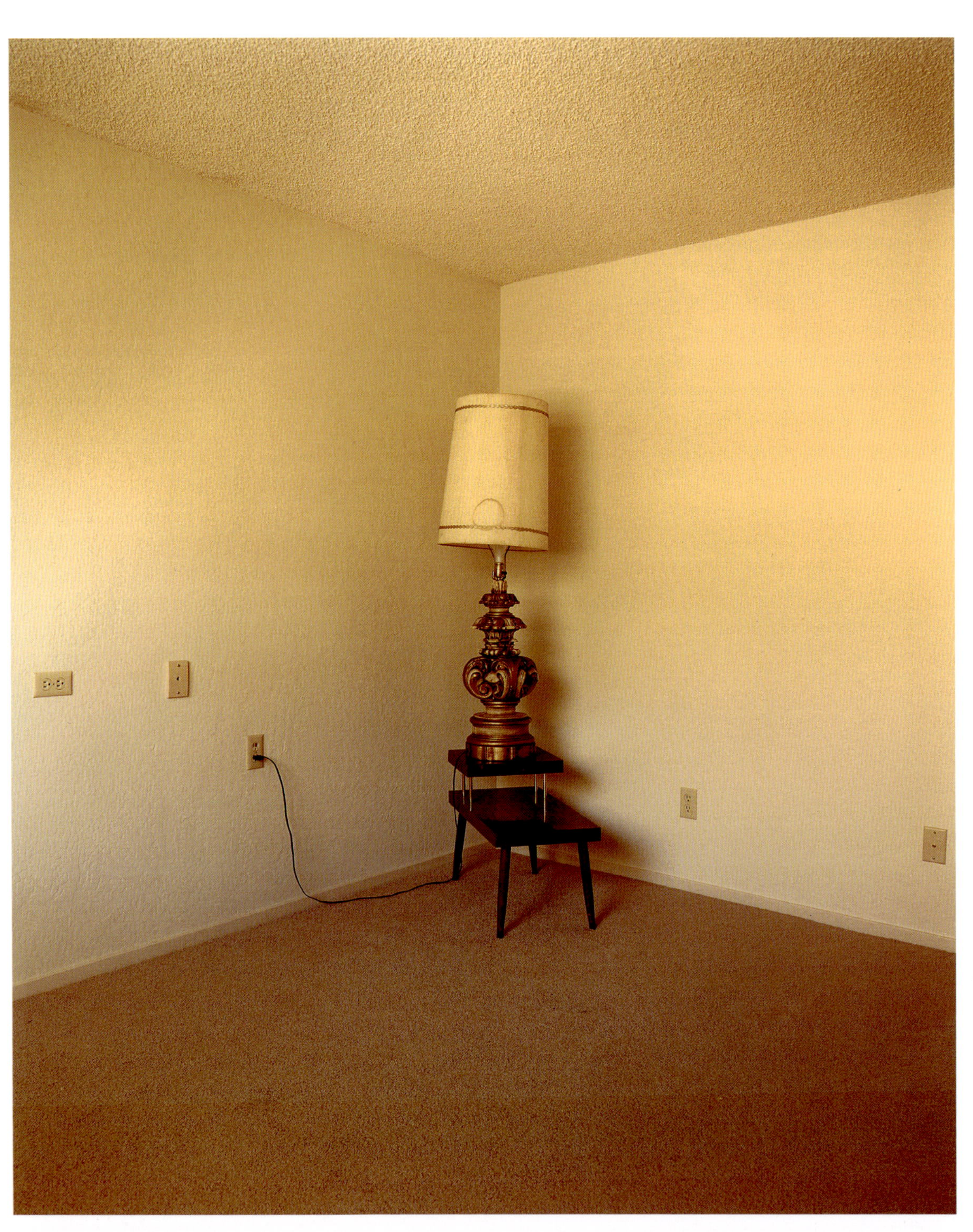

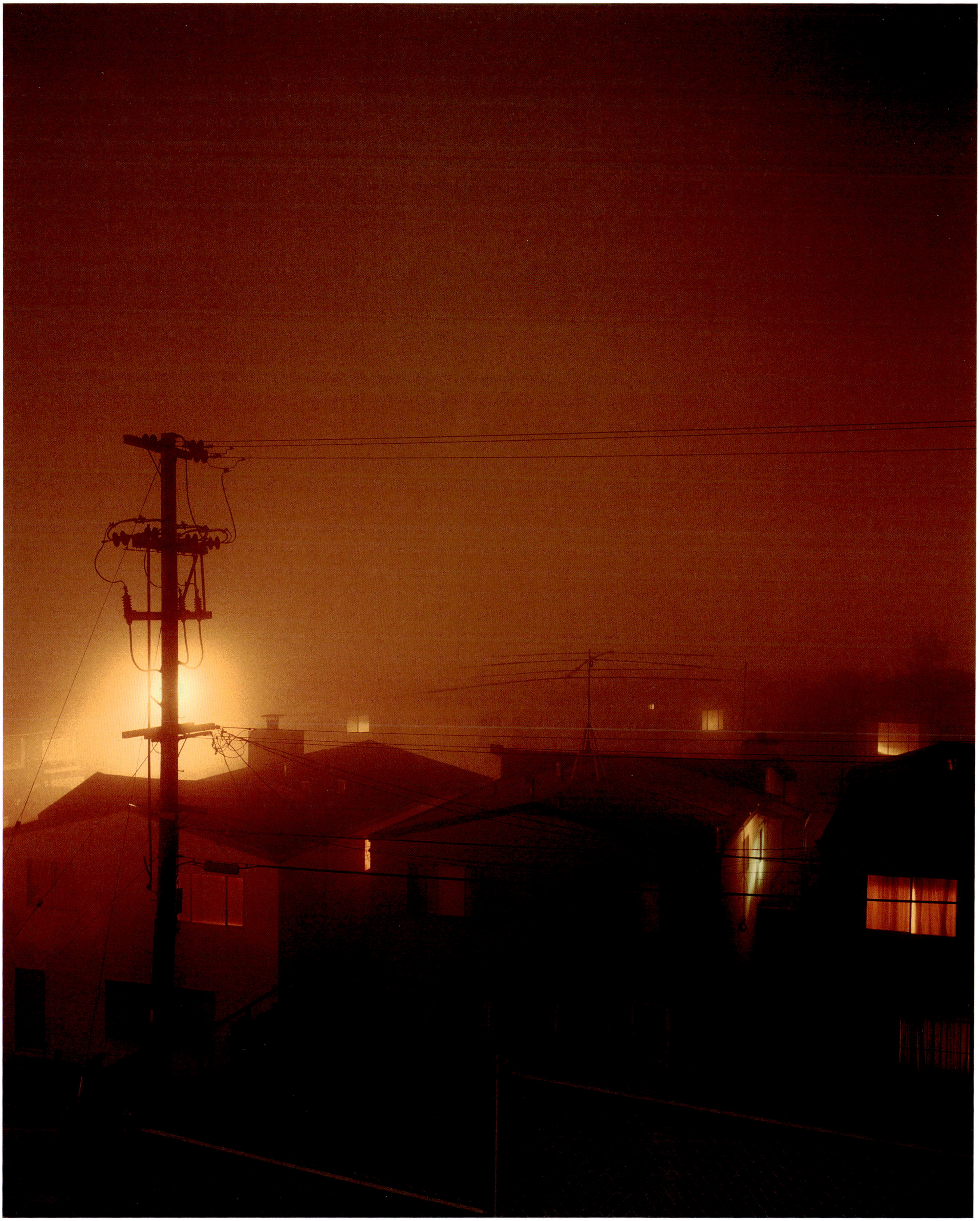

#1932 / Los Angeles, CA **#1941** / San Francisco, CA / *House Hunting*

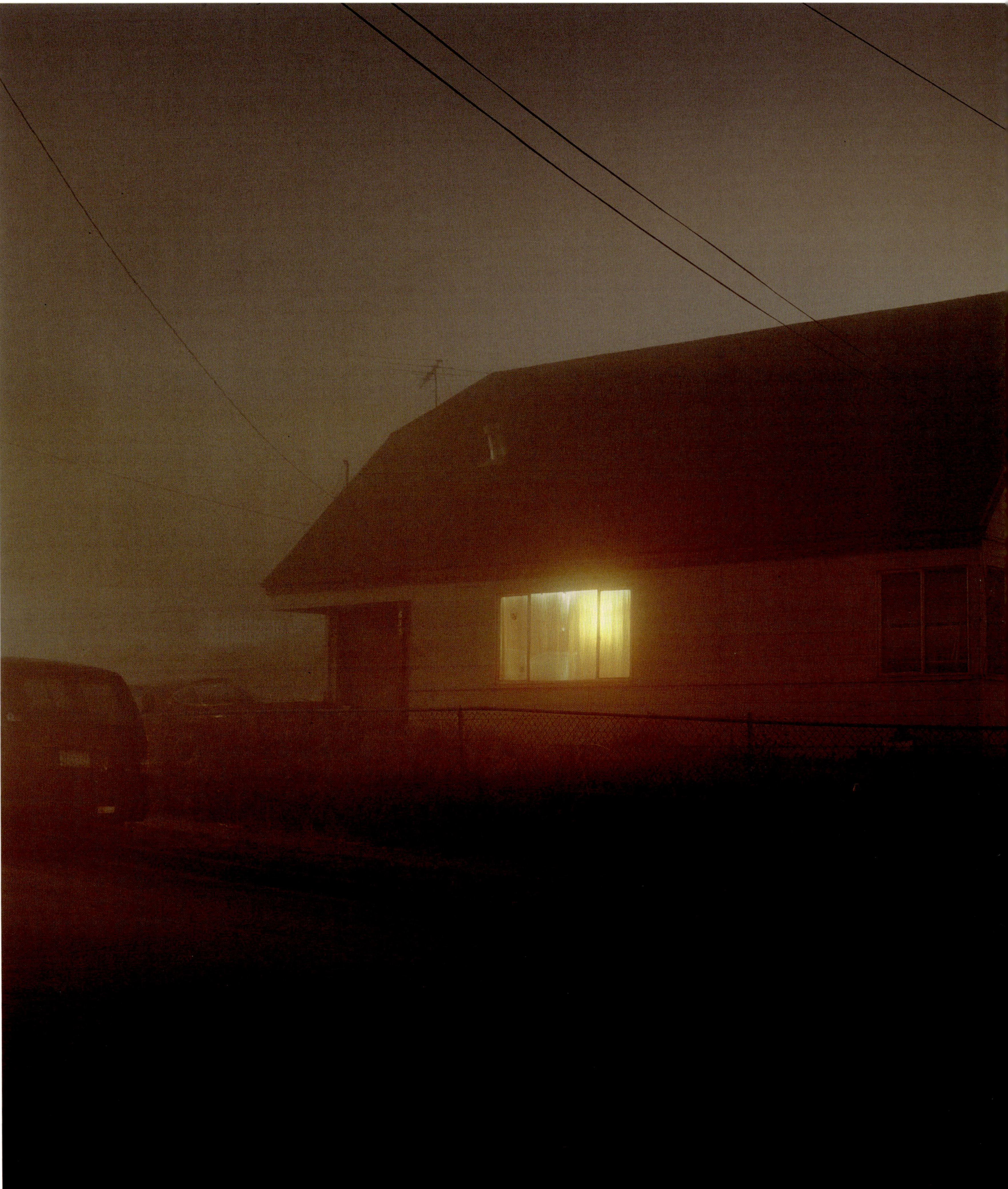

#1951-a / *Pacifica, CA / House Hunting*

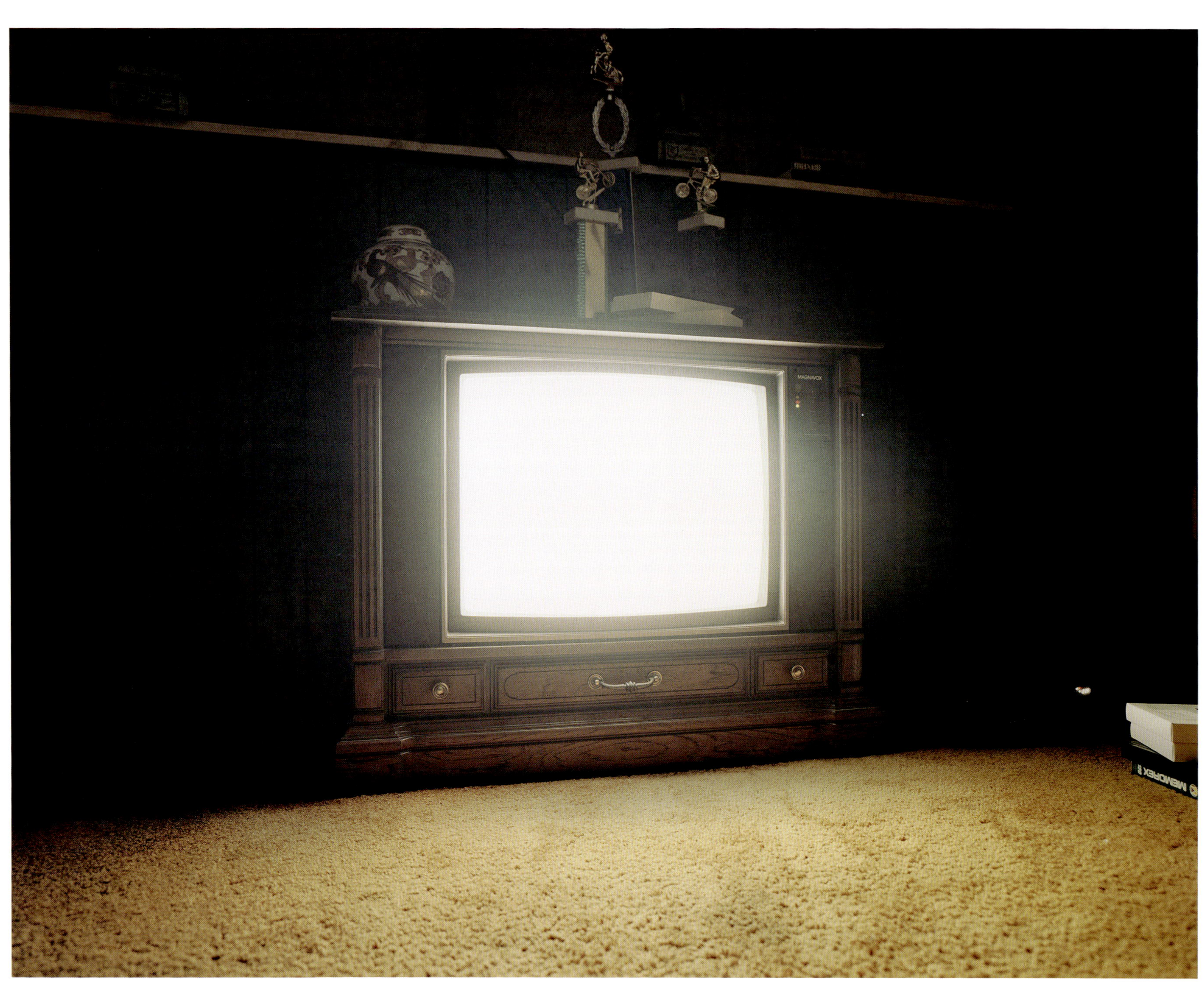

 1997

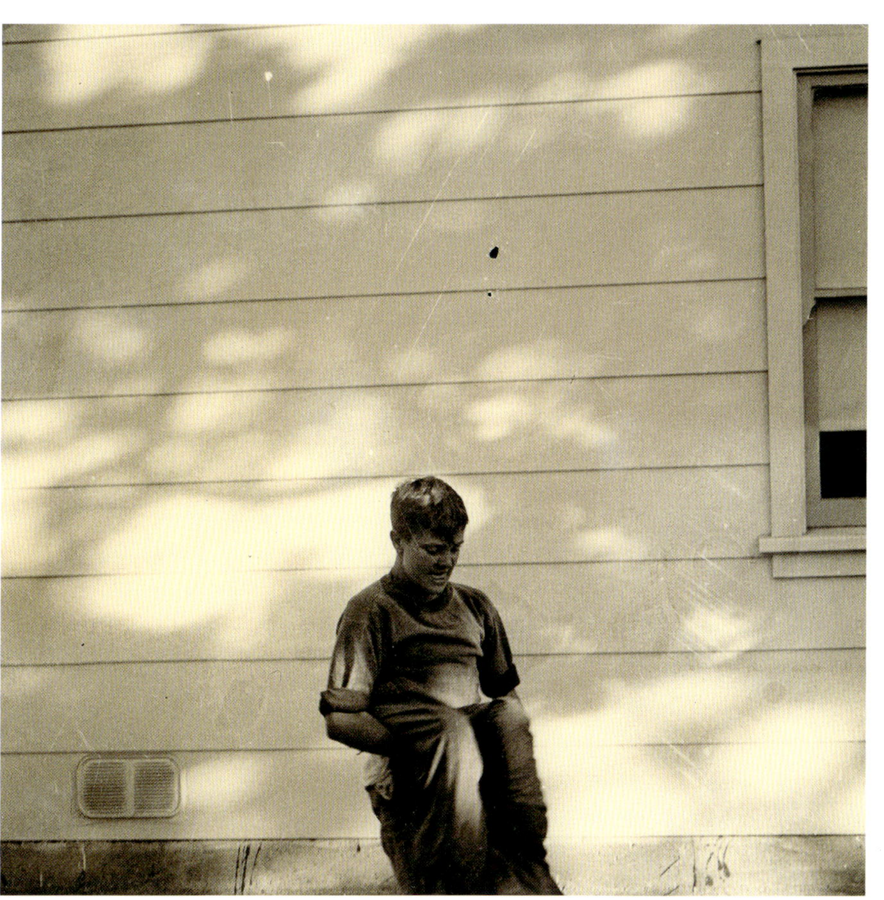

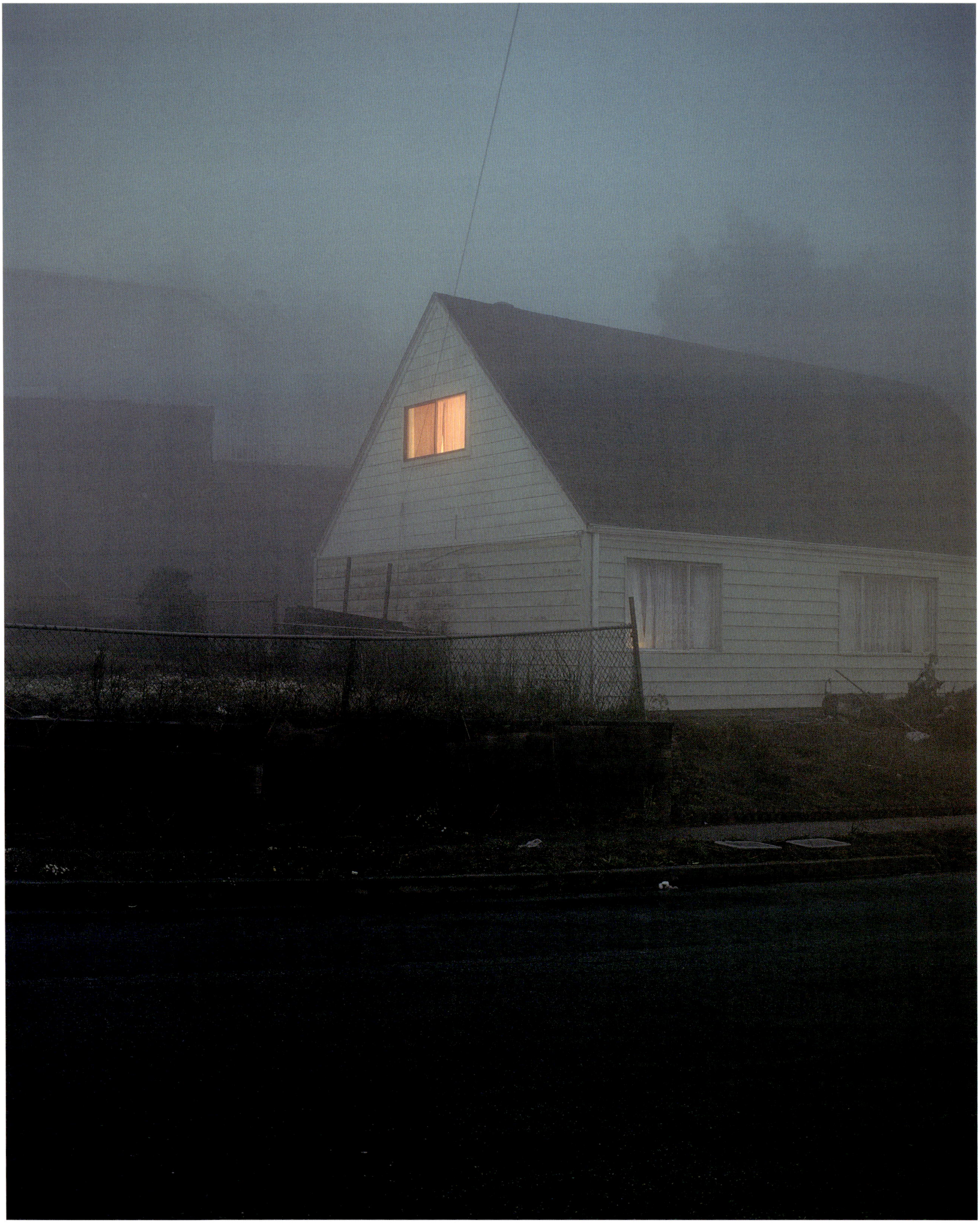

#1975-a / Pacifica, CA / *House Hunting*   **#2027-a** / Pacifica, CA / *House Hunting*   **#2020-a** / found / *Excerpts from Silver Meadows*

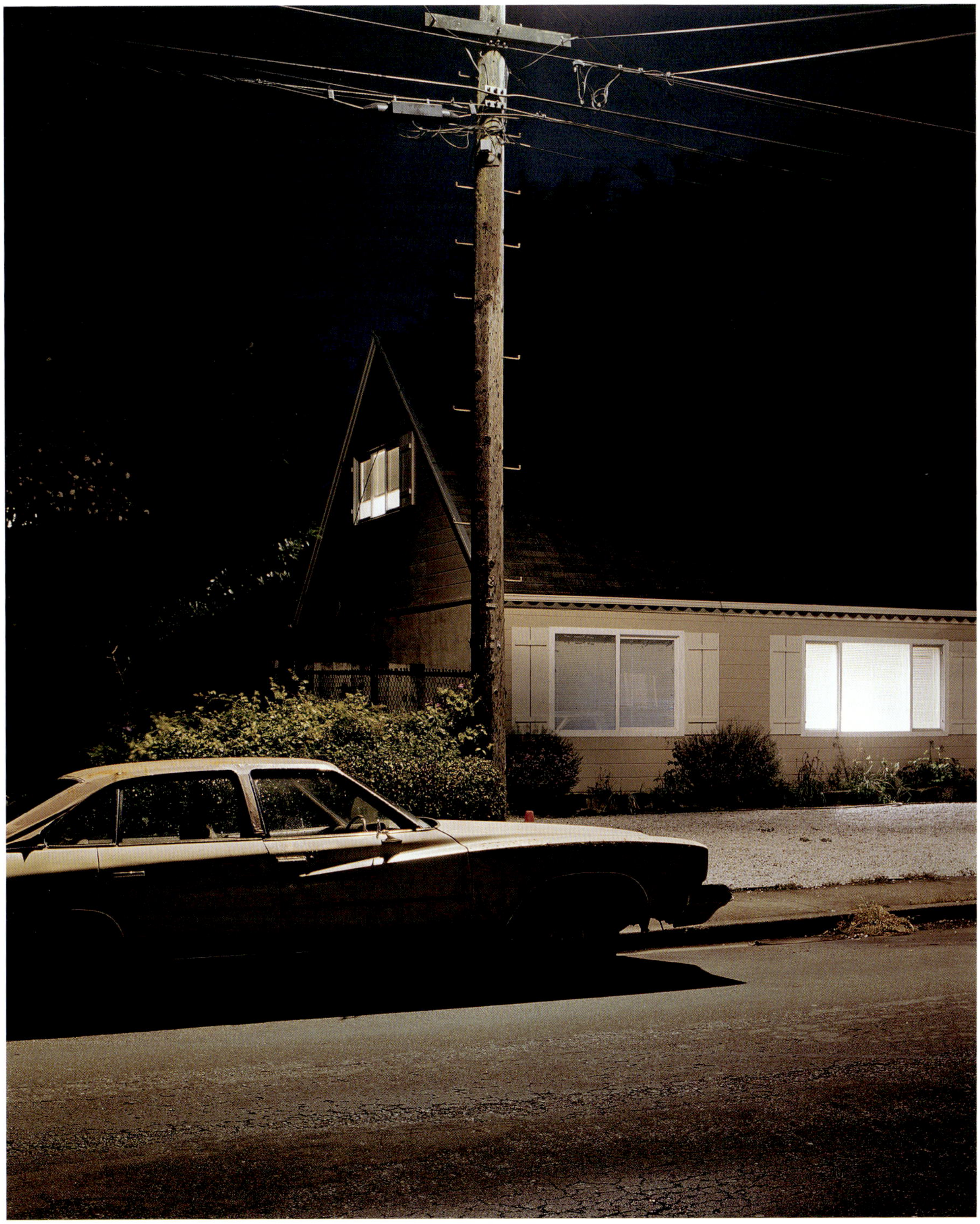

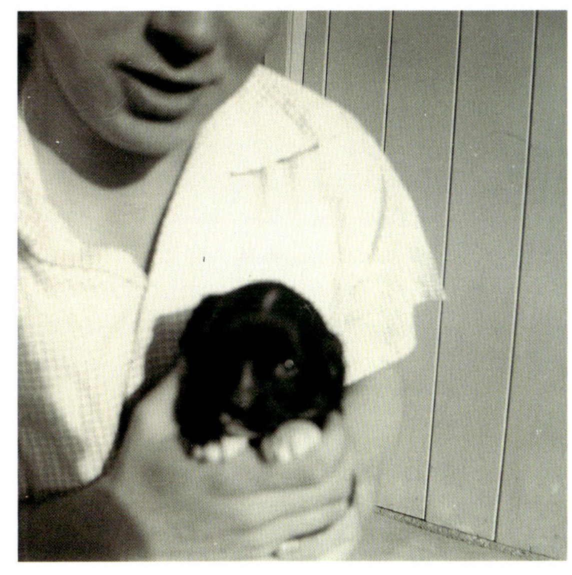

1997

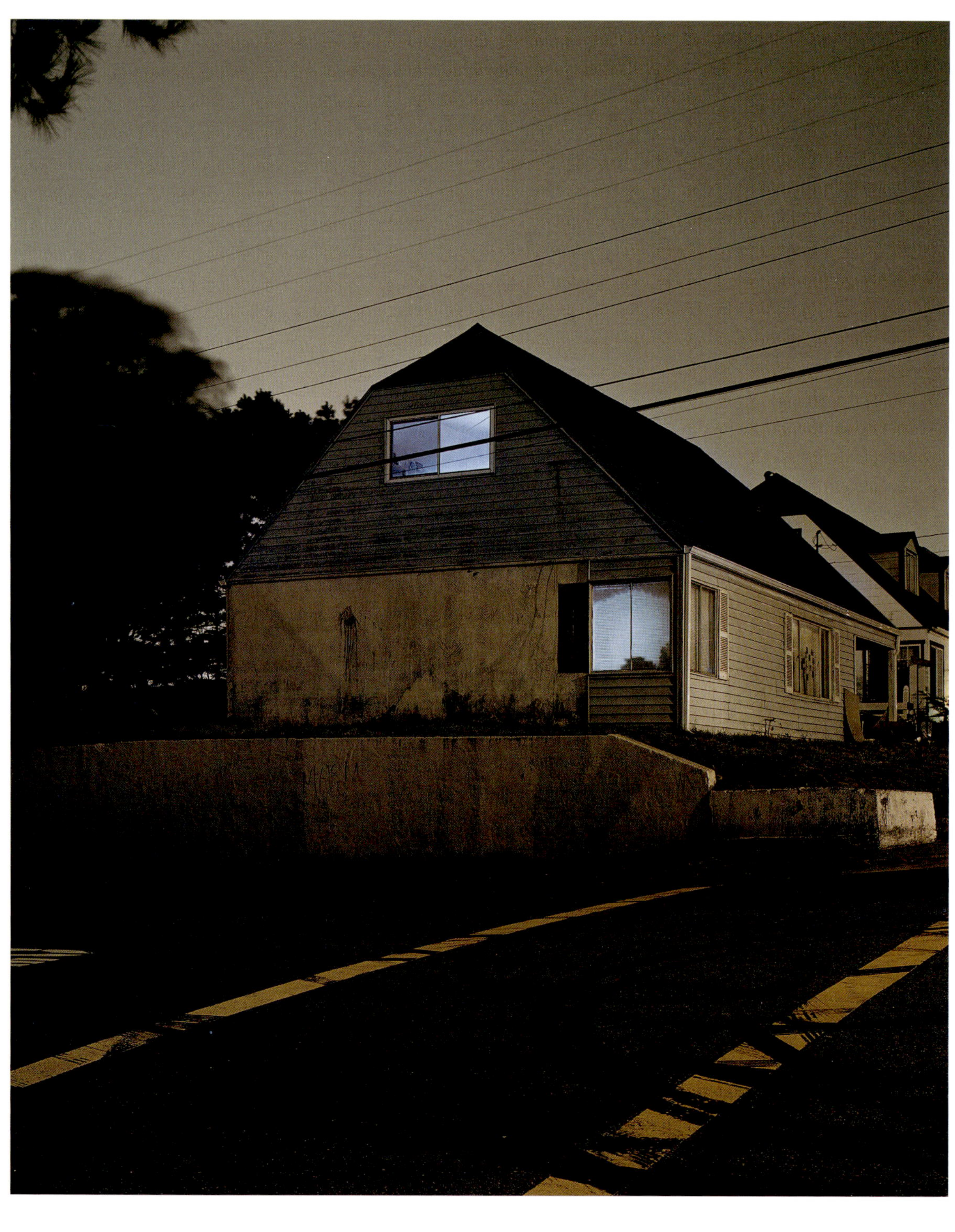

 1998

#2133 / Pacifica, CA / *House Hunting*   #2122 / Pacifica, CA / *House Hunting*

#2214 / Pacifica, CA / *Outskirts*

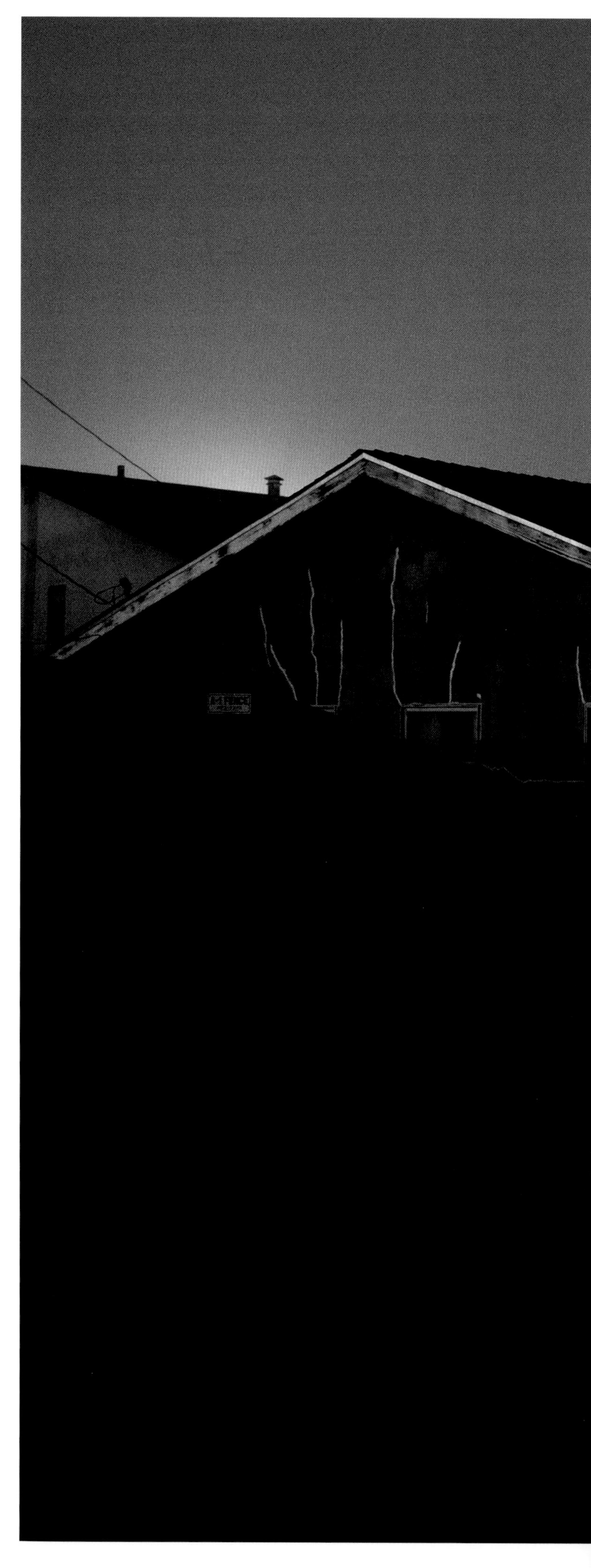

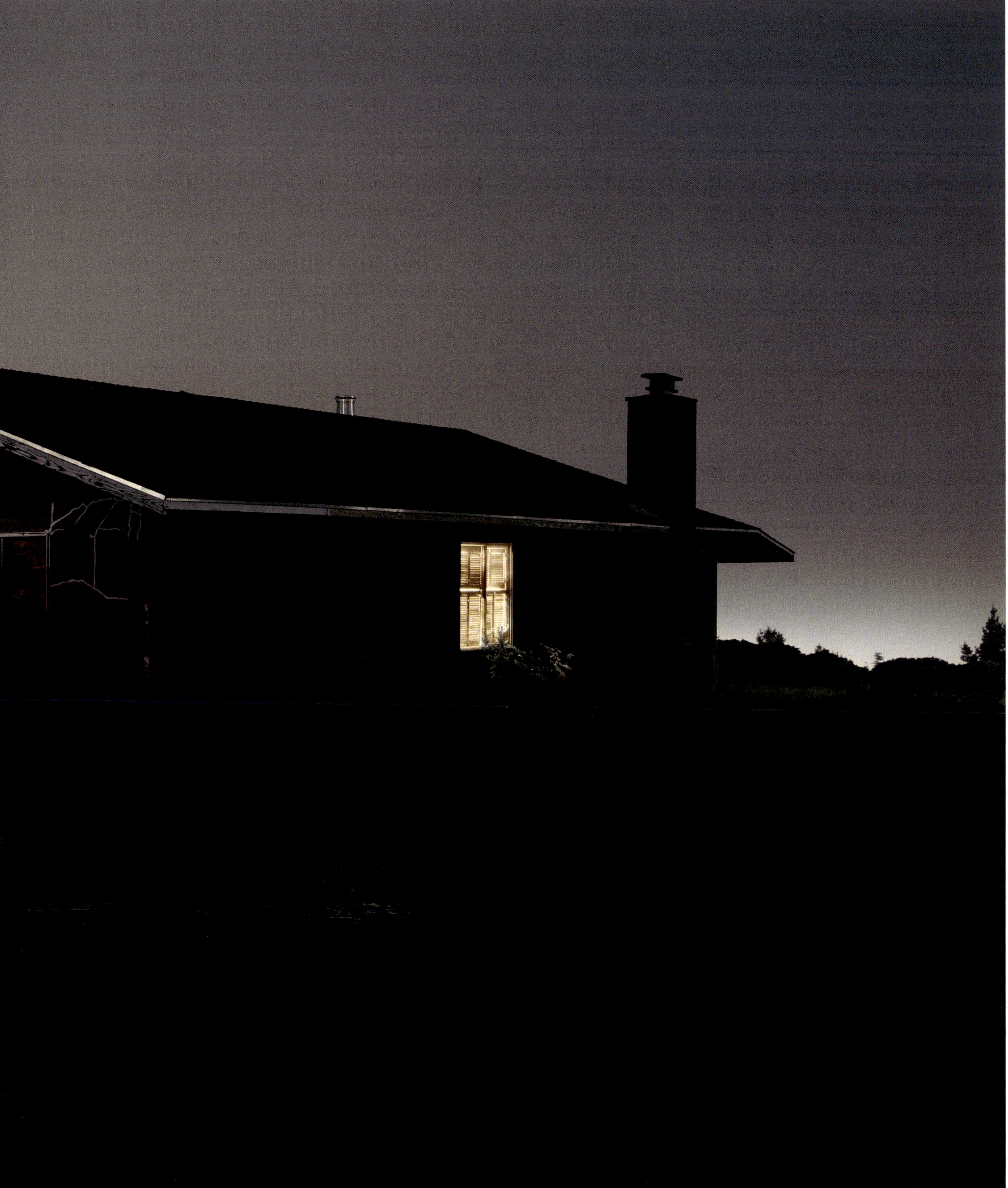

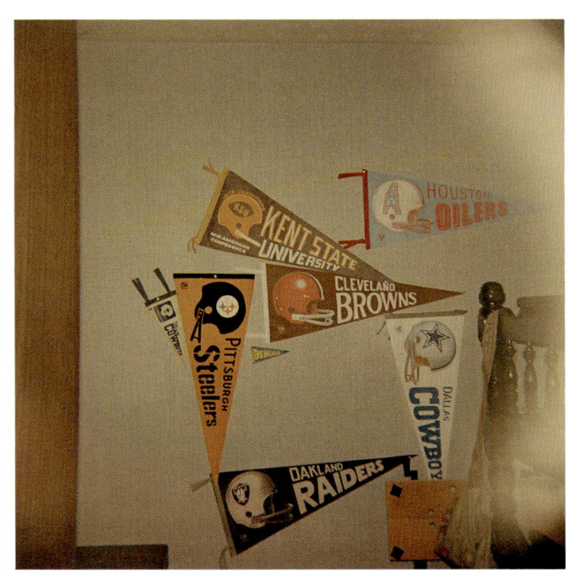
HOUSTON
OILERS
KENT STATE
UNIVERSITY
CLEVELAND
BROWNS
PITTSBURGH
Steelers
COWBOY
OAKLAND
RAIDERS

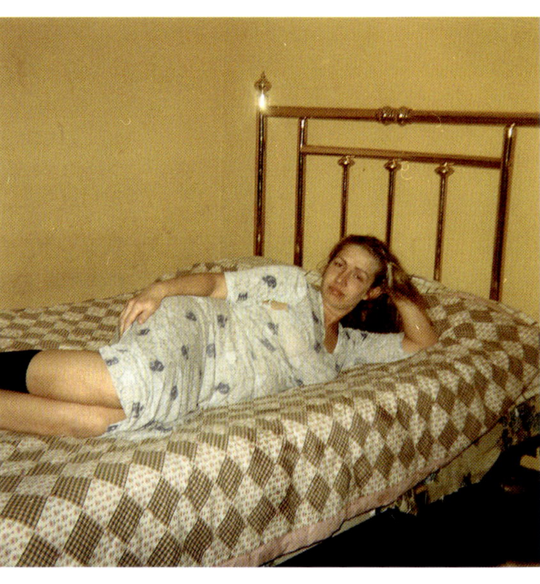

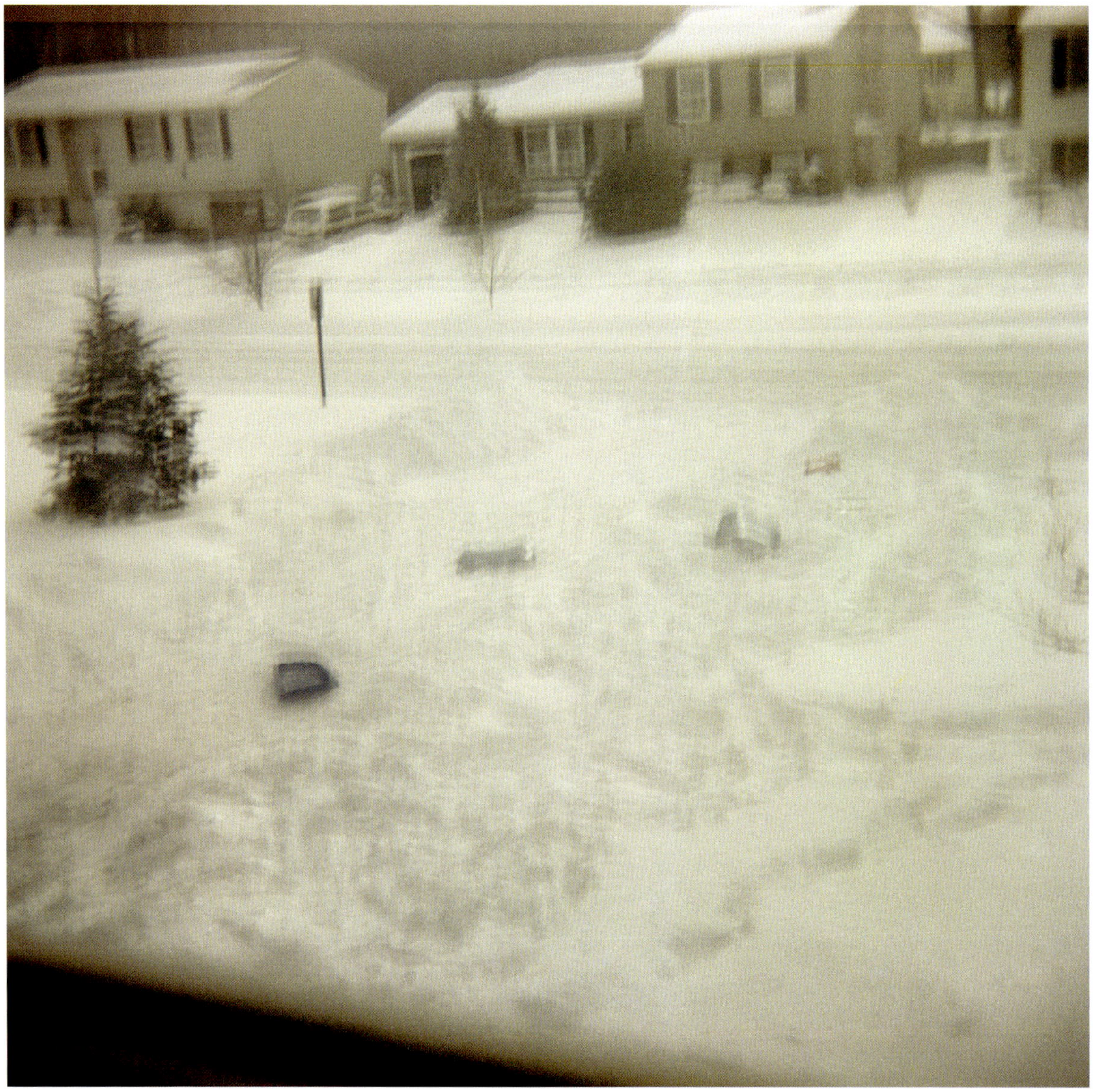

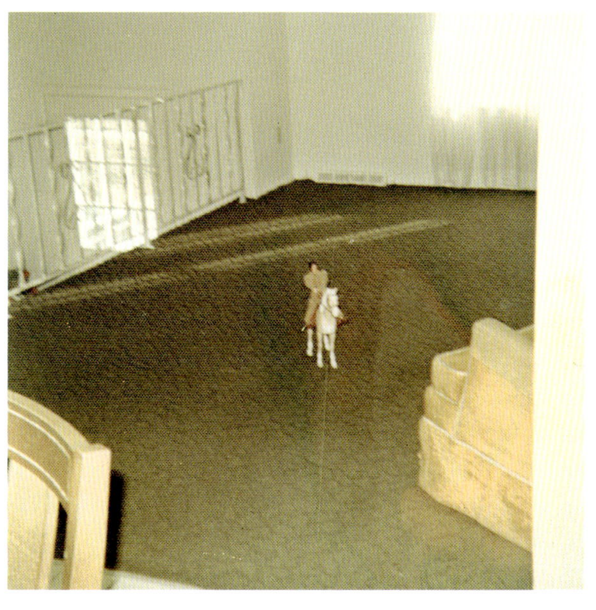

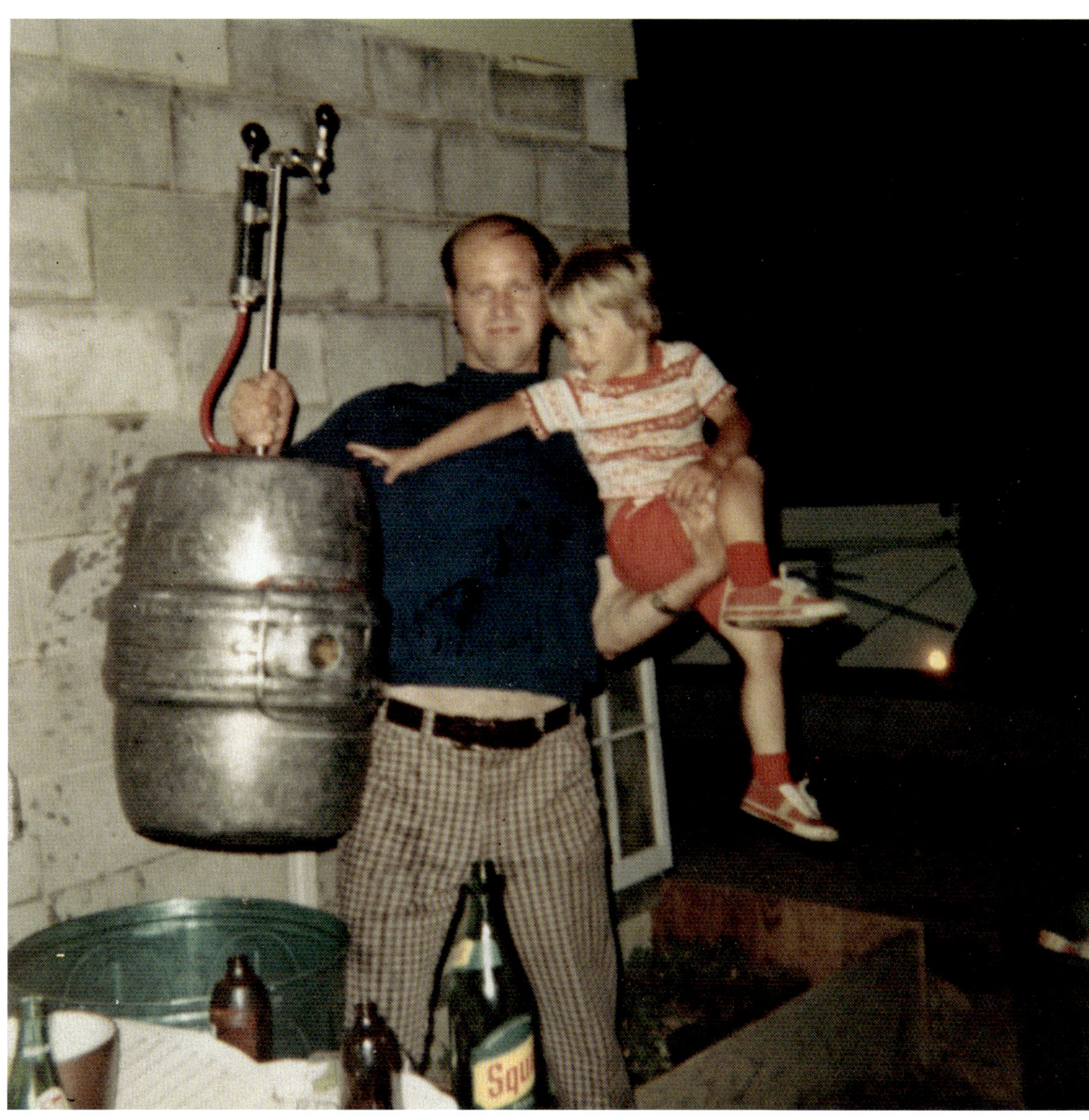

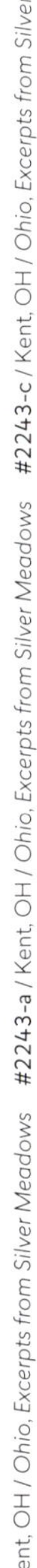

#2235-a / Kent, OH / Ohio, *Excerpts from Silver Meadows* #2236 / Kent, OH / Ohio #2237 / Kent, OH / Ohio, *Excerpts from Silver Meadows* #2243-a / Kent, OH / Ohio, *Excerpts from Silver Meadows* #2243-c / Kent, OH / Ohio, *Excerpts from Silver Meadows*

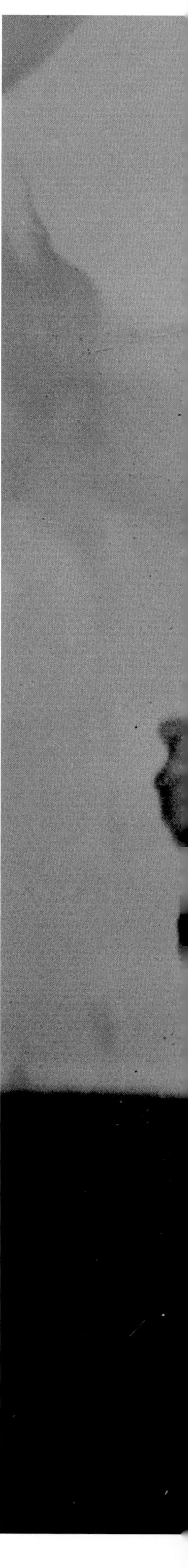

#2243-d / Kent, OH / Ohio, *Excerpts from Silver Meadows*

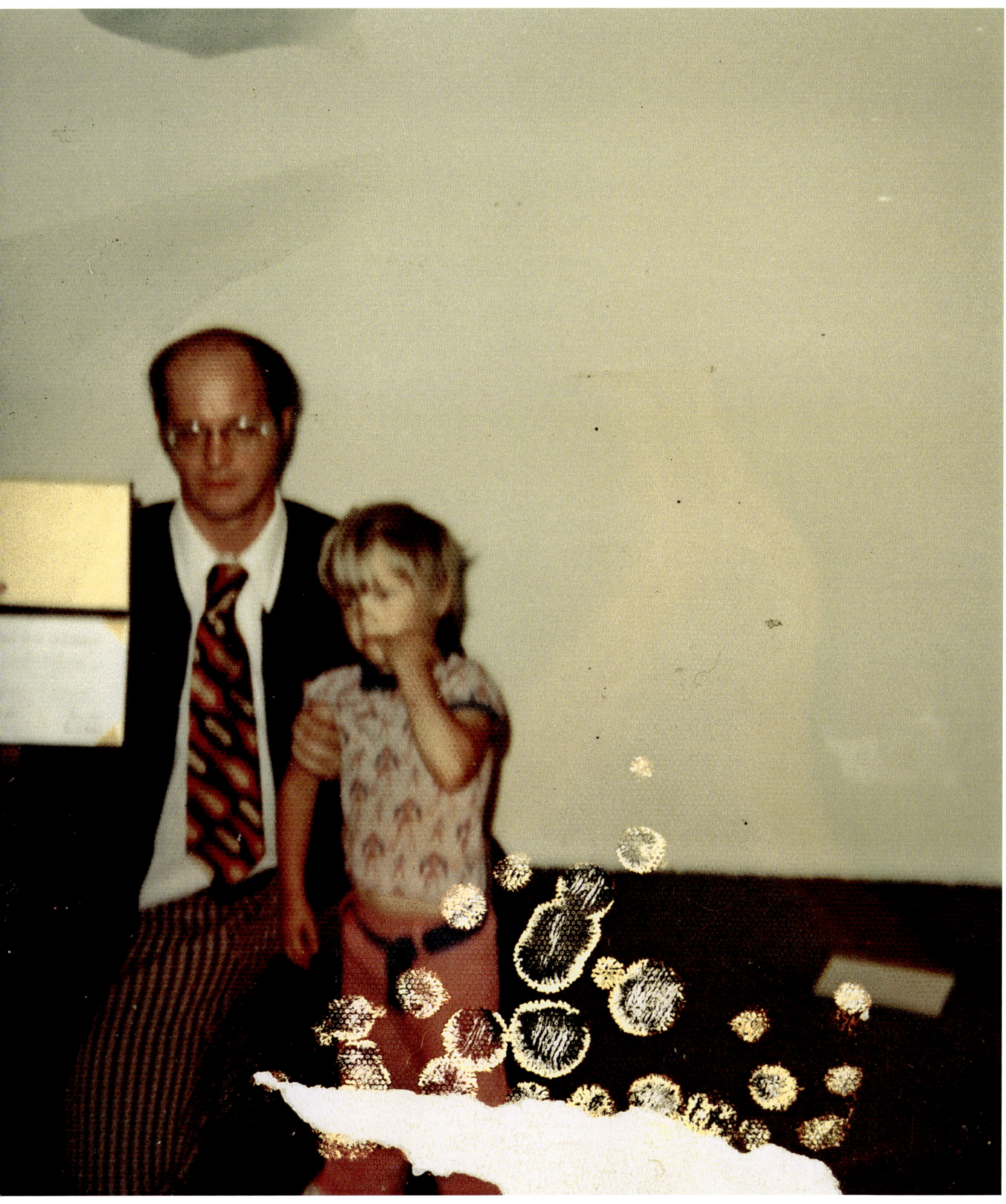

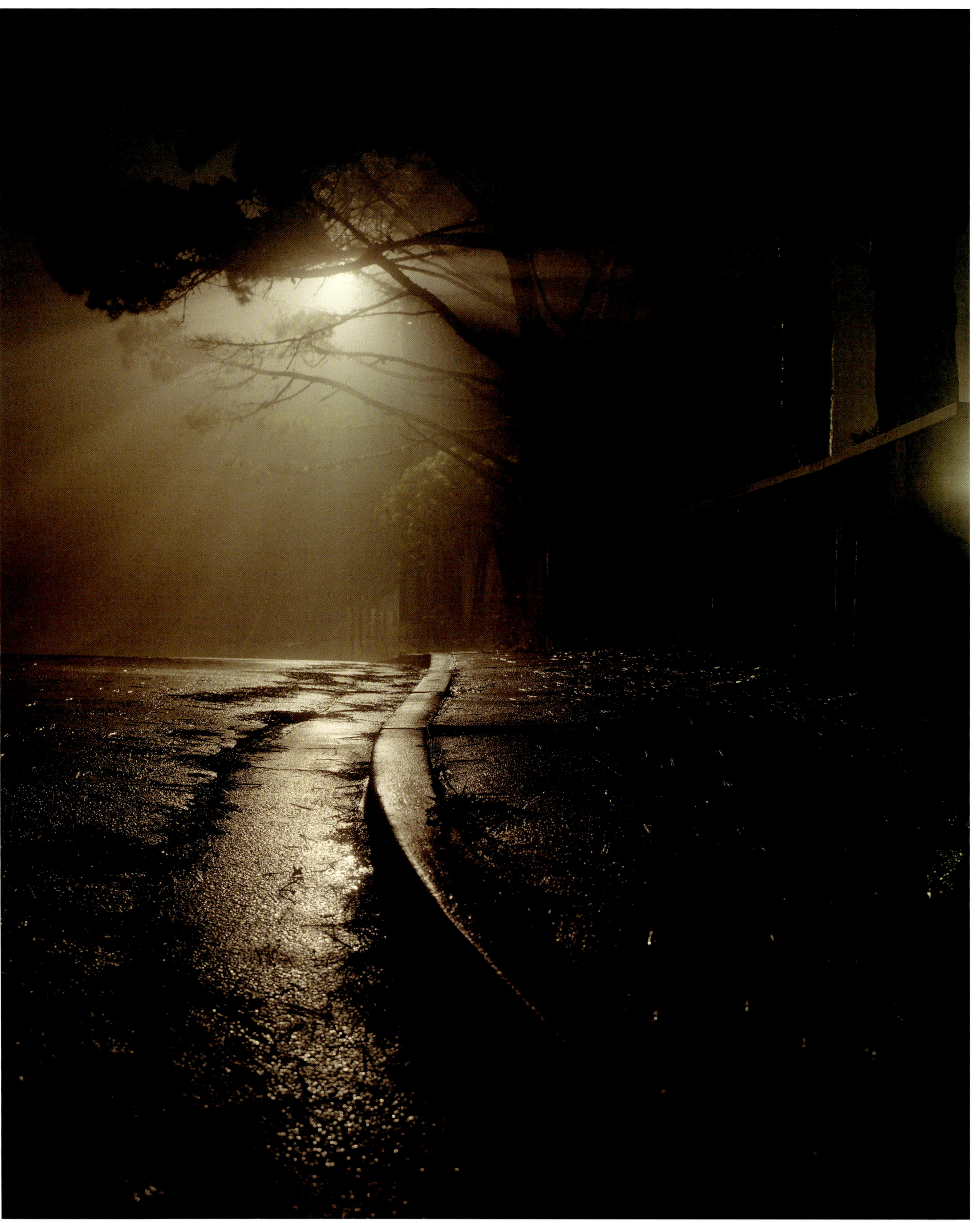

#2256-a / Pacifica, CA / *Outskirts*   #2275 / Pacifica, CA / *Roaming*

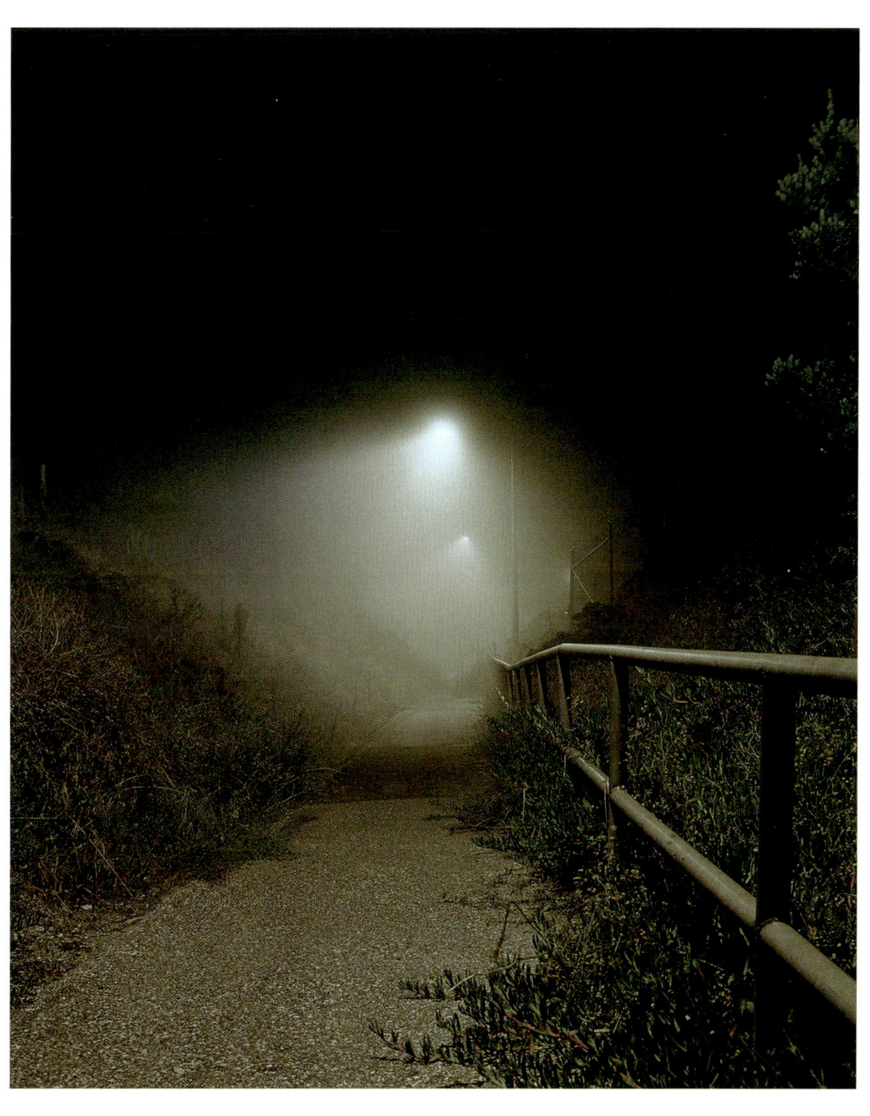

1999

#2312-a / Love Canal, NY / *House Hunting*

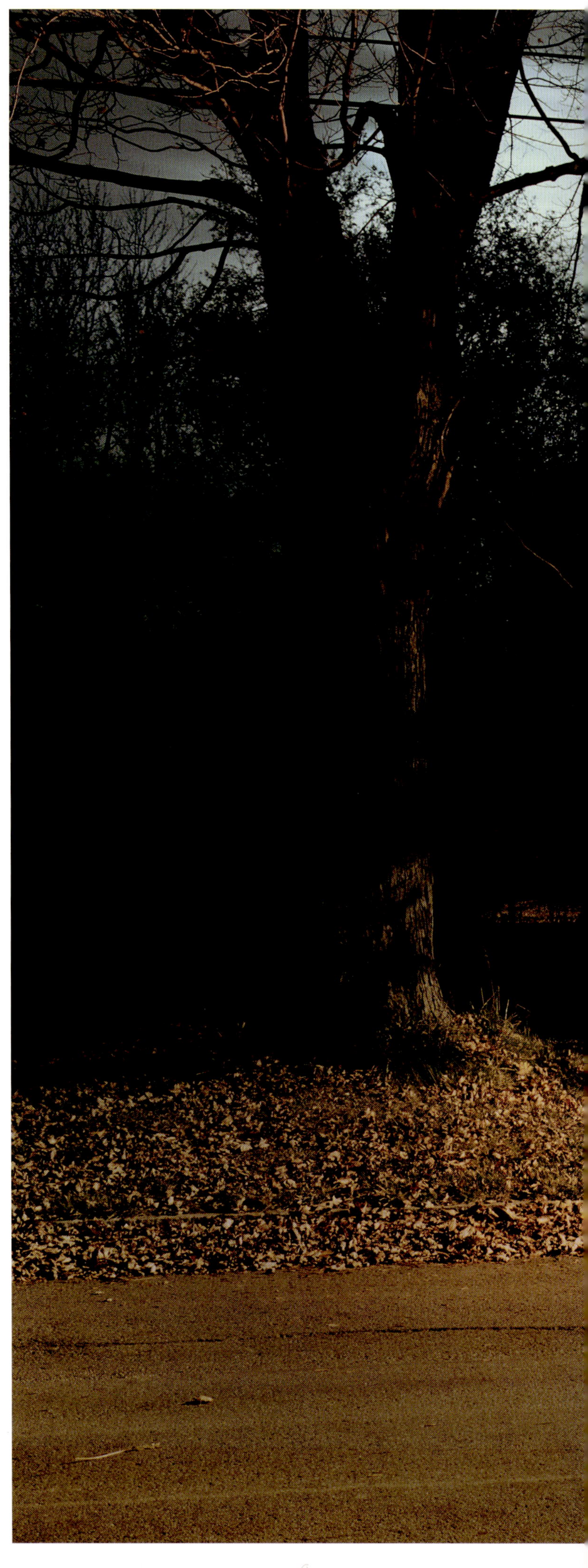

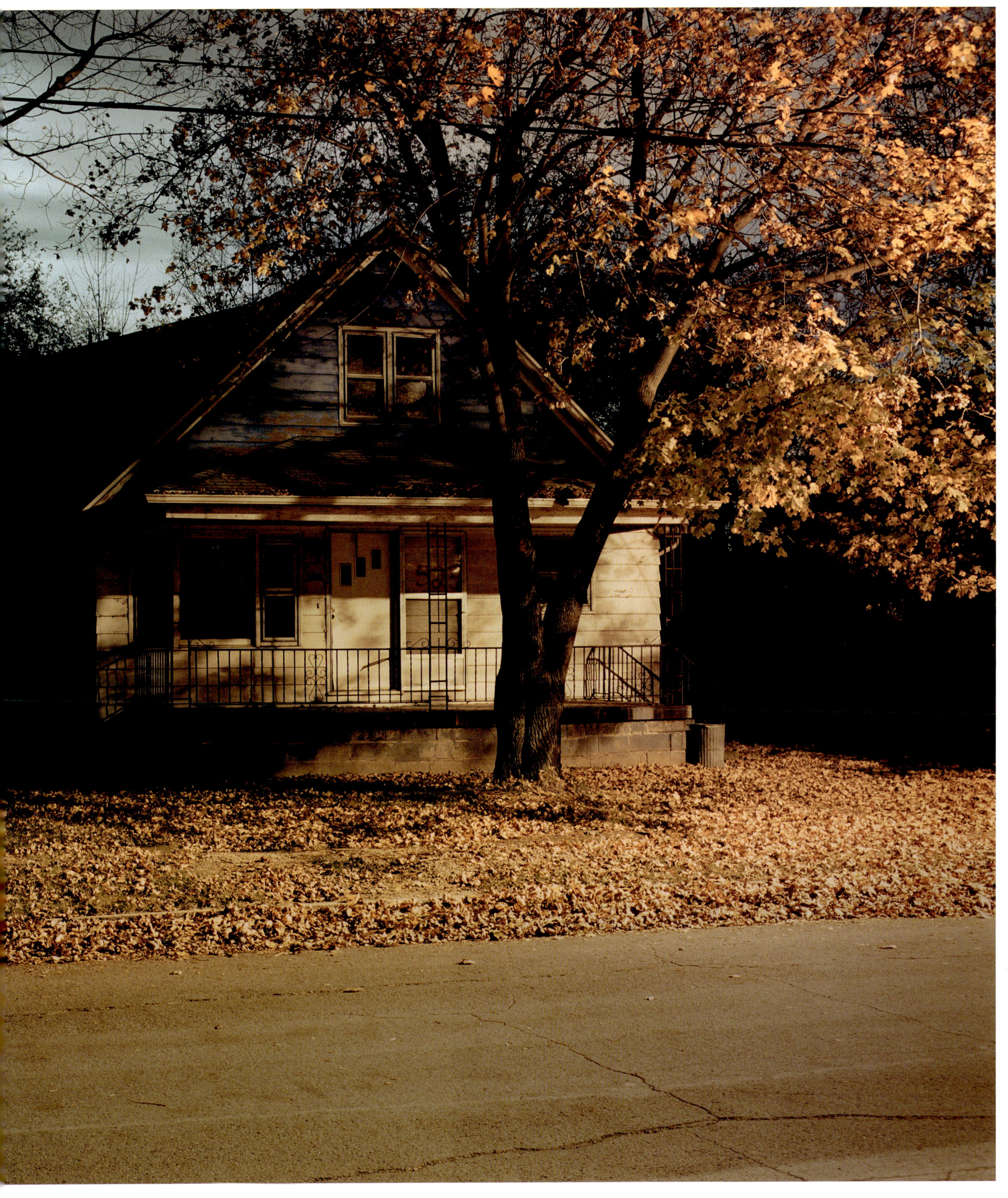

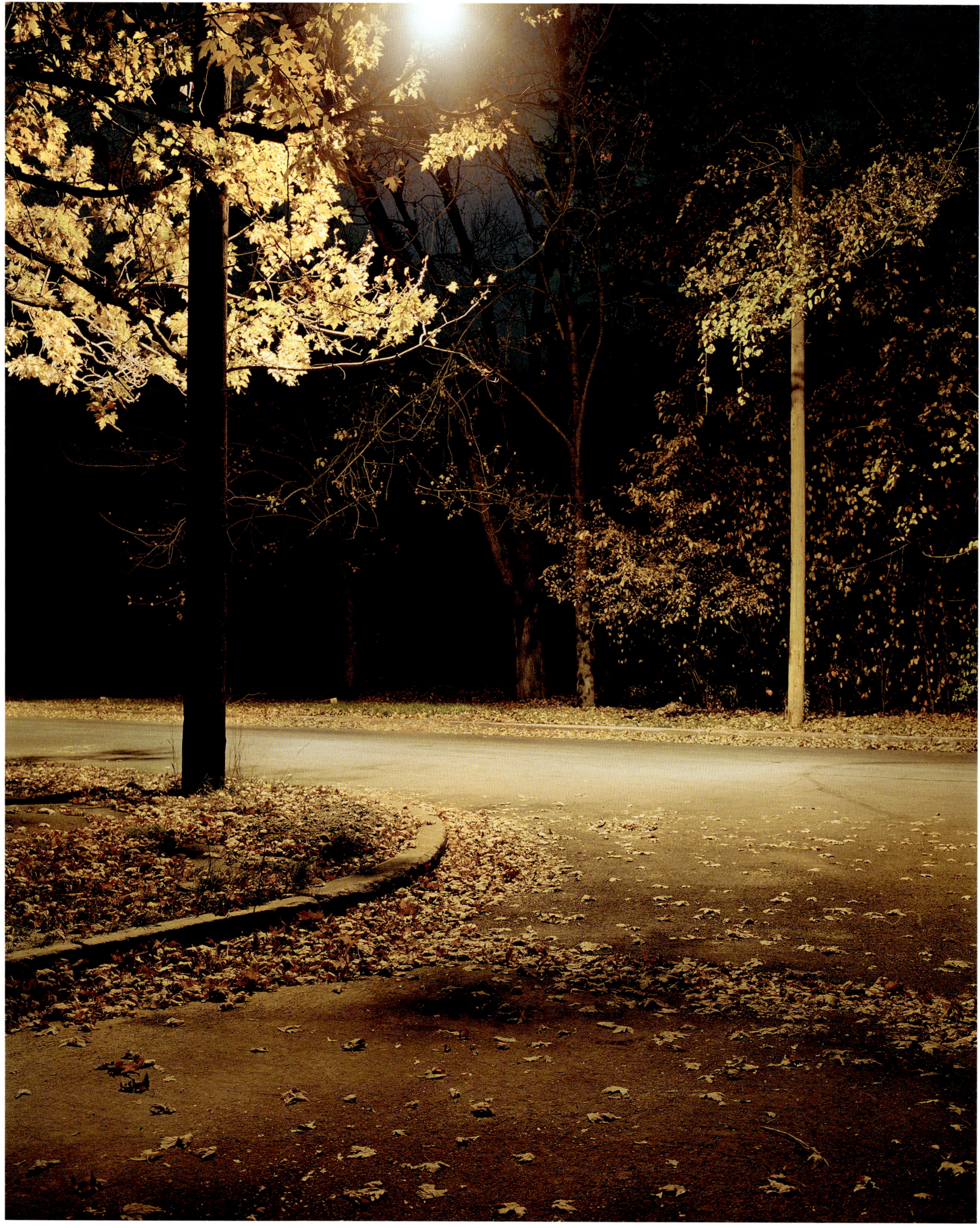

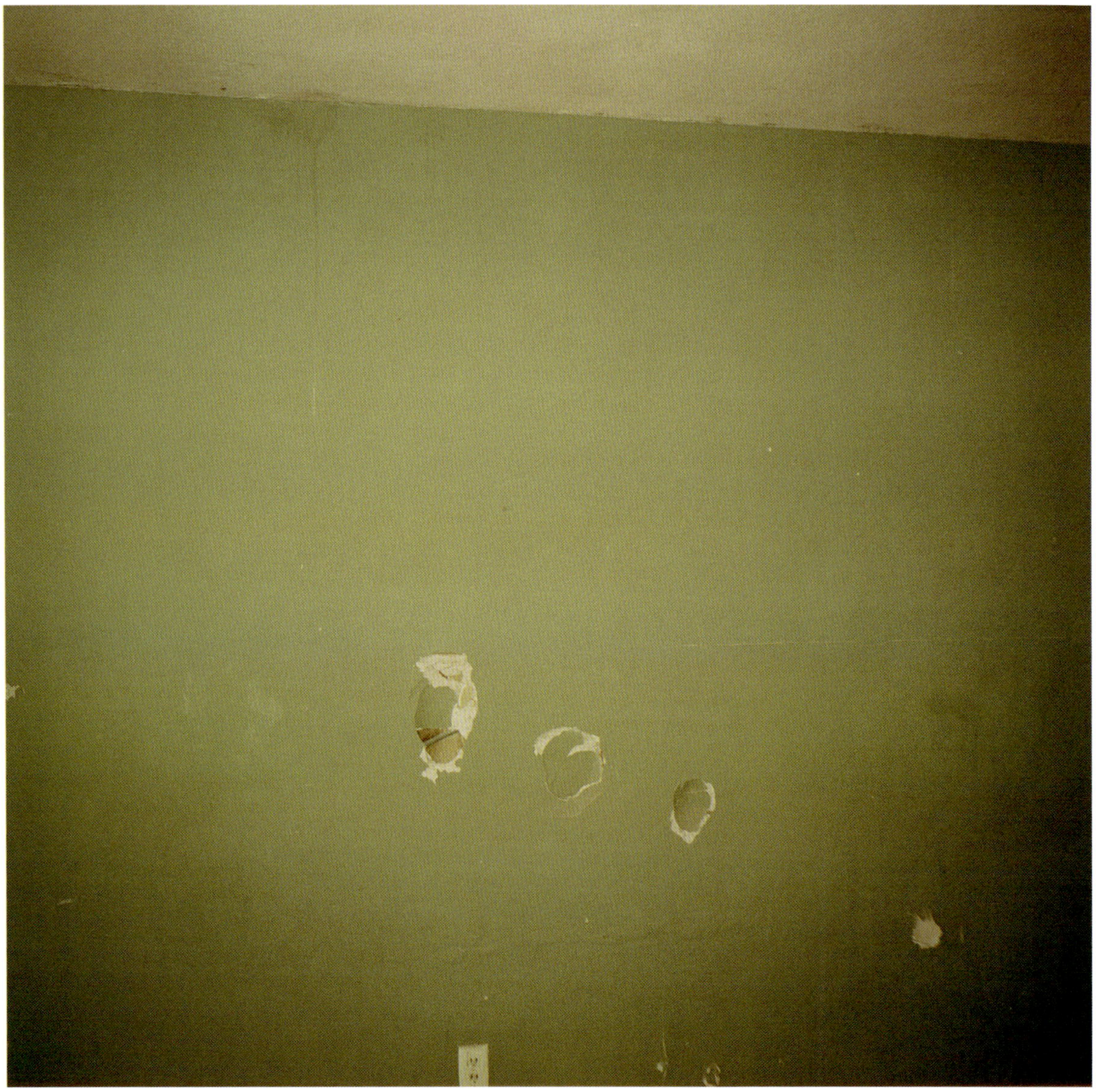

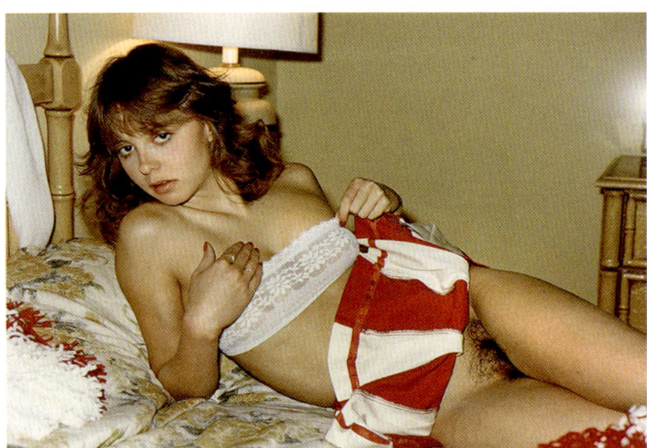

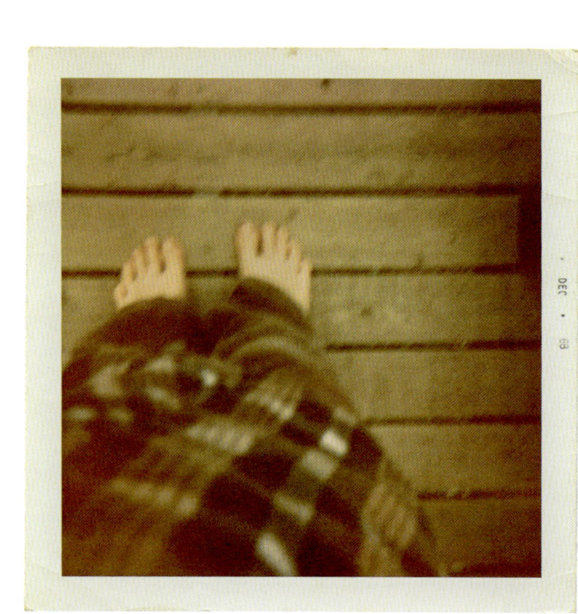

#2347-b / Salton Sea, CA / Ohio, *Excerpts from Silver Meadows*   **#2347-c-cheerleader** / found   **#2360** / Kent, OH / Ohio, *Excerpts from Silver Meadows*

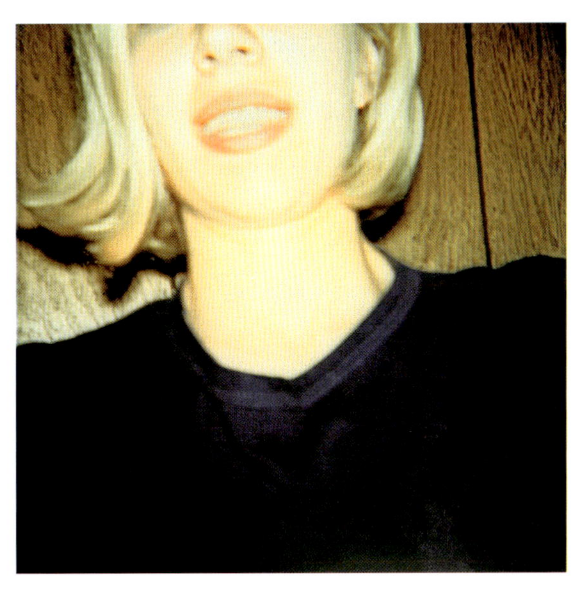

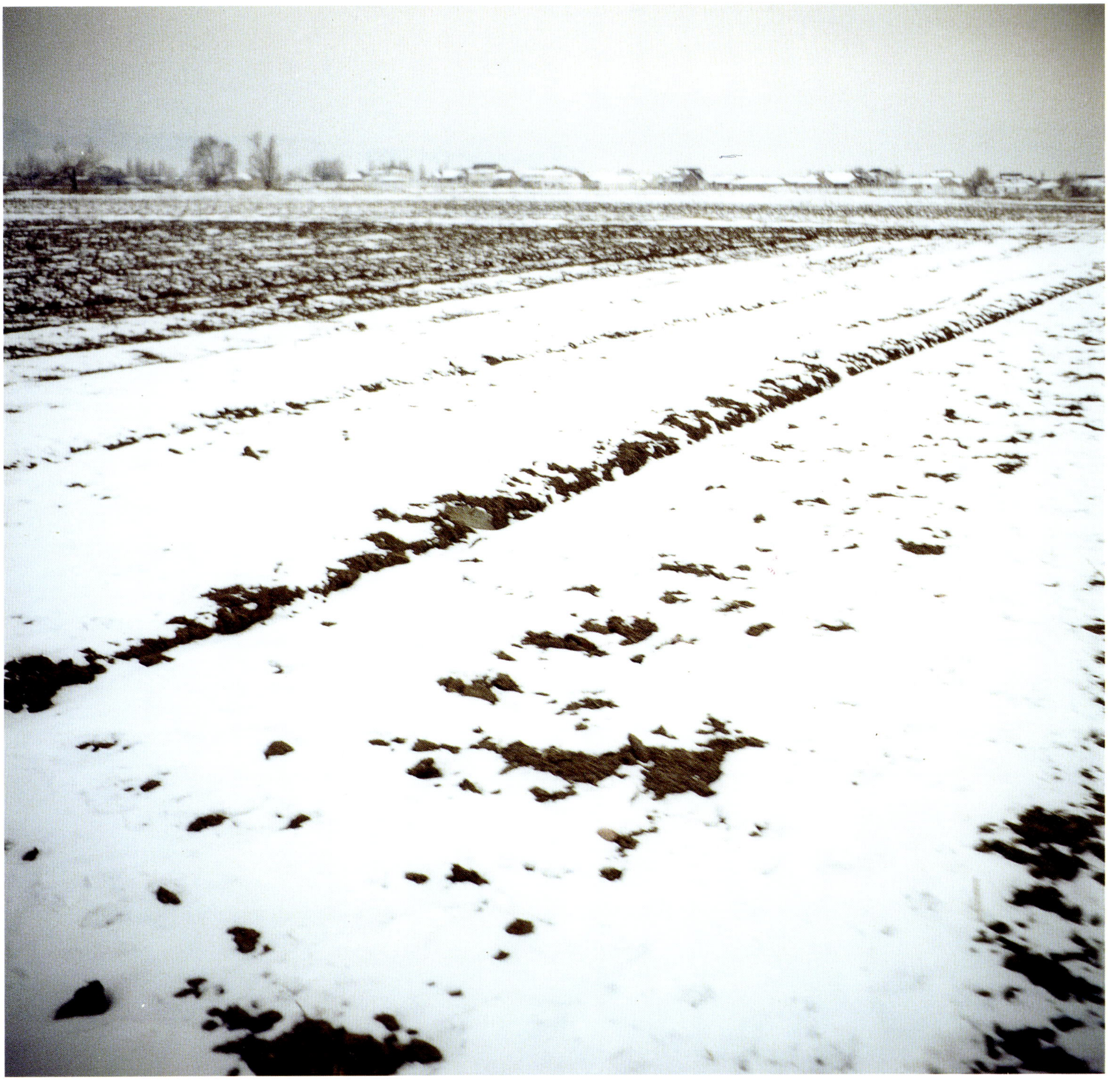

#2369 / Provo, UT / Ohio #2399 / Cuyahoga Falls, OH / Ohio, *Excerpts from Silver Meadows*

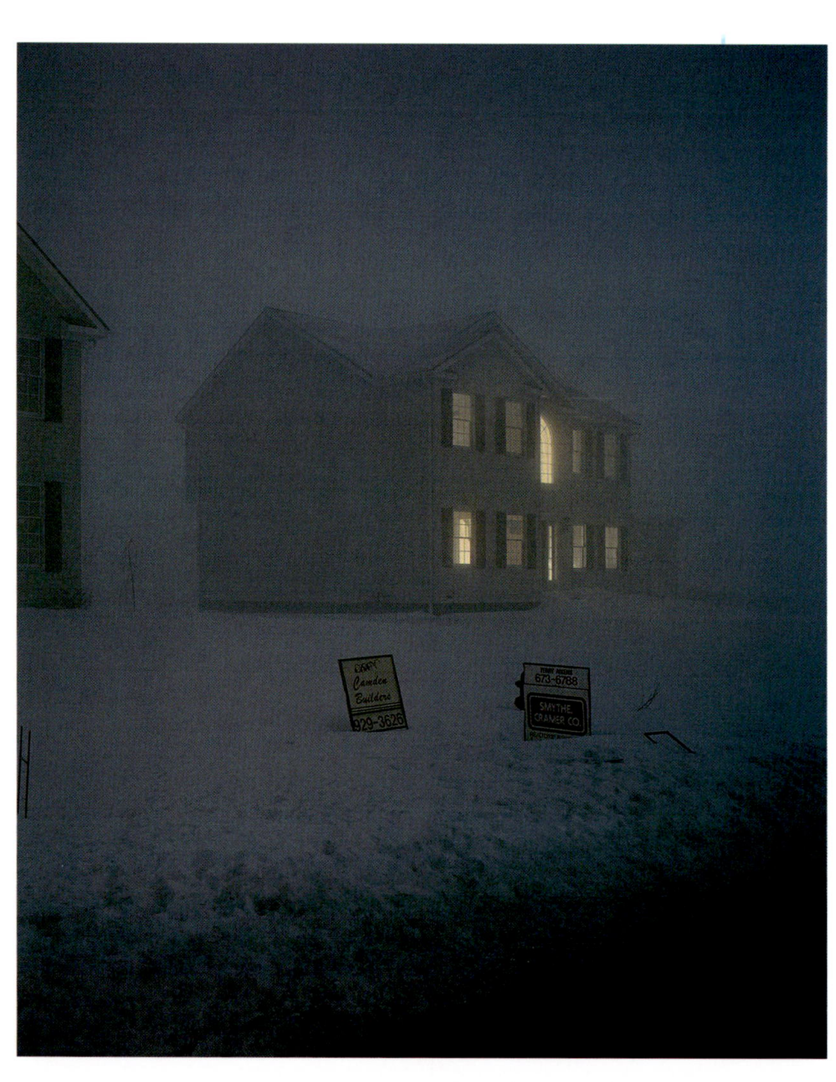
Camden
Builders
929-3626
673-6788
SMYTHE
CRAMER CO.

#2424-b / Stow, OH / Outskirts **#2424-a** / Stow, OH / *Outskirts, Roaming*

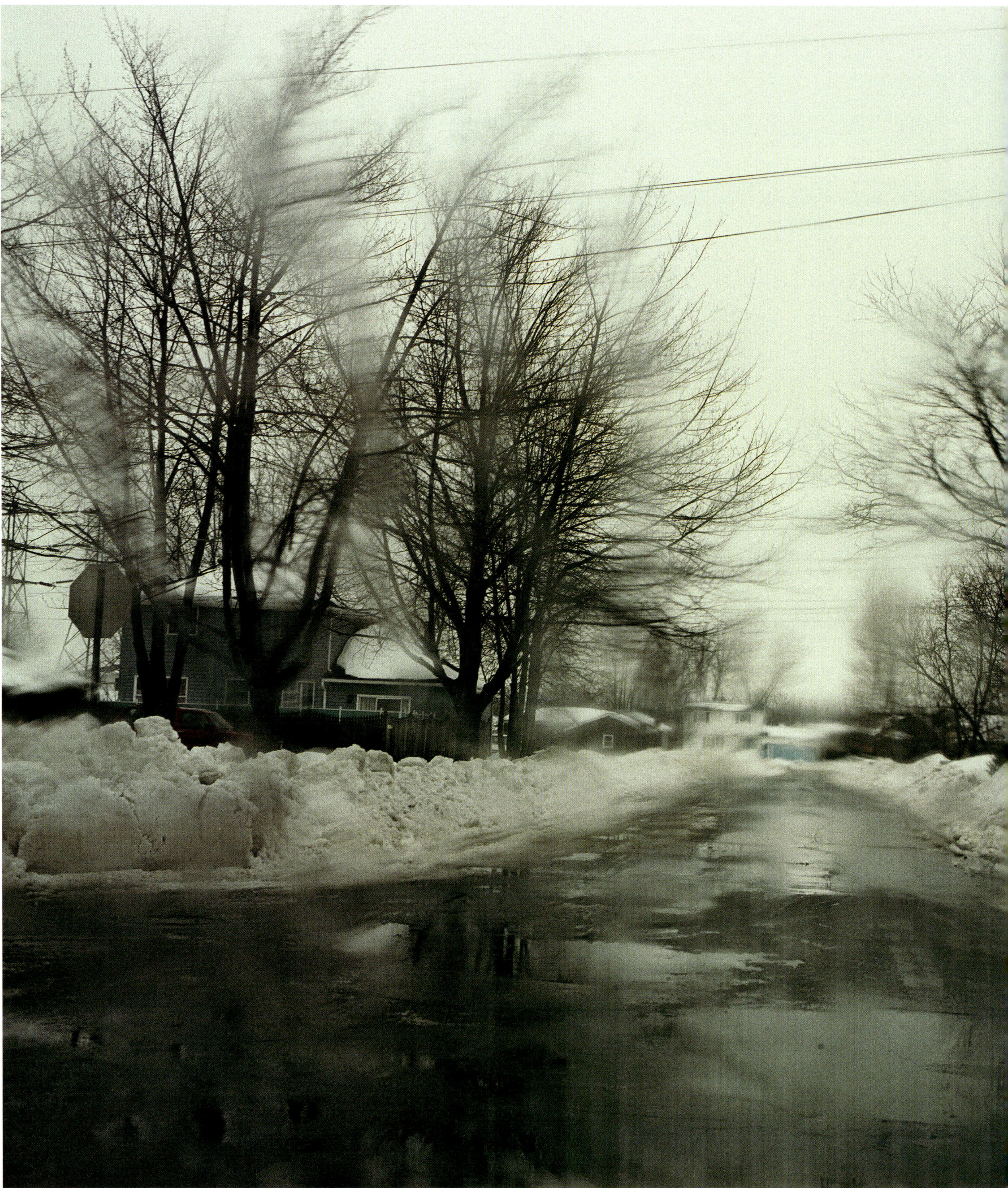

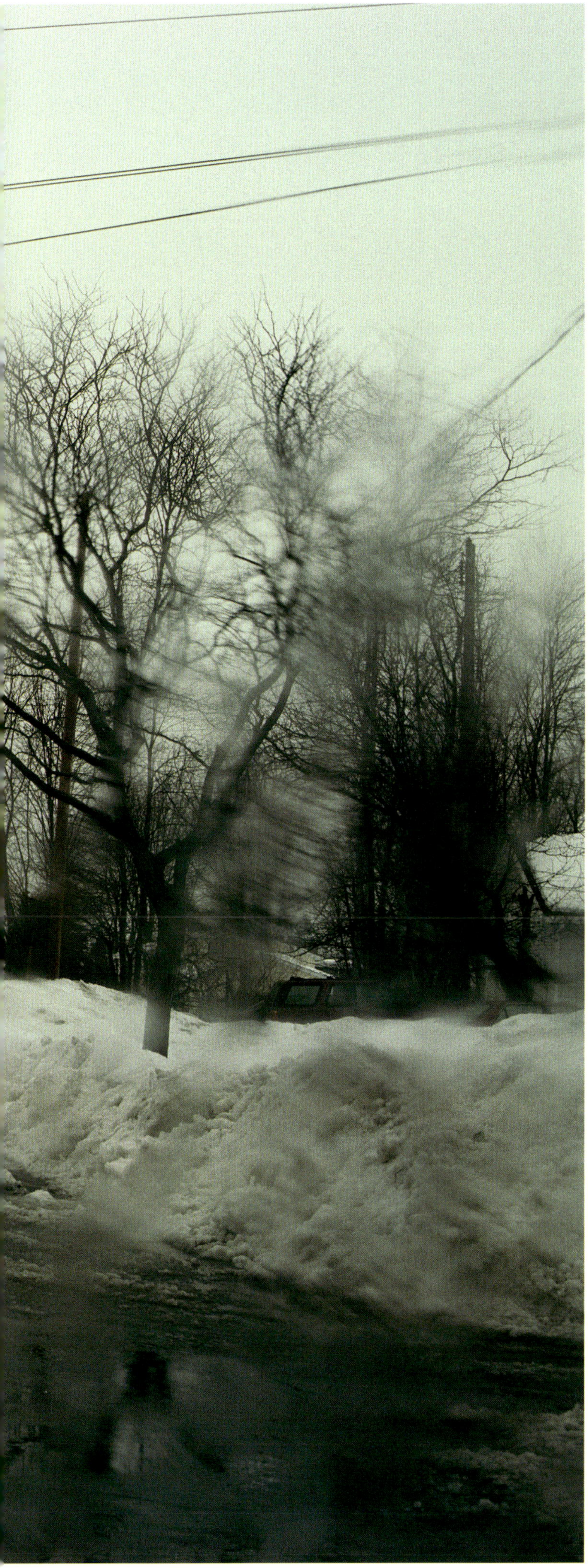

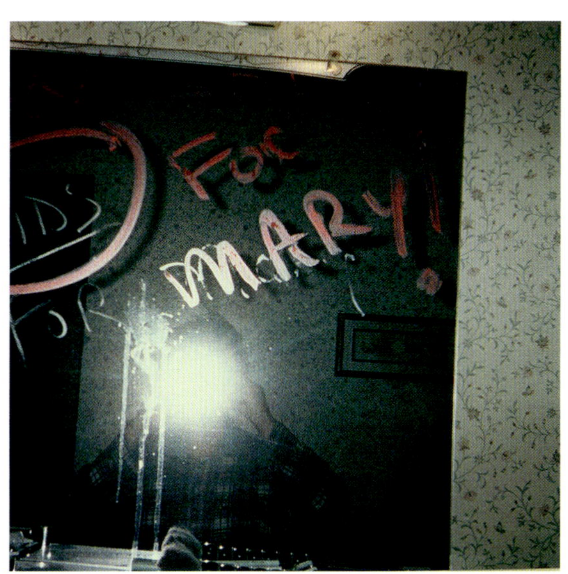

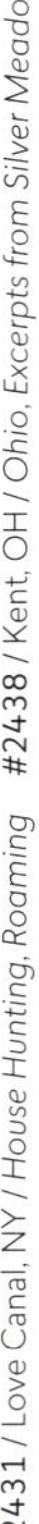
#2431 / Love Canal, NY / *House Hunting, Roaming*   **#2438** / Kent, OH / *Ohio, Excerpts from Silver Meadows*

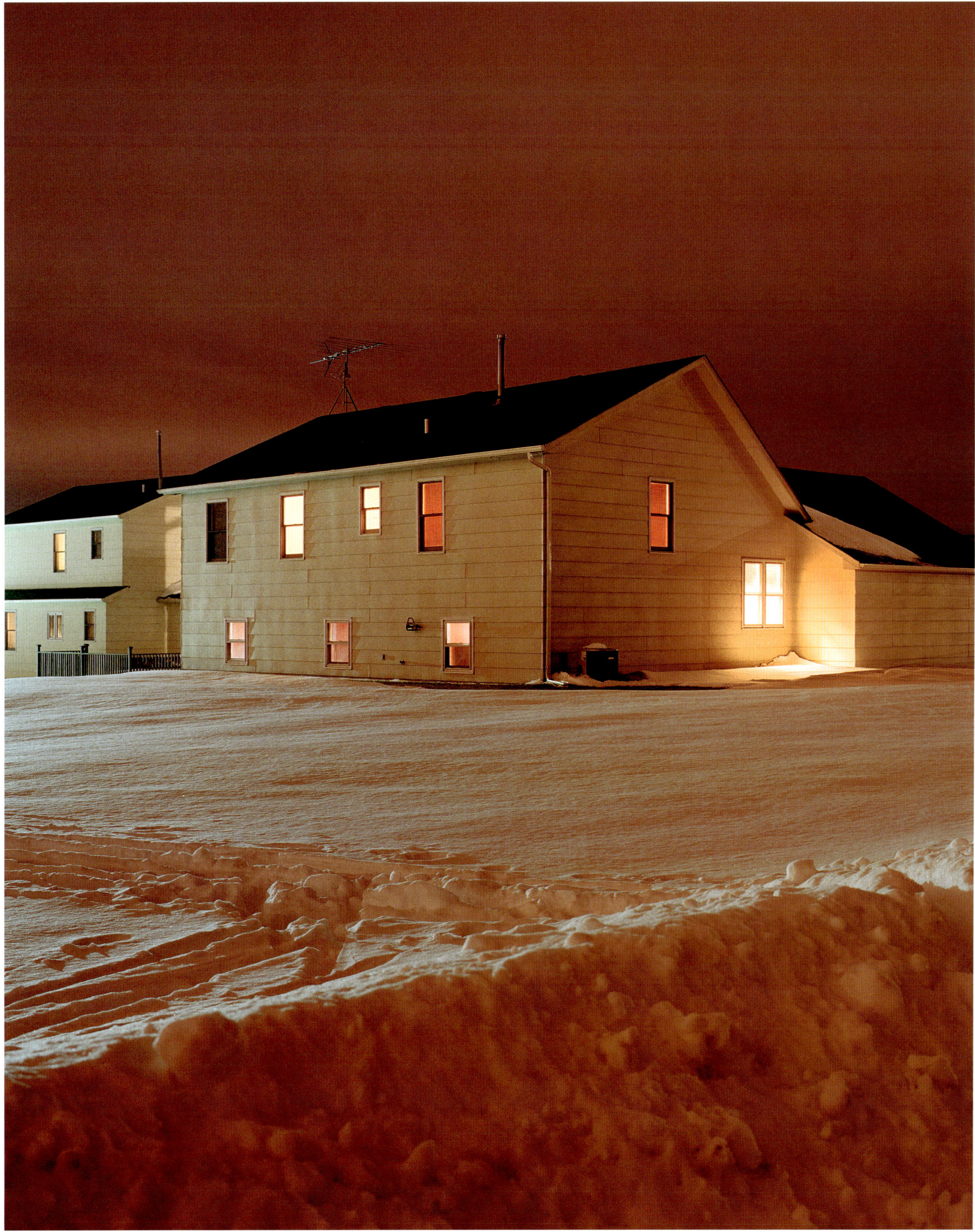

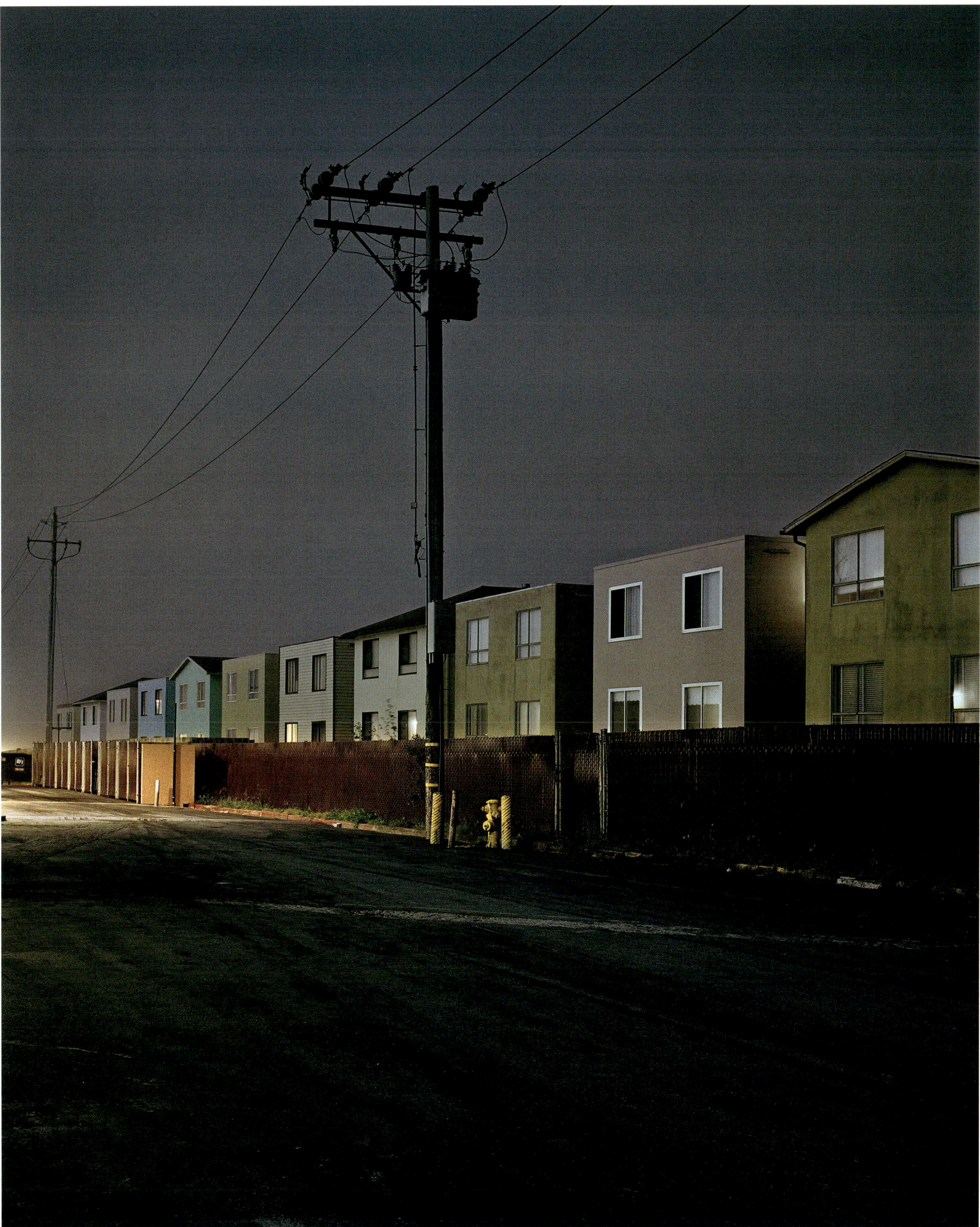

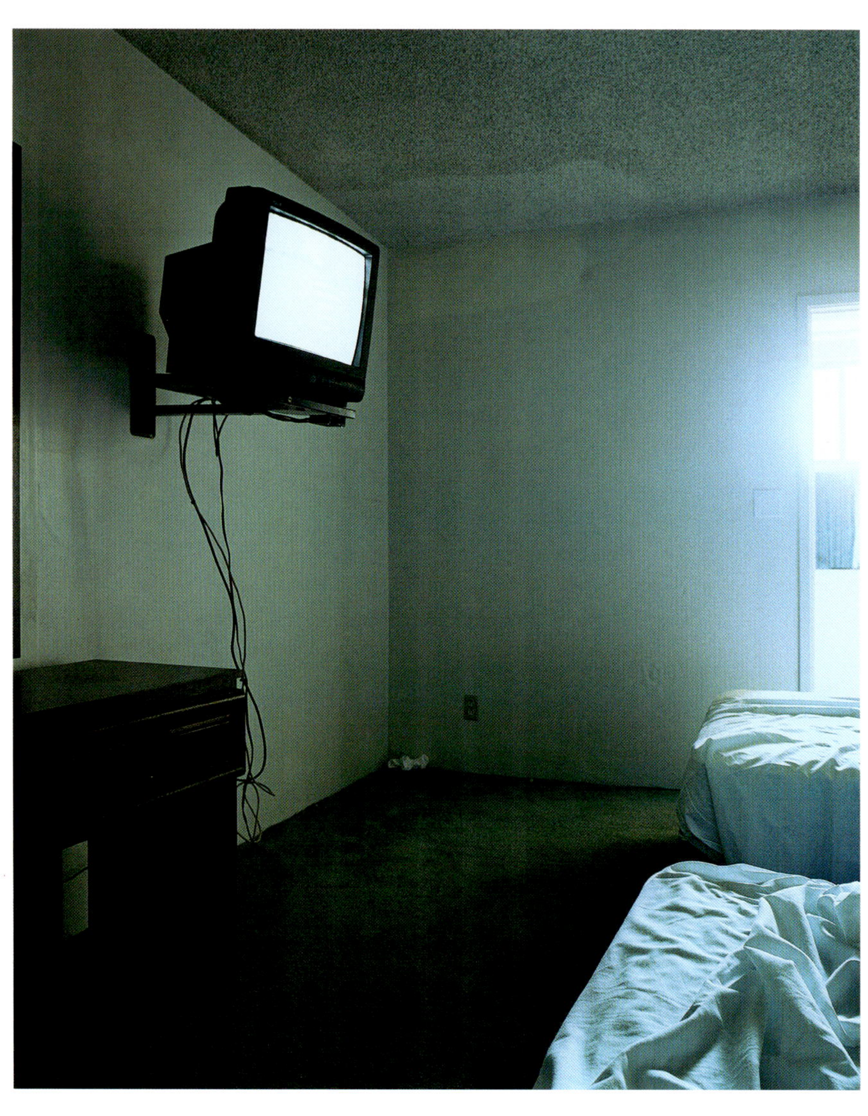

#2551 / Bakersfield, CA / *Between the Two* **#2548-b** / Bakersfield, CA / *House Hunting*

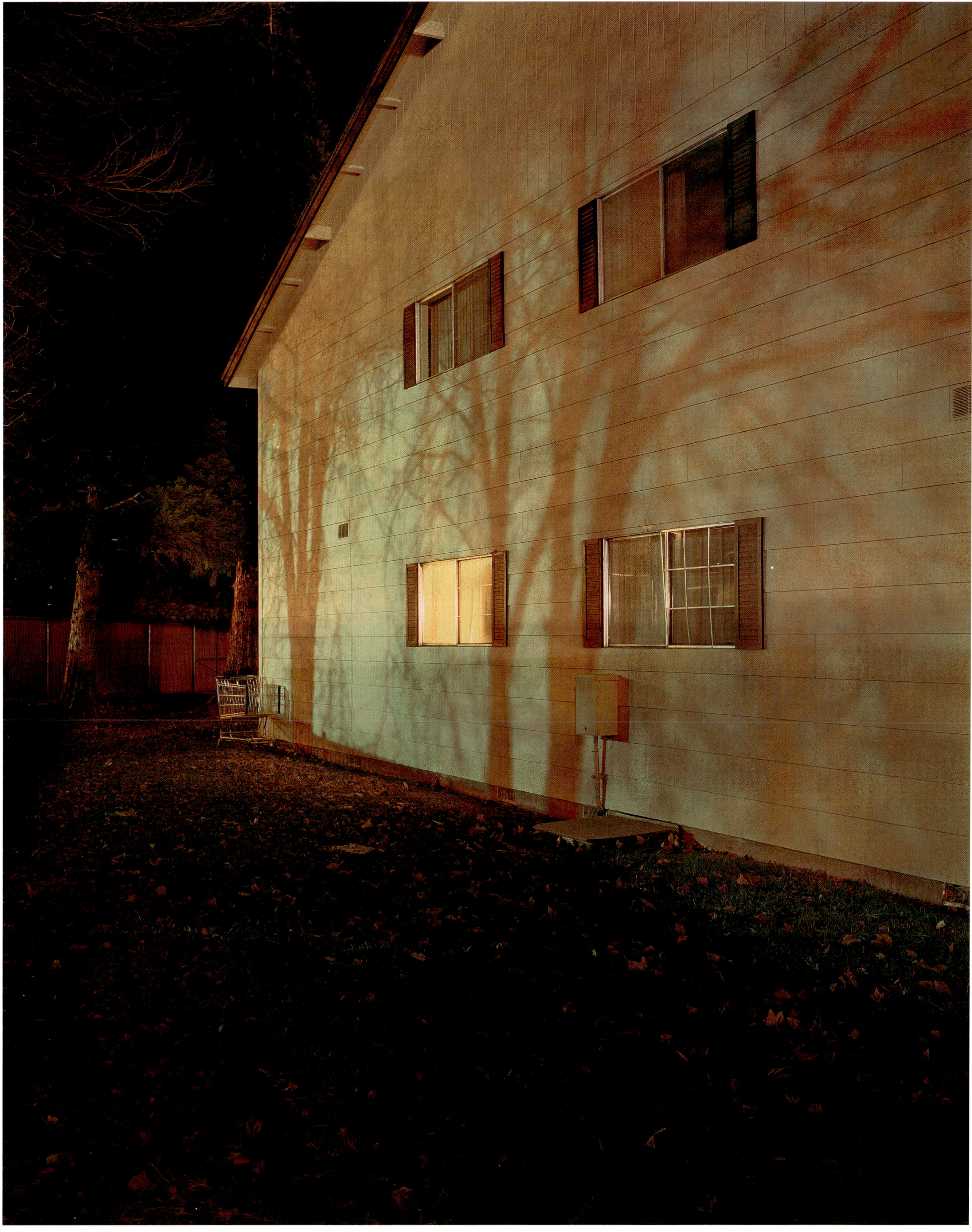

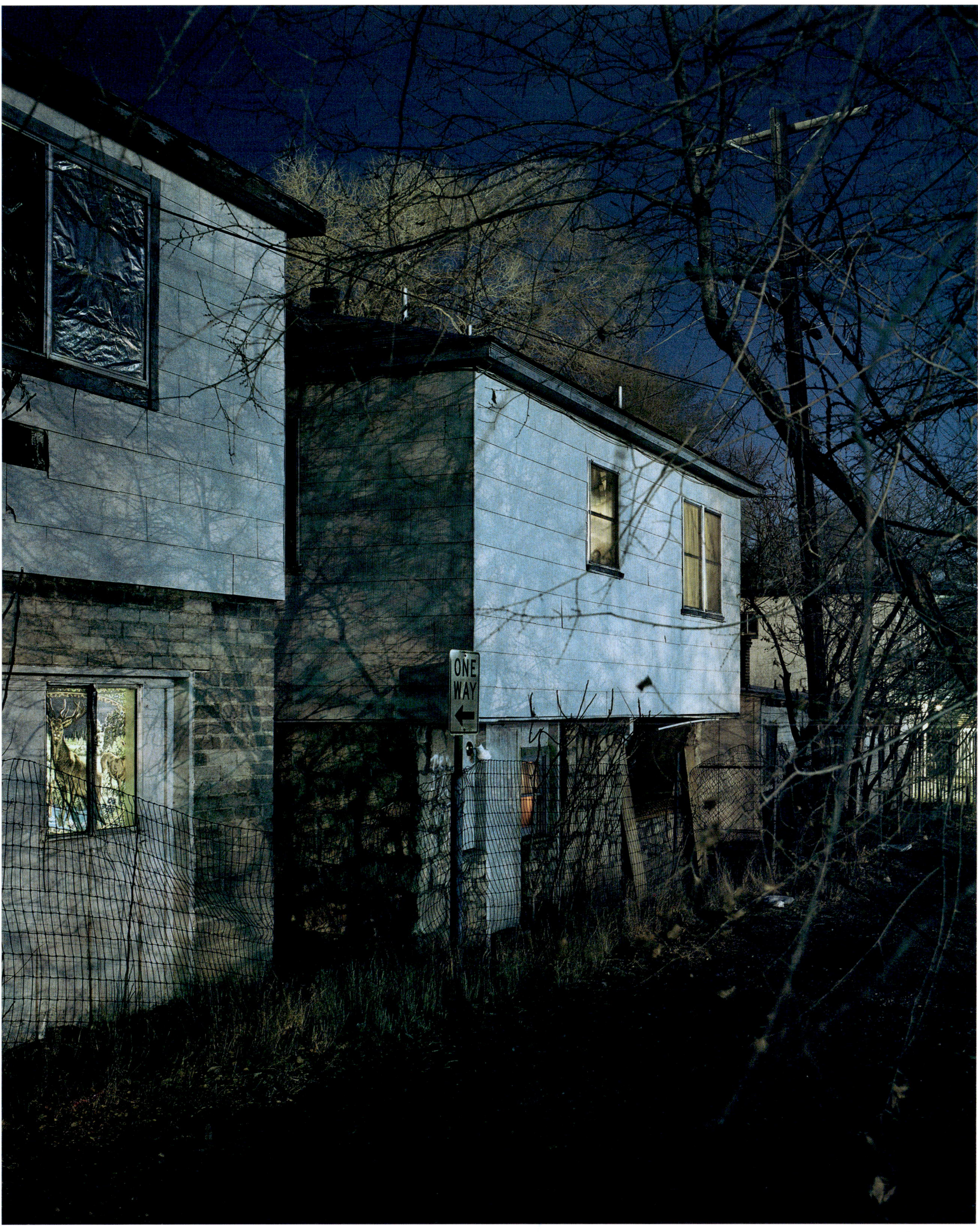
ONE
WAY

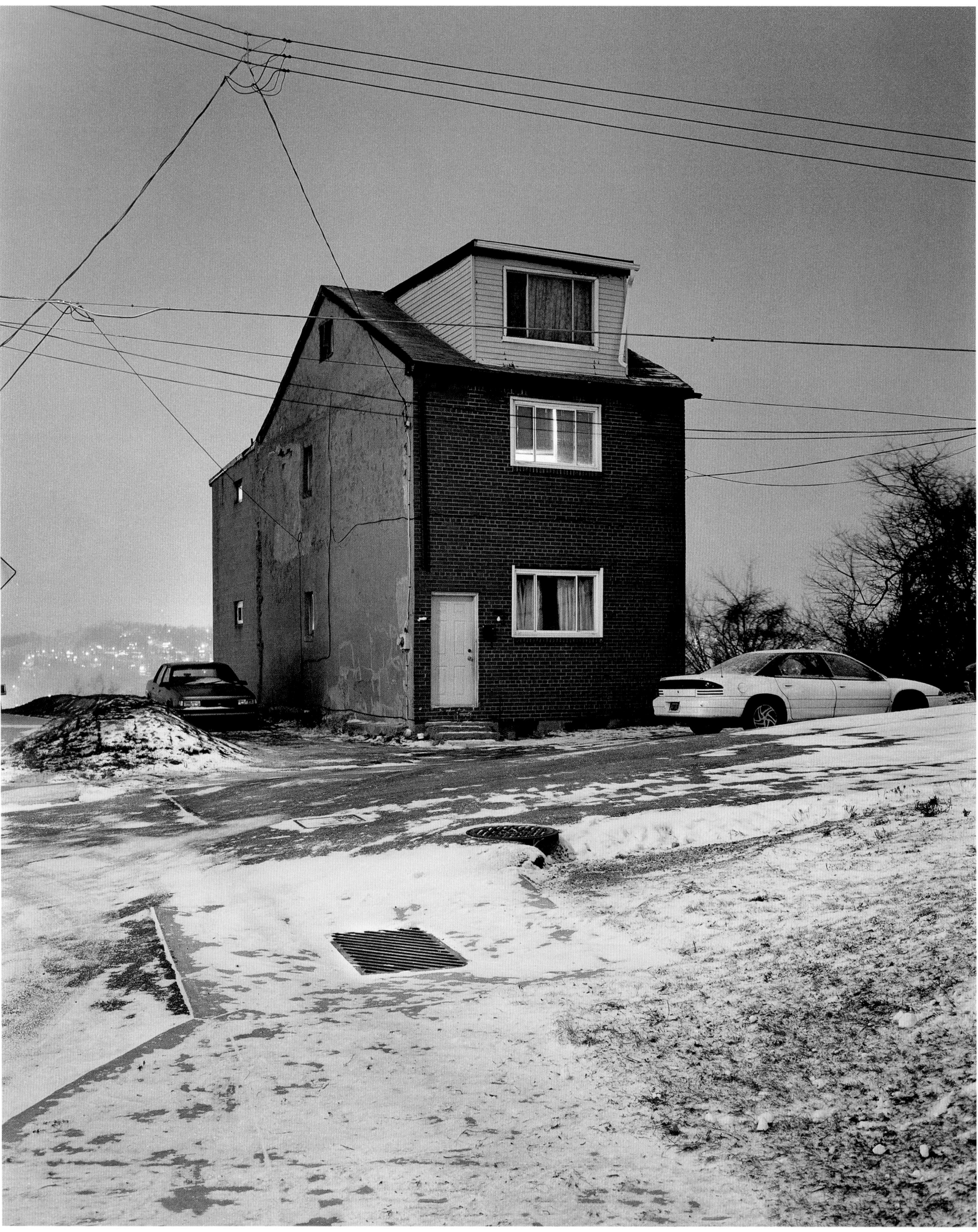

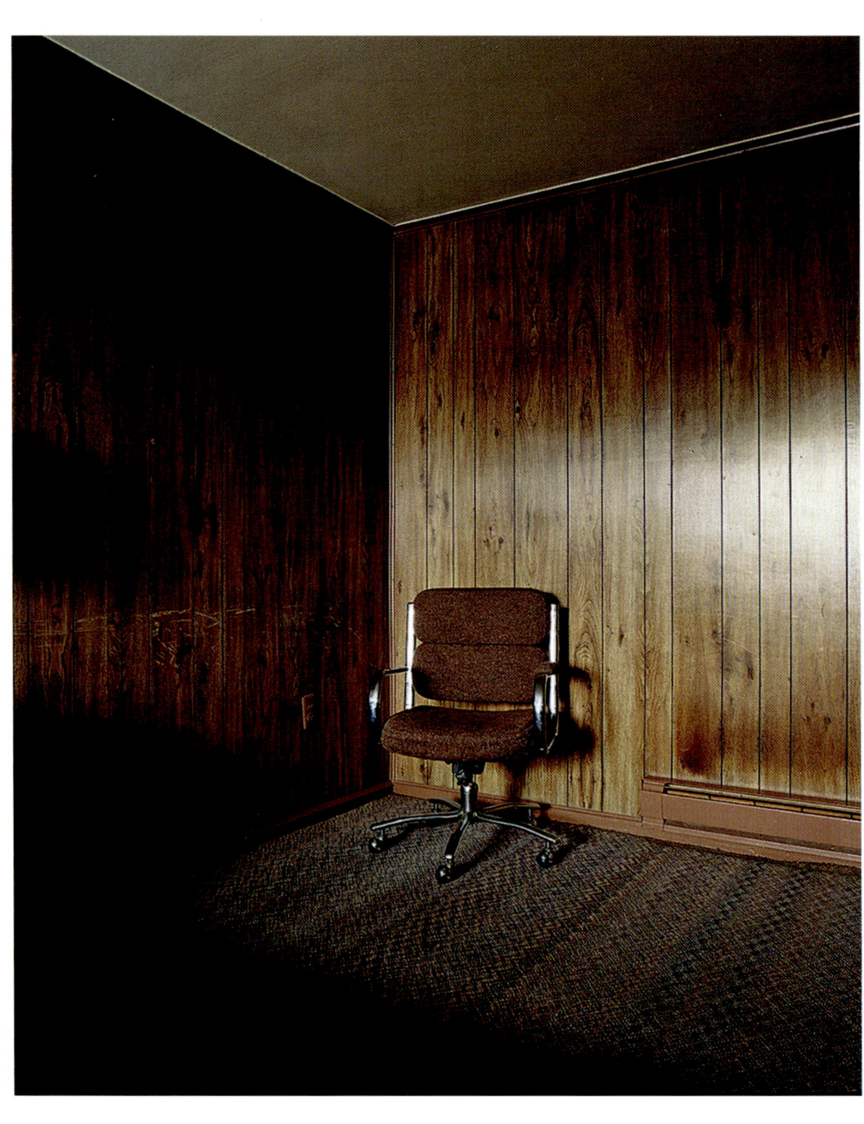

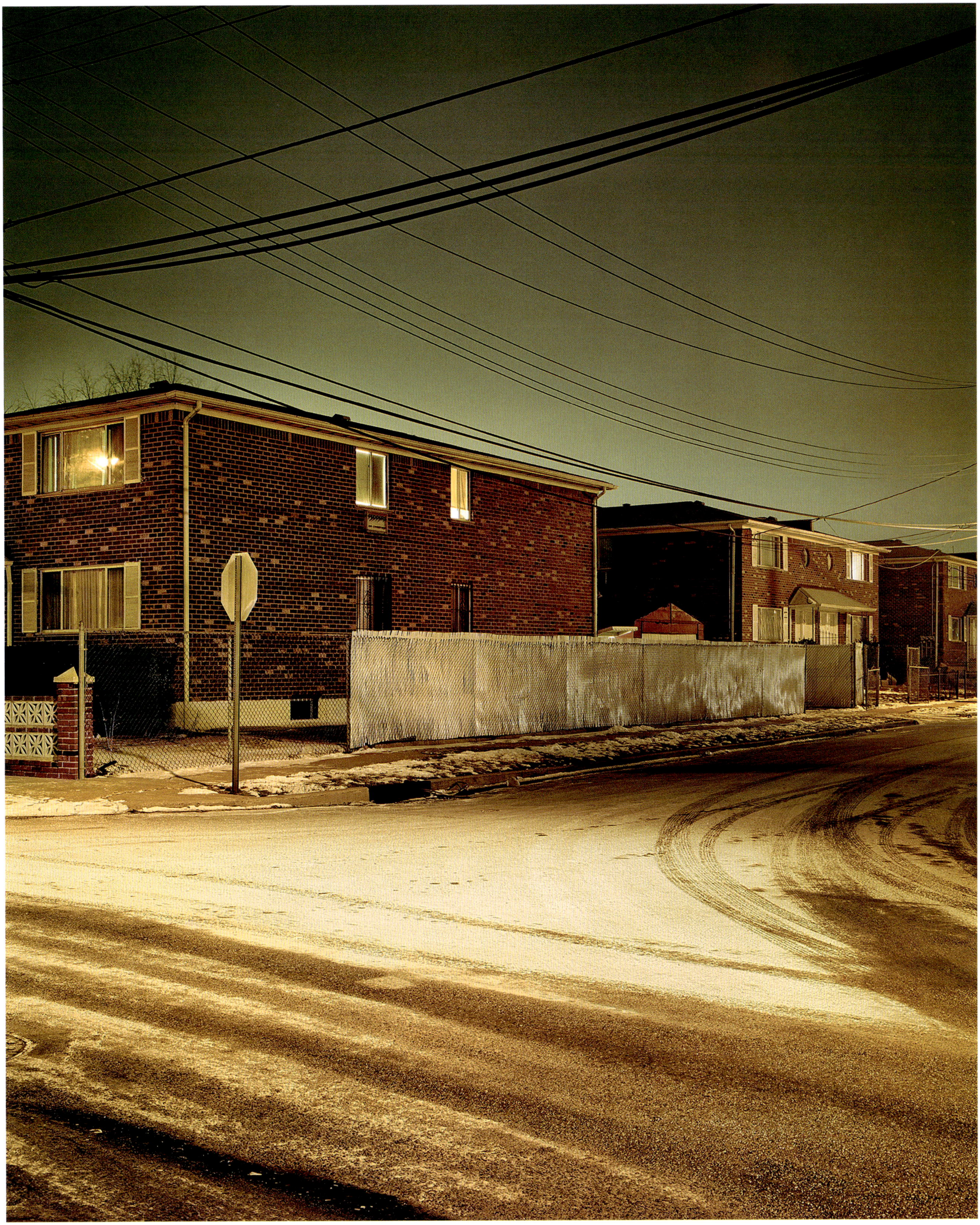

#2625 / Elizabeth, NJ / Between the Two #2632 / Queens, NY / Outskirts

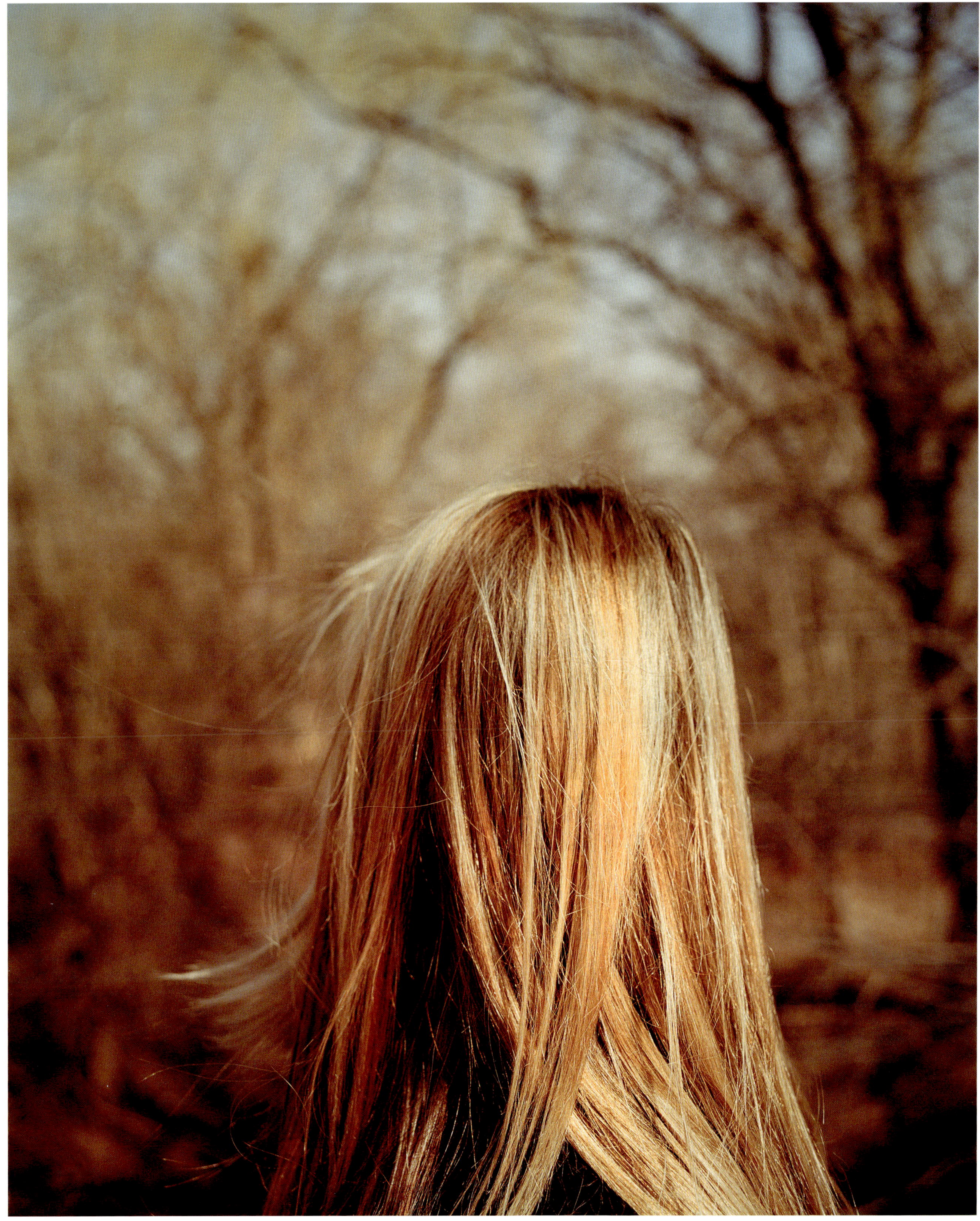

#2663 / Solon, OH / *Roaming*

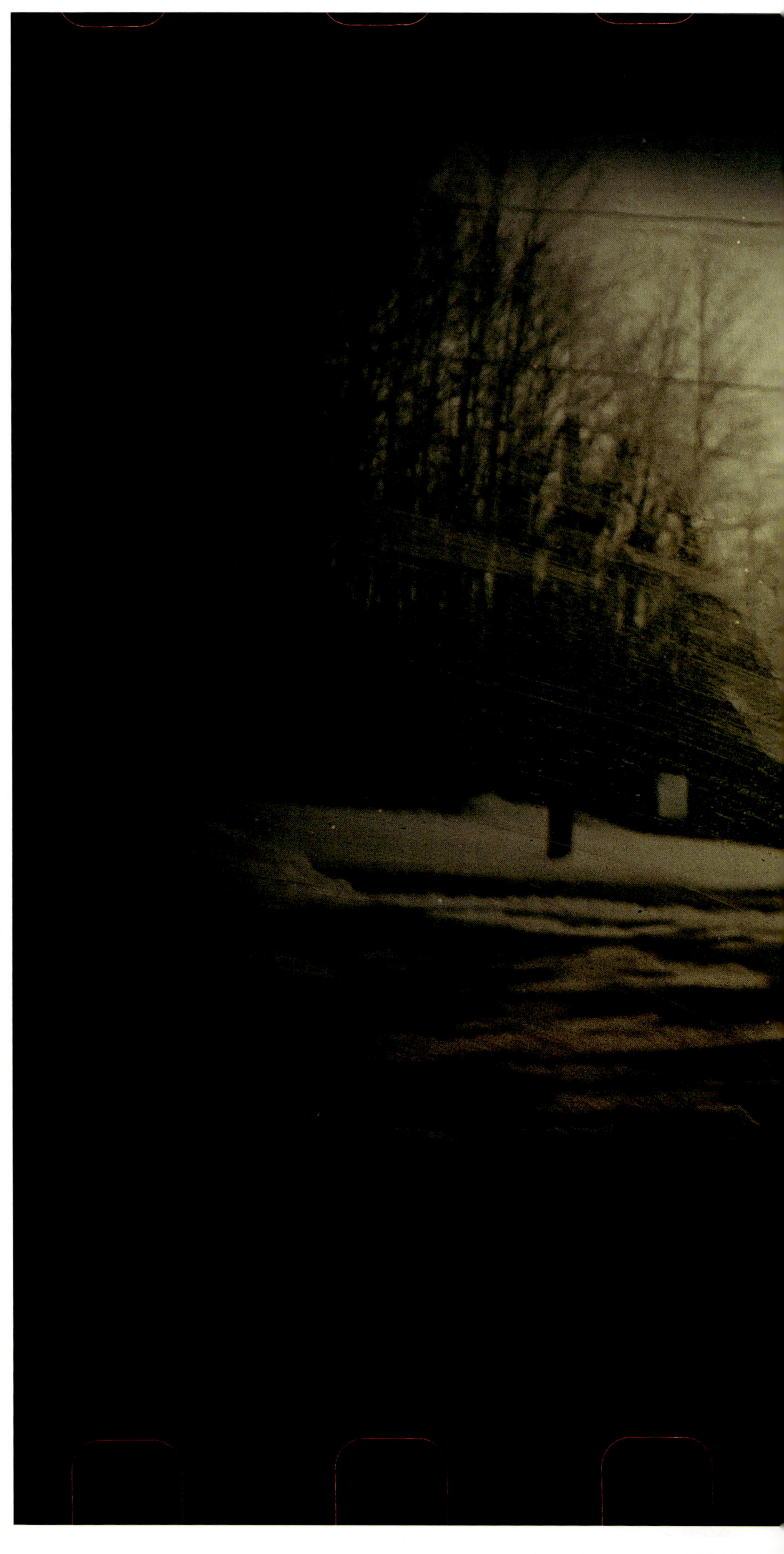

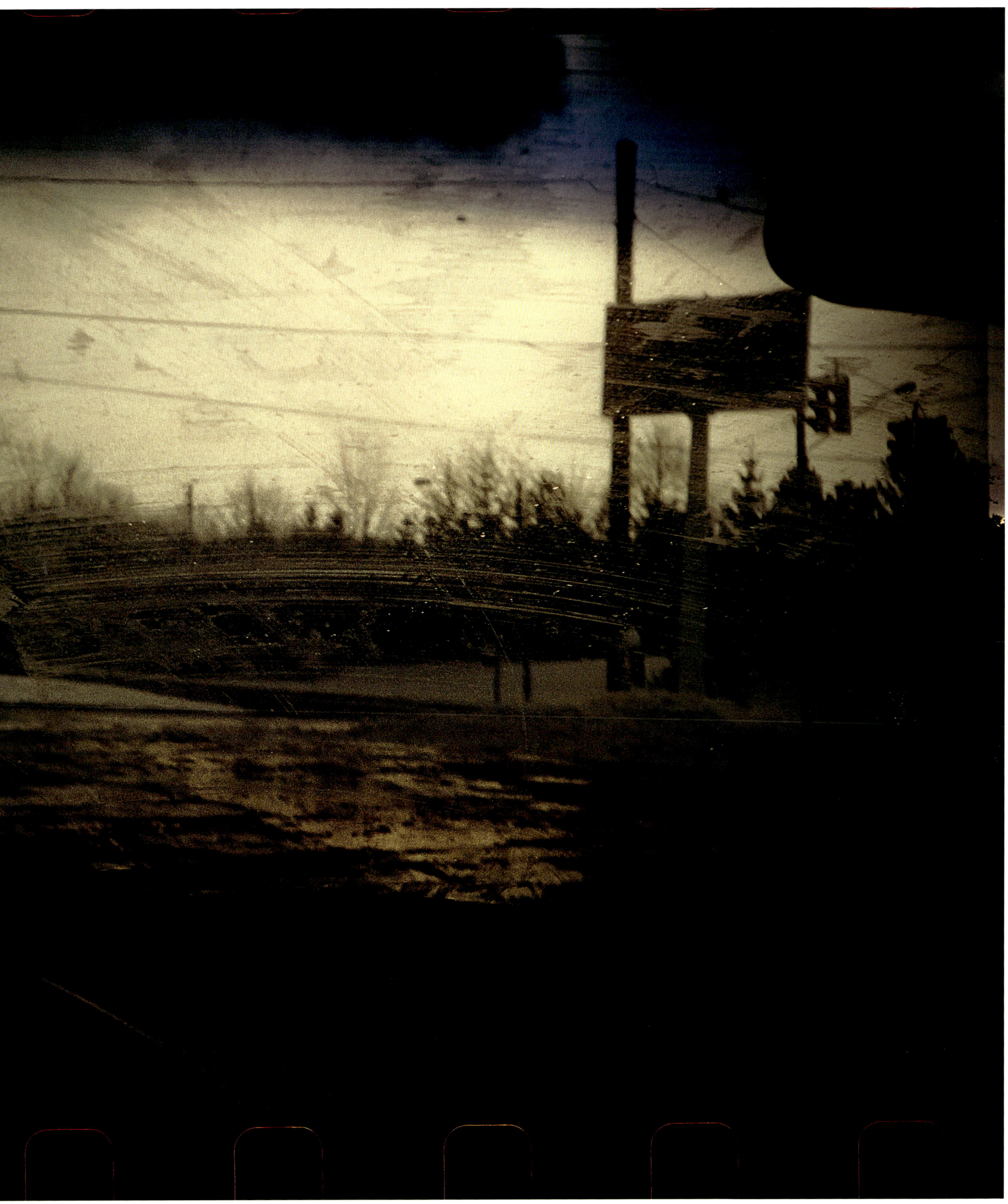

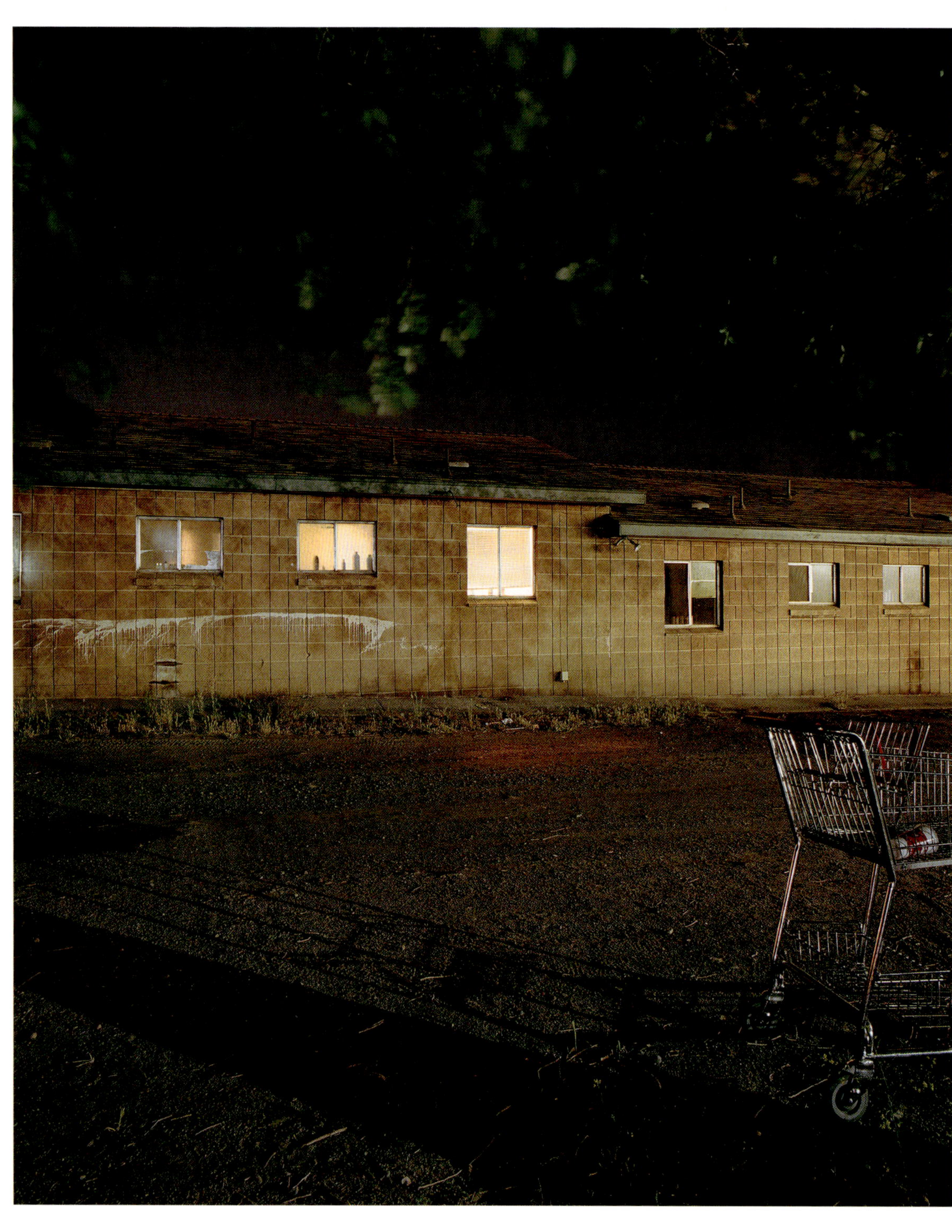

#2675 / Reno, NV #2676 / Reno, NV / Outskirts

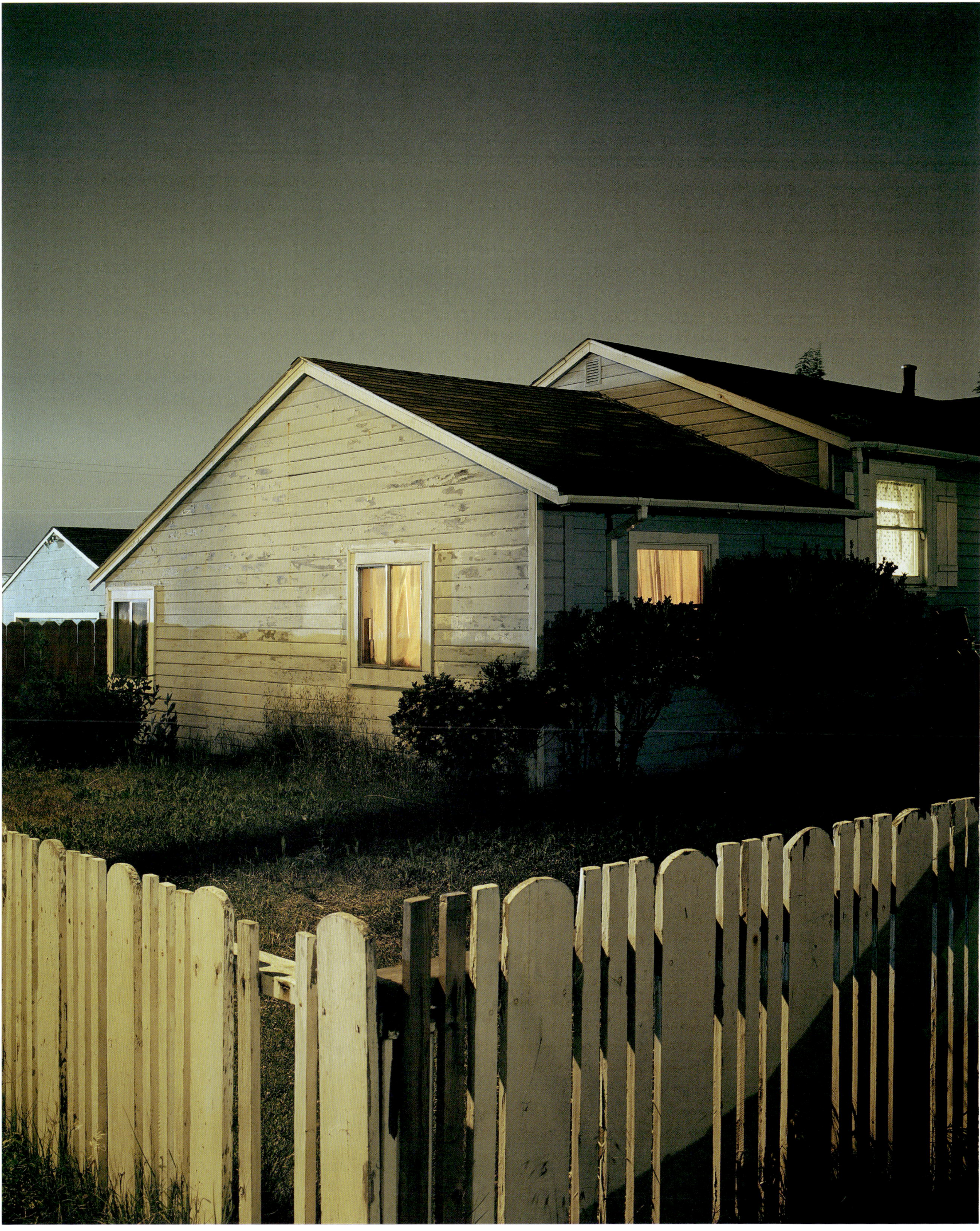

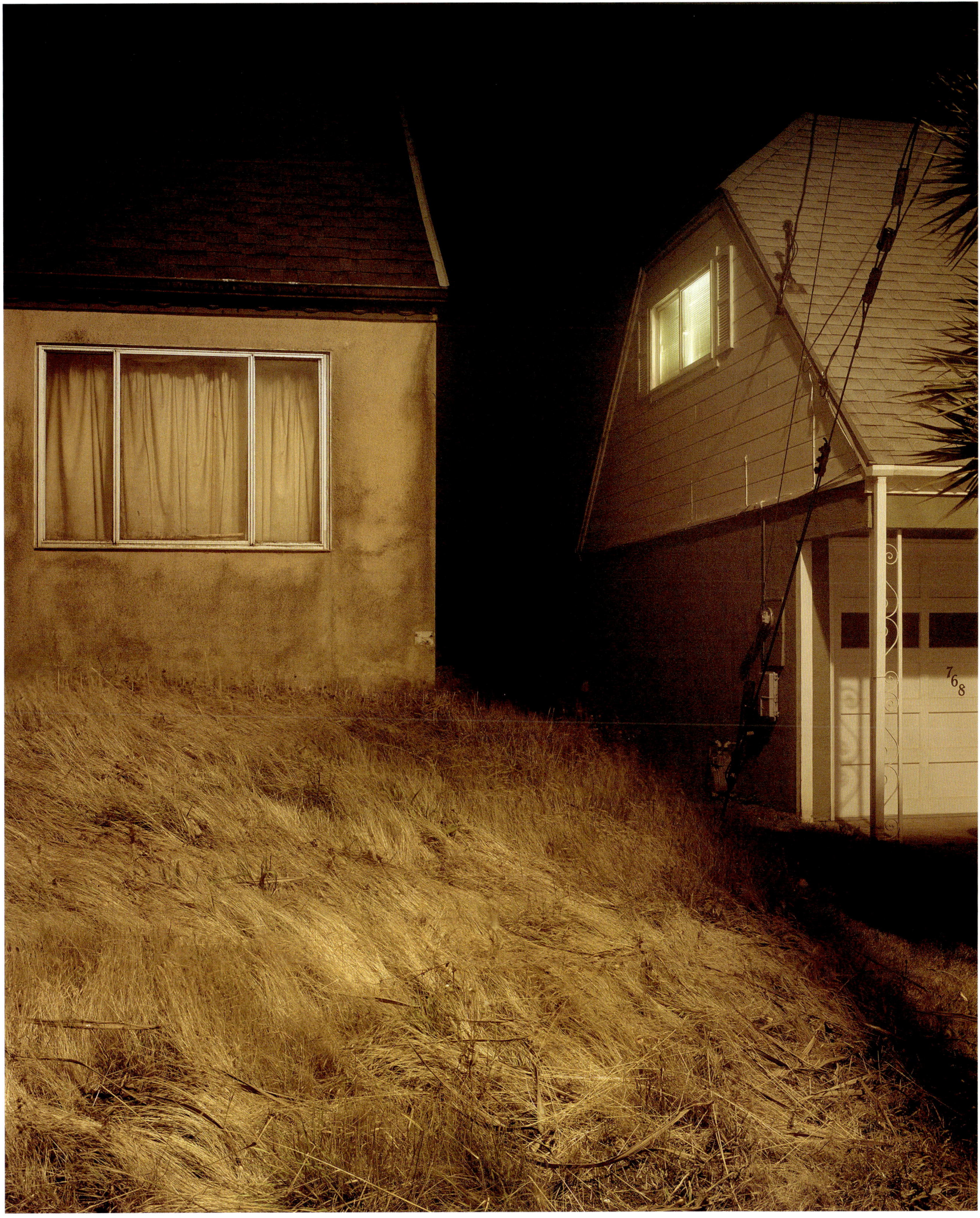
768

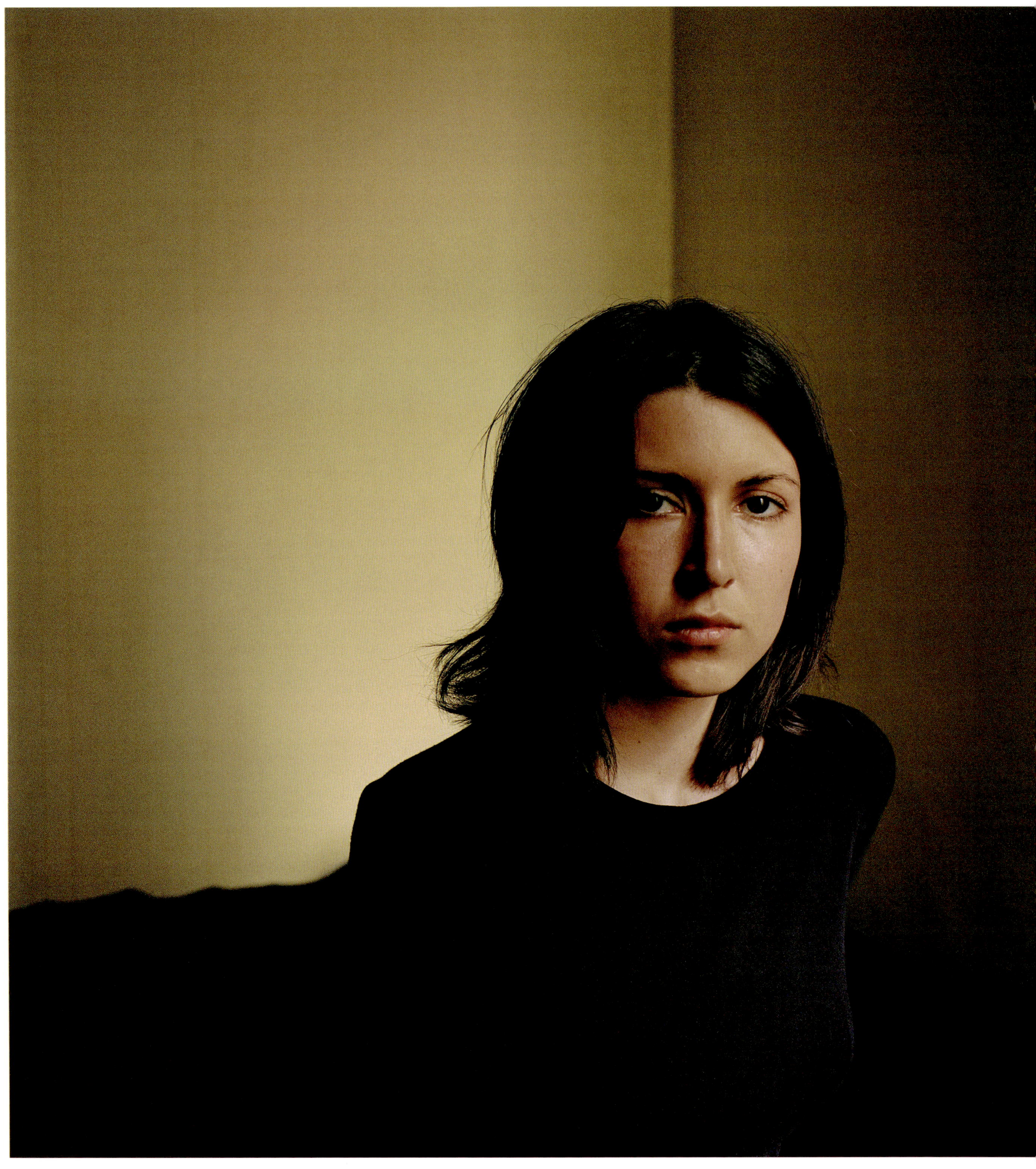

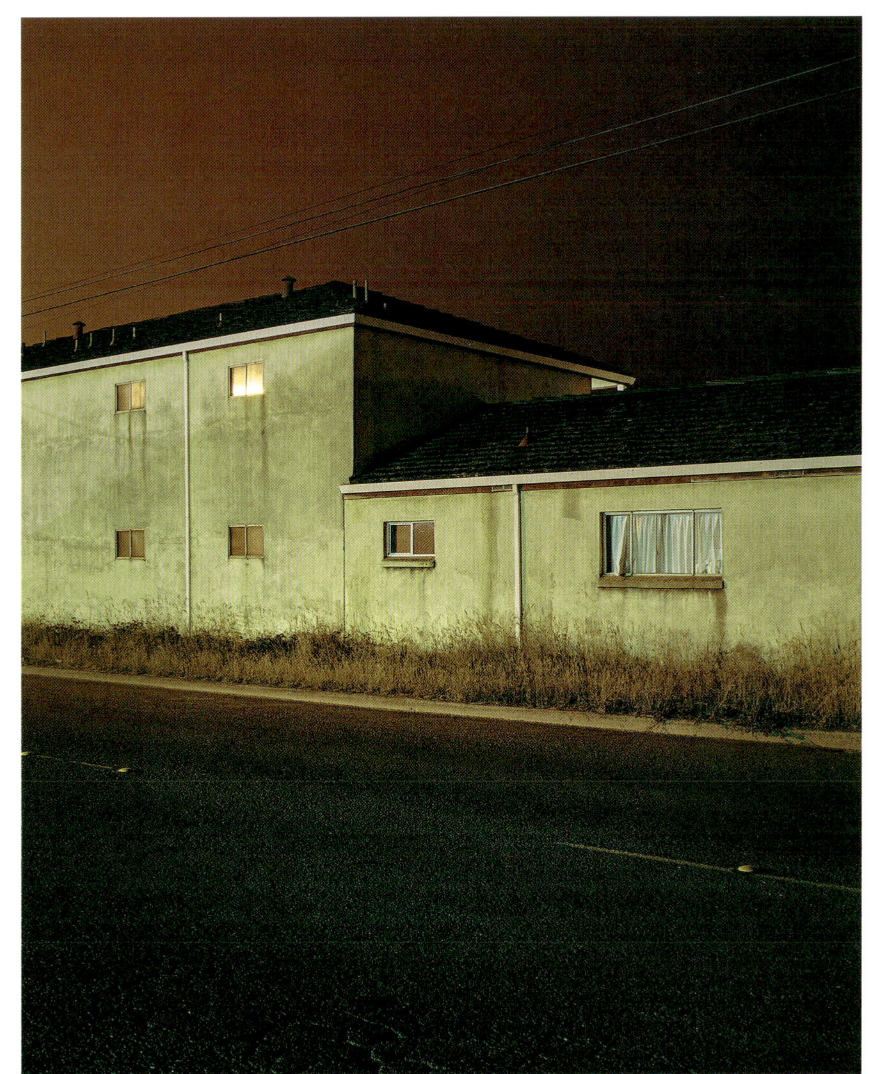

#2737 / San Francisco, CA / *Between the Two* **#2750** / Fort Bragg, CA / *House Hunting*

HOUSE HUNTING, OUTSKIRTS 2001–2002

House Hunting
Published 2001 by Nazraeli Press
13½×16½ inches
56 pages

Outskirts
Published 2002 by Nazraeli Press
13½×16½ inches
56 pages

"If you want to take a photo, you don't knock on someone's door to ask permission," Todd Hido says. I've tagged along on one of his drives, sitting shotgun as he pulls off the main roads to take the "unscenic" routes, so to speak. It didn't matter what city we were in, because Hido always drives along anonymous streets, choosing views that could be found "anywhere" in America, and, more important, "at any time." As always in his process, Hido is in search of something. He is "insatiable" in that search, he says, "even if I can't name exactly what I'm looking for."

Published in 2001, *House Hunting*—composed of color photographs of houses, made primarily at night—is, on one hand, a portrait of a certain America at a specific moment in history, an economically downtrodden place: dark and empty homes with the dirty laundry barely packed, or homes with the lights on that radiate no warmth. Simultaneously, it is a portrait of suburban America during any postwar decade, a raw look at the white paint chipping off the picket fence.

Hido's work has echoes of the '70s childhood he spent in his hometown of Kent, Ohio, a city scarred by the 1970 shooting of four college students by the Ohio National Guard during a Vietnam War protest. Then again, the images resonate less for their relationship to the photographer and more for their ability to connect and identify with almost any viewer. These are reserved photographs, overwhelmed with emotion and history but reluctant to say a word.

"I take photographs of houses at night because I wonder about the families inside them," Hido tells me. "I wonder about how people live, and the act of taking that photograph is a meditation." *House Hunting*, therefore, is more question than answer: a rumination without resolution.

It would seem that in order for these pictures to exist, the photographer would need to be a voyeur, but Hido denies being secretive. He says he keeps himself obvious, even when shooting in the dark. If somebody calls the police, he is quick to make the distinction between photographer and criminal. "You're allowed to take pictures in public," Hido says. "It's interesting that so many people regard their surroundings as inherently private." His work heightens that sense of false privacy—amplifies it, to show the cracks in the edifice.

The scale of *House Hunting*, at 16½ by 13½ inches, gave the artist pause when first proposed by the publisher: "I wasn't sure about it. I didn't want the book to end up crooked or shoved in someone's bookshelf." Instead, the large scale of the book demands a confrontation with its twenty-six carefully selected photographs, edited by Hido himself—a practice he insists on with each of his books. By so deliberately determining the contents of *House Hunting*, Hido establishes how critical each photograph is, in meaning and function.

The companion book to *House Hunting*, *Outskirts* (published 2002) has the same size, shape, and page count as its predecessor, and reinforces the formal and psychological differences between "homes"—single-family versus apartment buildings, for example. In *Outskirts*, Hido also travels beyond residences, into the unmanicured back alleys of shopping centers and commercial districts, where "a natural intensification of light" illuminates "a different kind of darkness," he says. "The unkempt, uncared-for backside of a building is where you find its reality."

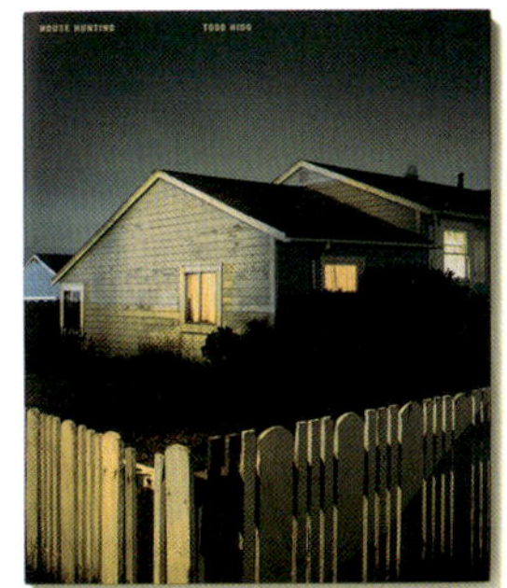
HOUSE HUNTING
TODD HIDO

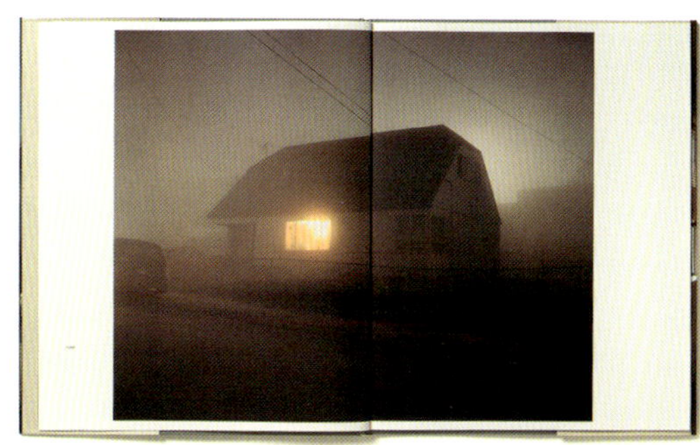

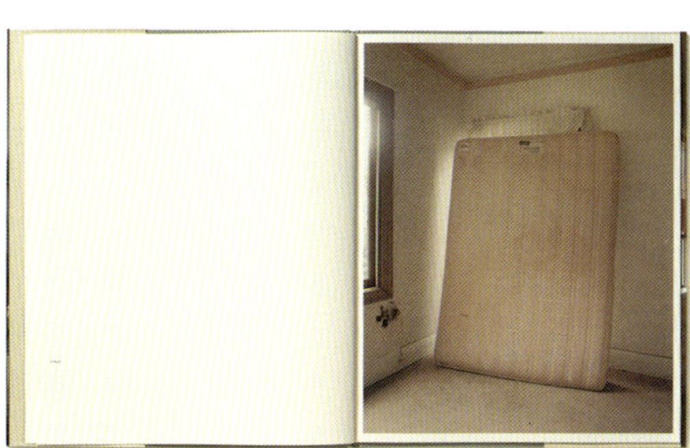

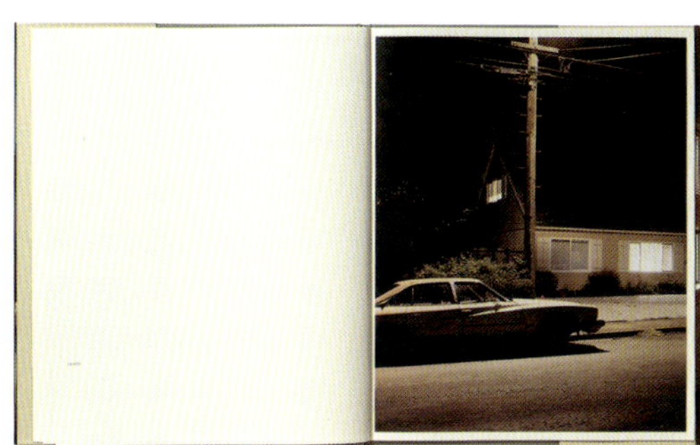

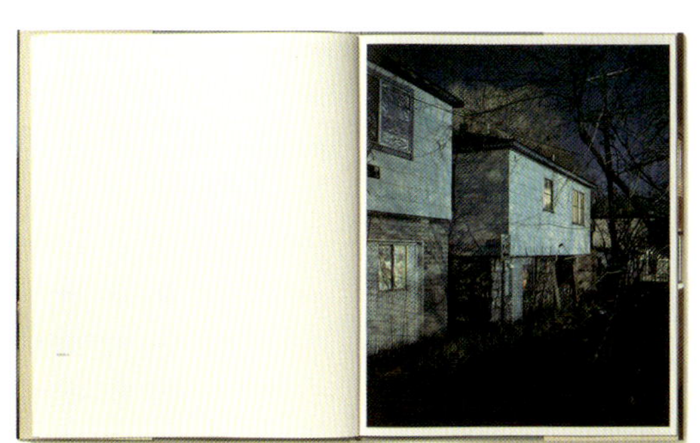

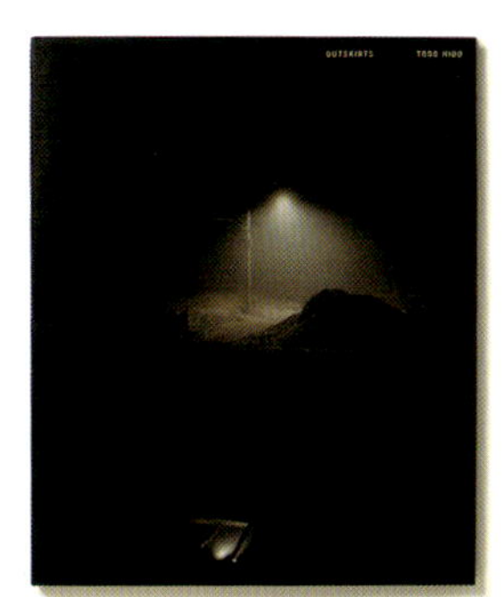
OUTSKIRTS
TODD HIDO

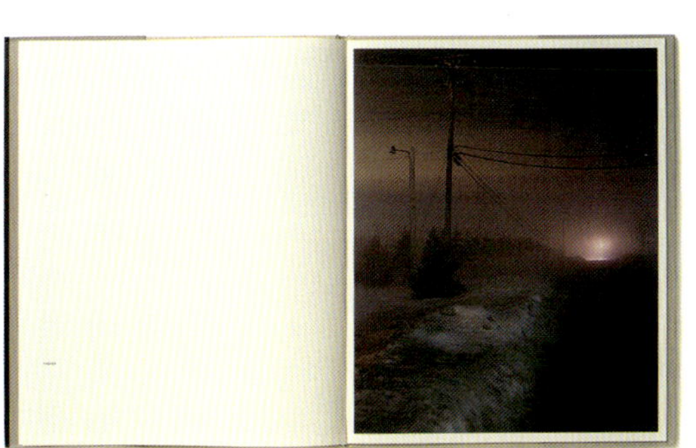

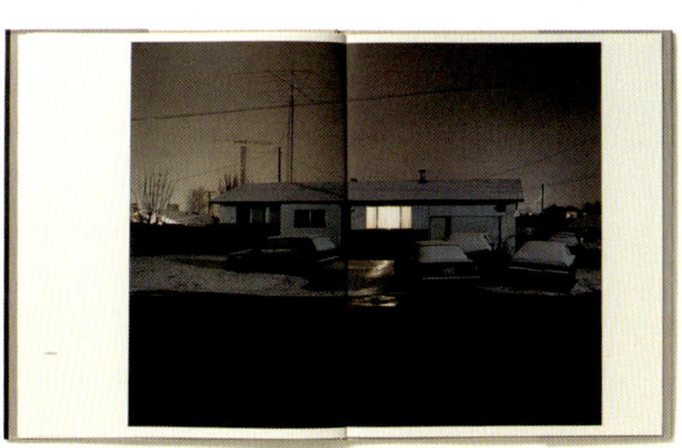

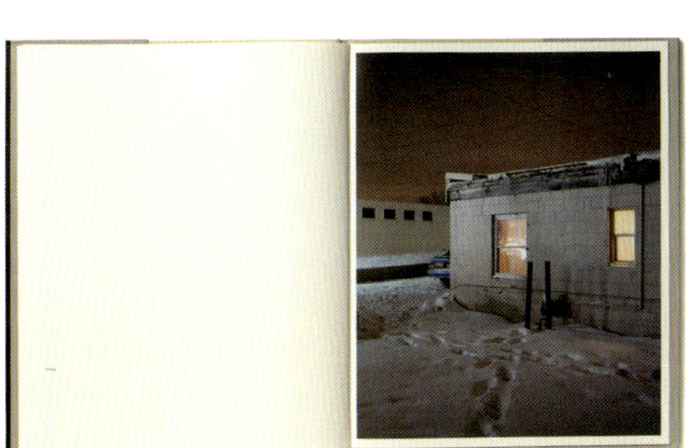

CHRONOLOGY 2001–2004

2001 Nazraeli Press publishes *Taft Street*

2002 Receives best first monograph award for 2001 from photo-eye for *House Hunting*

2002 Nazraeli Press publishes *Outskirts*

2002 First solo museum exhibition: *Open House*, Kemper Museum of Contemporary Art, Kansas City, Missouri

2002 Moves to Oakland, California

2002 Begins photographing the Sacramento–San Joaquin River Delta, California

2002 Included in the festival Le Printemps de septembre: photographie et arts visuels, Toulouse, France

2003 Begins photographing in eastern Washington State

2003 Group exhibition: *Fabula*, National Museum of Photography, Film and Television, Bradford, West Yorkshire, England

2003 Group exhibition: *Terrain Vague: Photography, Architecture, and the Post-Industrial Landscape*, Carnegie Museum of Art, Pittsburgh

2004 Group exhibition: *The Gray Area*, Wattis Institute for Contemporary Arts, California College of the Arts, San Francisco

2004 Nazraeli Press publishes *Roaming*

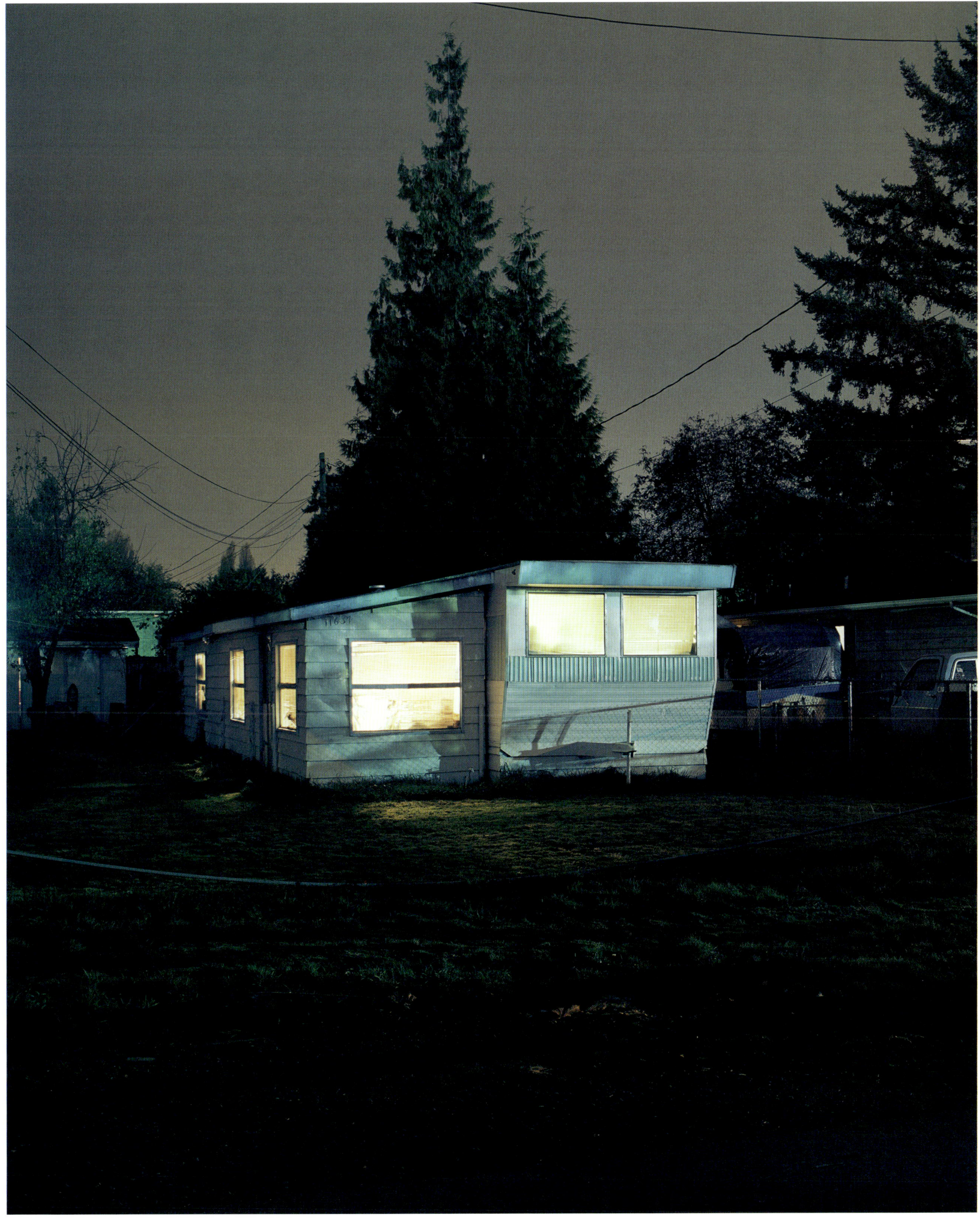

#2810 / Seattle, WA / *Excerpts from Silver Meadows*

#2840 / Kent, OH / *Outskirts, Excerpts from Silver Meadows* **#2820** / Detroit, MI / *Excerpts from Silver Meadows* **#2844** / Dearborn, MI / *Outskirts*

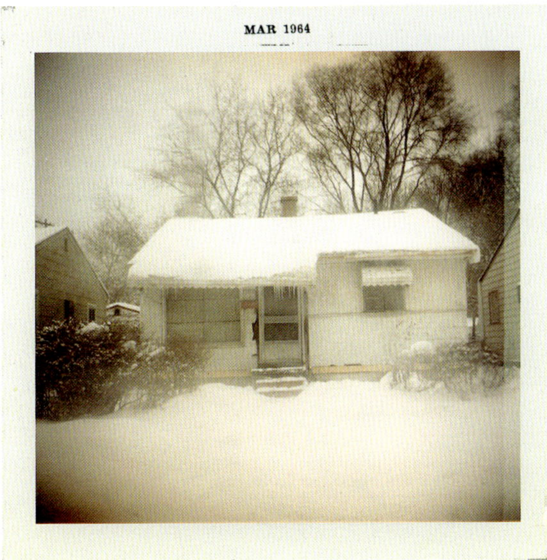
MAR 1964

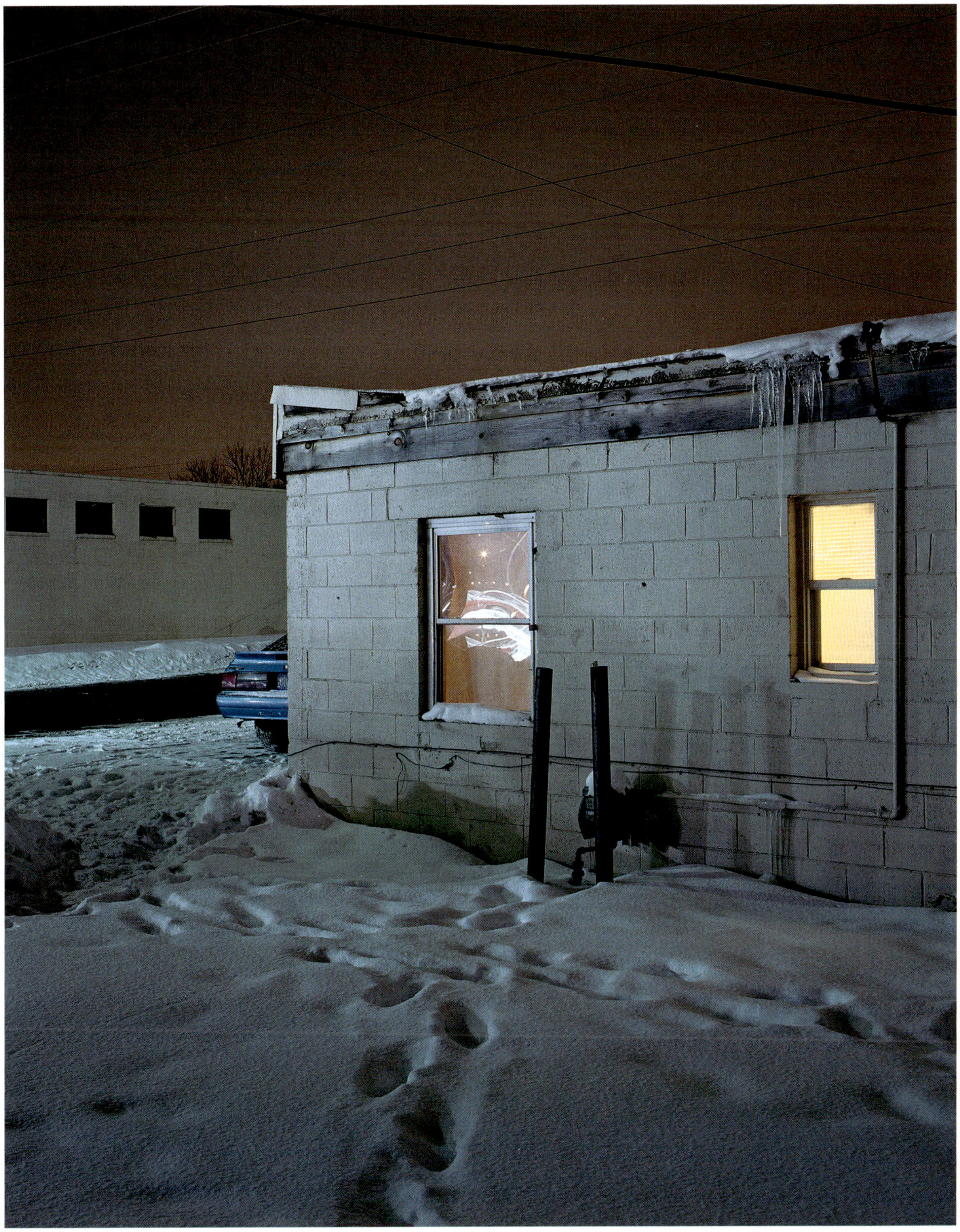

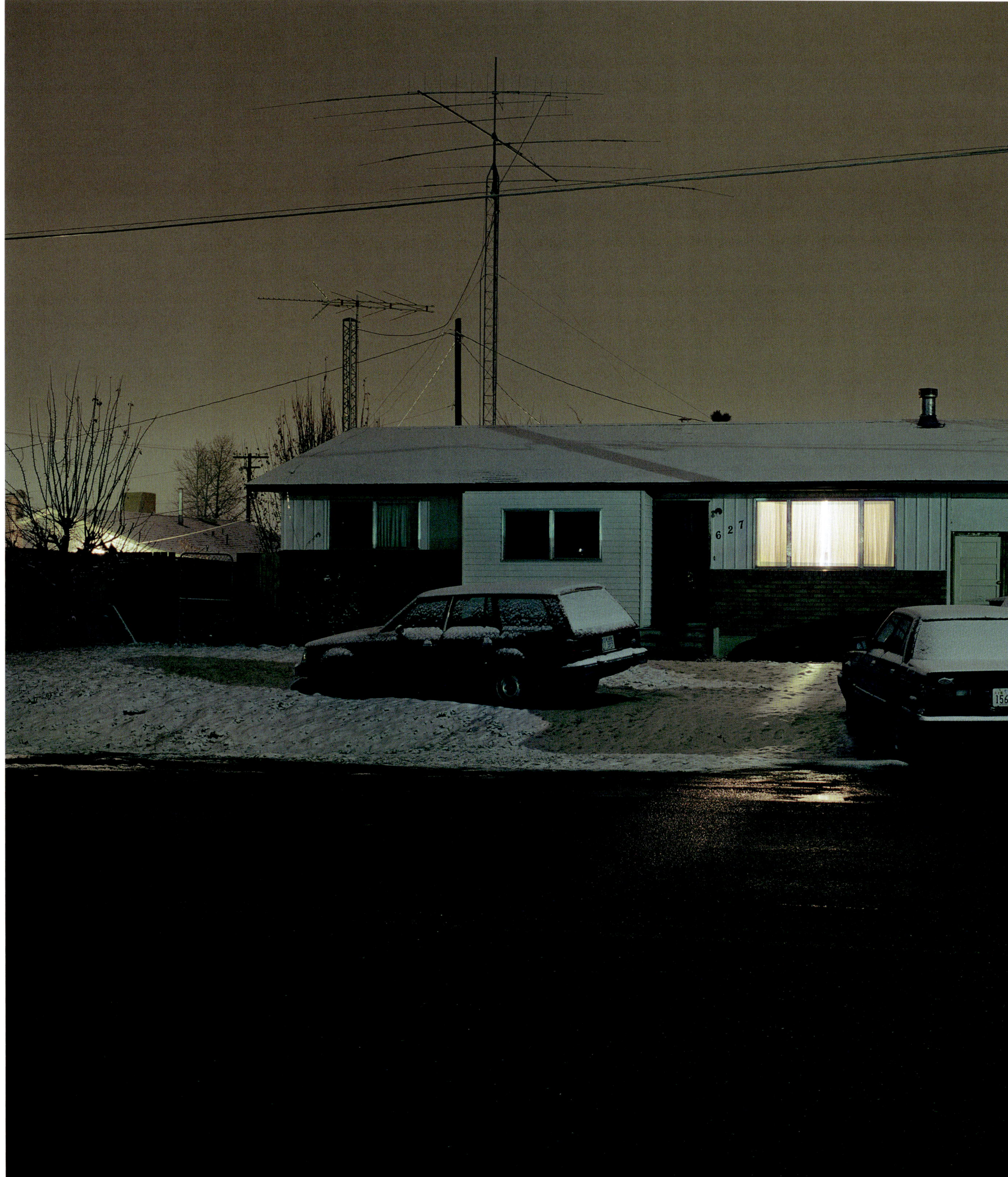
627

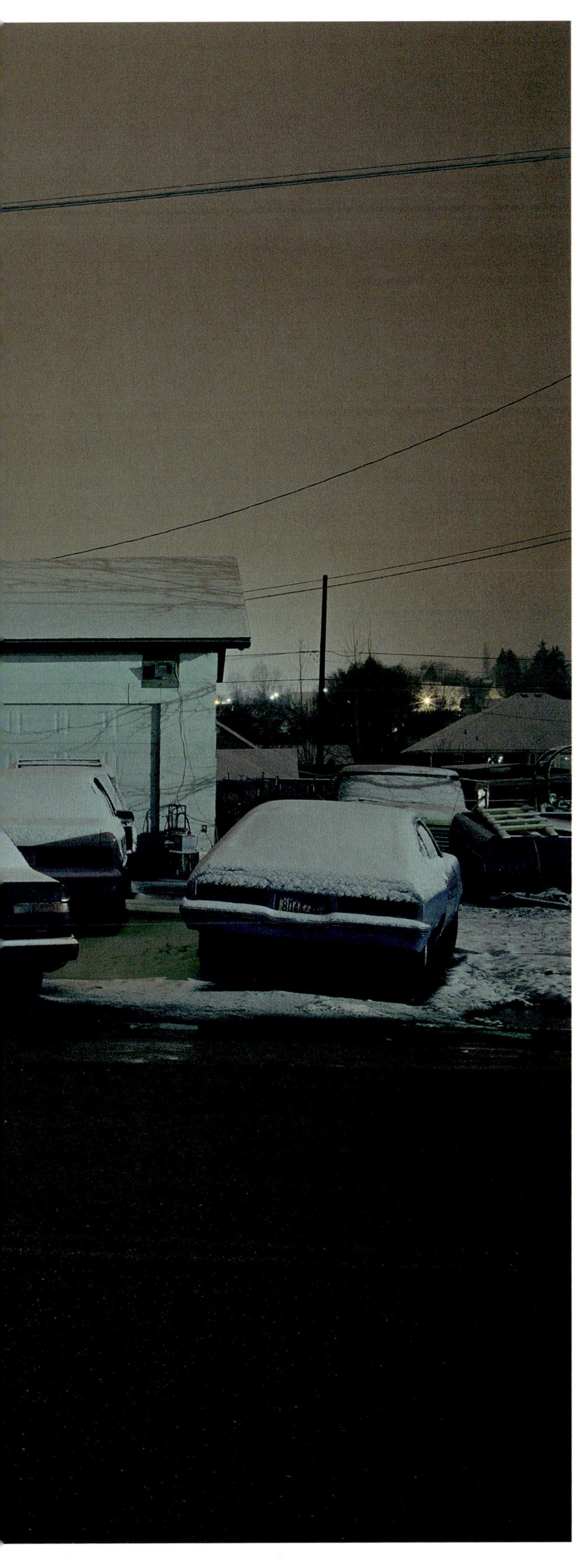

#2871-a / Provo, UT / *Outskirts*

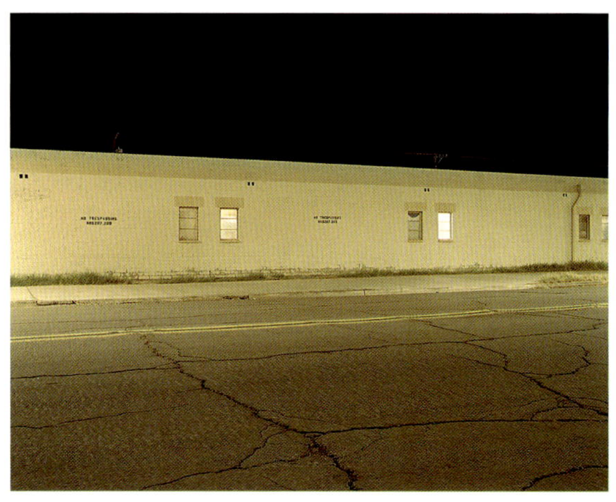

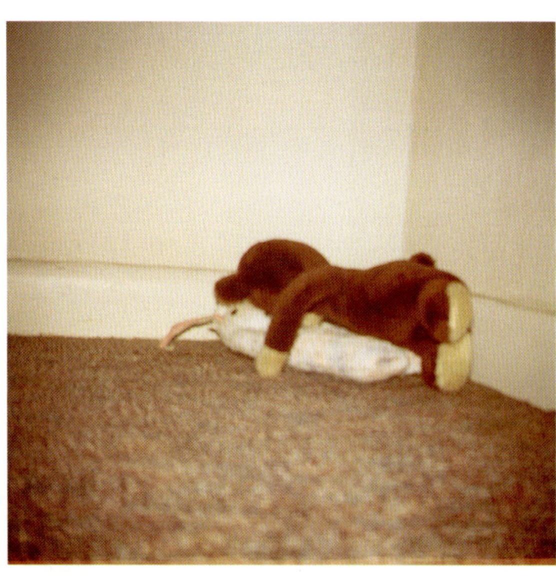

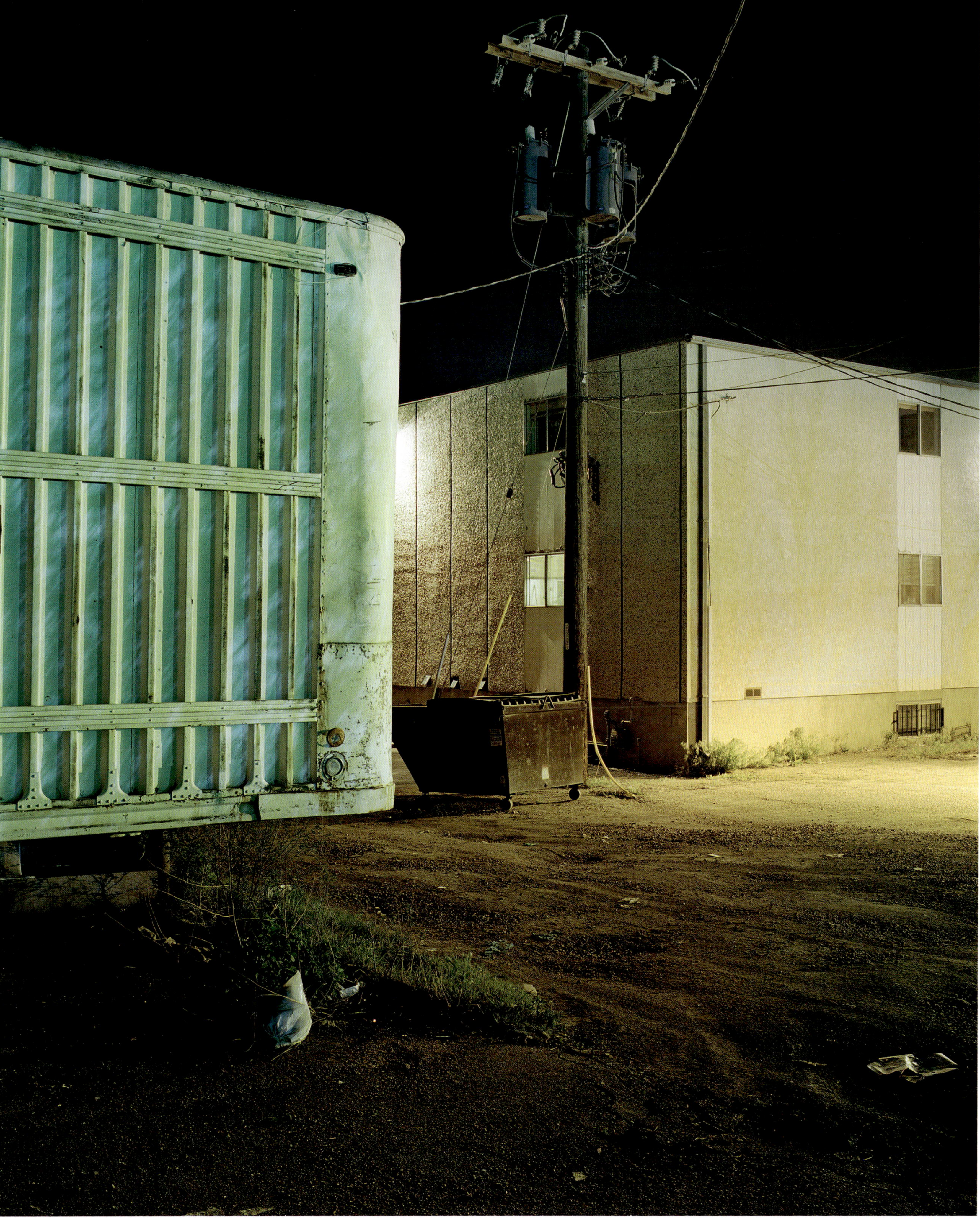

#2872 / Las Vegas, NV / Outskirts #2998-b / Colorado Springs, CO / Ohio, *Nymph Daughters, Excerpts from Silver Meadows* #2899-a / Colorado Springs, CO / Outskirts

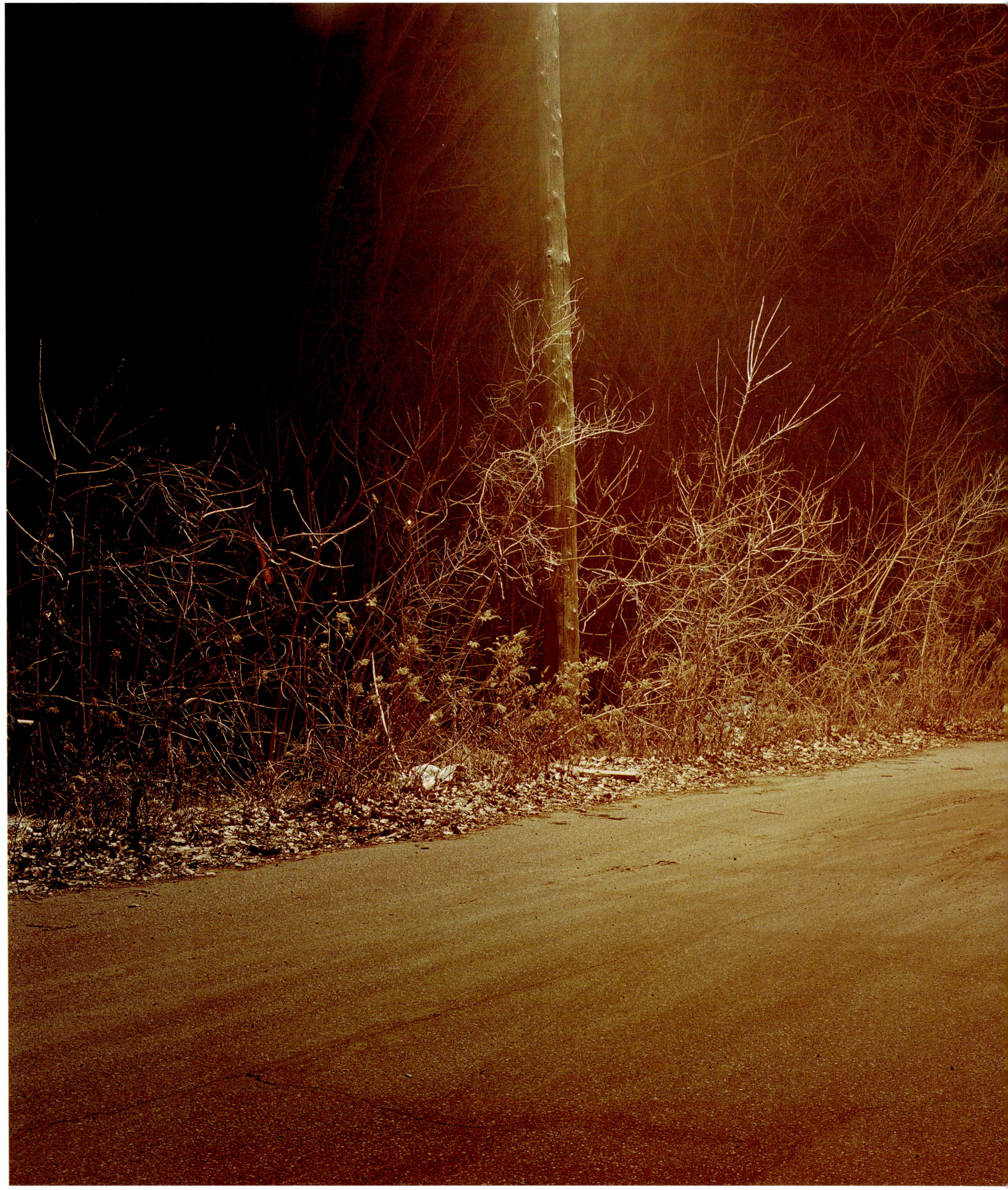

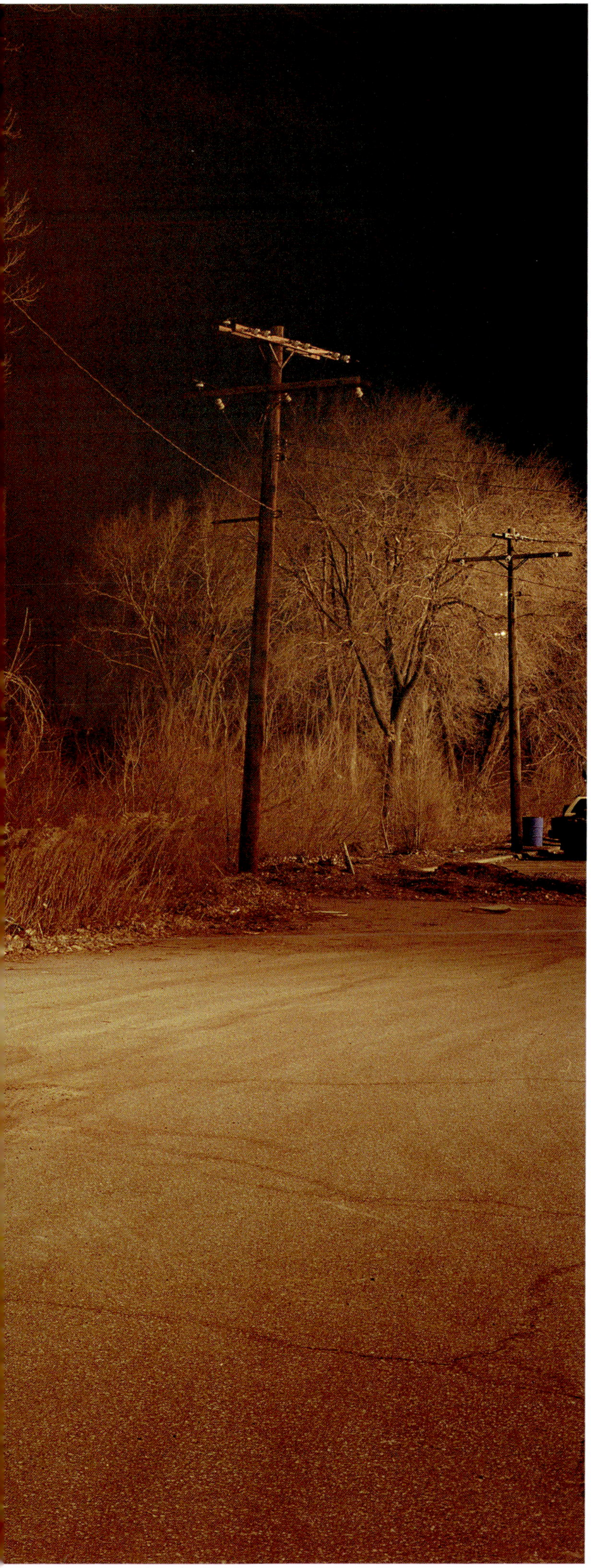

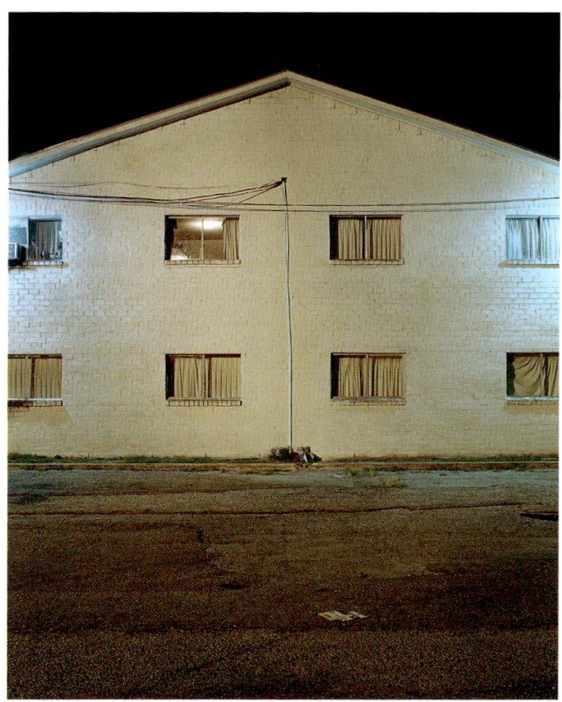

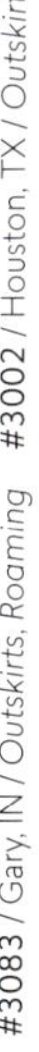

#3083 / Gary, IN / Outskirts, *Roaming* **#3002** / Houston, TX / Outskirts

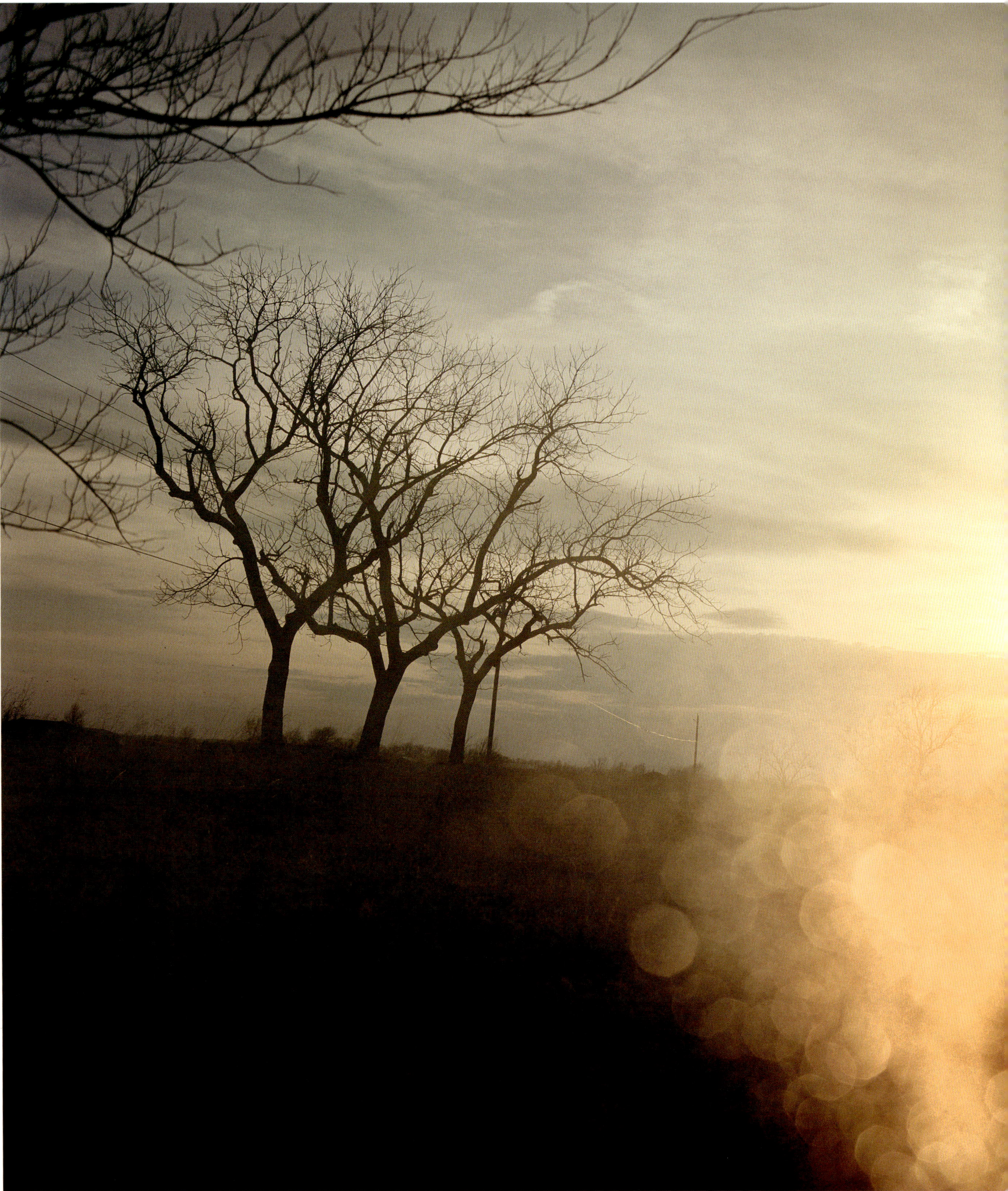

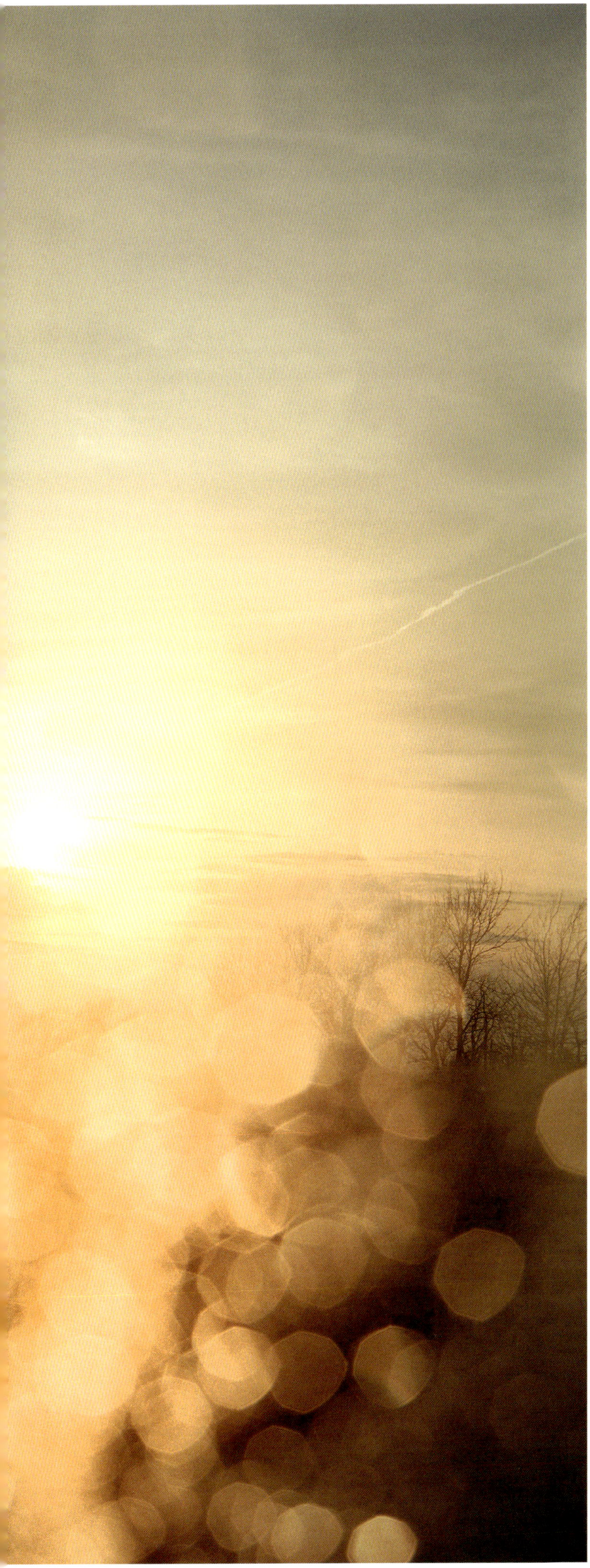

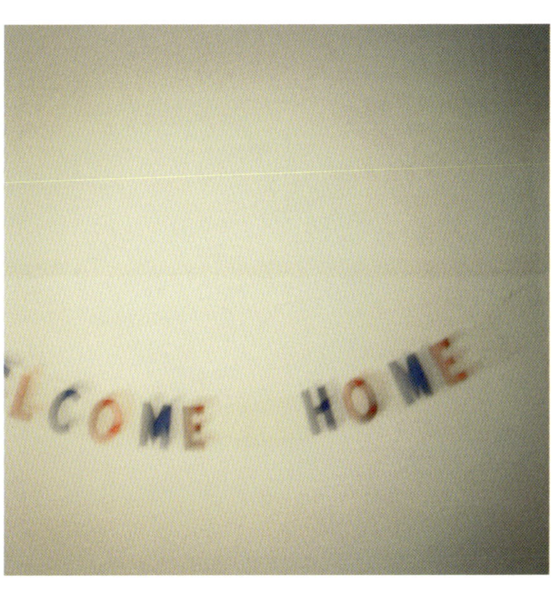

#3114-b / Kansas City, KS / *A Road Divided*   #3142 / Oakland, CA / Ohio, *Excerpts from Silver Meadows*

#3176 / Atlantic City, NJ / *Roaming* **#3101-a** / Indianapolis, IN

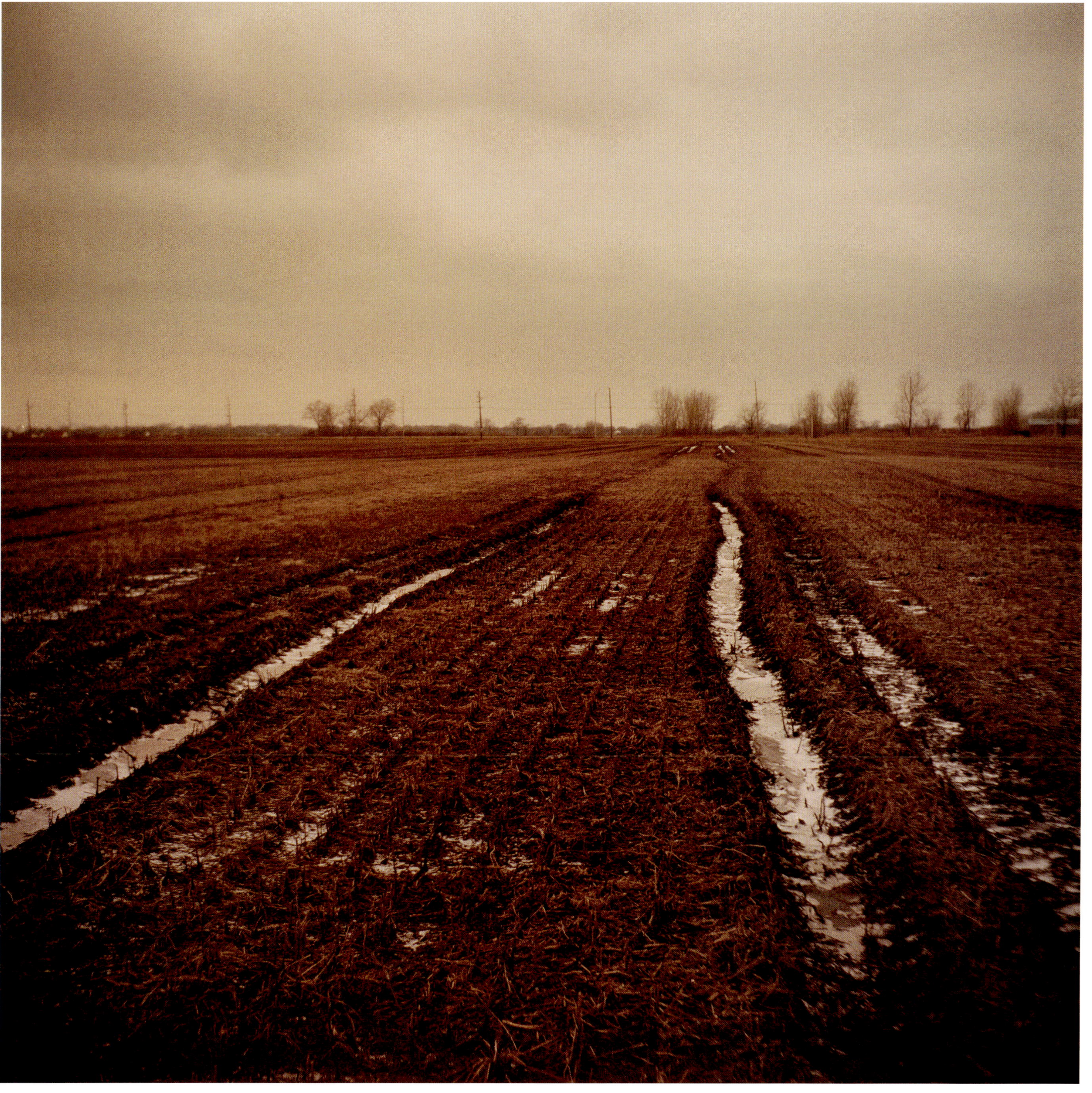

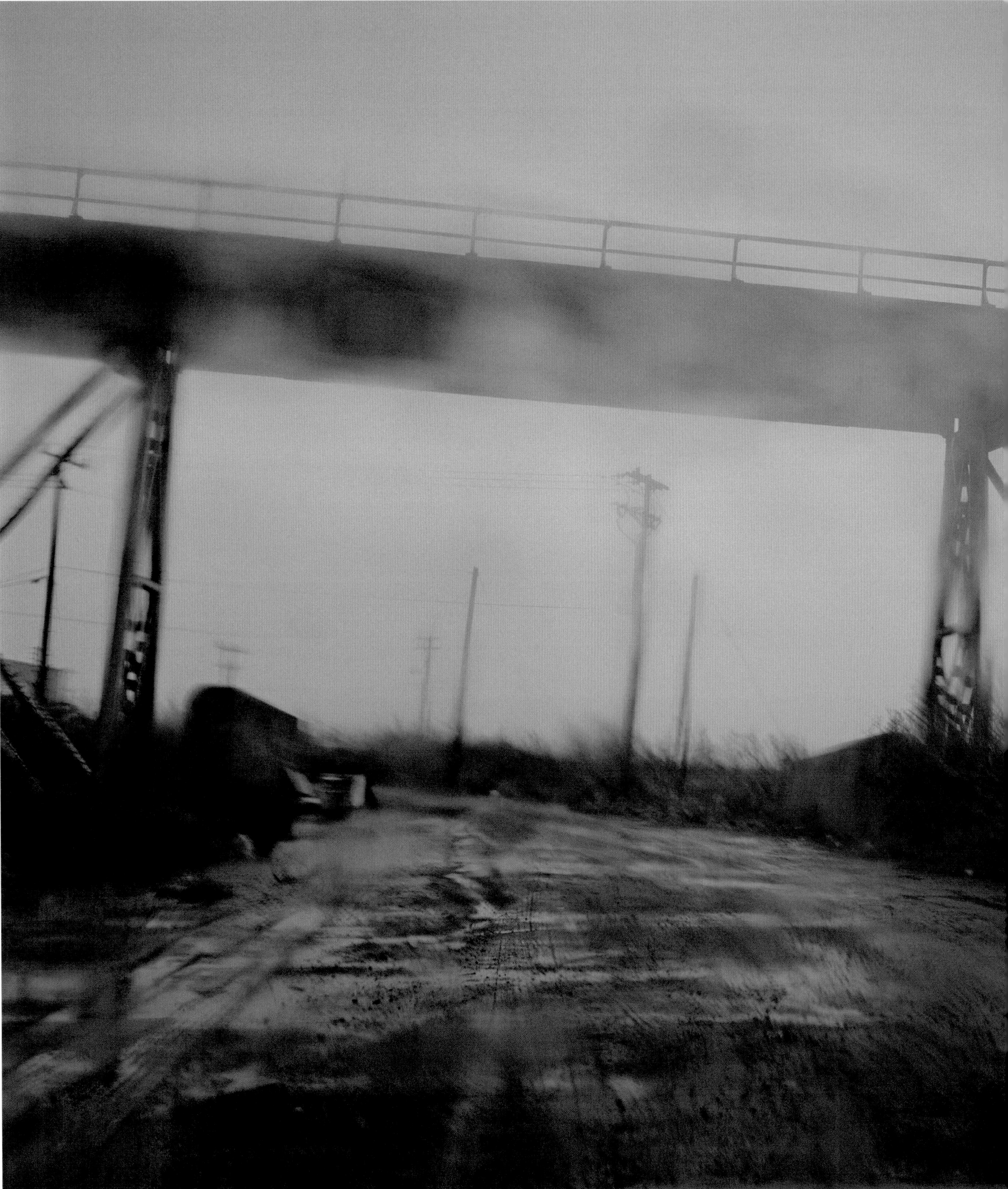

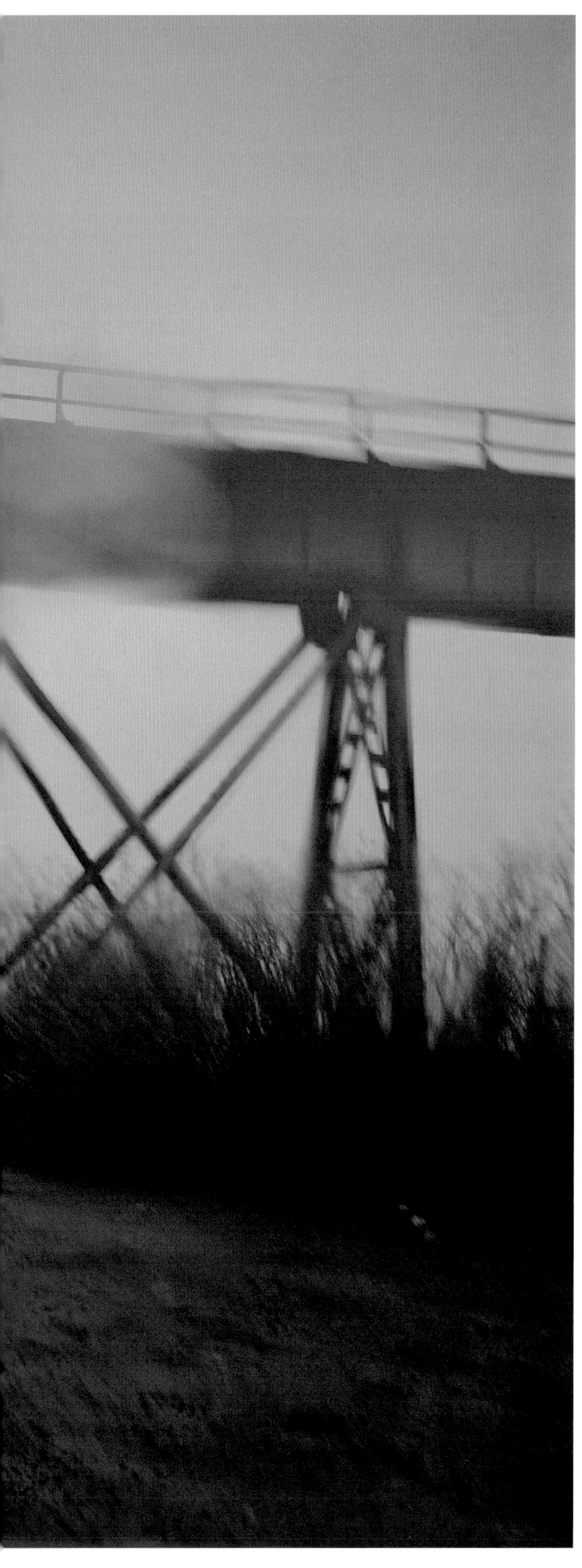

#3179 / Benicia, CA / *Roaming*

#3225 / Spangle, WA / *Roaming*

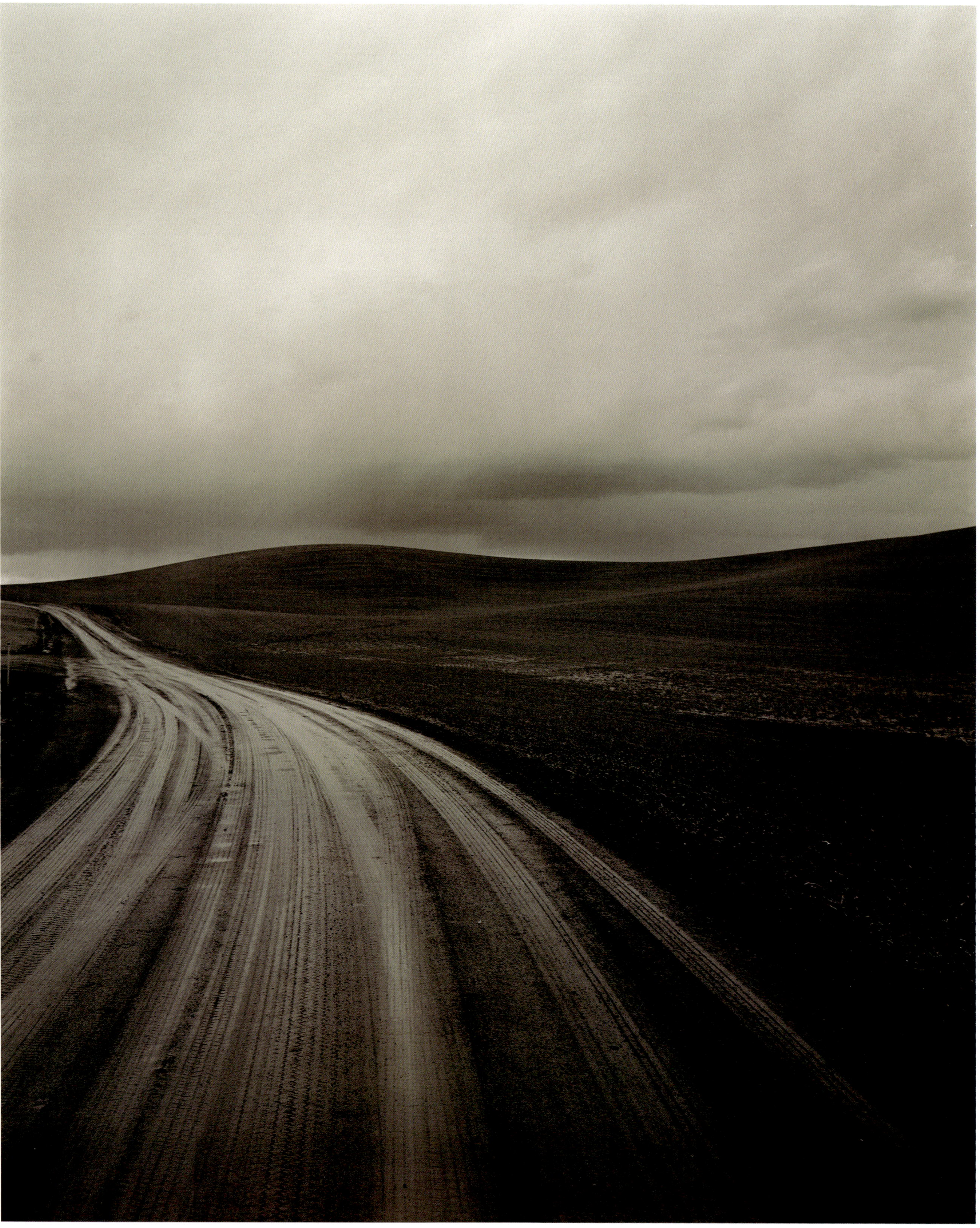

#3235 / Spangle, WA / *Roaming* #3258-b / Denver, CO / Ohio

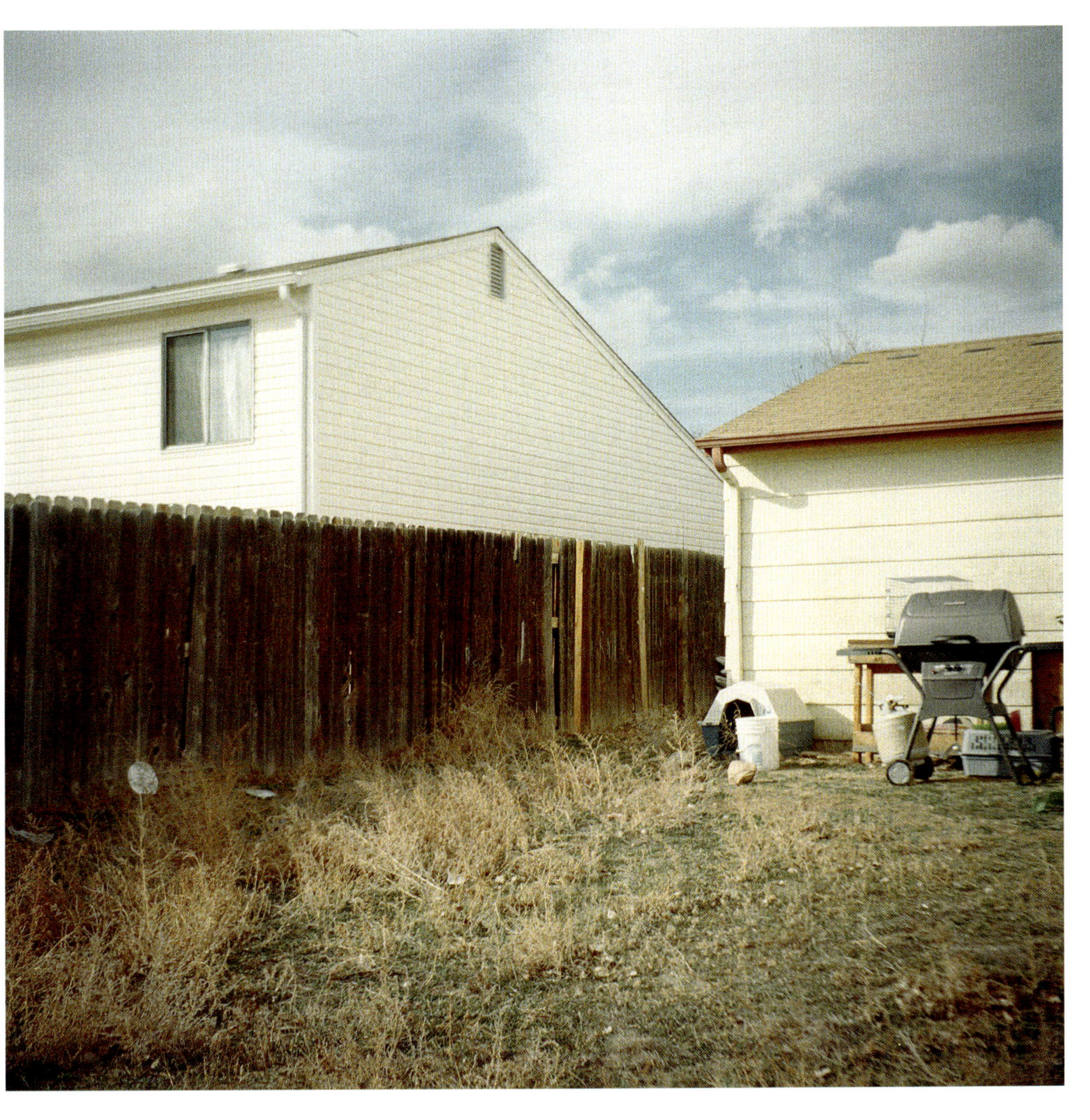

#3277 / Patterson, CA / *Roaming*

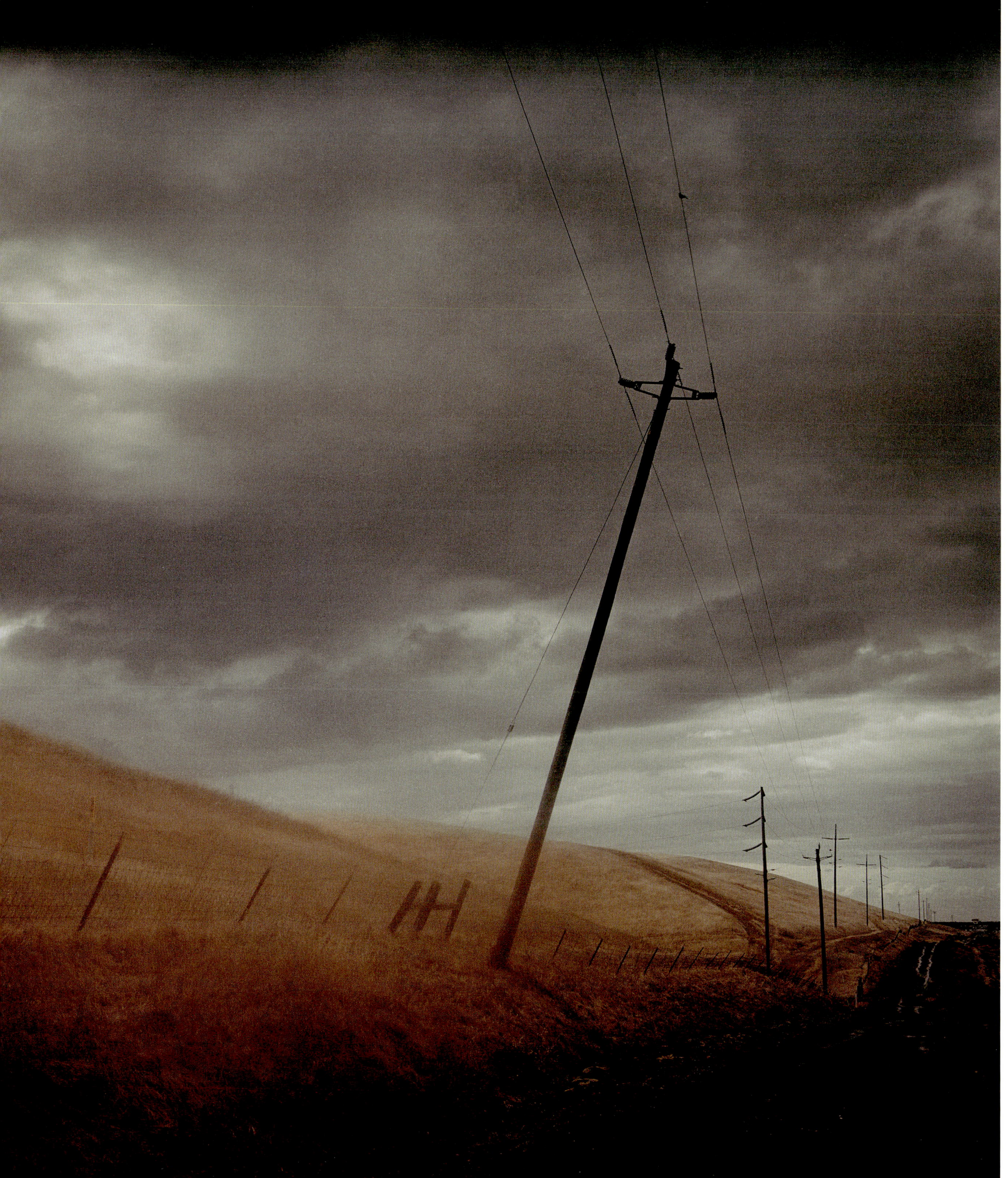

ROAMING 2004

Hido didn't want to be seen as a "one-trick pony." After the critical and general success of *House Hunting* and *Outskirts*, he wanted to create a book that had no homes in it. He also made a concerted effort to shoot primarily in the daytime. In that way, *Roaming*, which is a book of landscape photographs taken over ten years and published in 2004, demonstrates a purposeful shift in Hido's work. *Roaming* is a physical move out of the driveway and onto the open road, once the sun has risen.

Psychologically, however, this book of landscapes exhibits the same rumination as his previous books. It is a meditation on—or preoccupation with—how people live. The photographer and viewer may have left the hazy suburban "homes" portrayed in *House Hunting* and *Outskirts*, but the sensation remains. Go as far as you can, but you never leave yourself. Rather than consecutive, the photographs in *Roaming* feel persistent: a reoccurring feeling rattles between the internal and external world, behind the windshield, no matter the scenery outside.

Hido keeps at least three water bottles with him in his car. One time, I watched him spray his windshield with this water before taking a landscape. "I've learned from sheer disappointment that sometimes I need to take pictures, but it isn't raining outside," he said. Sometimes he will spray glycerin on the windshield for a different effect, a technique he compares to changing paintbrushes. The size, direction, and position of drops of water on the car window inform the photograph that results, and, within these fictitious raindrops, Hido says he can "compose" the real picture he wants to see. Ultimately, each of his photographs is a composition. It is a way of giving shape to a mental state, as opposed to capturing an actual setting.

Every one of Hido's landscapes, free of the human figure, is nonetheless littered with human presence. The photographs show telephone poles, electrical wires, the road, and the window through which they're seen—both the means and barriers to communication.

"I can't take photographs of pure nature," says Hido. "The view I'm photographing doesn't exist unless you can drive up to it." These are not retreats into the outdoor or "natural" world; they are attempted (and, ultimately, failed) escapes from an internal one.

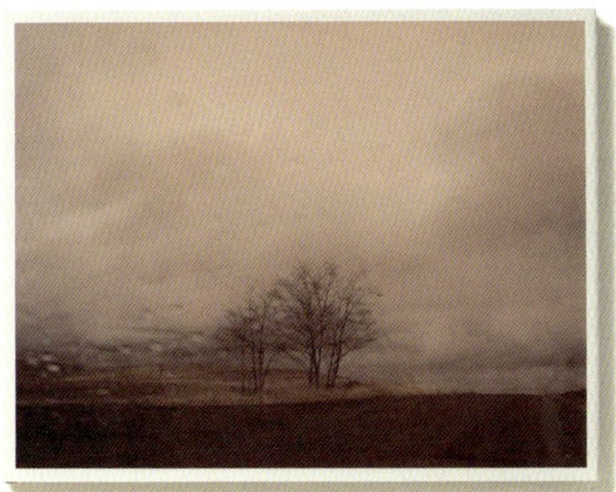

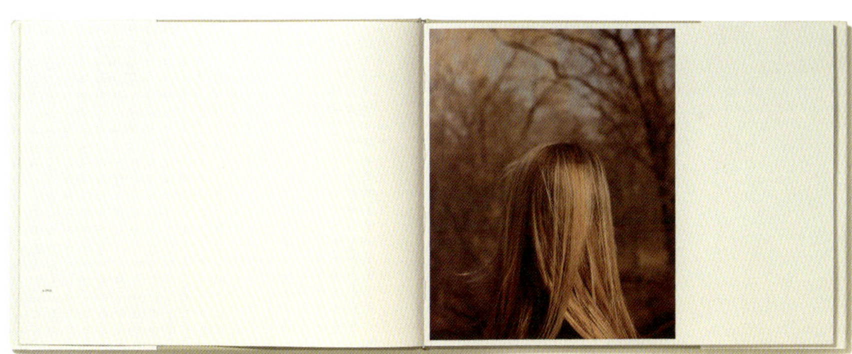

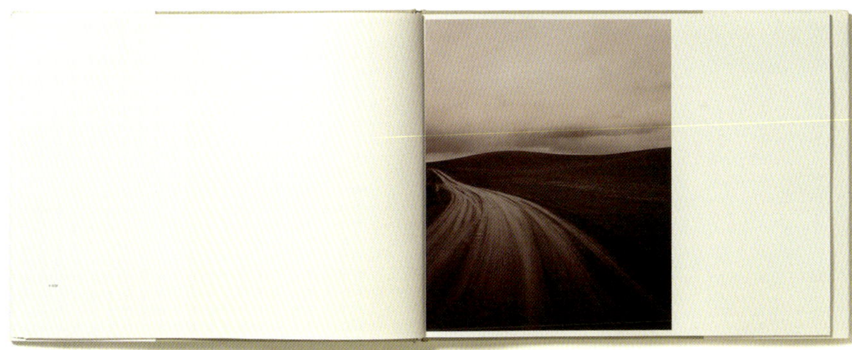

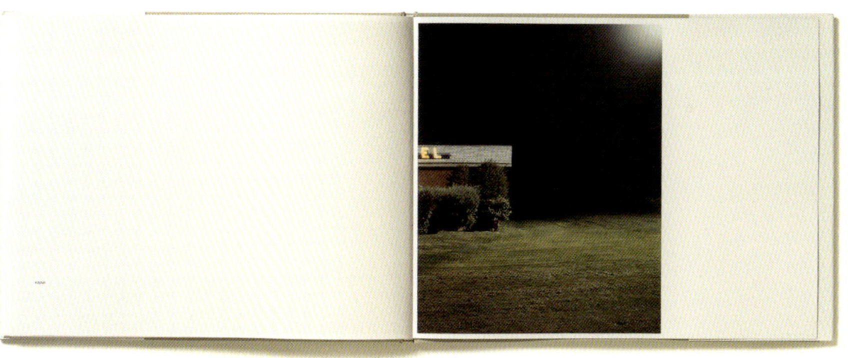

Roaming
Published 2004 by Nazraeli Press
13¾×11 inches
56 pages

CHRONOLOGY
2004–2006

2004 Begins photographing with models
2005 Begins photographing with 126 mm Instamatic camera
2005 Begins taking annual winter trip back to Ohio
2005 Group exhibition: *Marks of Honour*, Foam, Amsterdam
2006 Becomes adjunct professor at California College of the Arts
2006 Moves studio to downtown Oakland, California
2006 Expands studio production to include assistants
2006 Group exhibition: *Spectacular City*, NWR-Forum, Düsseldorf, Germany
2006 Nazraeli Press publishes *Between the Two*

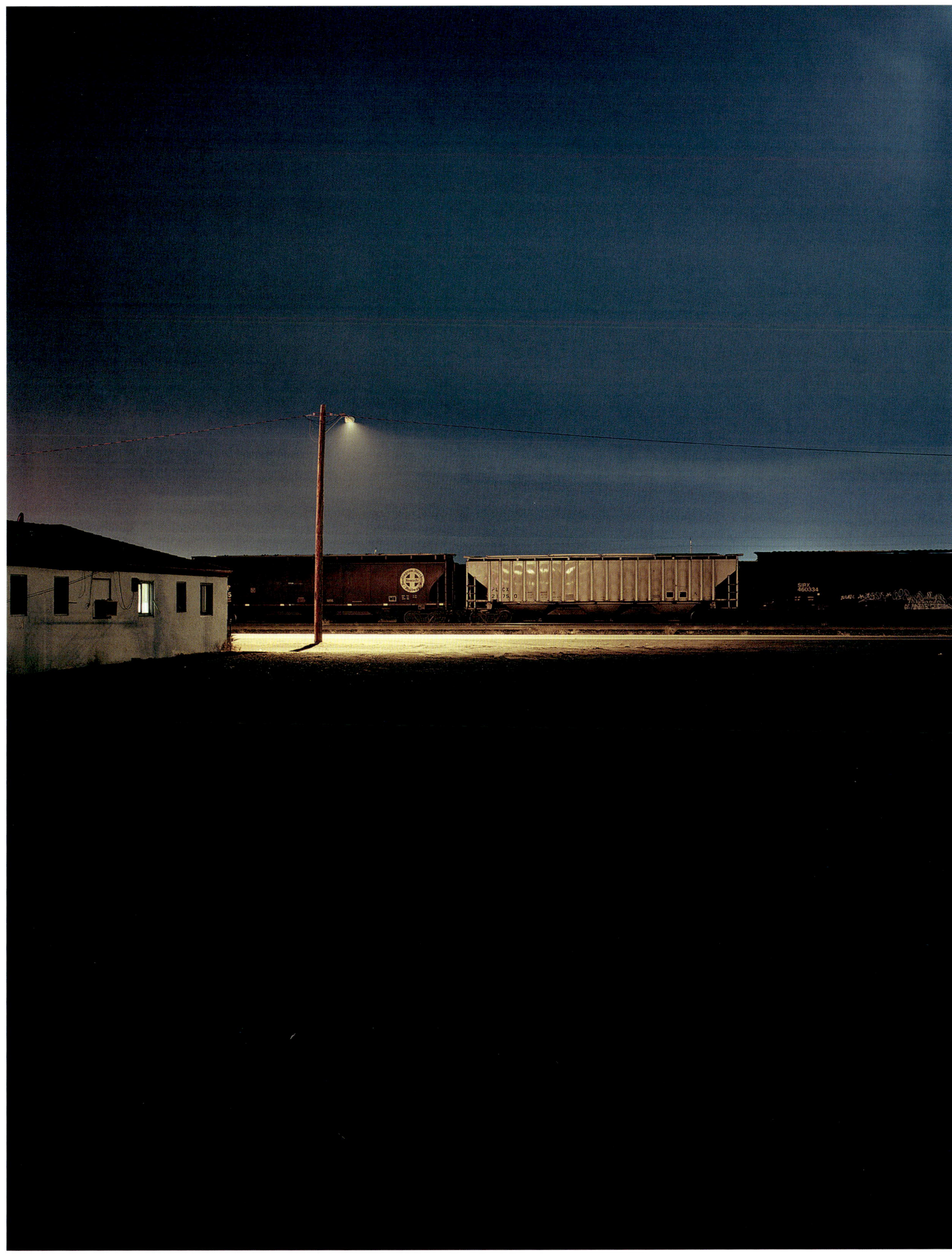

#3511 / Pasco, WA

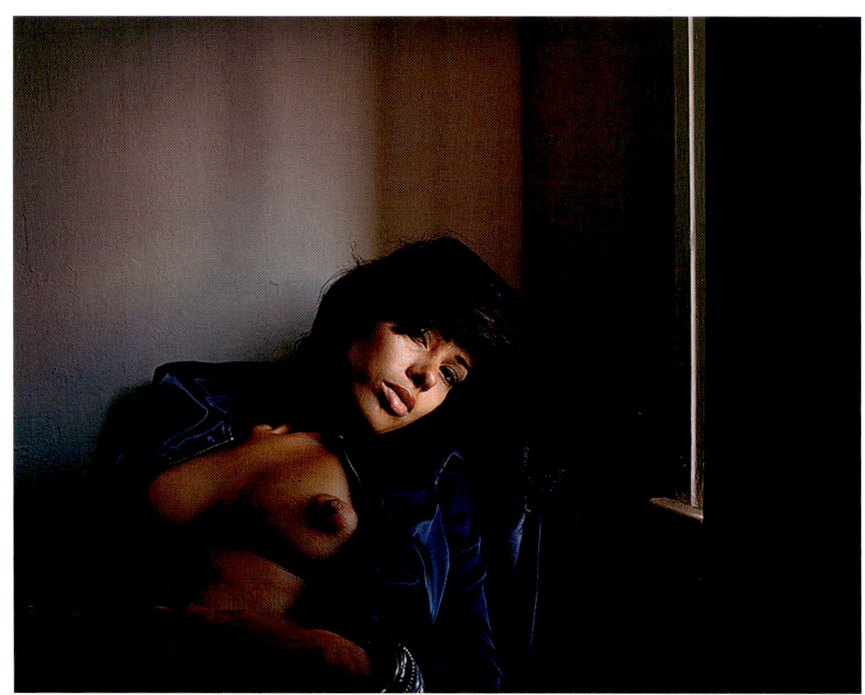

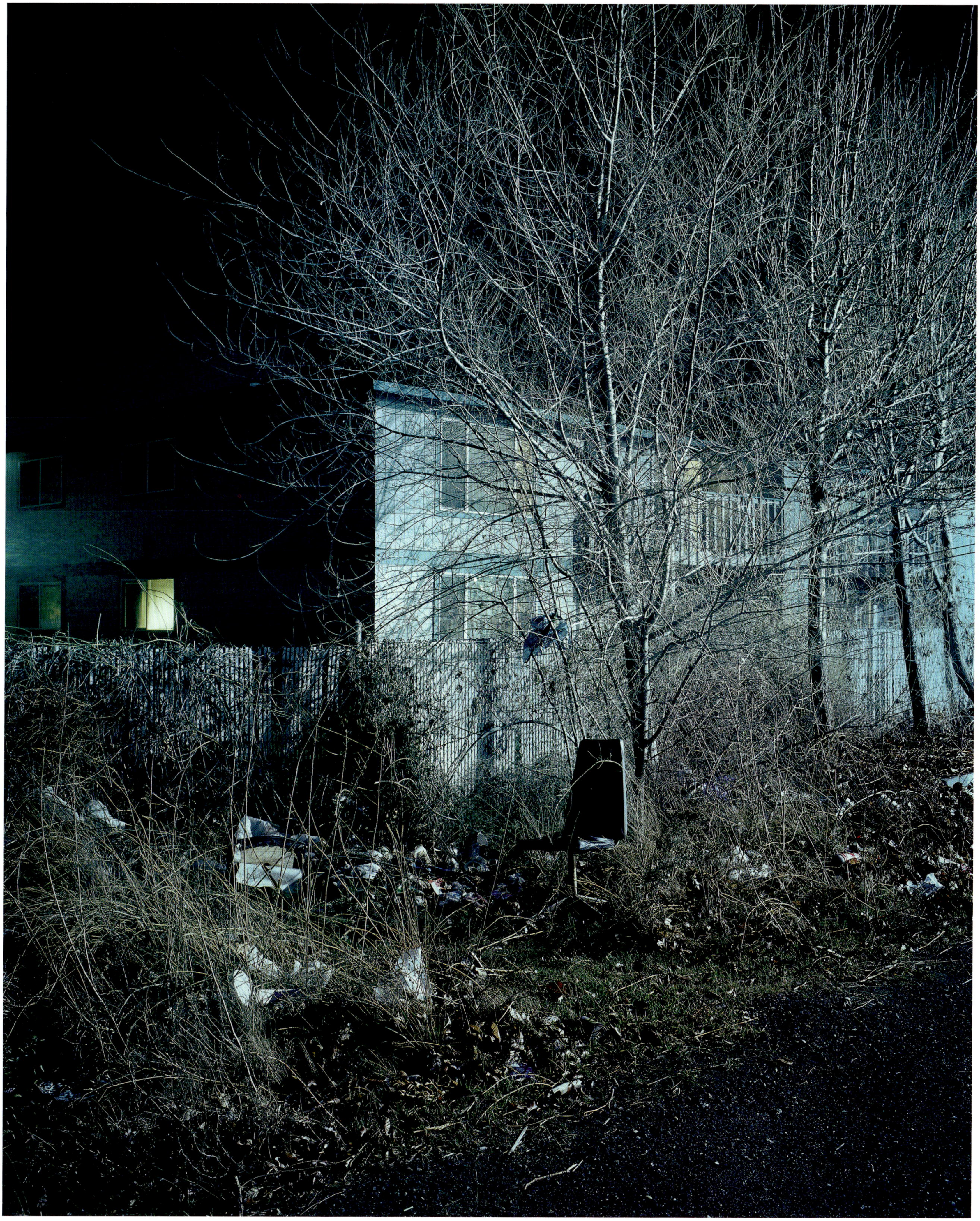

#3356 / San Francisco, CA / *Between the Two* **#3510** / Fairfield, CA / *Excerpts from Silver Meadows*

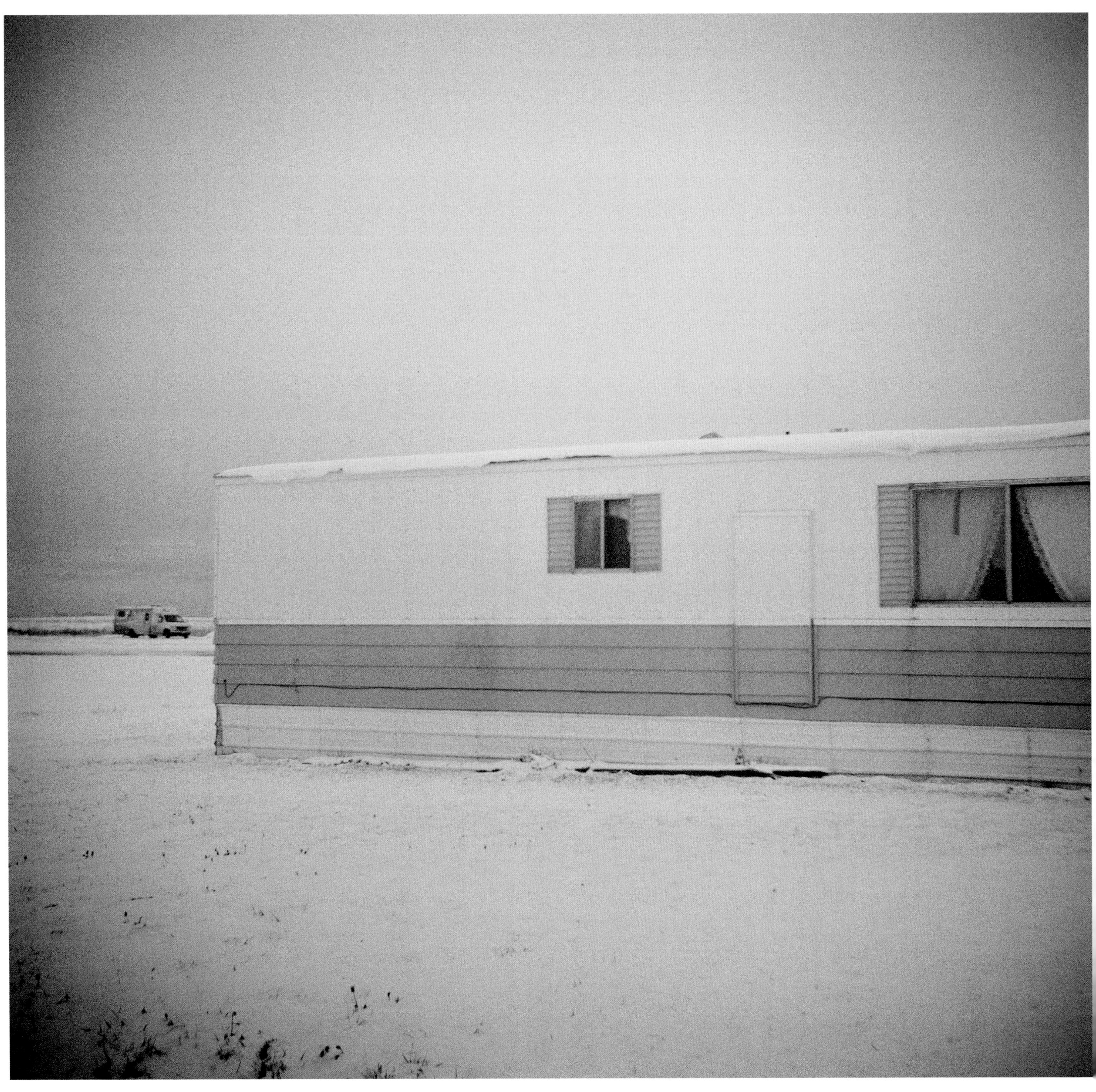

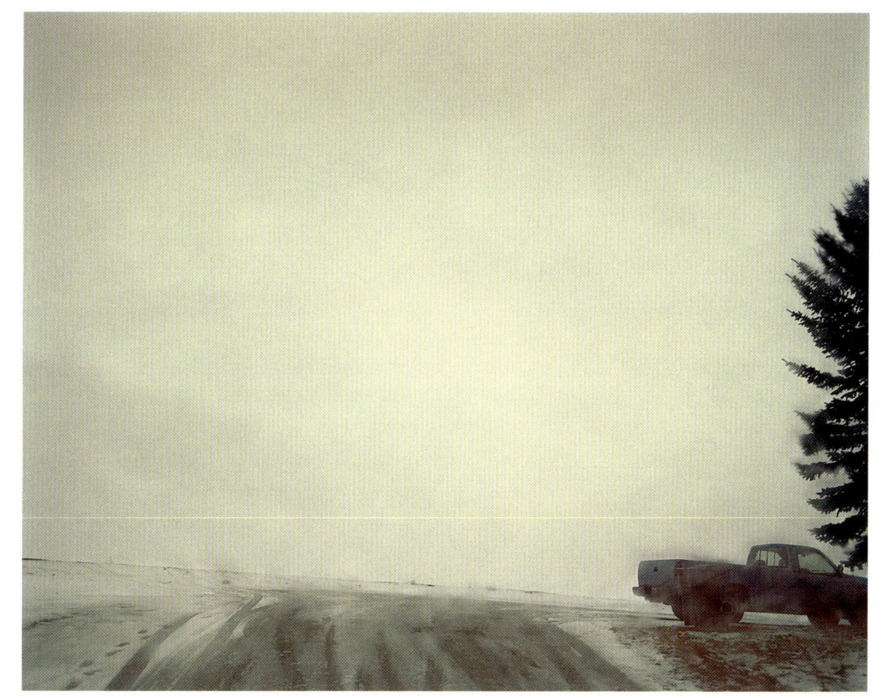

#3520 / Spangle, WA **#3515** / Spangle, WA / *A Road Divided*

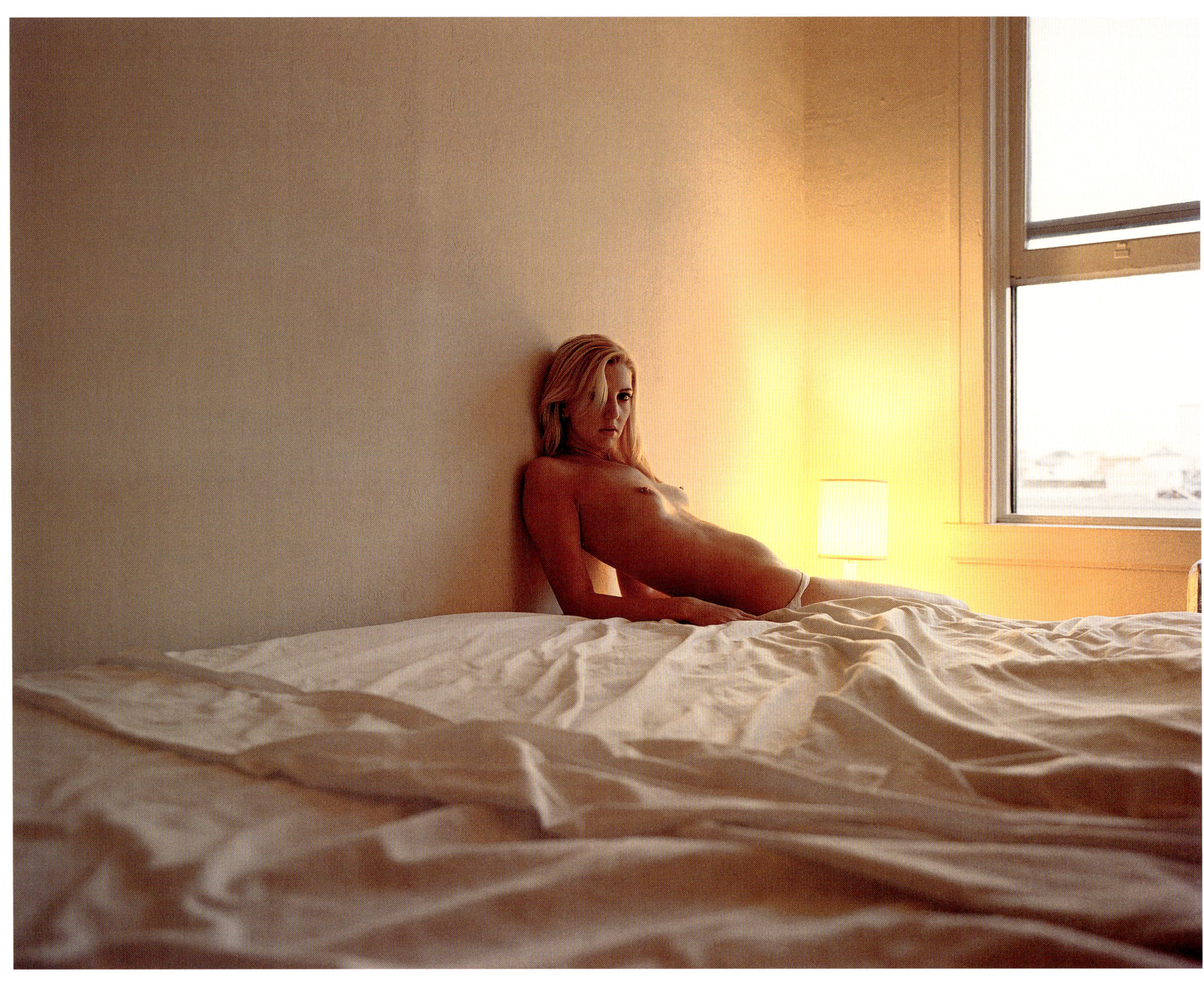

#3680 / San Francisco, CA / *Between the Two*

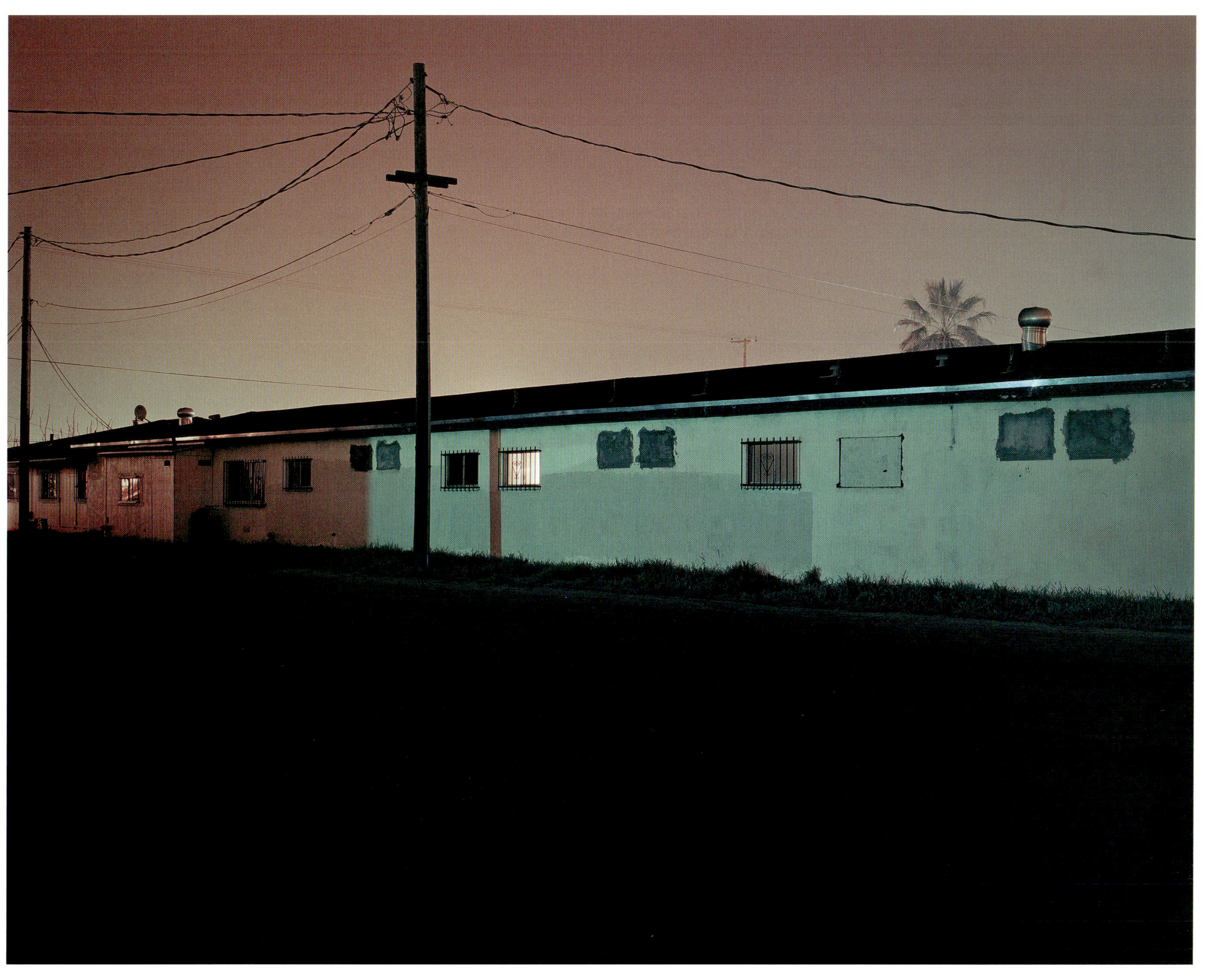

#3533-a / Modesto, CA / *Between the Two*

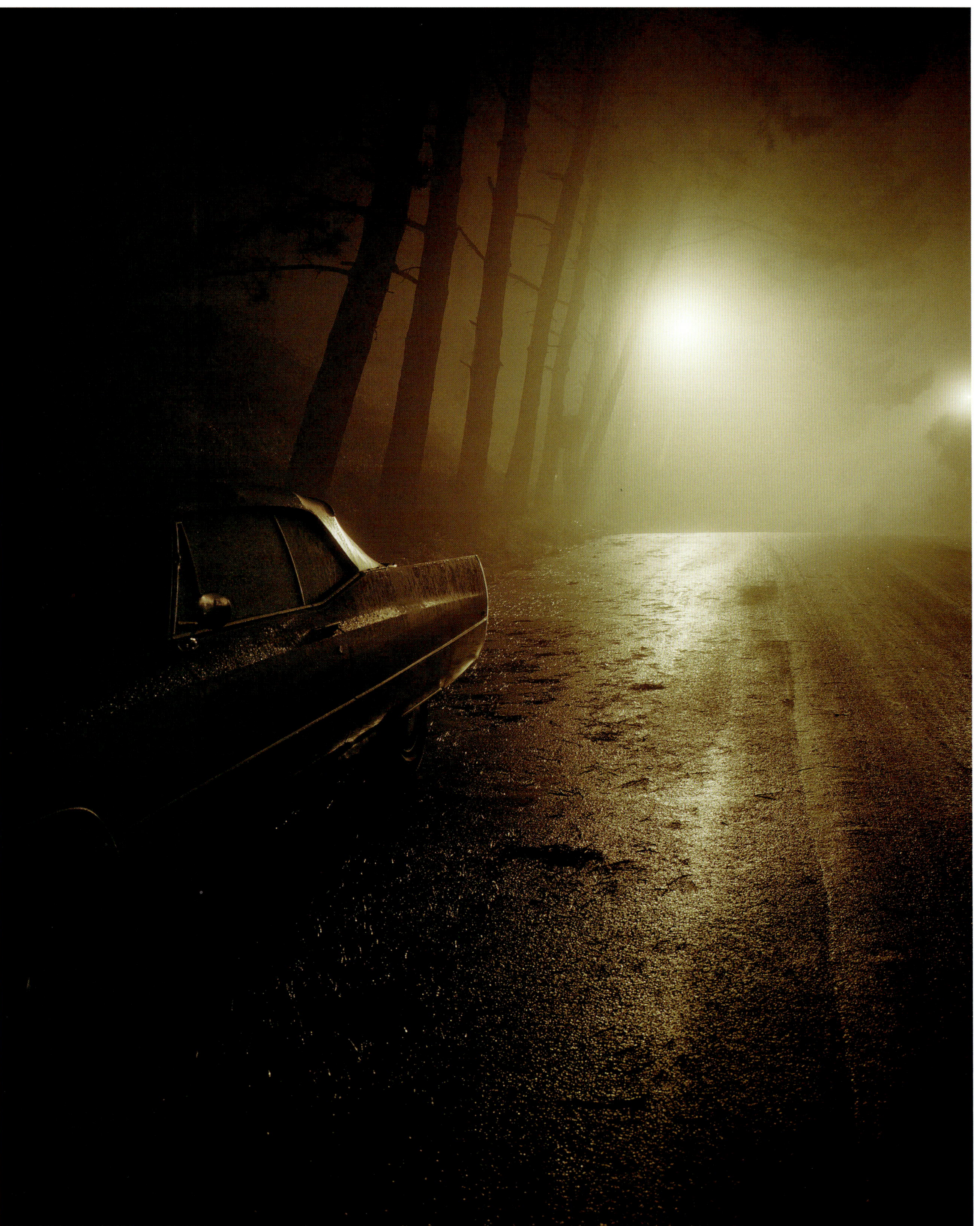

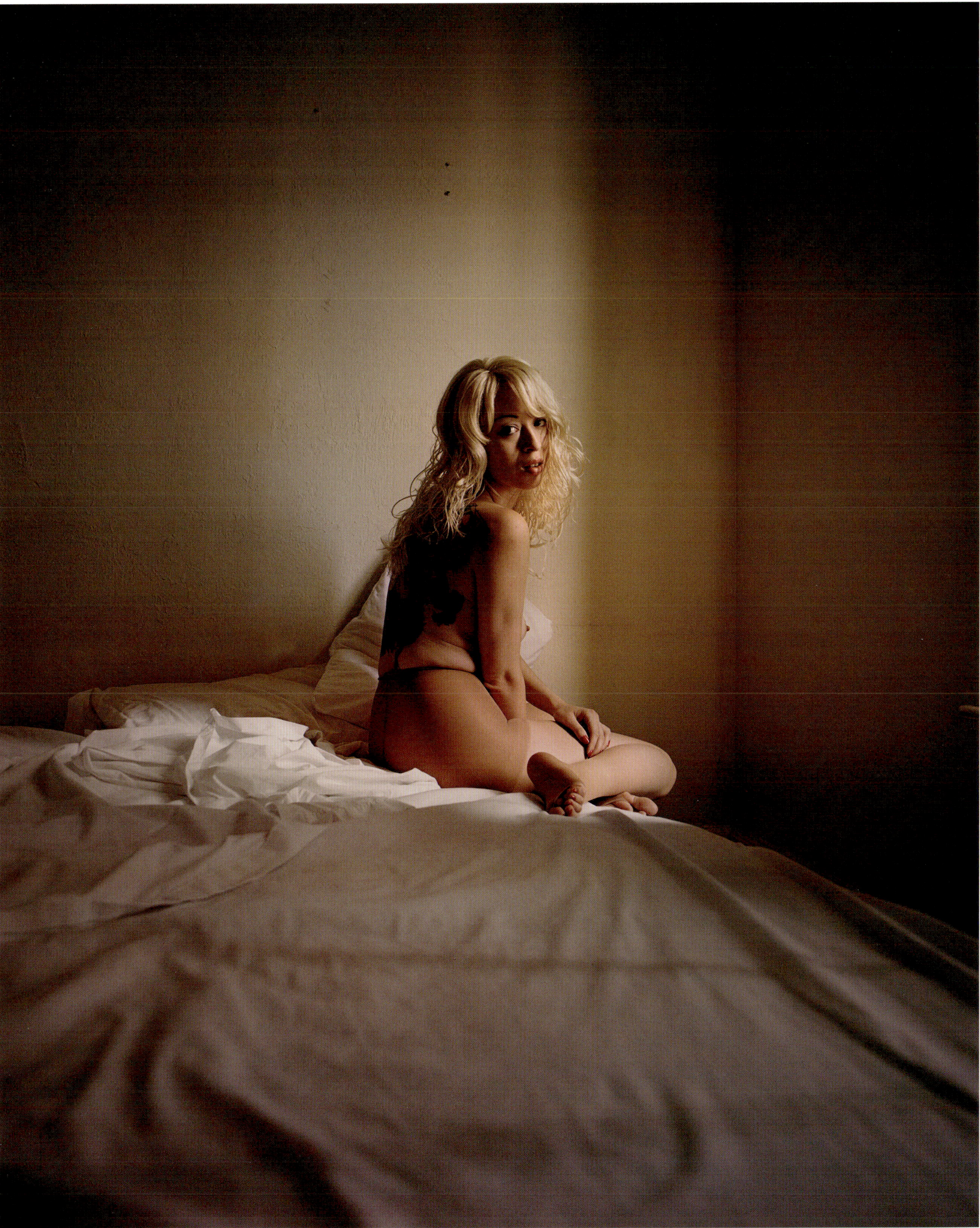

#3764 / San Francisco, CA / *Between the Two* **#3878** / Richmond, CA / *Between the Two*

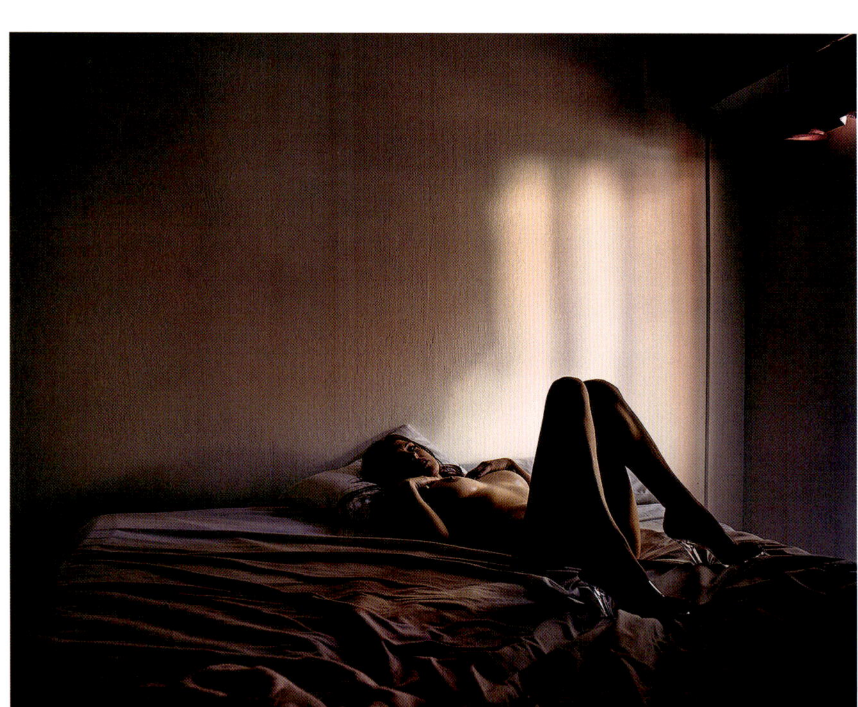

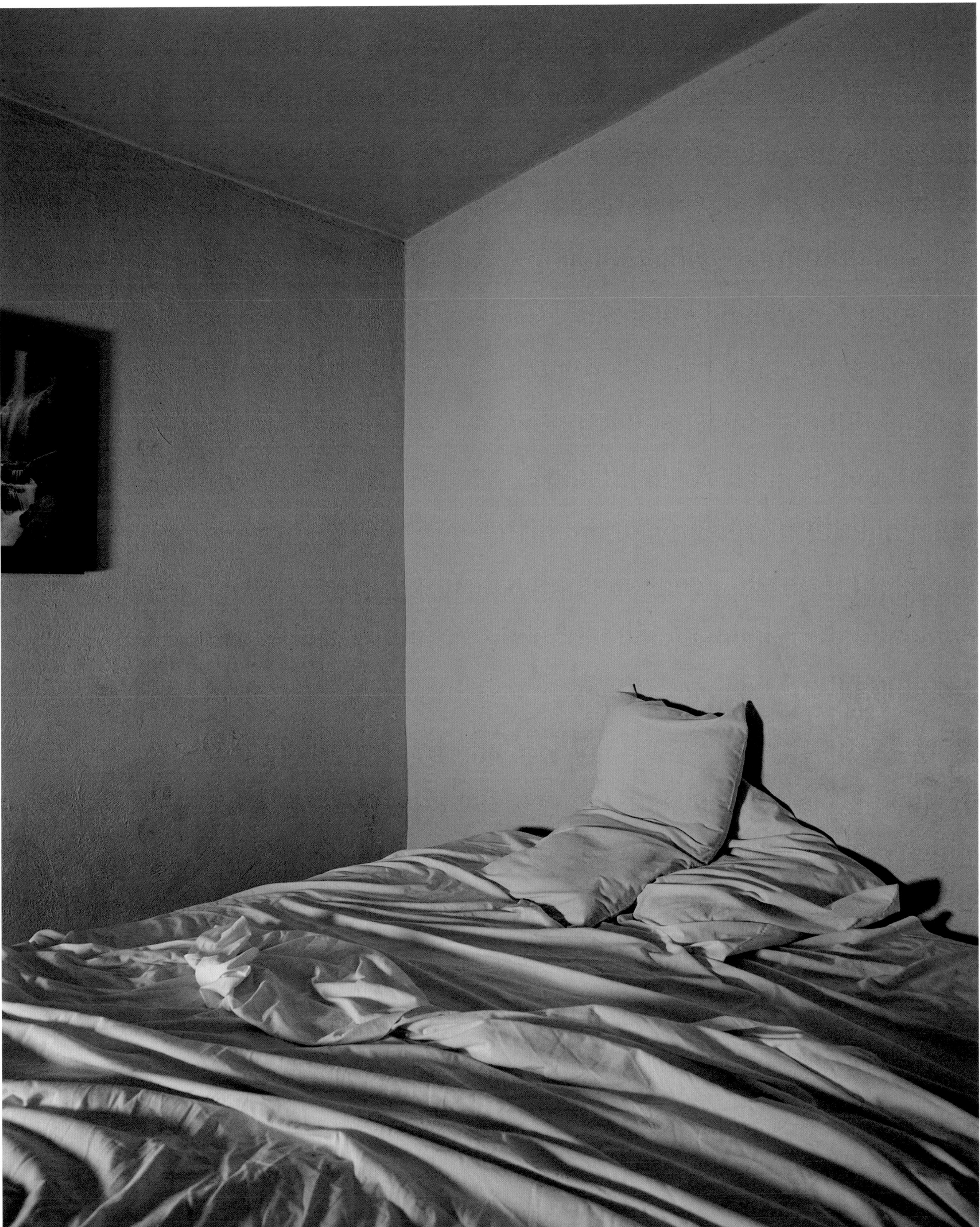

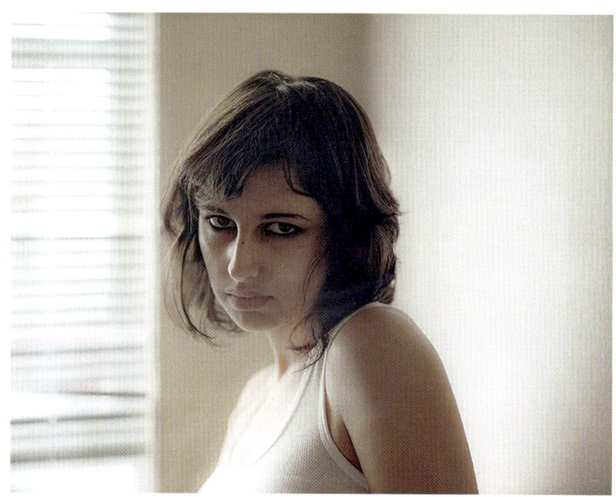

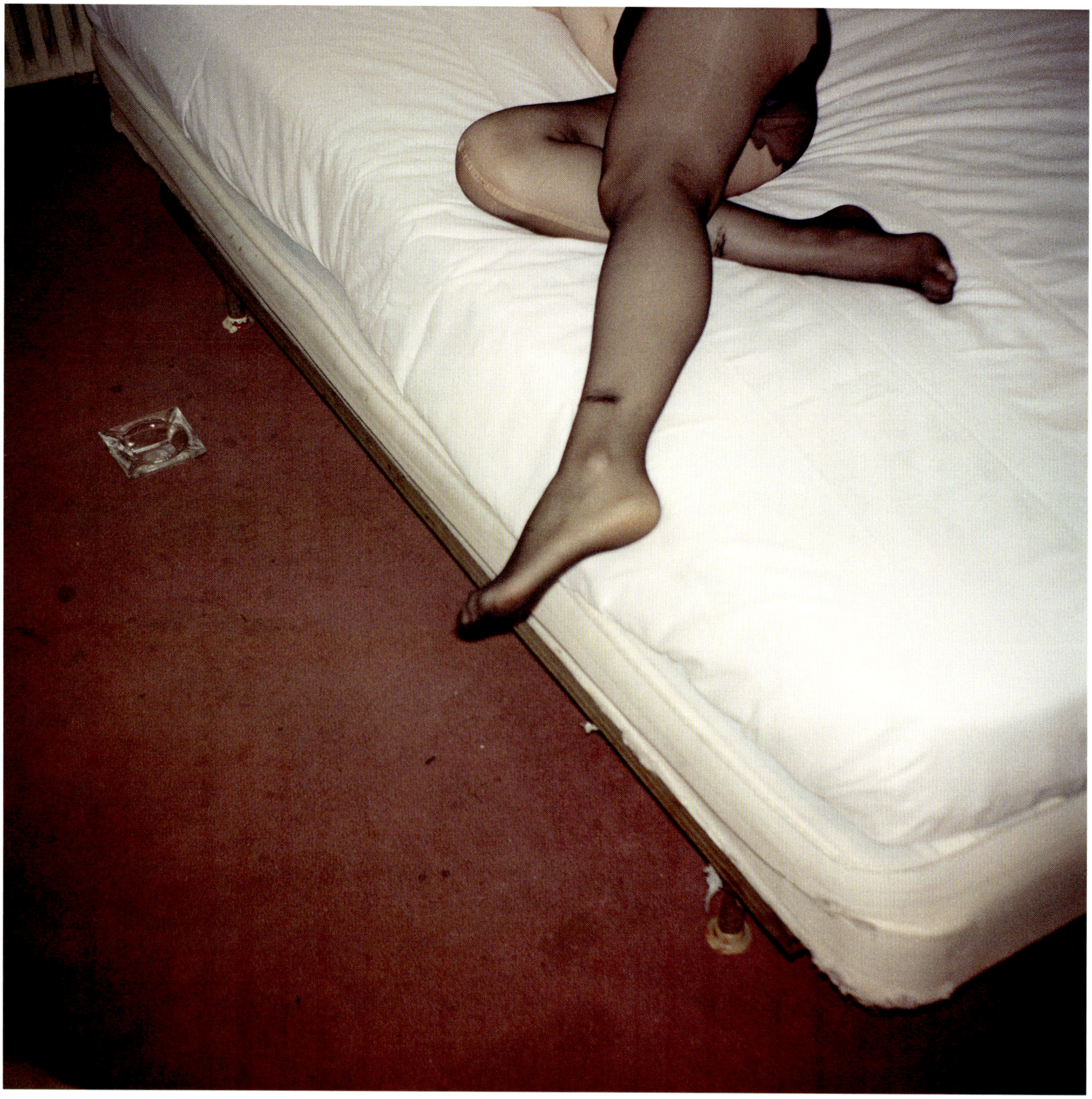

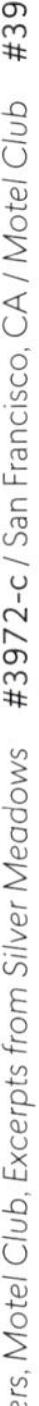
#3946 / San Francisco, CA / *Between the Two*   #3972-b / San Francisco, CA / *Nymph Daughters, Motel Club, Excerpts from Silver Meadows*   #3972-c / San Francisco, CA / *Motel Club*   #3973 / San Francisco, CA / *Between the Two*

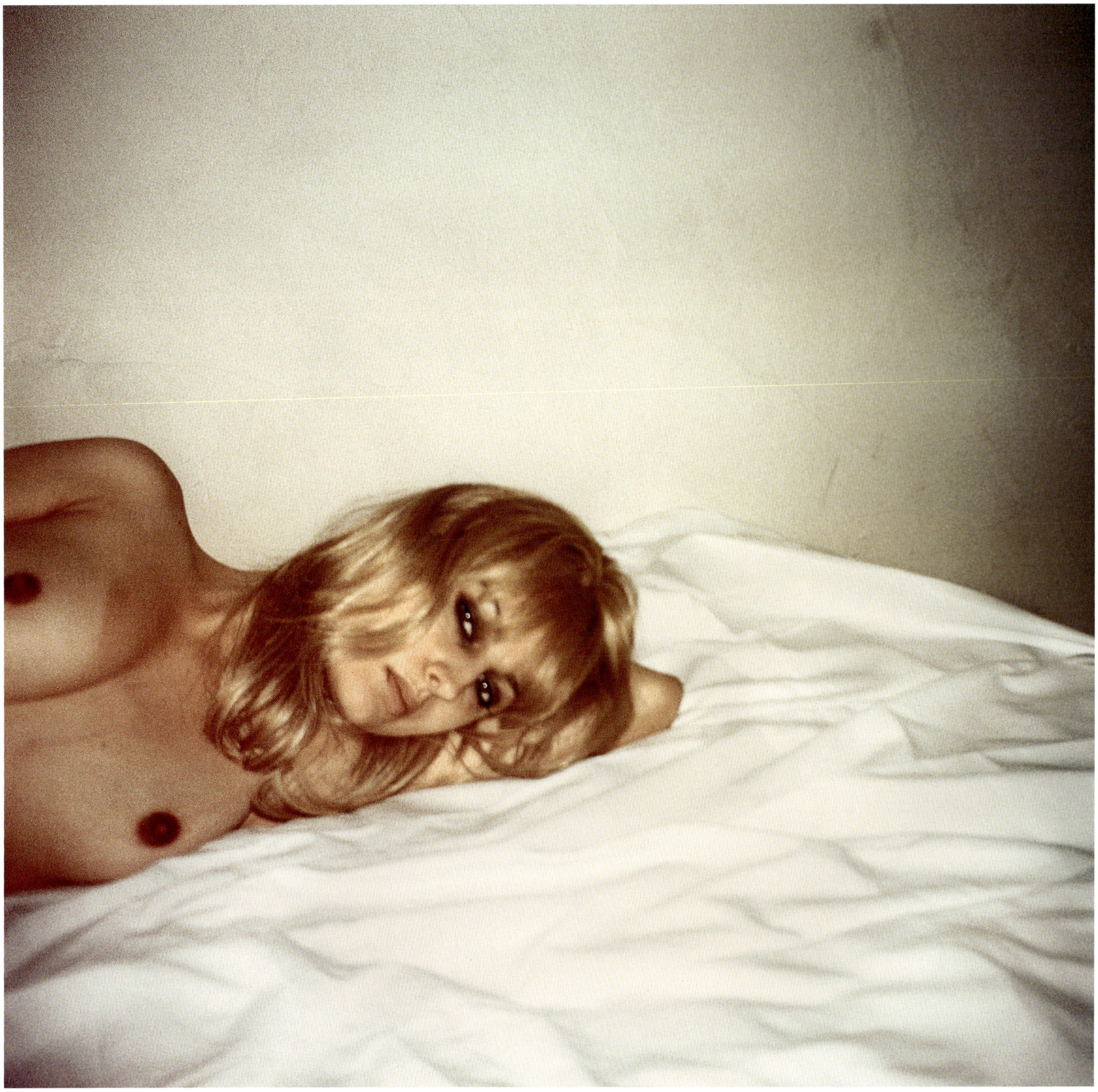

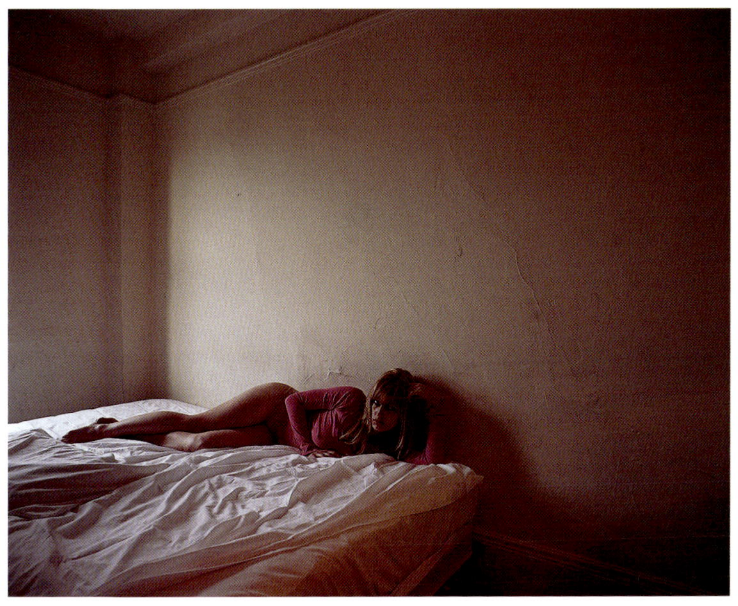

#3997-a / San Francisco, CA **#4022** / Stockton, CA **#3972-d** / Seattle, WA / *Motel Club, Excerpts from Silver Meadows*

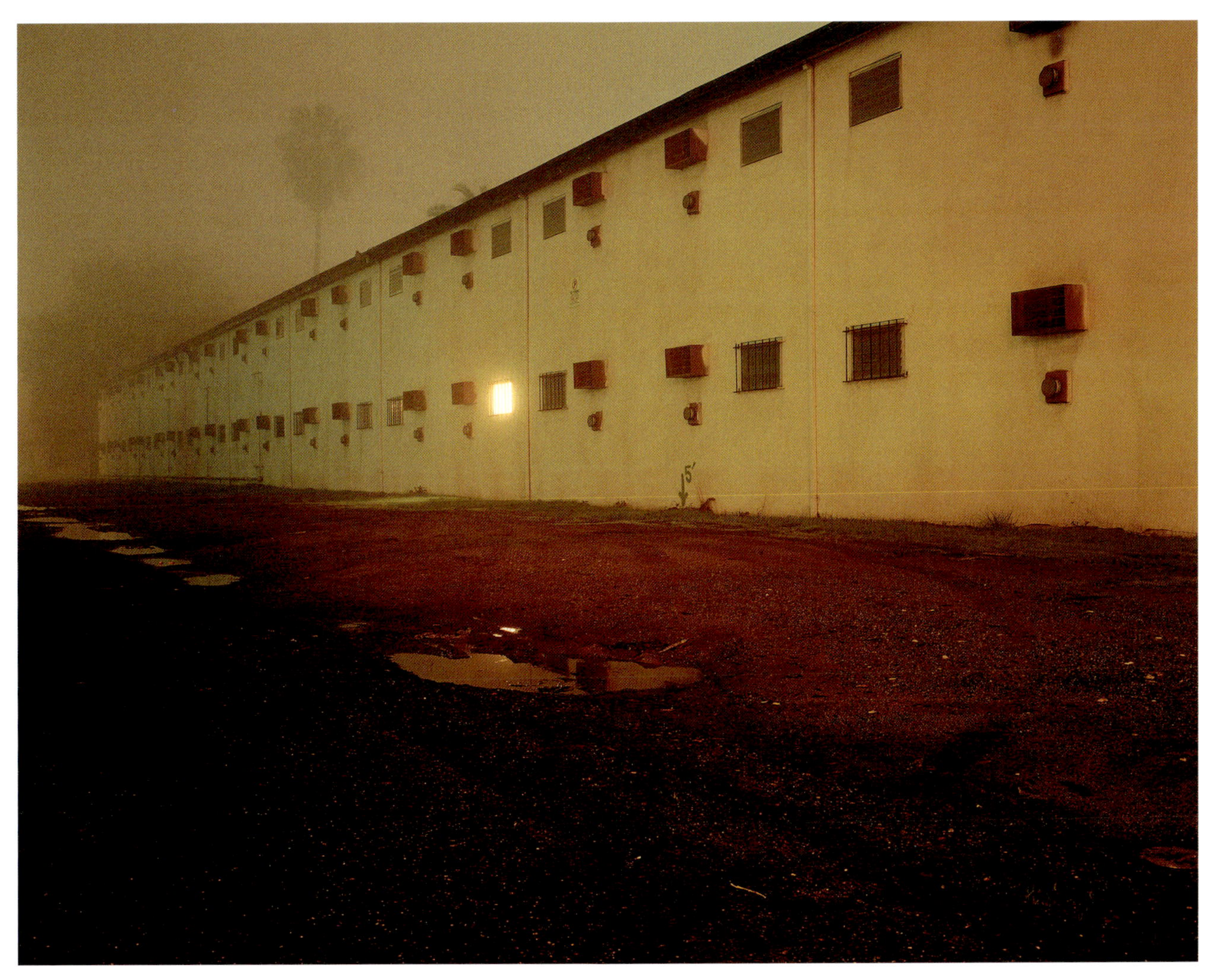

OFFICE

#4045 / Sacramento, CA / *Between the Two*

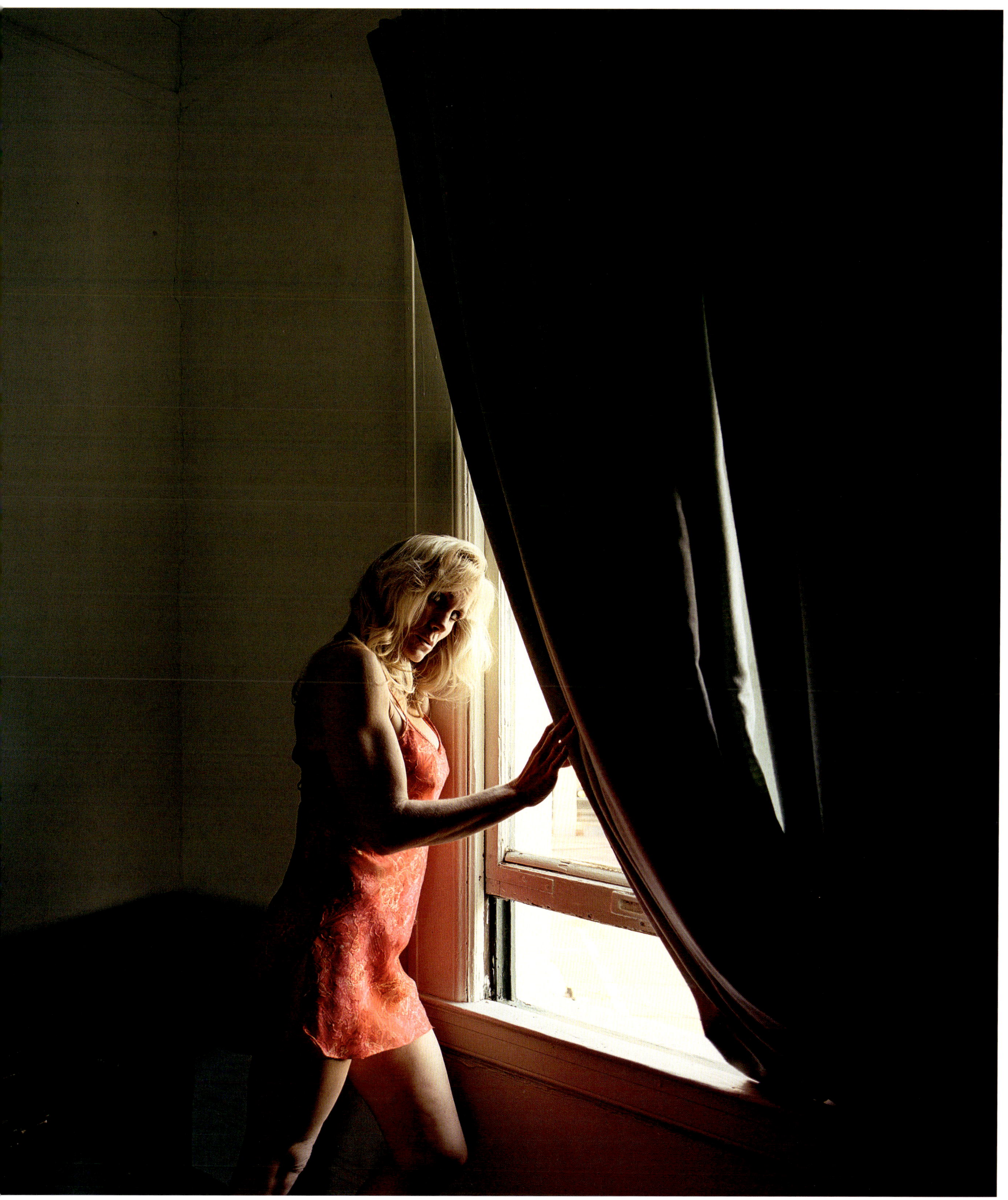

#4078 / Rio Vista, CA / *Between the Two*

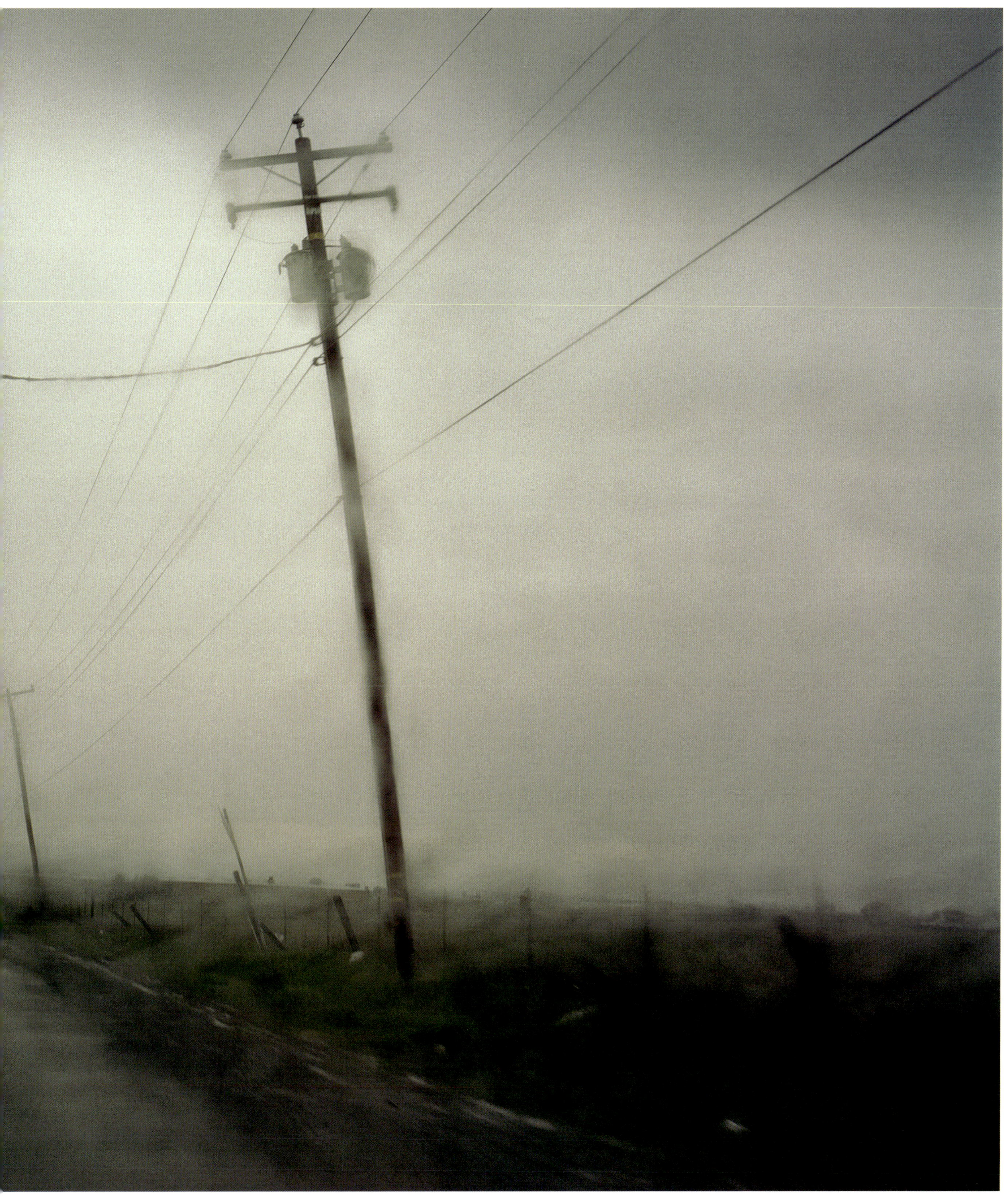

#4153 / San Francisco, CA / *Between the Two*

#4155-a / Benicia, CA / *Between the Two*

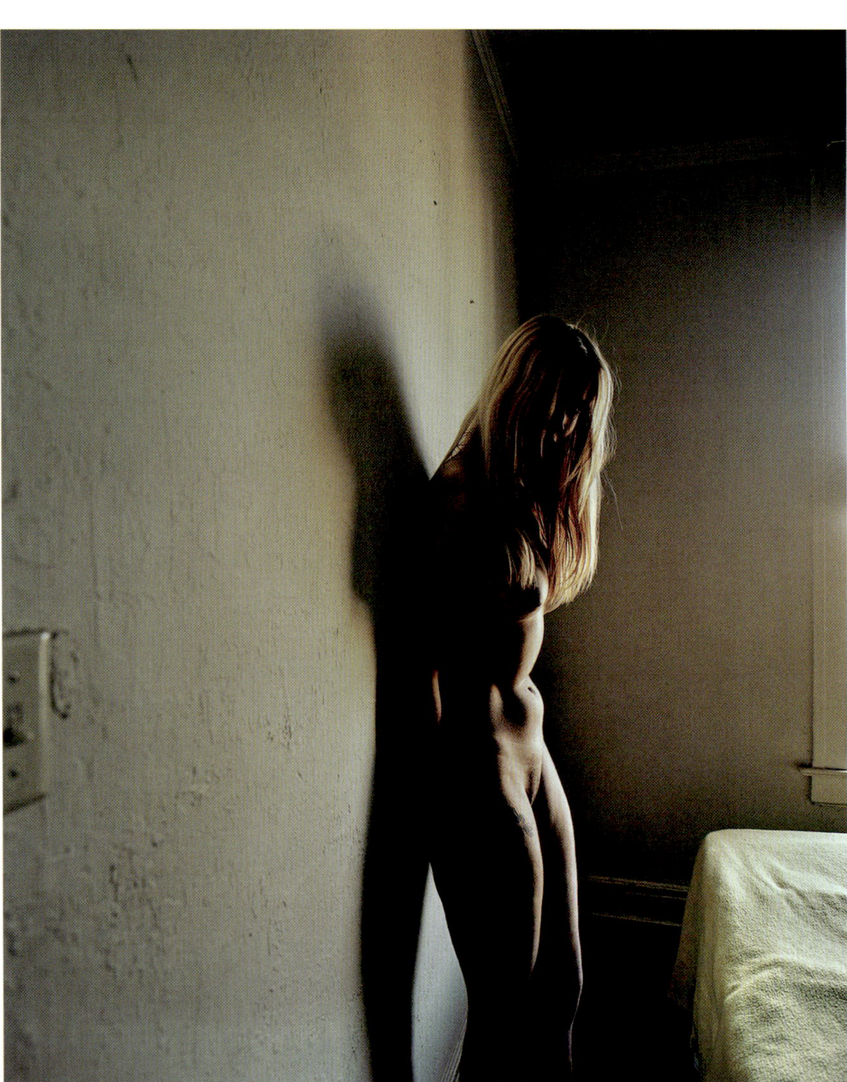

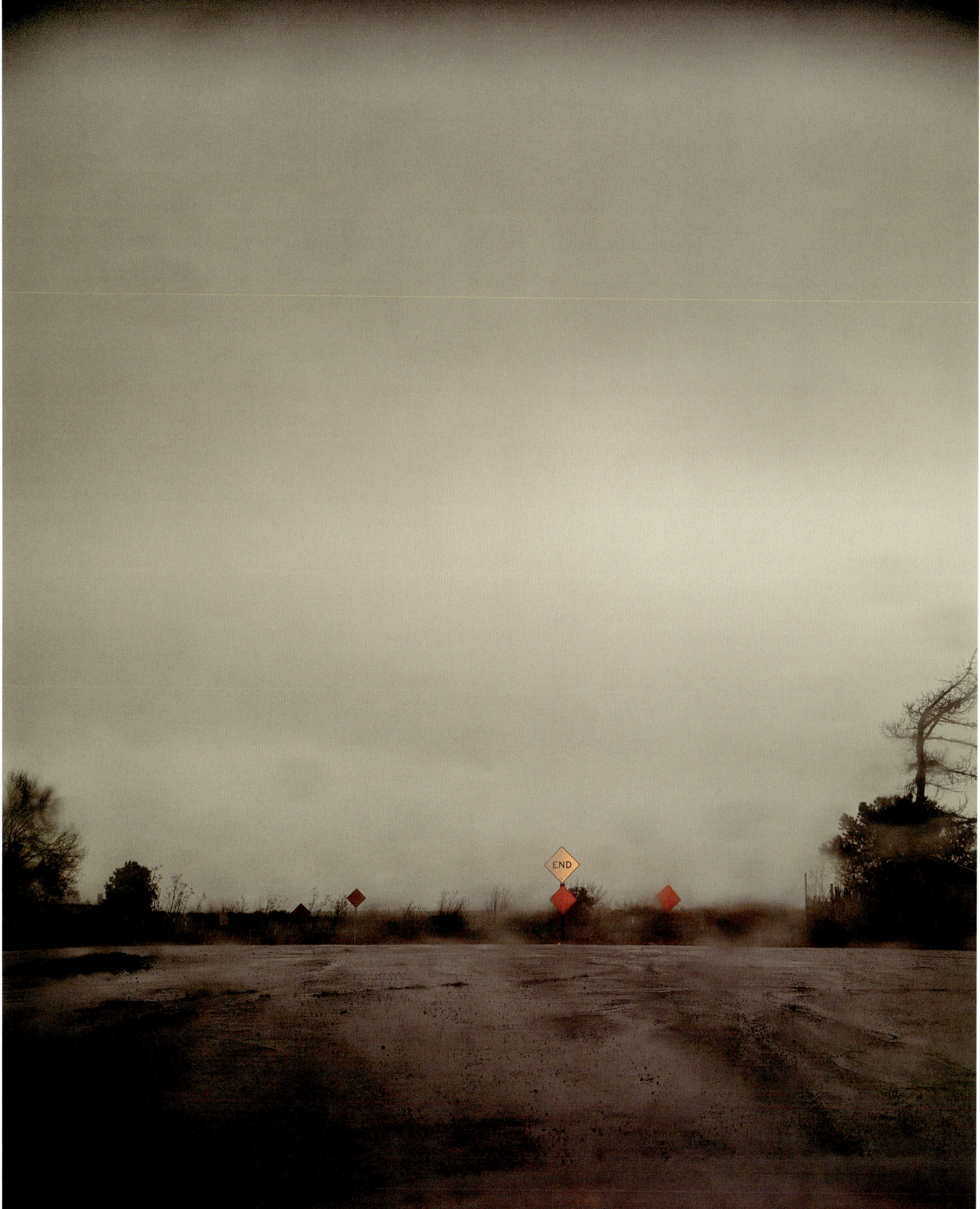
END

#4160 / San Francisco, CA

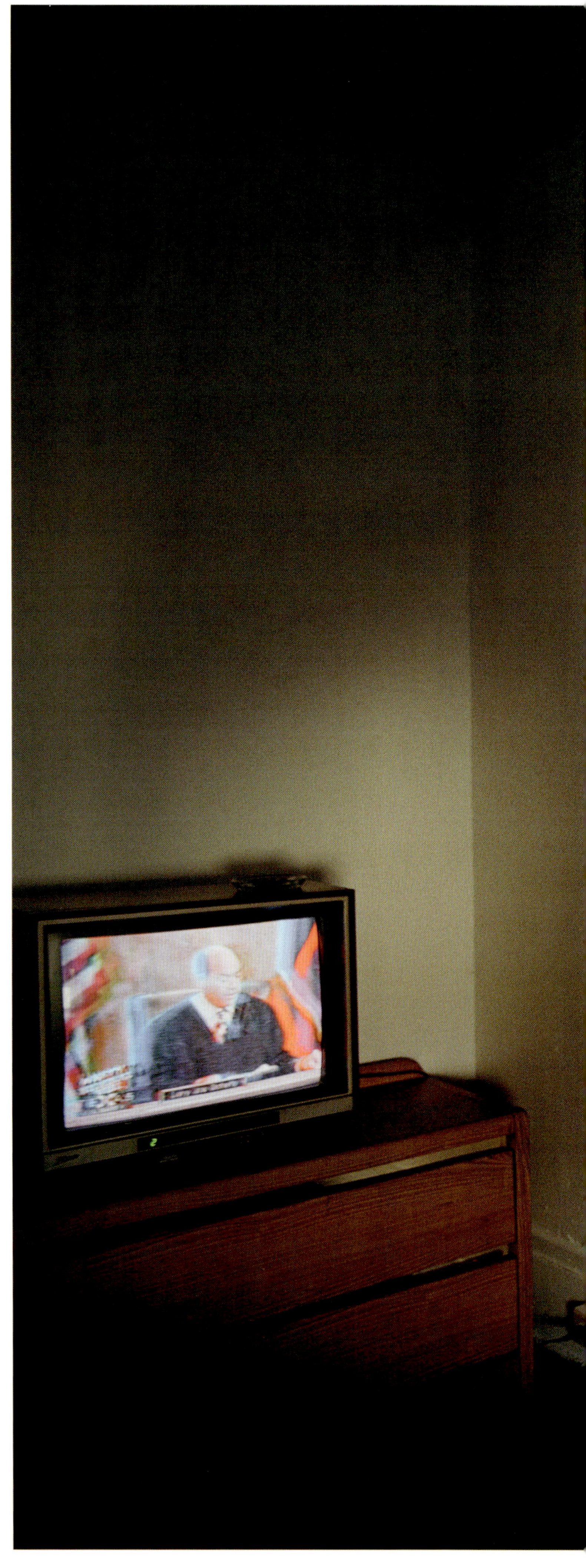

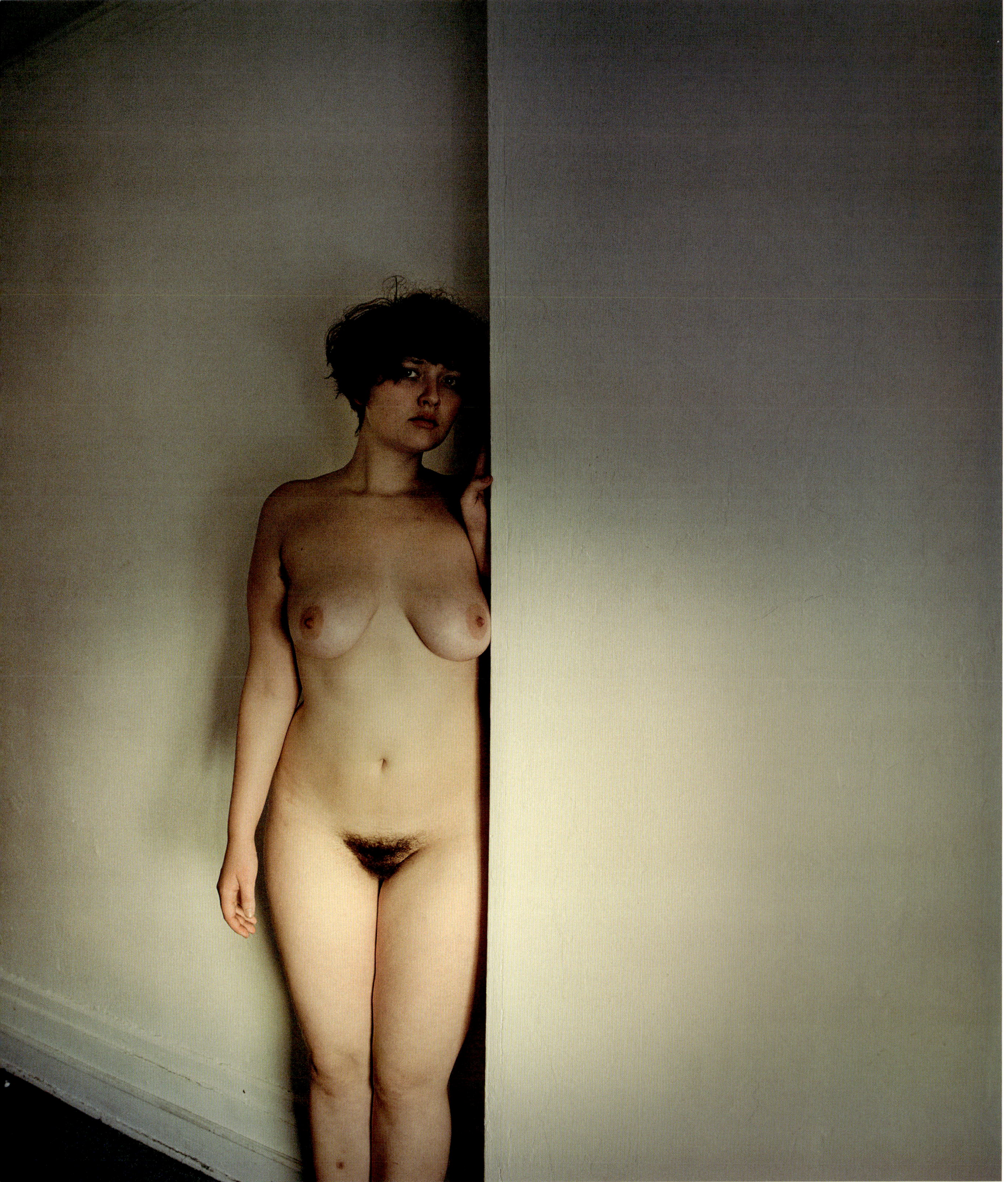

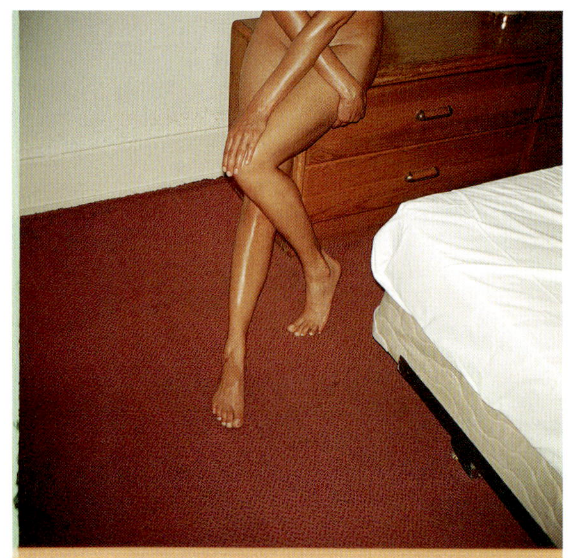

#4283-b / San Francisco, CA #4313 / San Francisco, CA / *Between the Two*

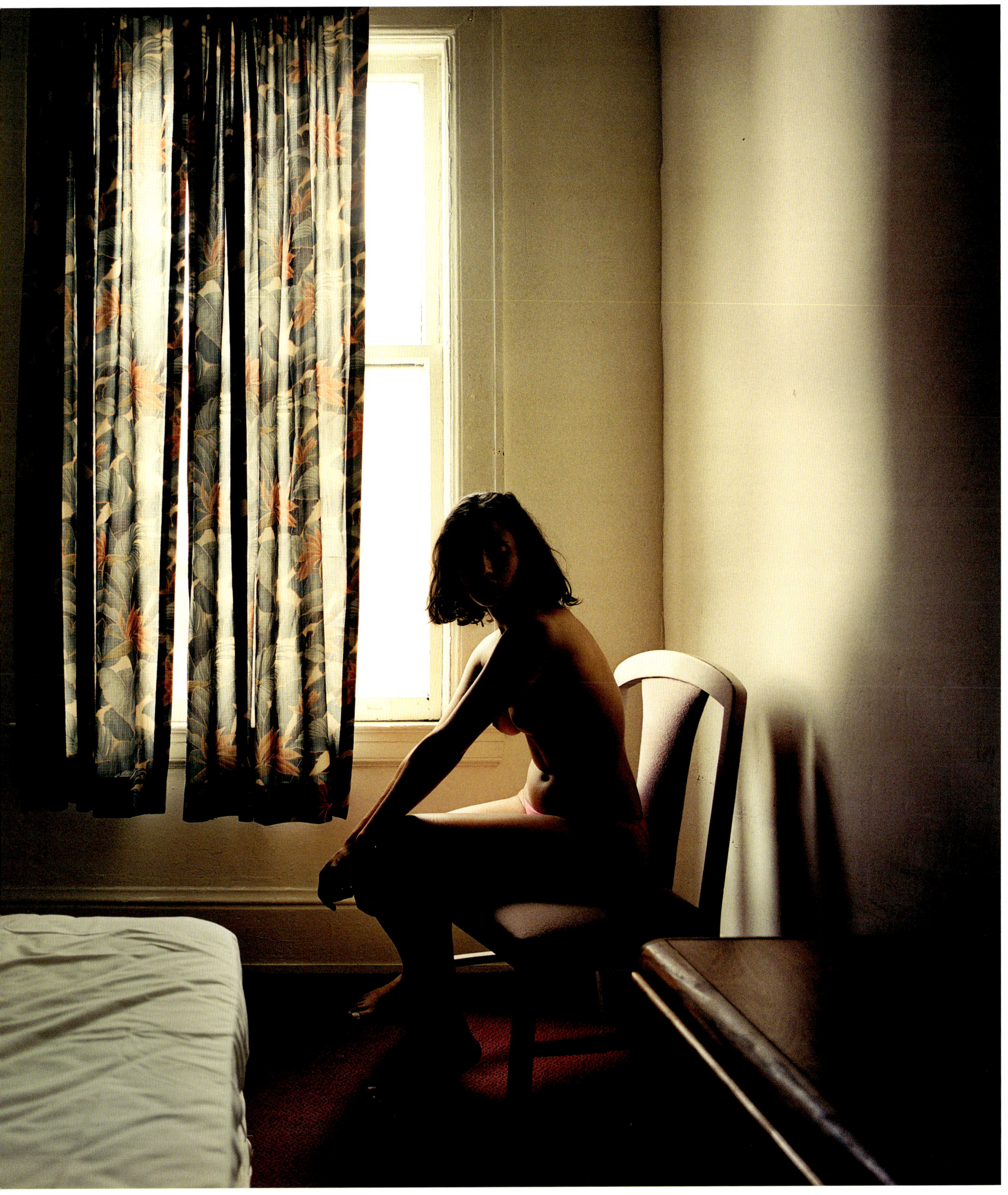

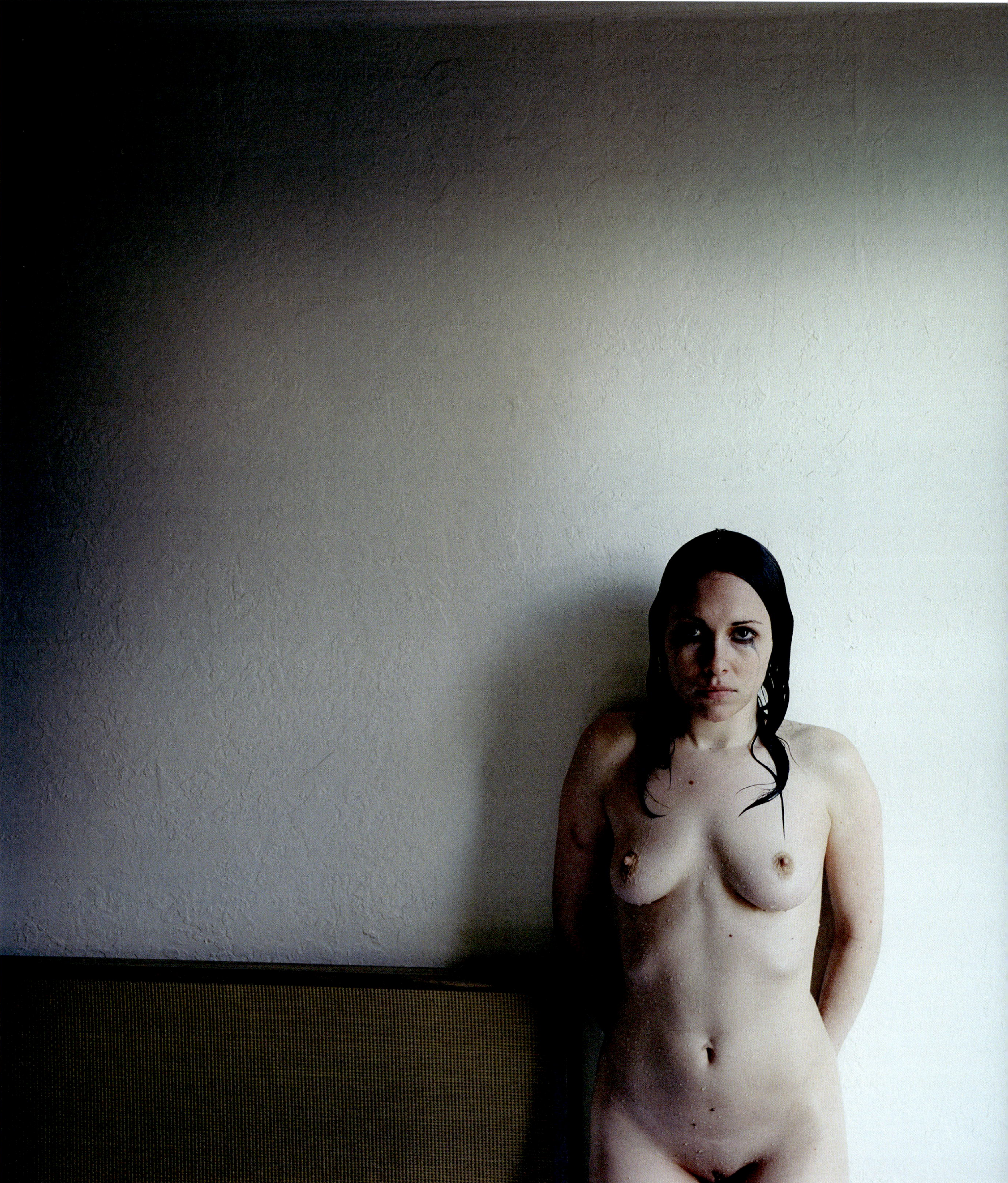

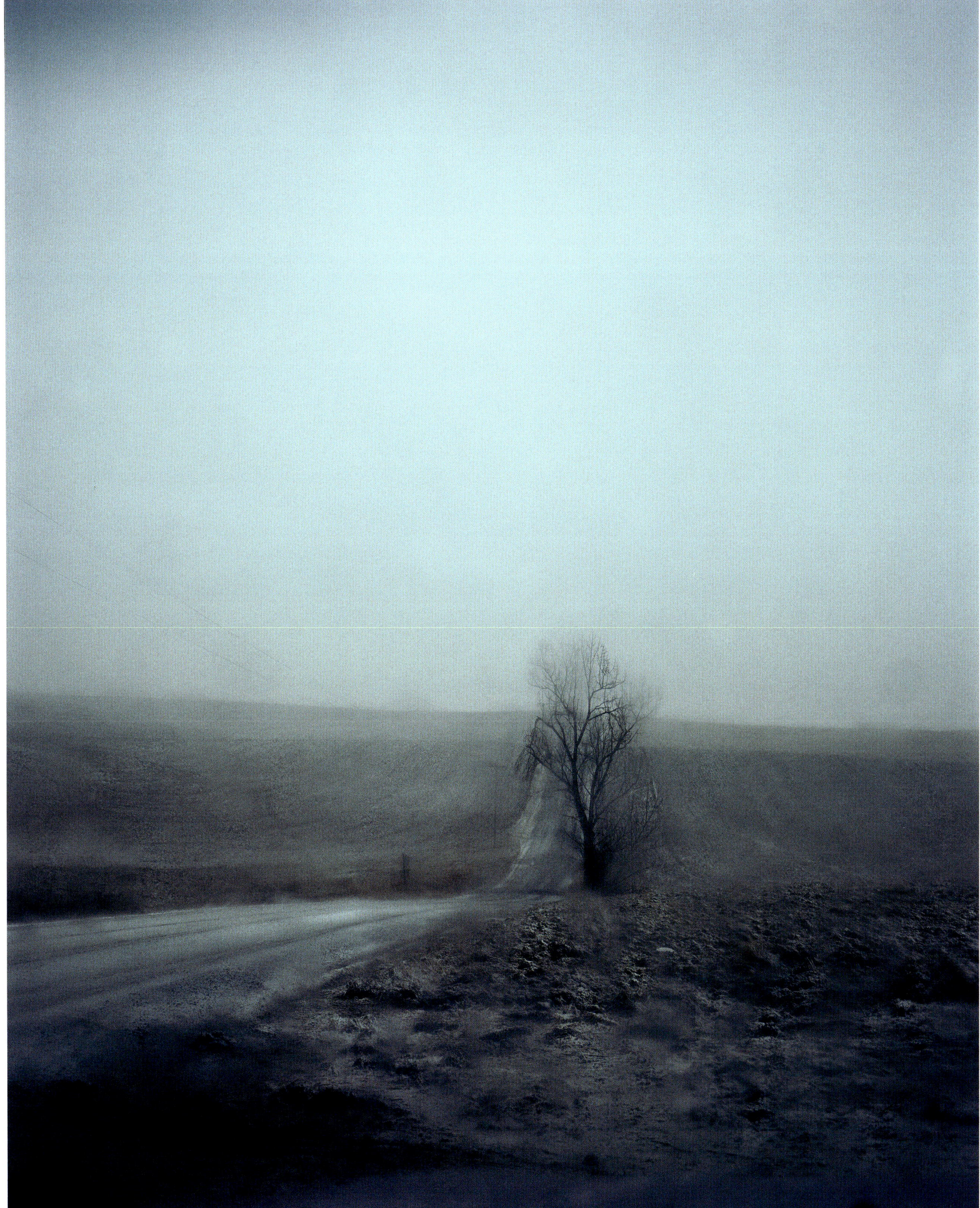

#5114 / Pasco, WA **#5203-a** / Sacramento, CA / *Motel Club, Excerpts from Silver Meadows*

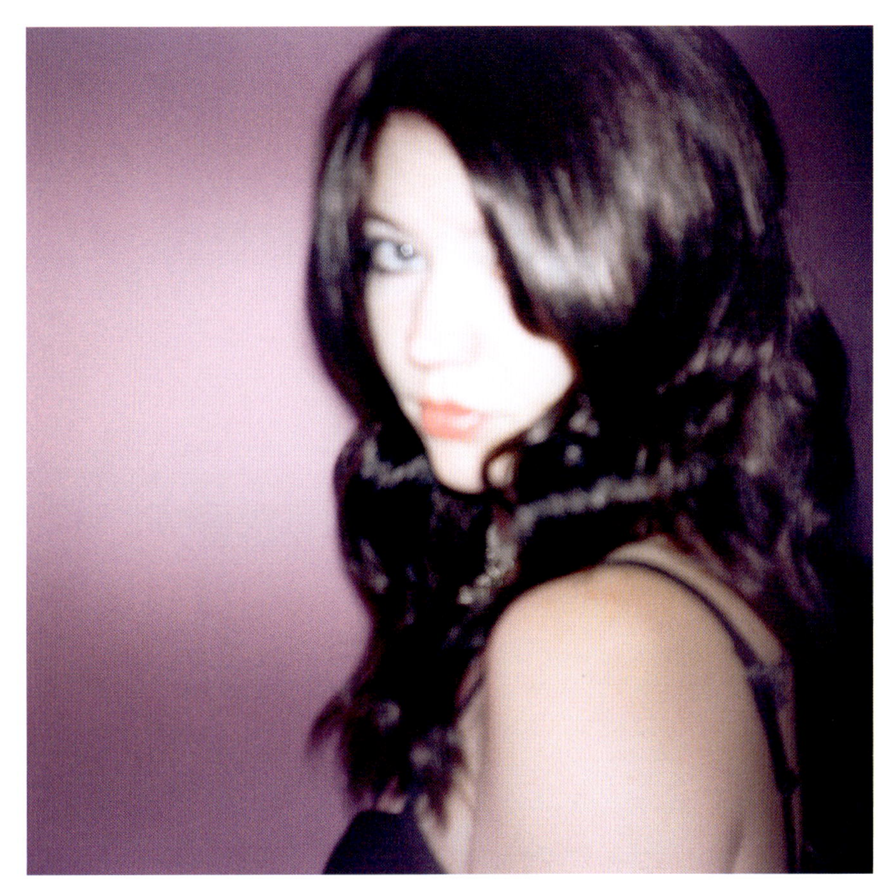

#5437 / Fresno, CA / *Between the Two*

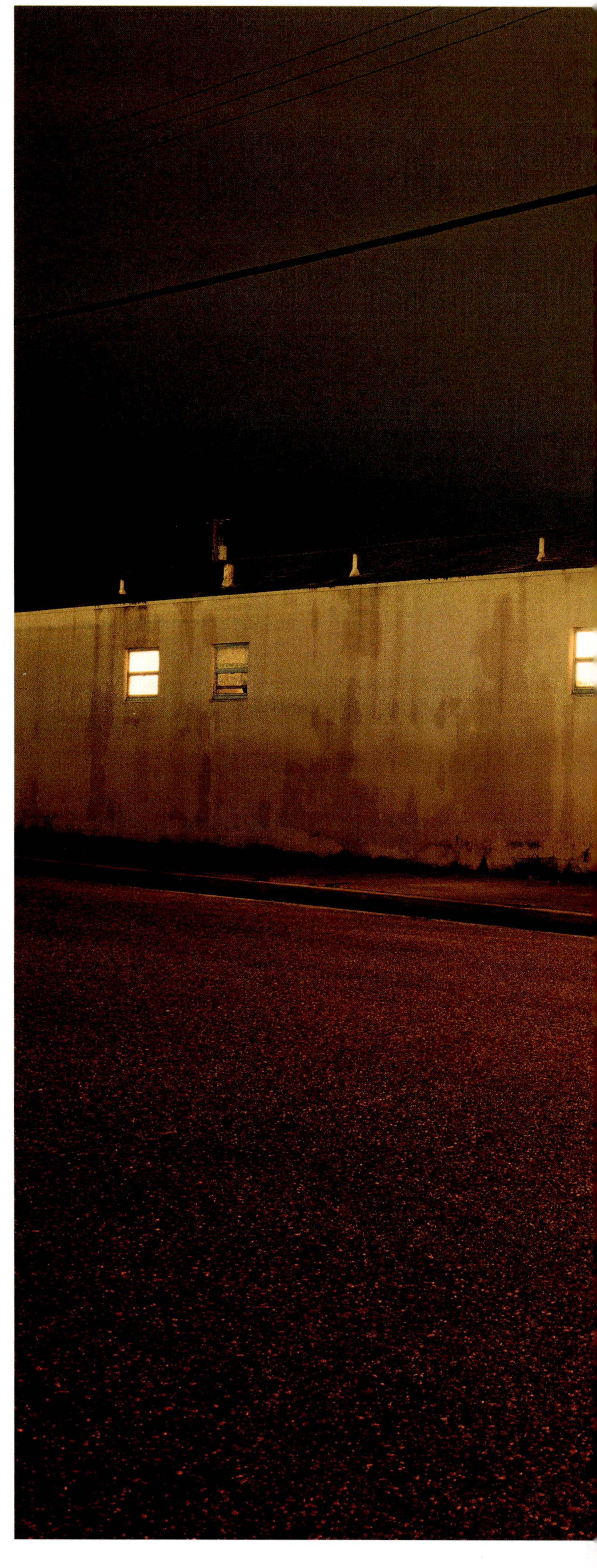

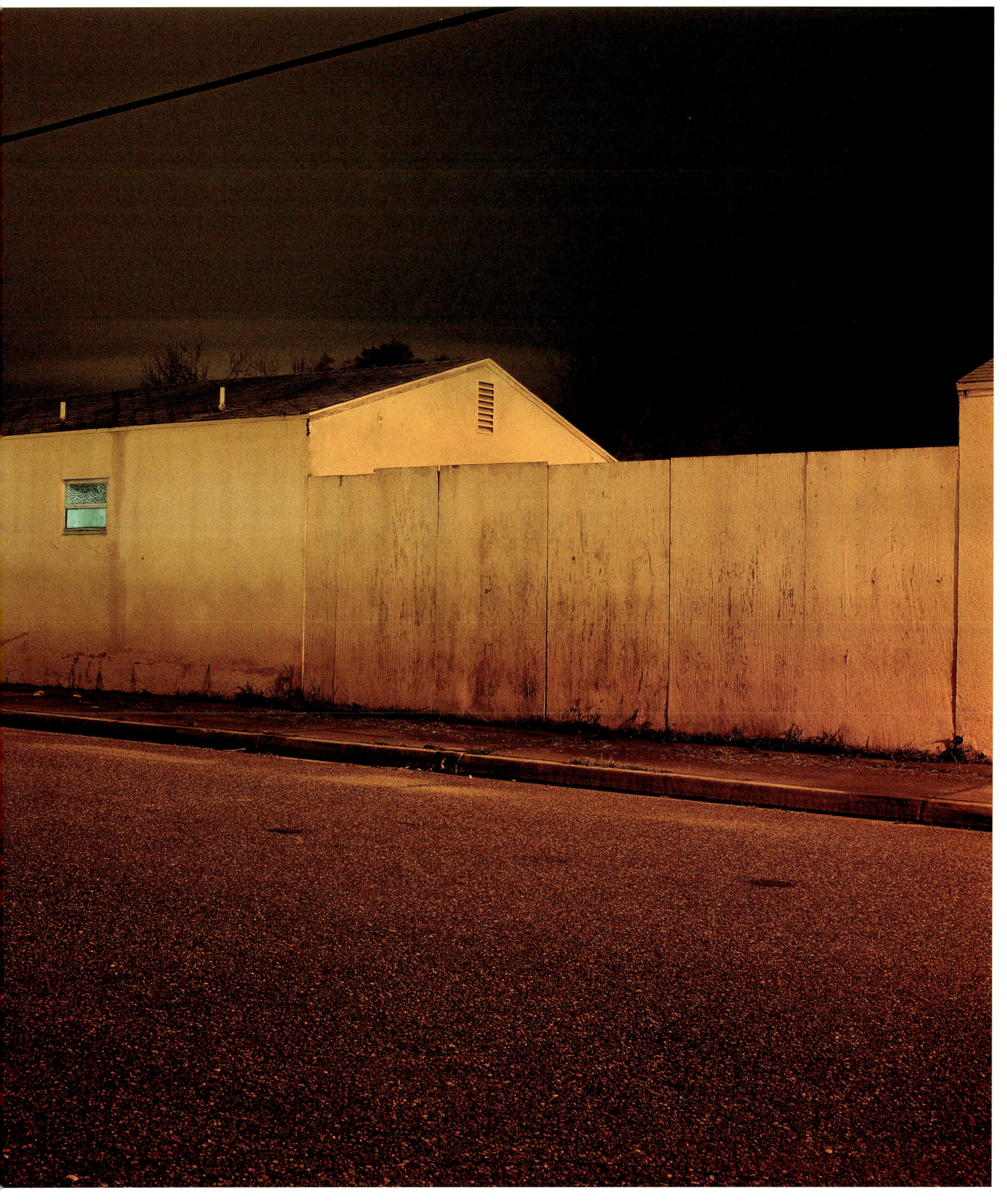

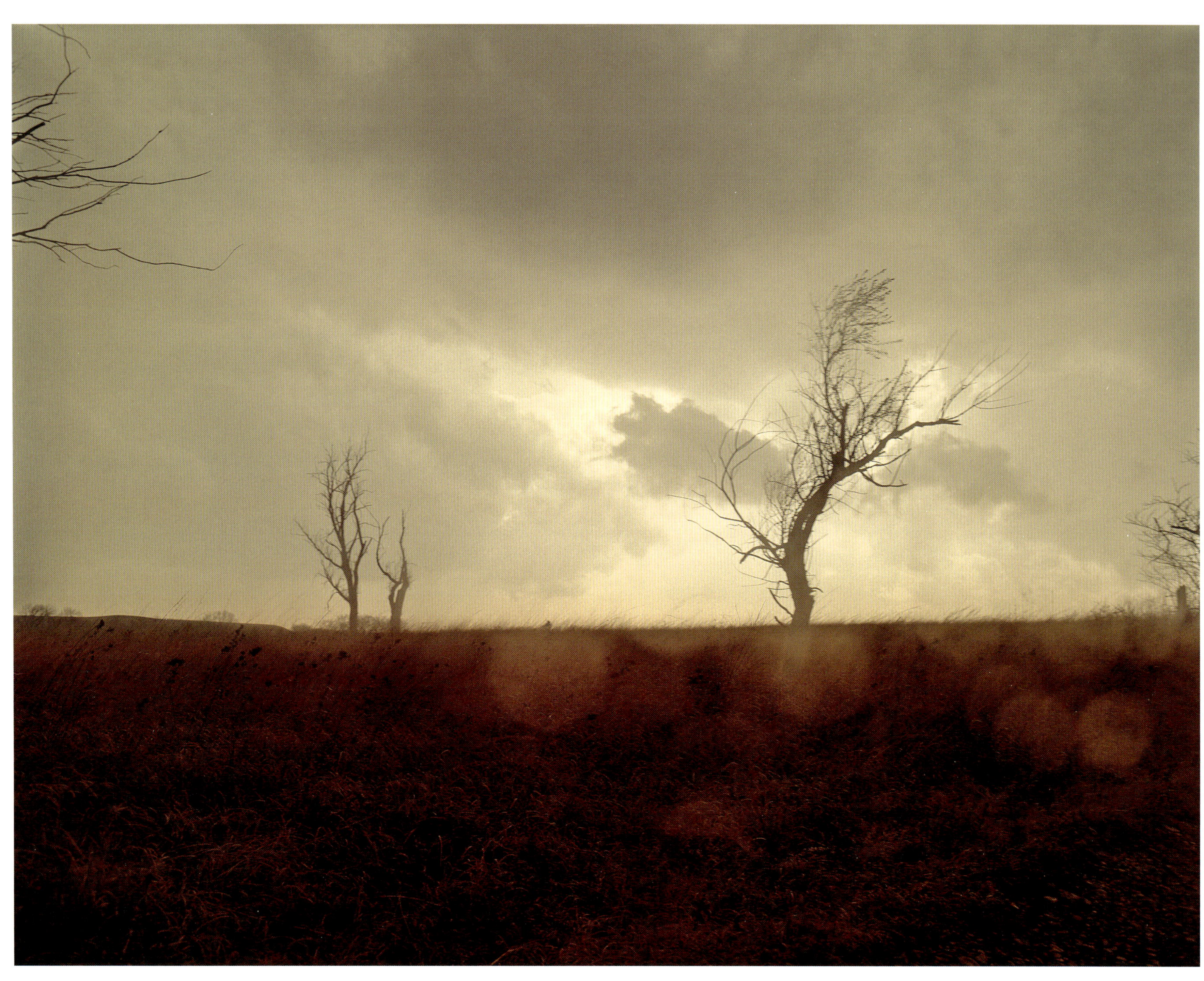

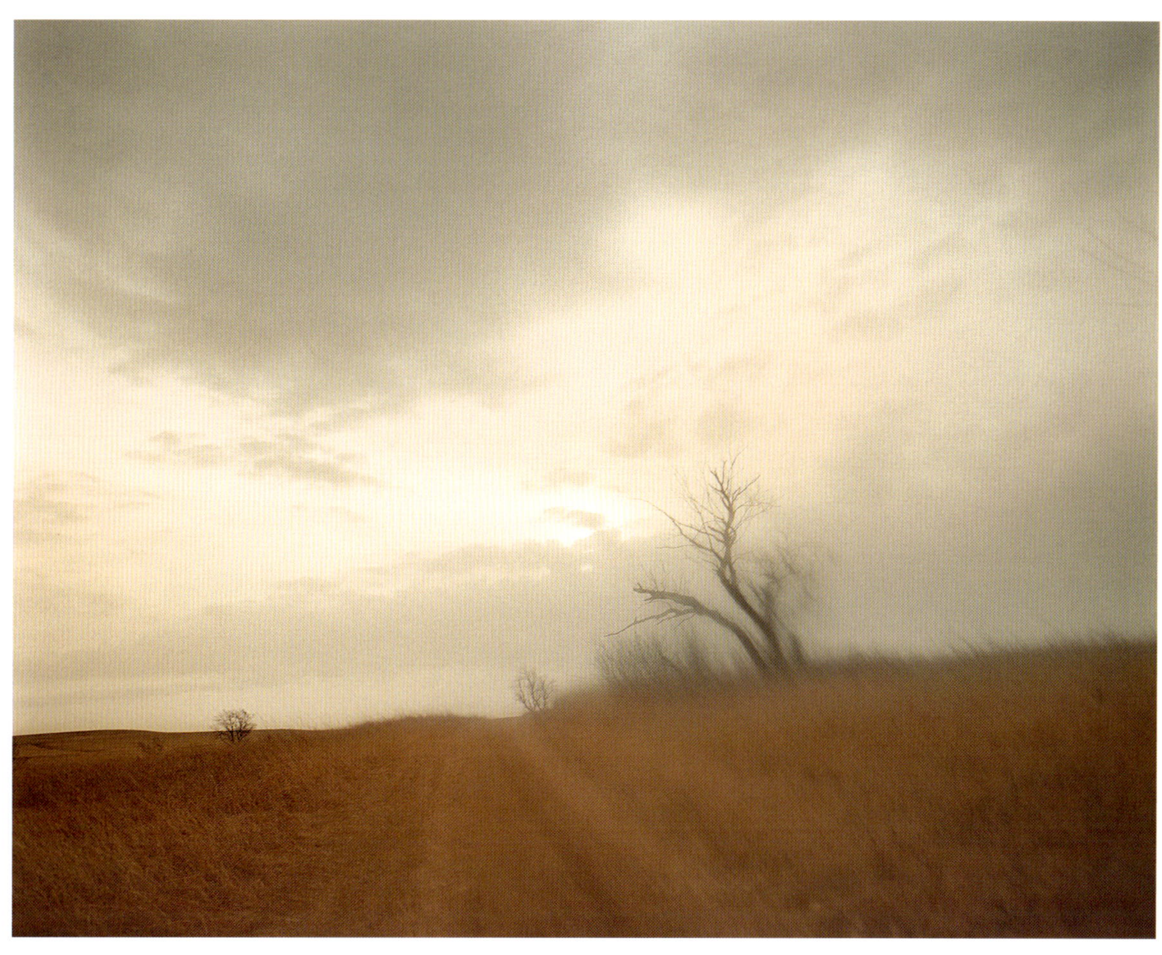

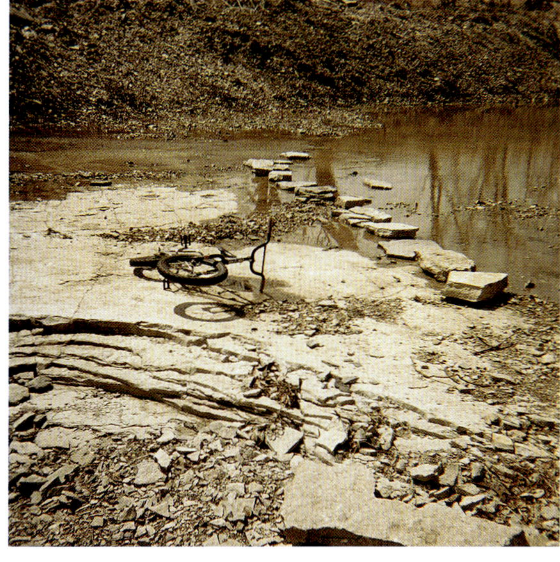

#5462 / Council Grove, KS / *A Road Divided* **#5484** / Council Grove, KS / *A Road Divided* **#5486-a** / Council Grove, KS / *Ohio, Excerpts from Silver Meadows*

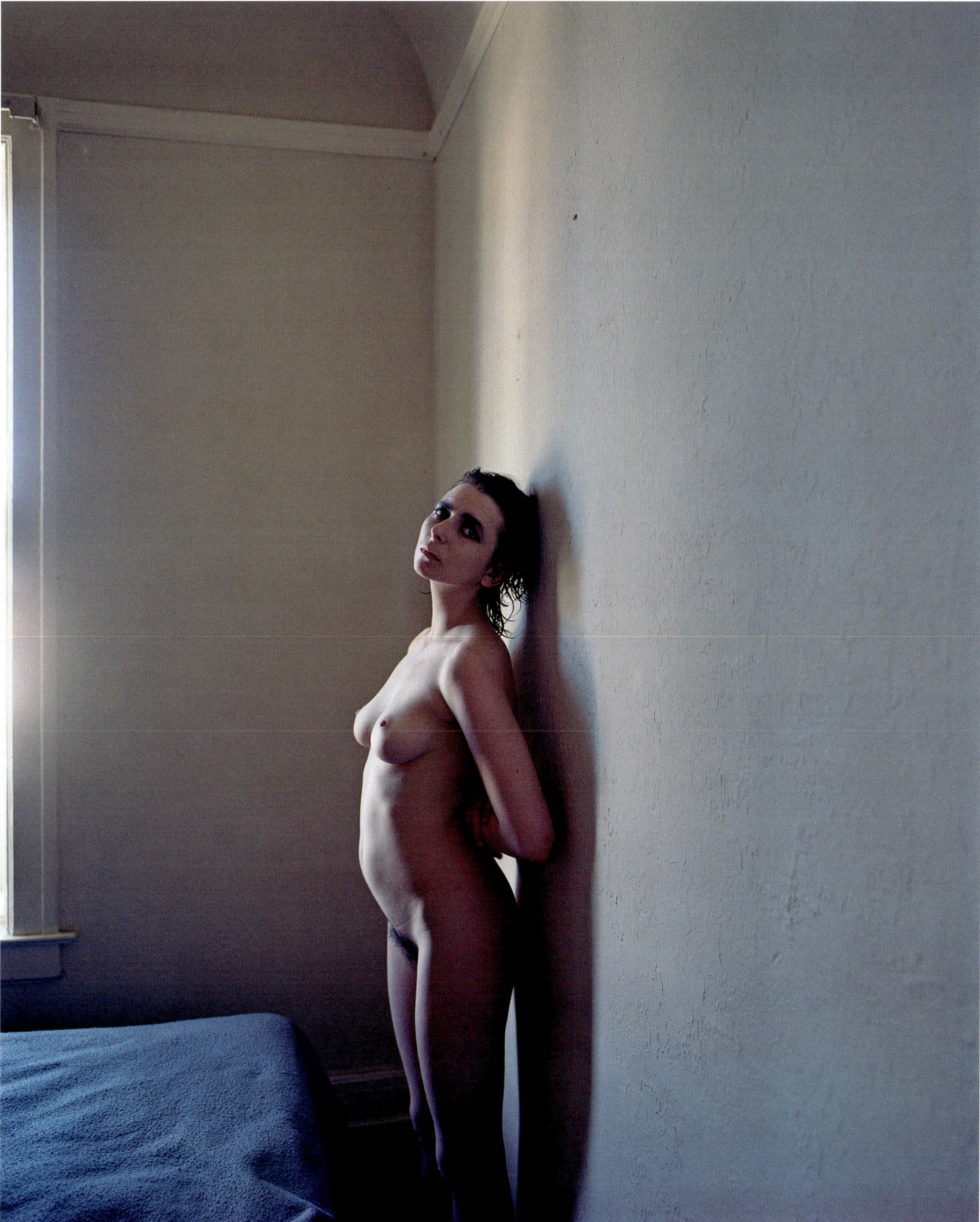

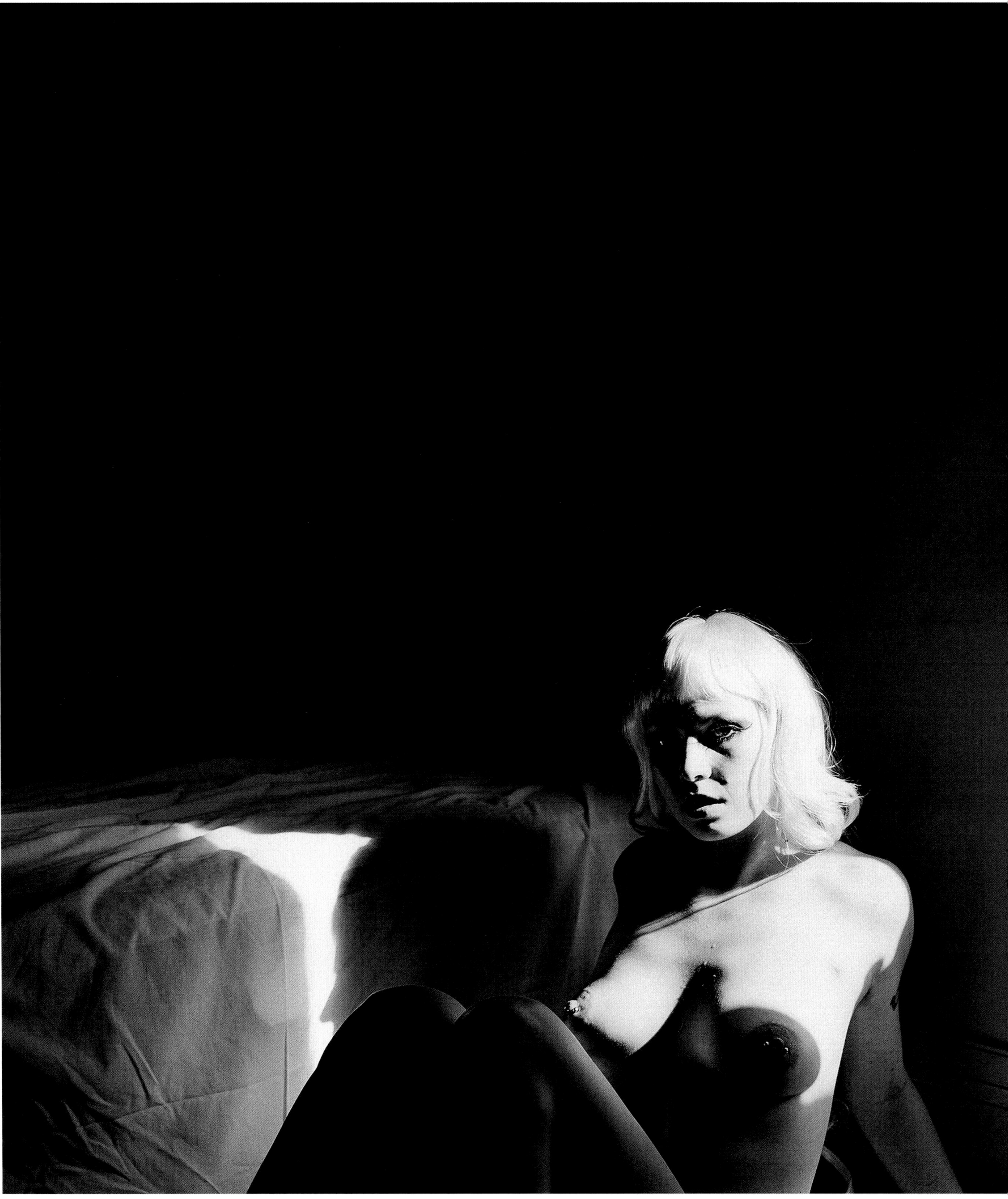

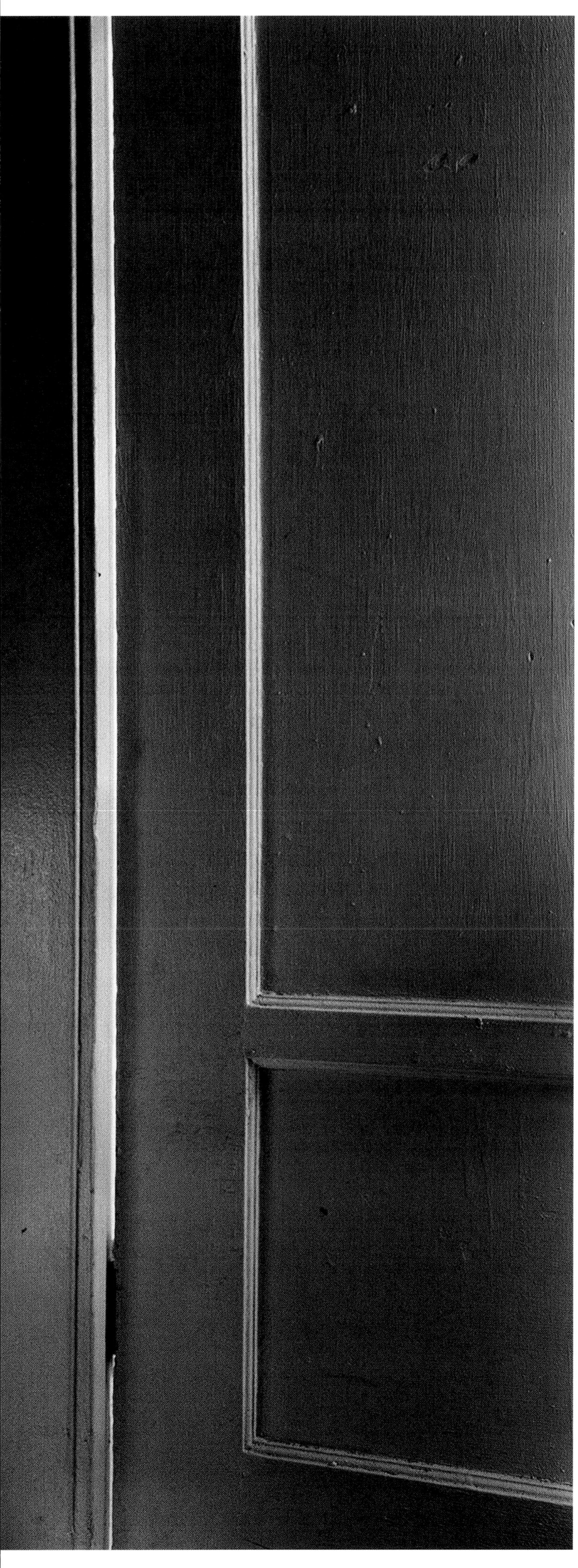

#5594 / Oakland, CA / *Between the Two*

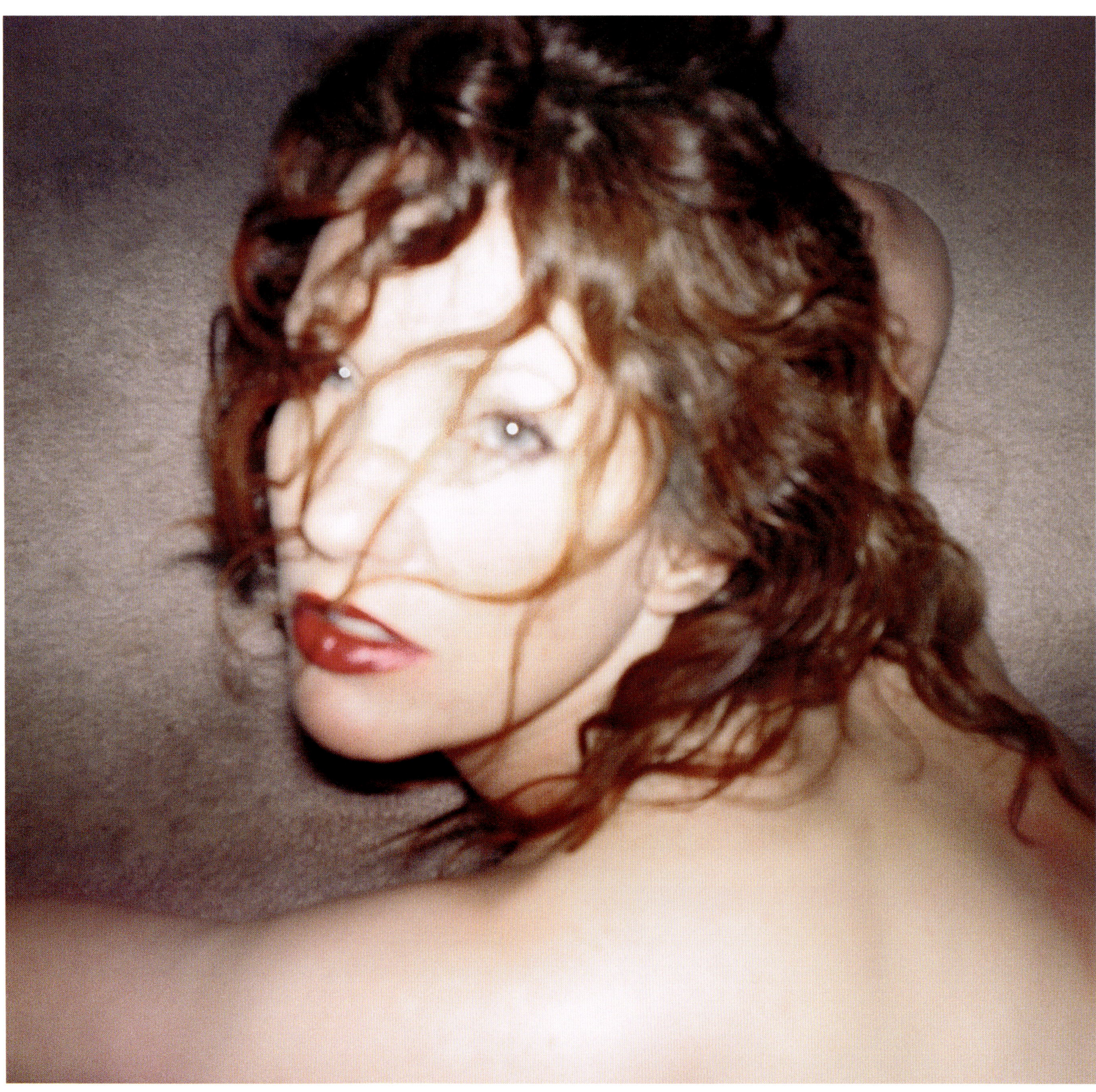

#5804-a / San Francisco, CA / *Motel Club*

#5407 / San Francisco, CA

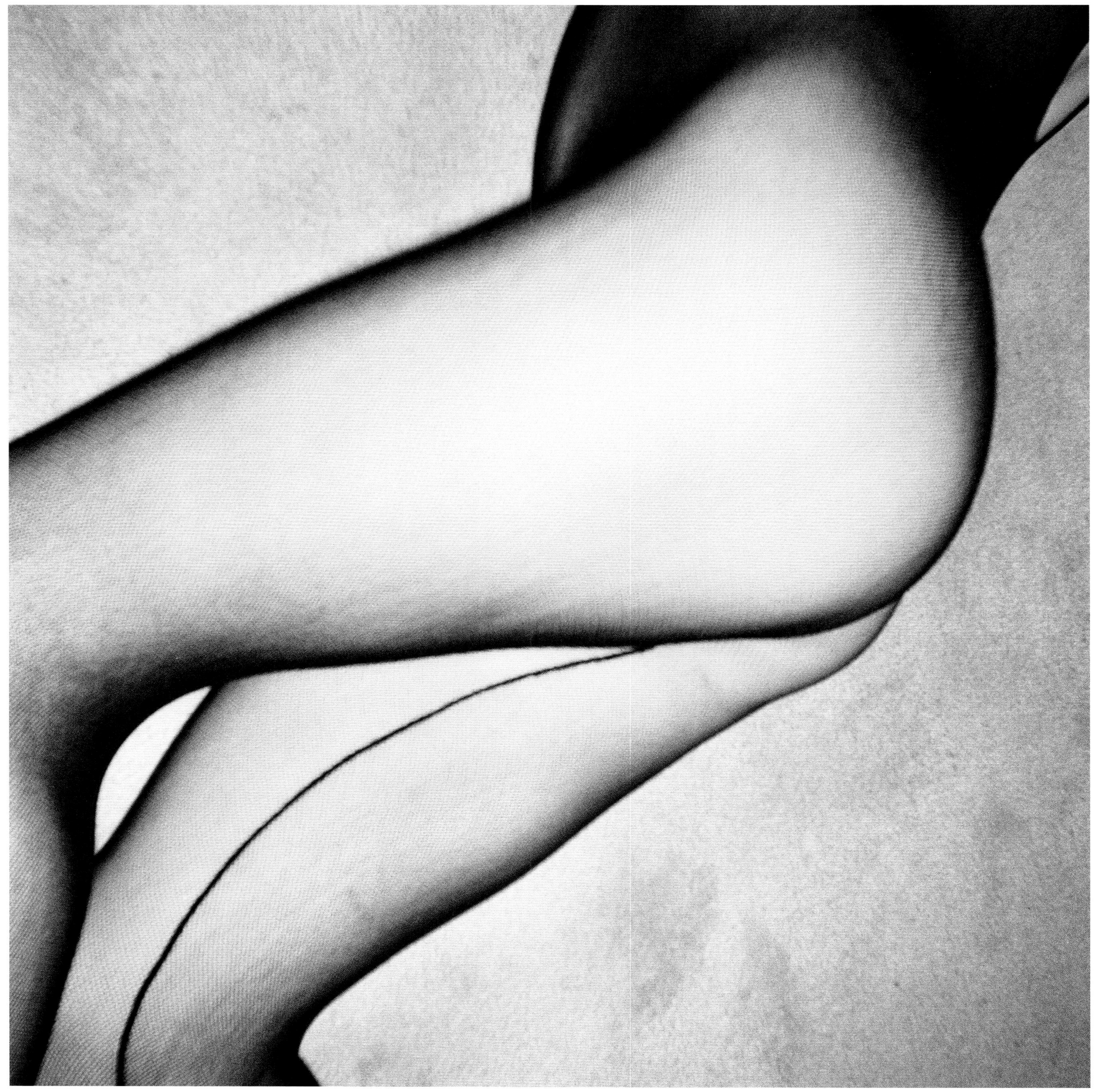

BETWEEN THE TWO
2006

Until the publication of *Between the Two* in 2006, Hido had not published or exhibited his portrait work, though he worked on it consistently. Portraits are the primary drive of this book, which maintains its introversion even while allowing for direct encounters and eye contact with people, whose existence was only implied in previous books.

Primarily, the camera finds women in anonymous American settings: the bare motel room, the suburban basement bedroom. Their expressions, captured on film, range from defiance to resignation, but primarily they demonstrate an inscrutability. The photographs are intimate and direct. Though there is a strong connection between photographer and model, the connection between photograph and viewer is stronger still, though undefined. The title of the book points to those spaces between photographer and subject, photograph and viewer, and one photograph and the next, in which a narrative (or tension) inevitably forms. "It is an unmistakable nod to the book being about relationships," acknowledges Hido.

Hido savors a quote by late photographer Lewis Baltz that defines photography as "a profound corner that sits in between literature and film." Hido likes to loiter on this corner. Without script, plot, before, or after, Hido shows characters, situations, and spaces that are at once malleable to personal interpretation and exhibit an extremely precise point of view. What can only be a Todd Hido photograph also lends itself to as many interpretations as there are humans.

"I think the people who really connect with my work see something of themselves in it; they don't necessarily see me," says Hido. "The thing I hear most often is 'that reminds me of': that reminds me of the town I grew up in. That reminds me of this house or that girlfriend. That weather brings me back to this point in my life."

"Take an image of a suburban street," the artist continues, "and some people see the most fucked-up place they've ever been, while others go back to their wonderful childhoods. I learned early on that ambiguity was one of art's best tools."

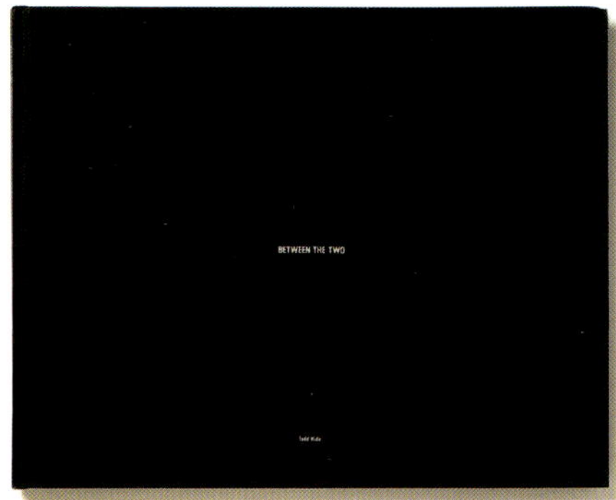

Between the Two
Published 2006 by Nazraeli Press
15×12 inches
76 pages

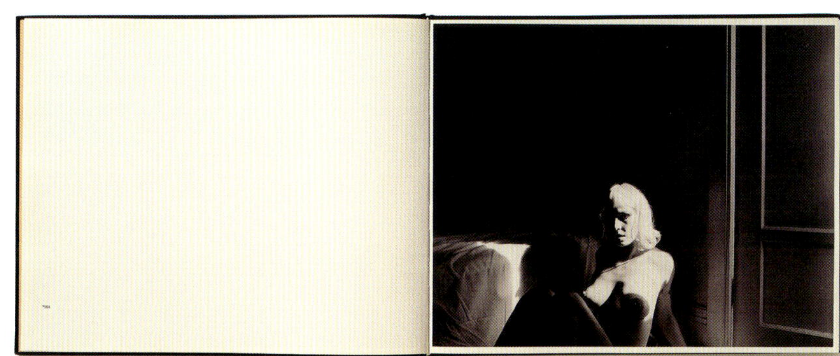

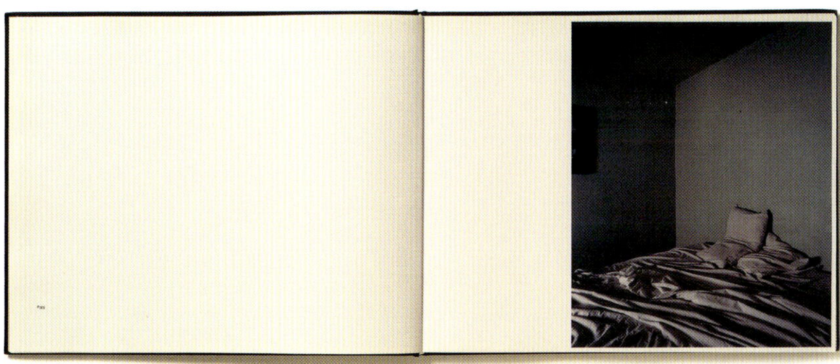

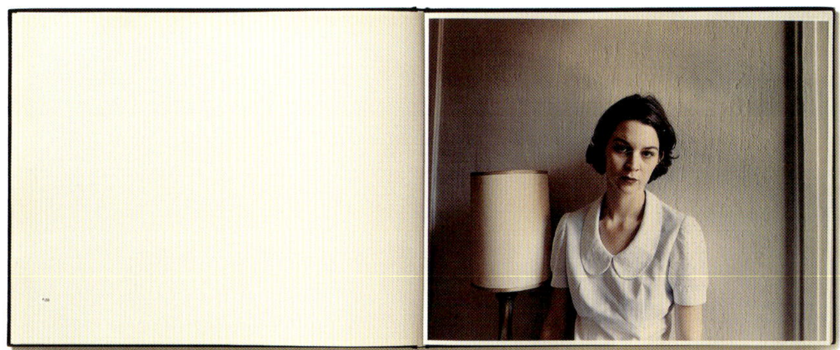

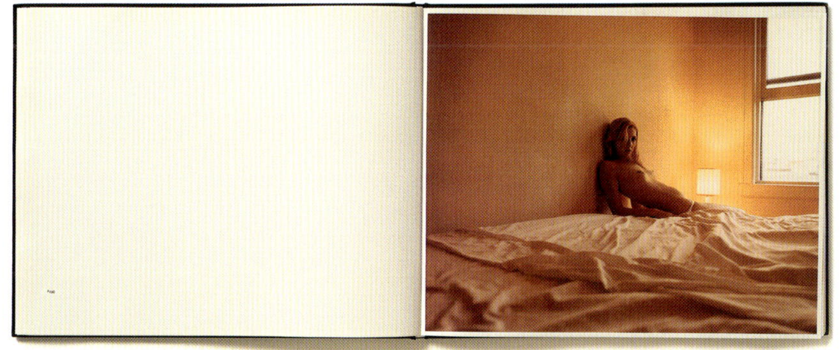

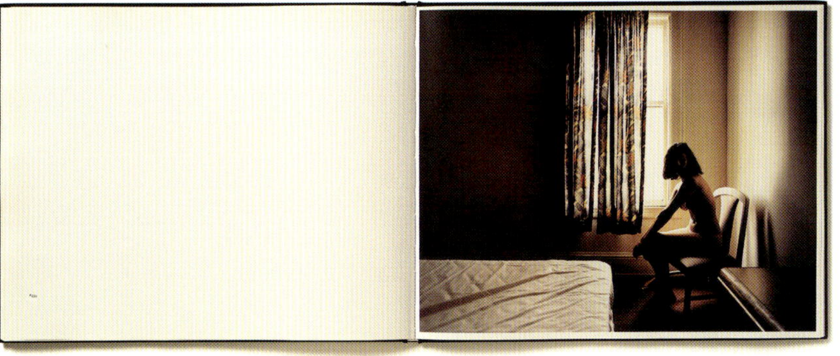

CHRONOLOGY 2006–2010

2006 Begins collaborating with a hair and makeup artist and wardrobe stylist

2009 TBW Books publishes *Ohio*

2009 Nazraeli Press publishes *Witness*

2009 Photographs appear on covers of reissued Raymond Carver books, published by Vintage Books

2010 First photographs taken in home studio

2010 Meets long-term collaborator and model Khrystyna Kazakova

2010 Begins altering found images

2010 Group exhibition: *US Today and After*, Lyon Septembre de la Photographie, France

2010 Nazraeli Press publishes *A Road Divided*

#6017-a / Stockton, CA / Ohio, *Excerpts from Silver Meadows*

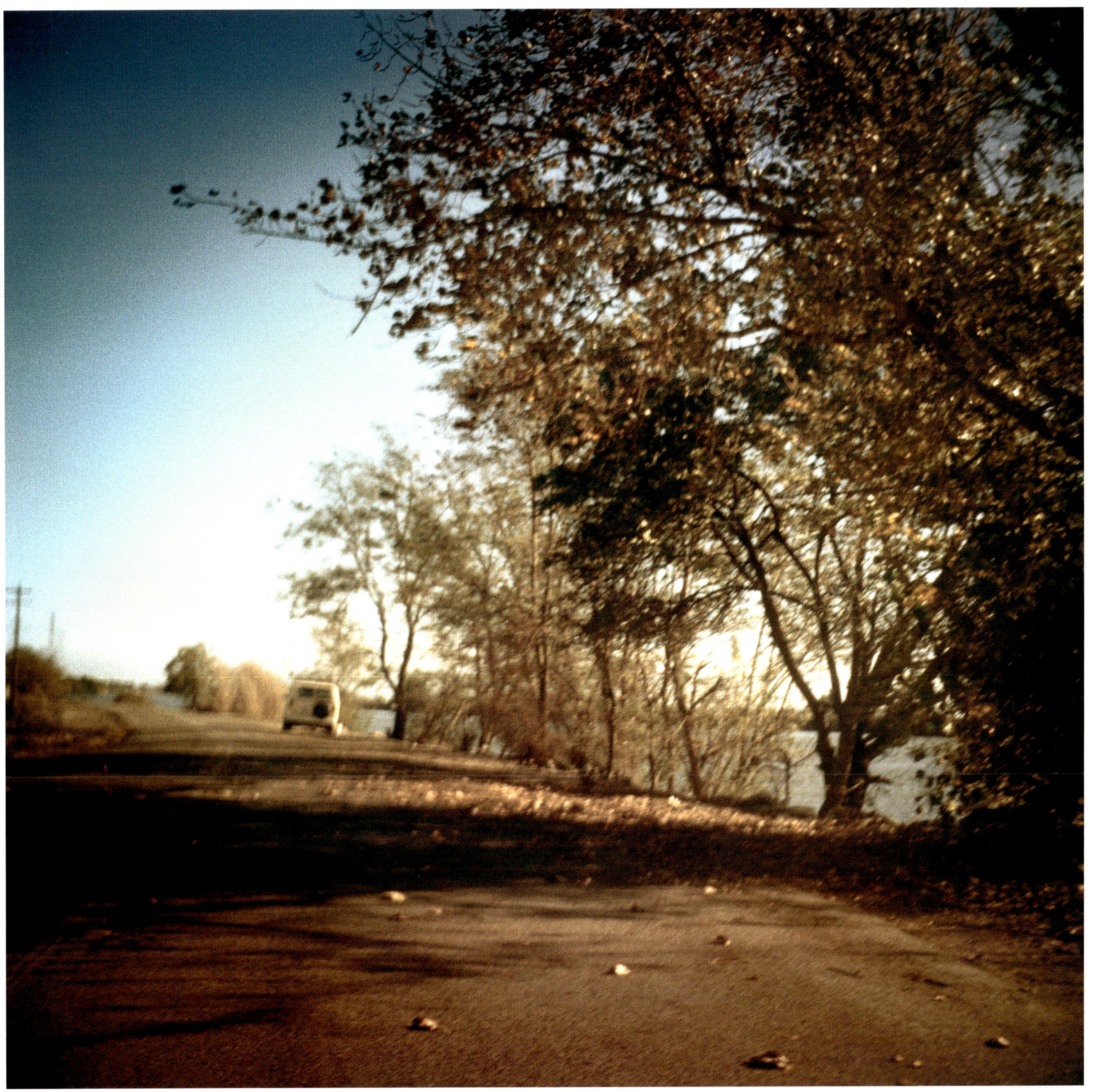

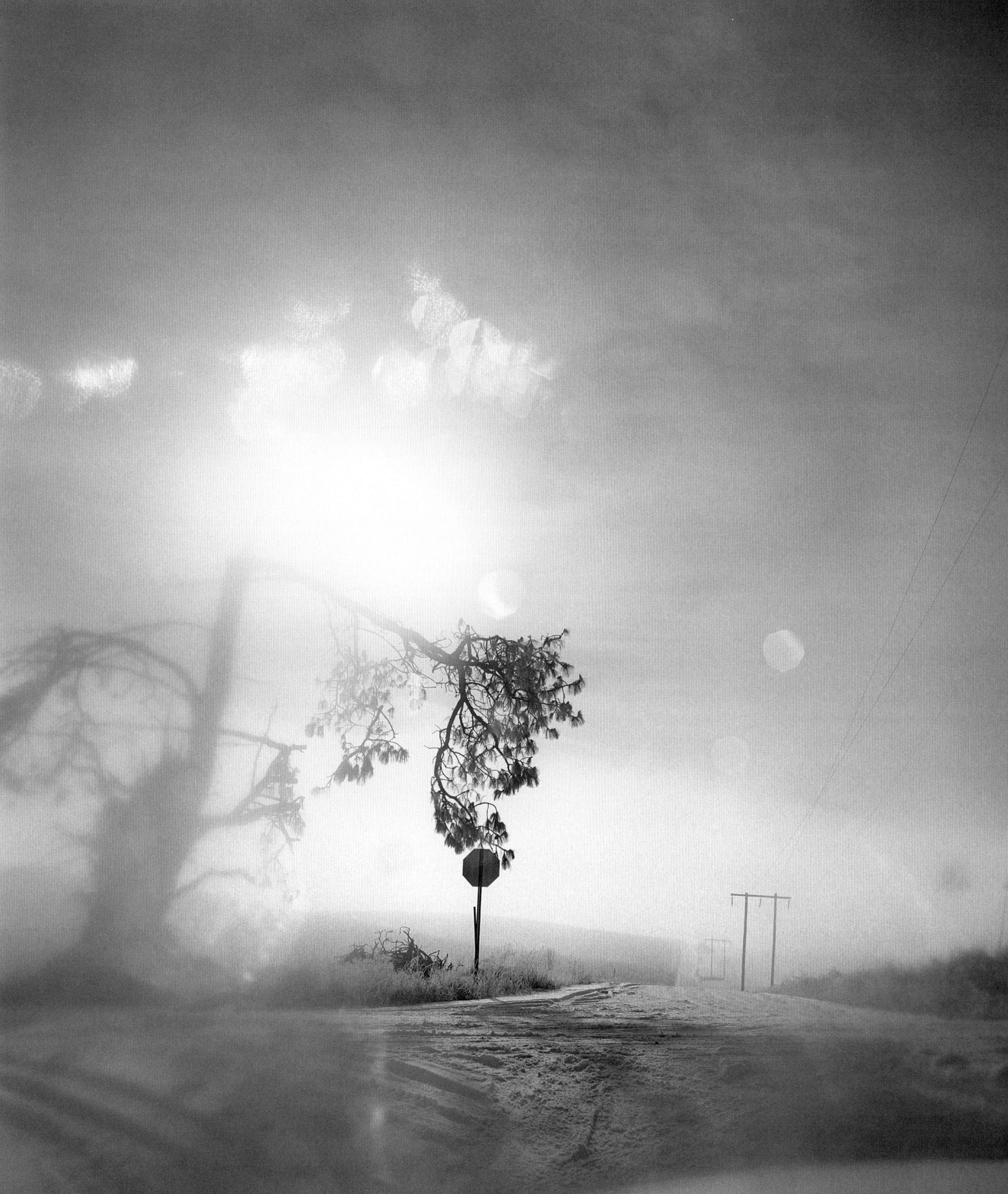

#6097 / Rockford, WA / *A Road Divided*

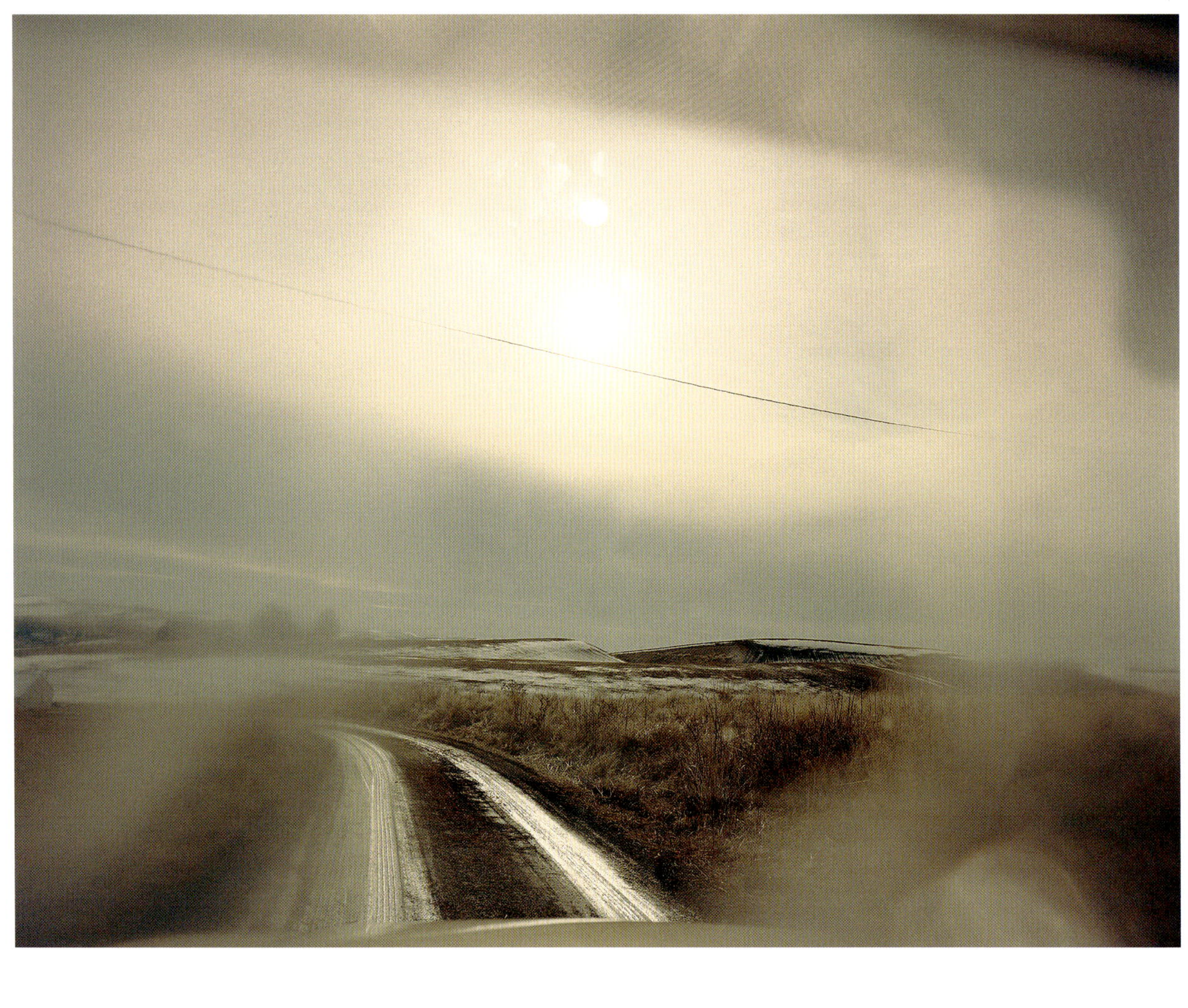

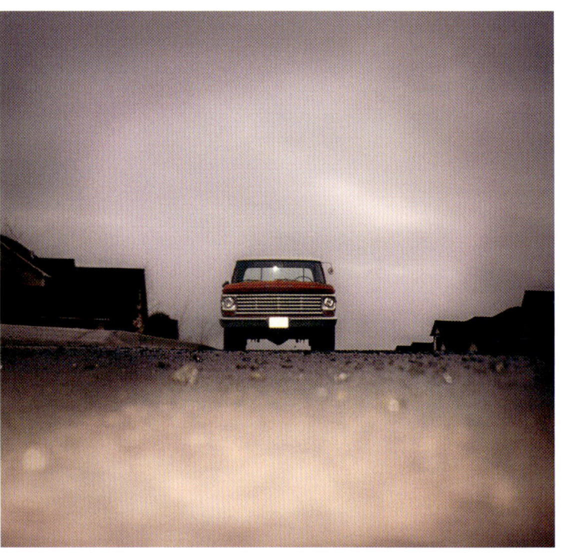

#6237 / Rosalia, WA / *A Road Divided* **#6315-a** / Potlatch, WA / *Excerpts from Silver Meadows* **#6349** / Kansas City, KS / *Excerpts from Silver Meadows*

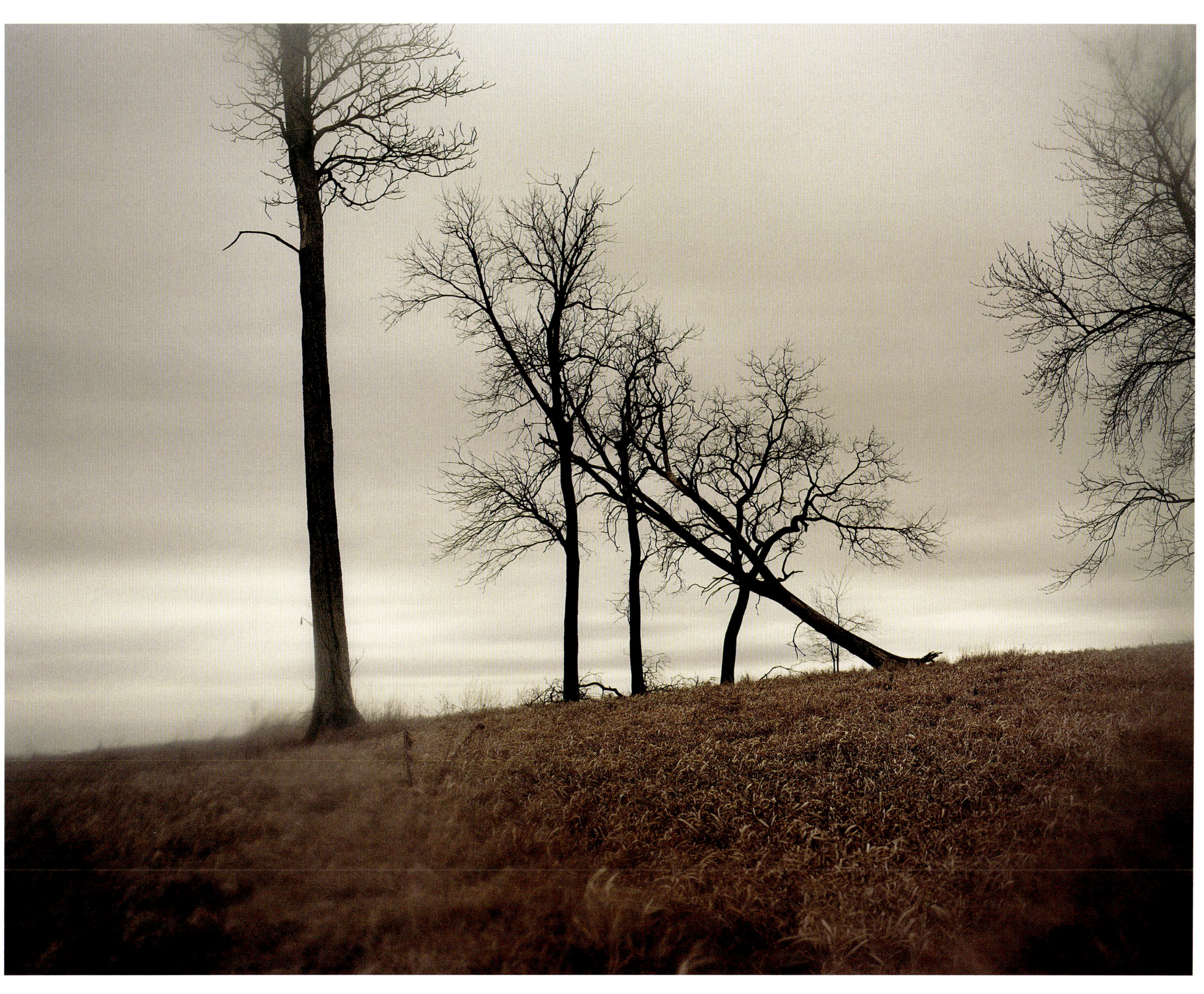

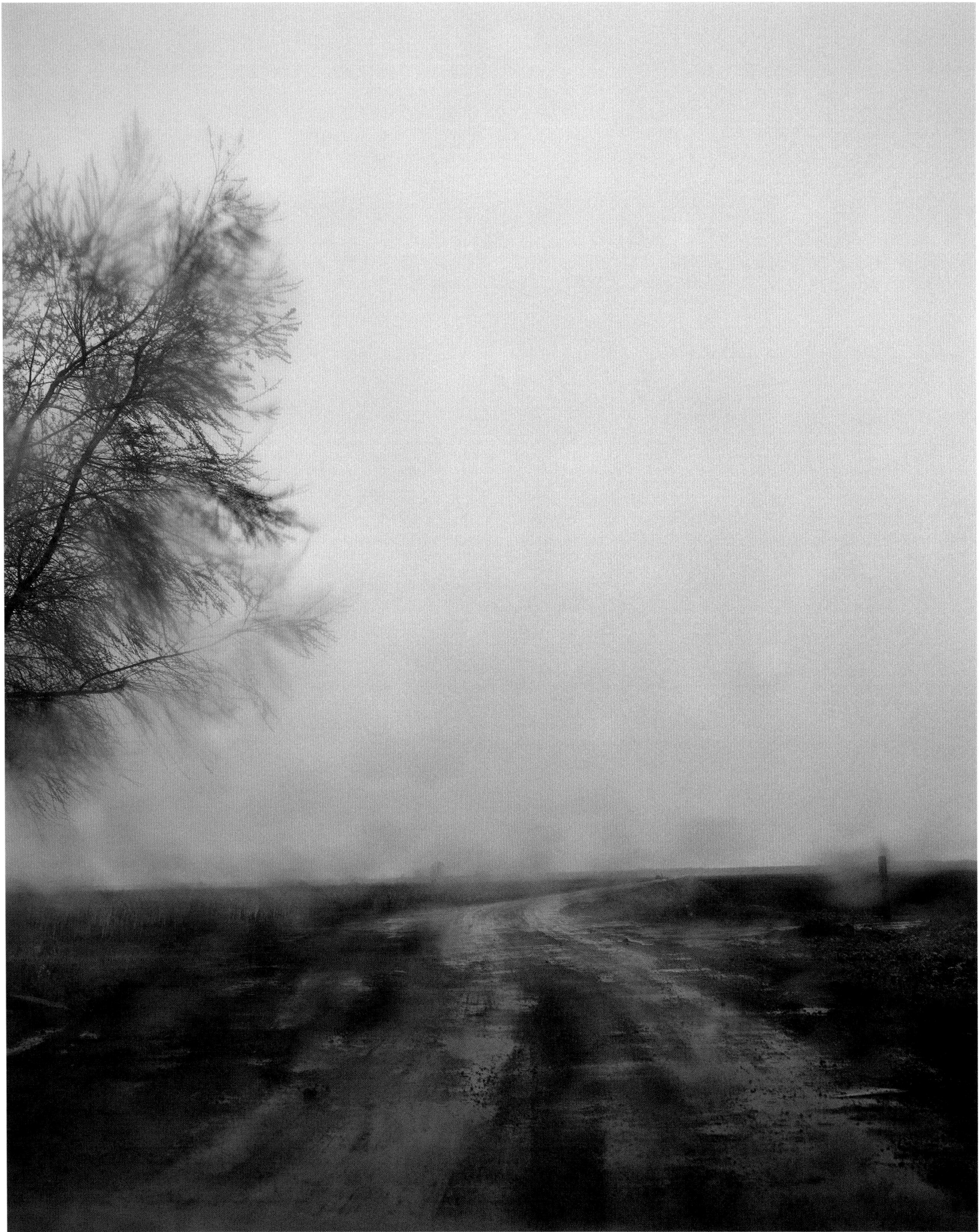

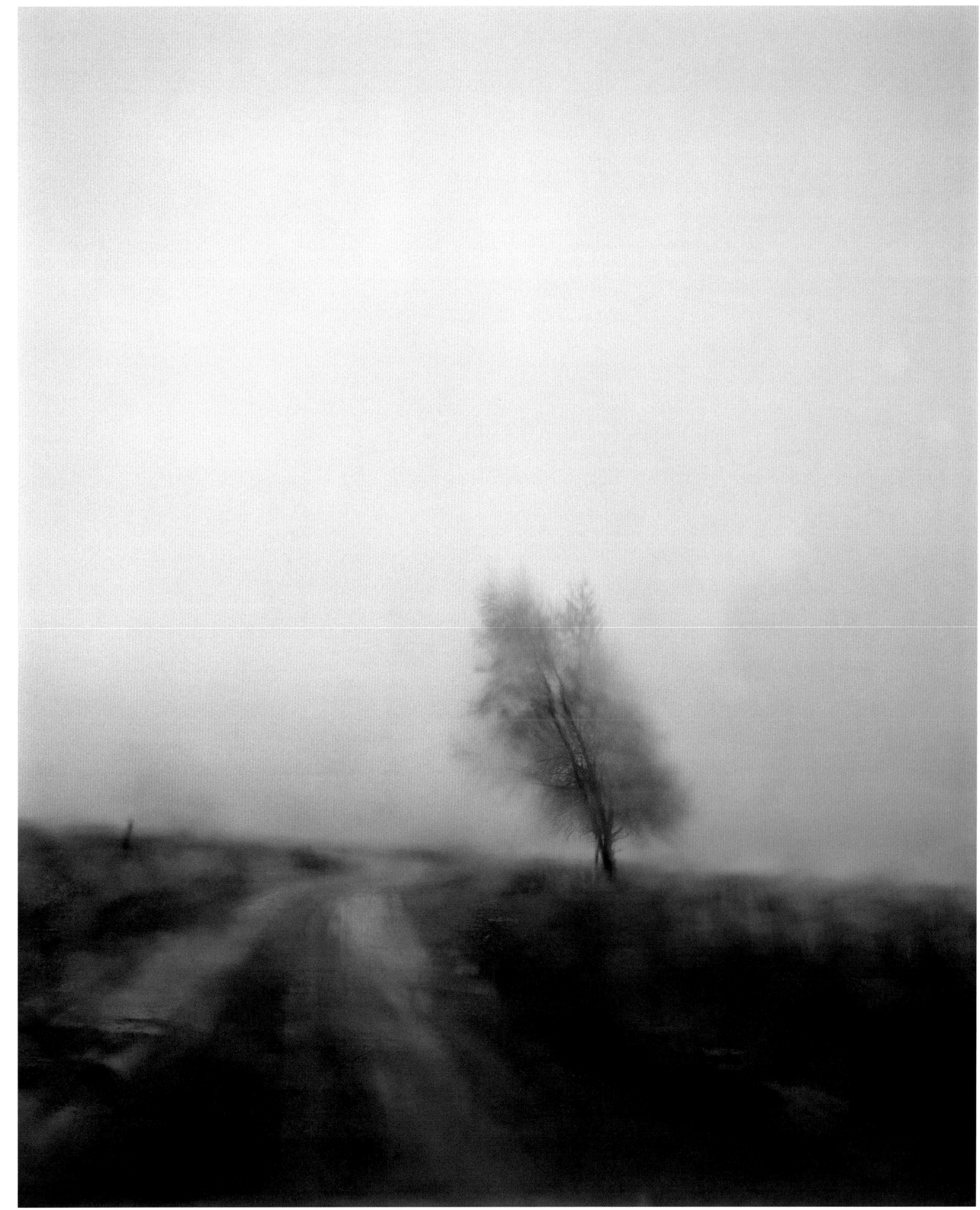

#6415 / Lodi, CA / *A Road Divided* **#6405** / Lodi, CA / *A Road Divided*

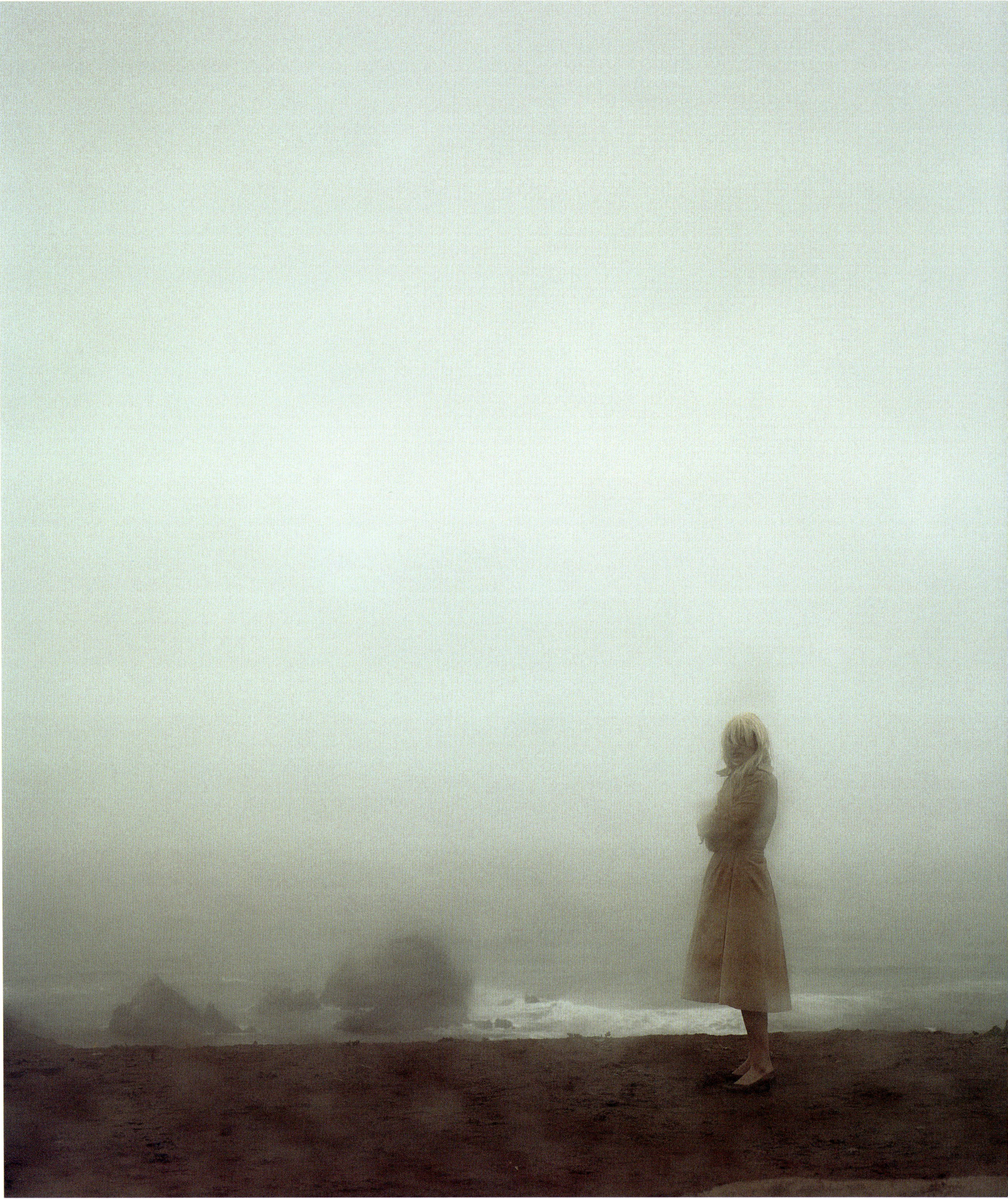

#6426 / San Francisco, CA

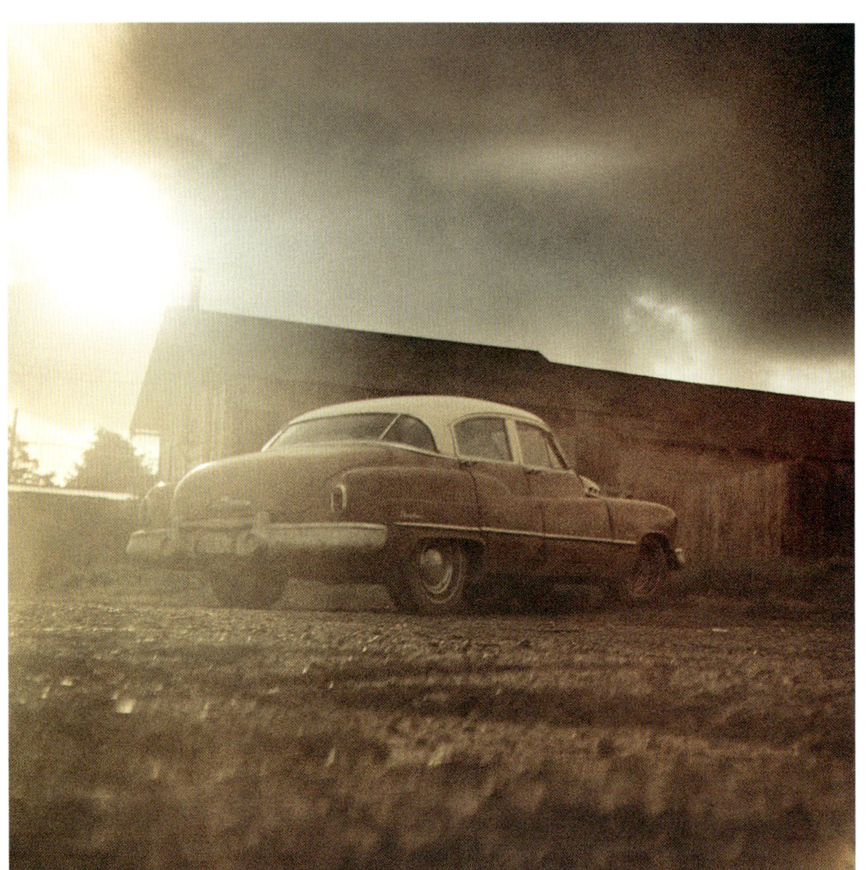

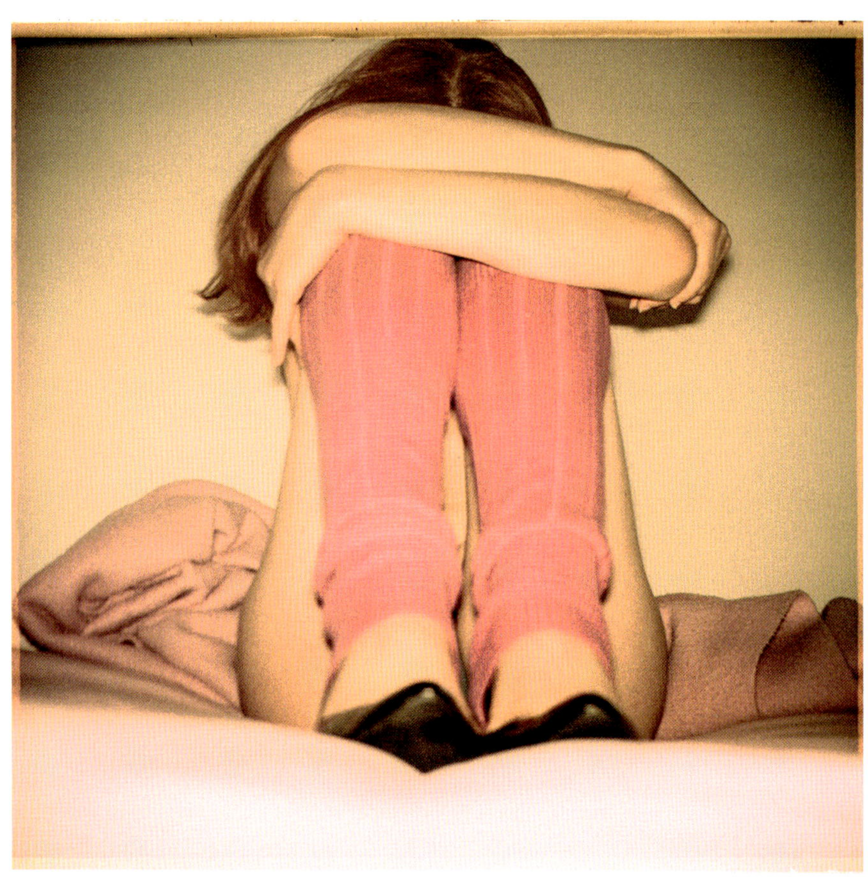

#6515-a / Redding, CA / *Motel Club* **#6909-d** / Concord, CA

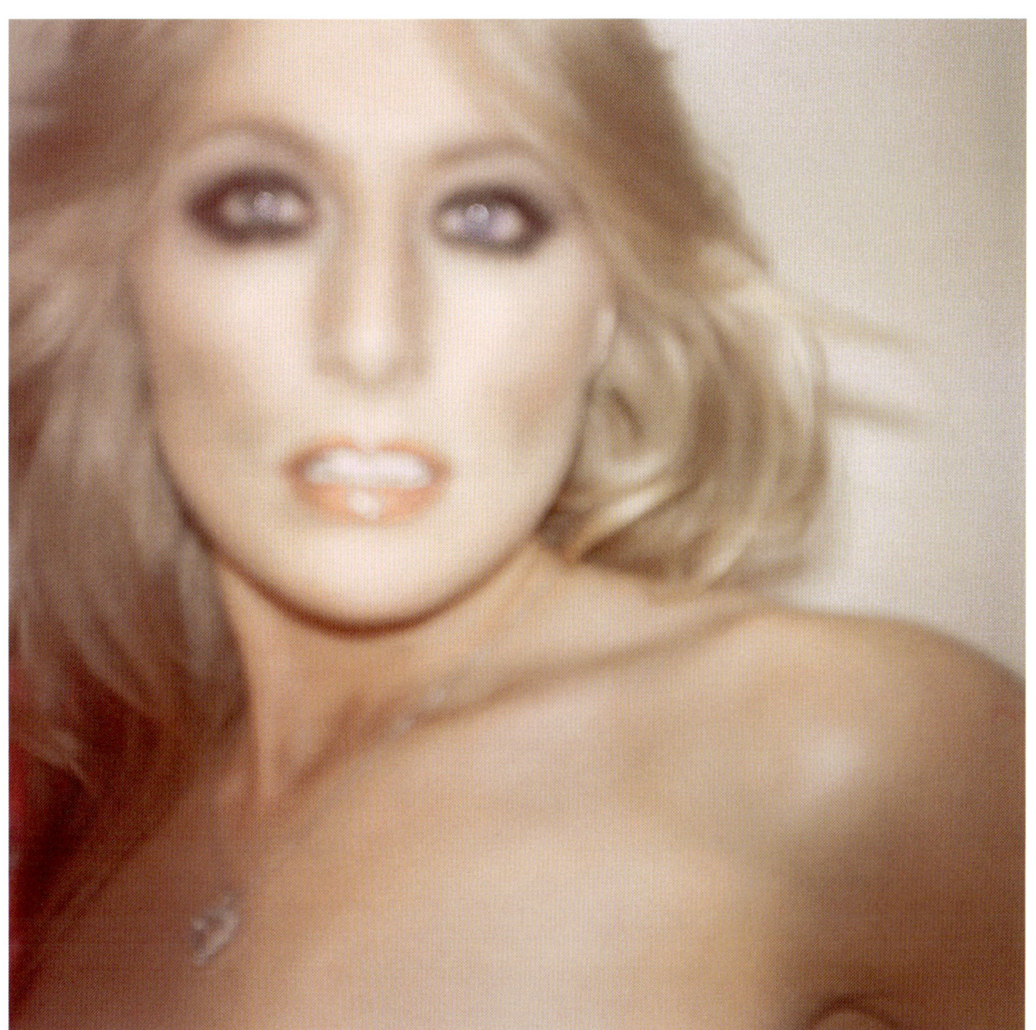

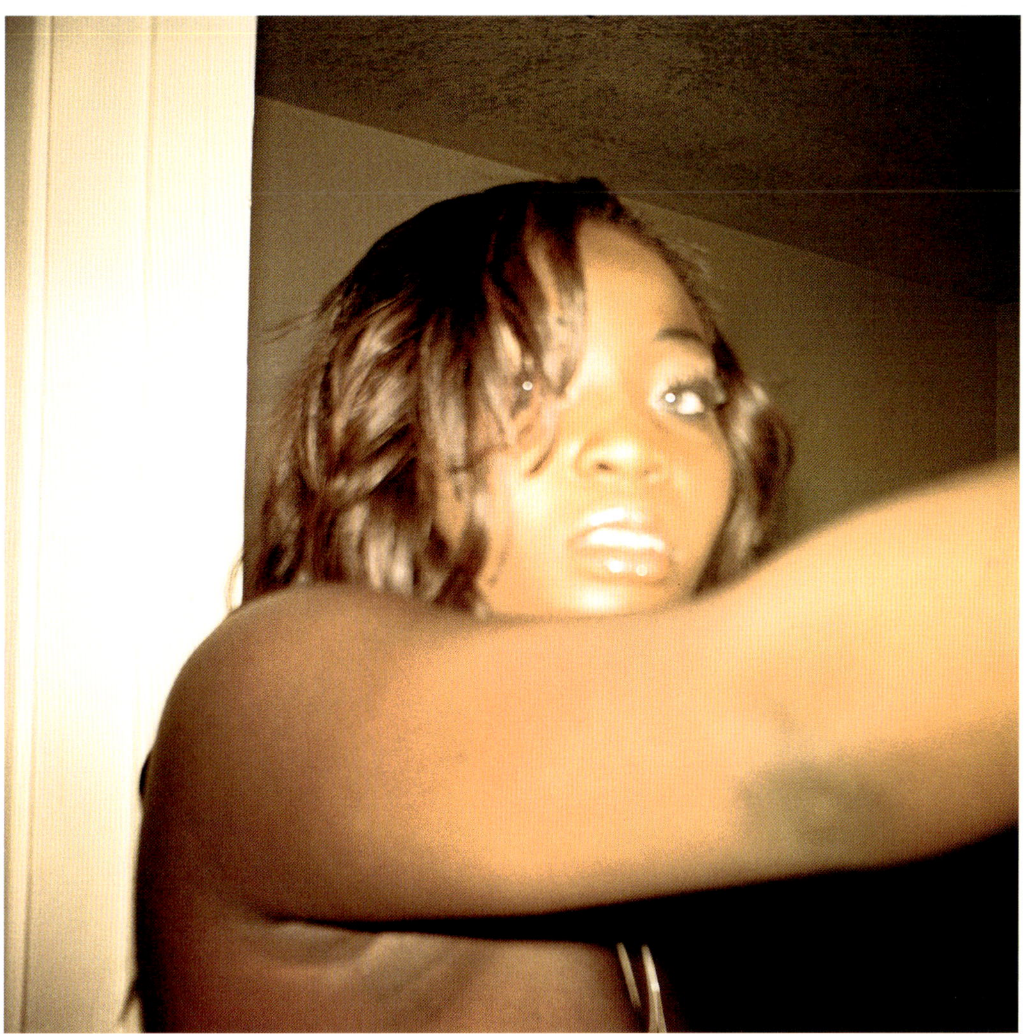

#6459-a / Oakland, CA / *Motel Club, Excerpts from Silver Meadows*

#6913-a / Concord, CA / *Excerpts from Silver Meadows*

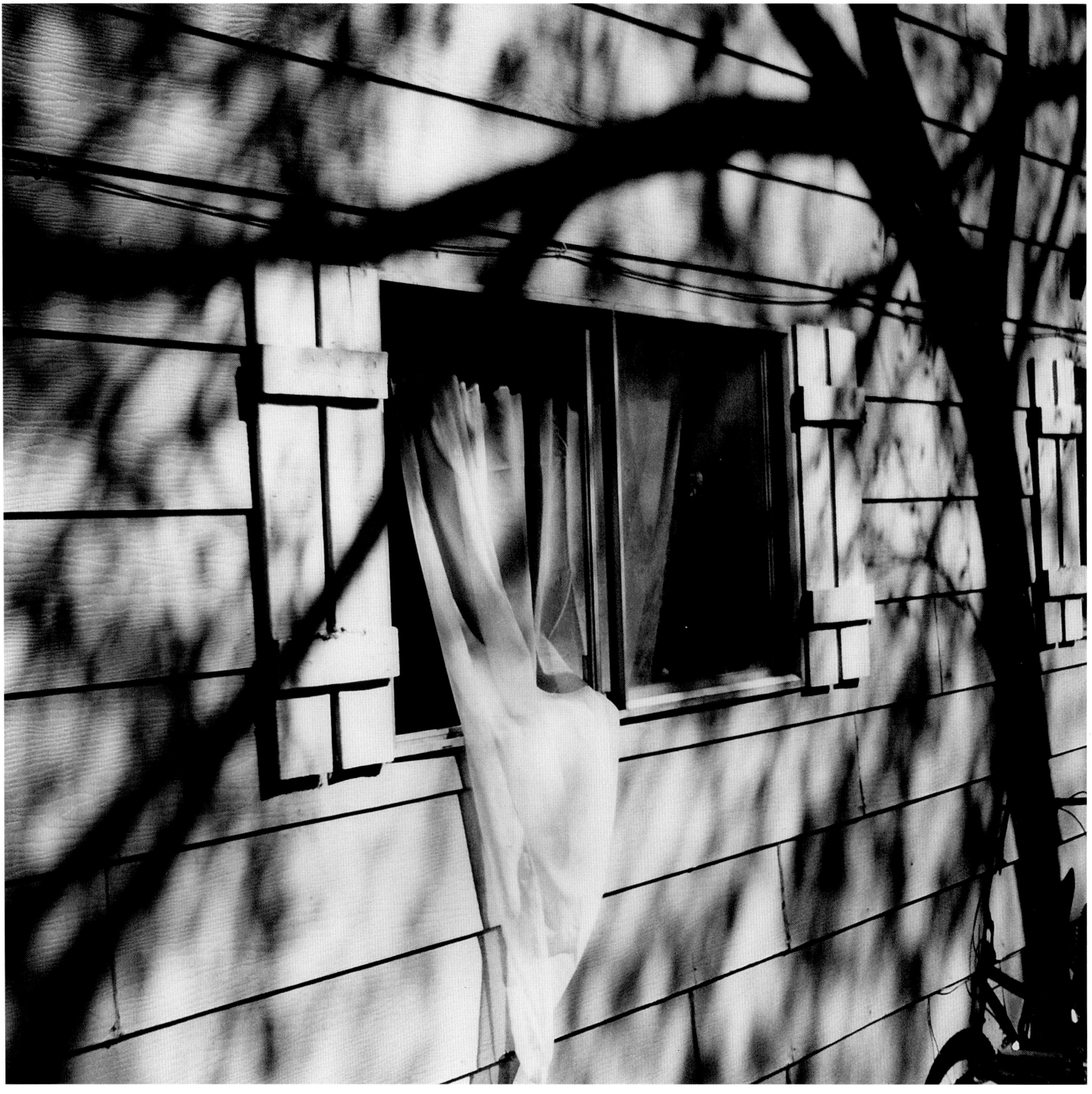

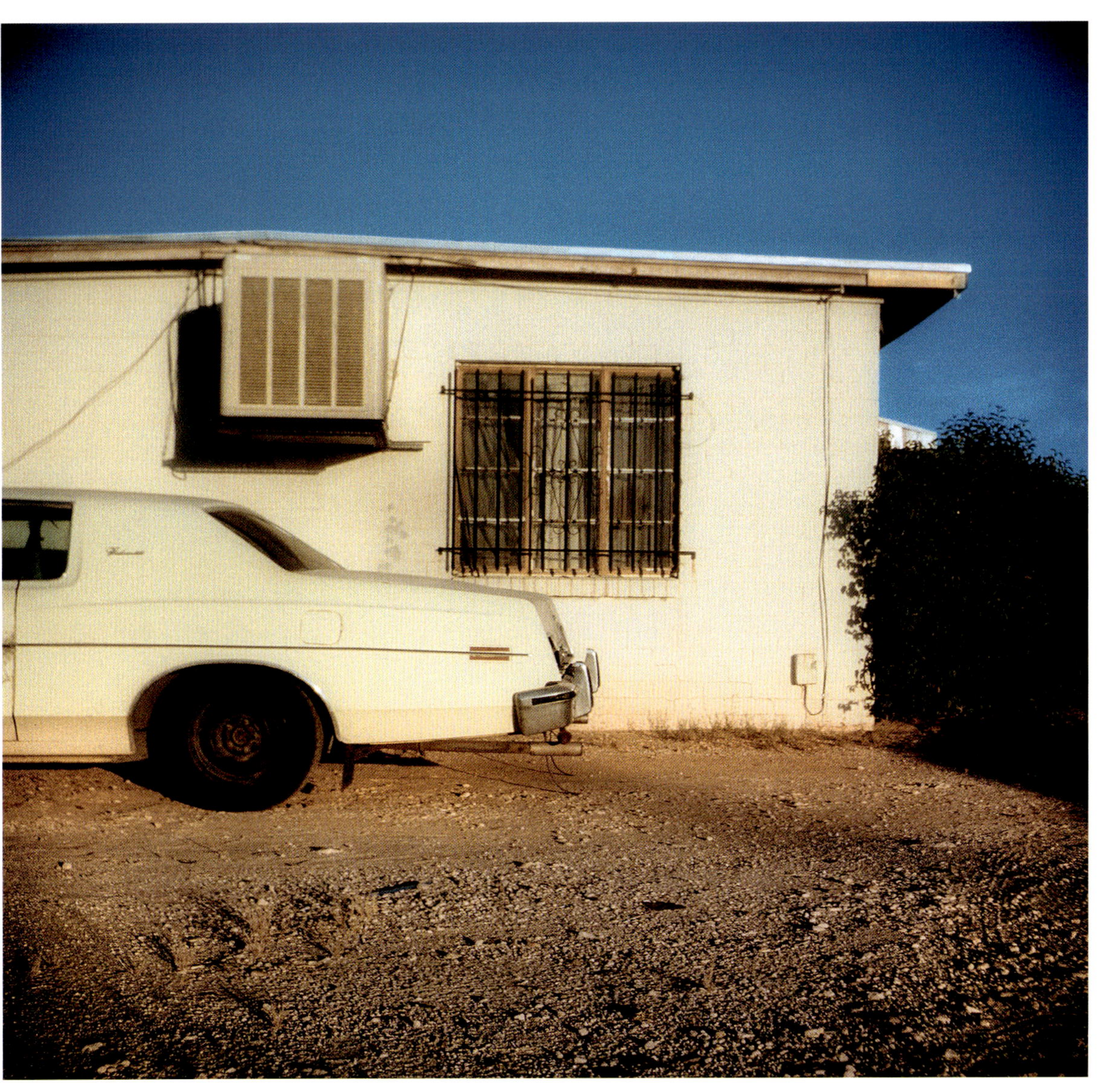

#6955-a / Reno, NV **#7144-a** / Tucson, AZ

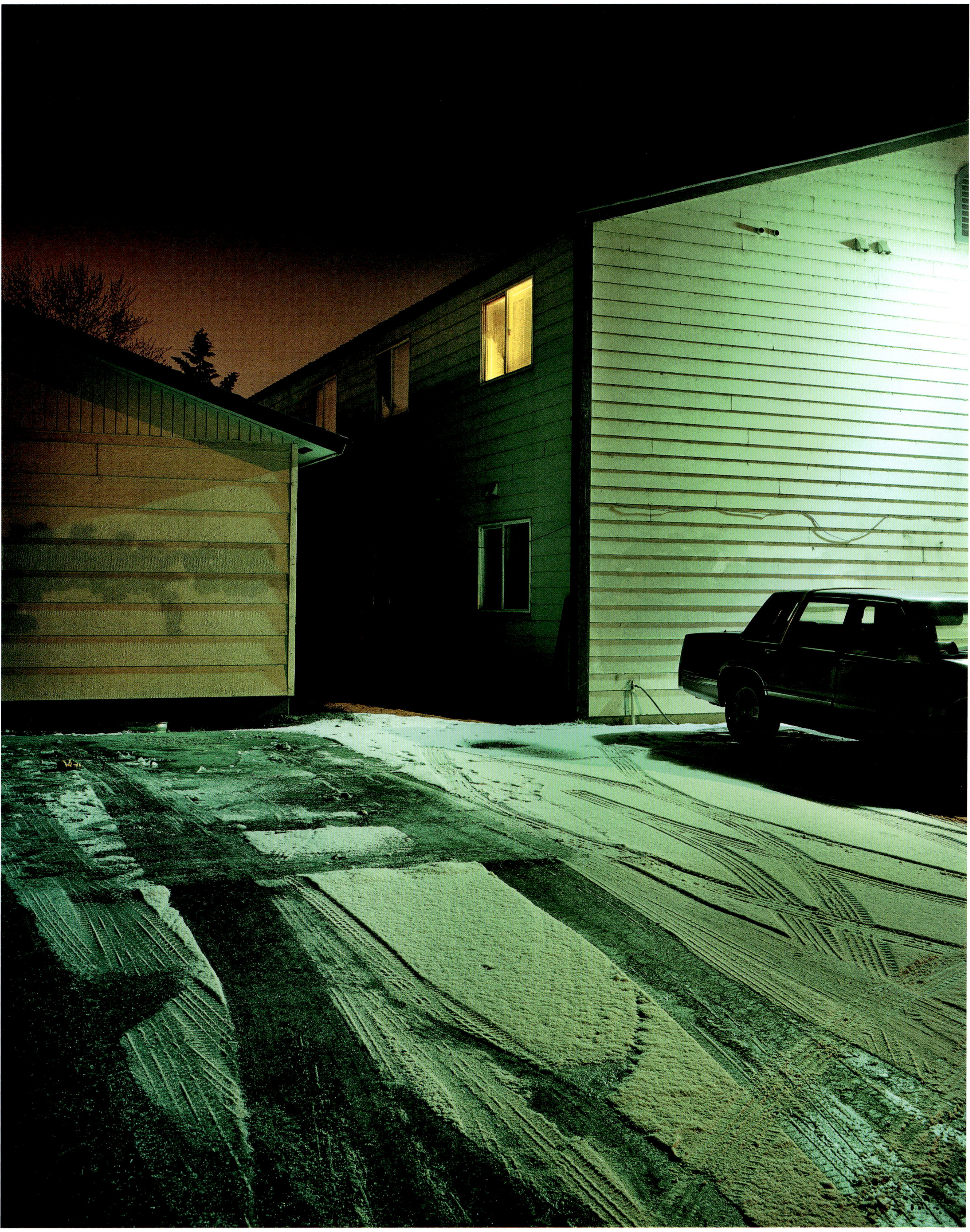

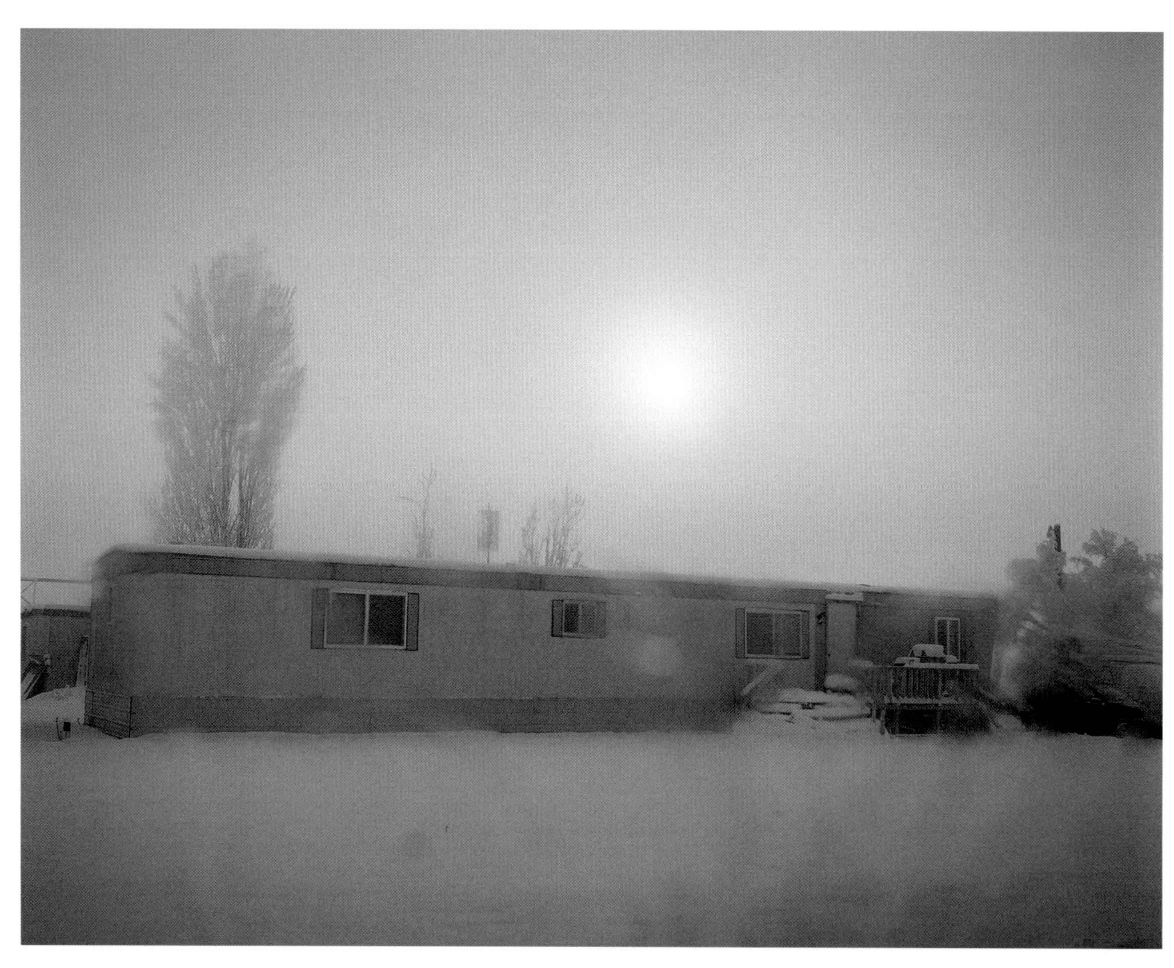

#7409 / Moses Lake, WA / *A Road Divided* **#7412** / Moses Lake, WA / *A Road Divided*

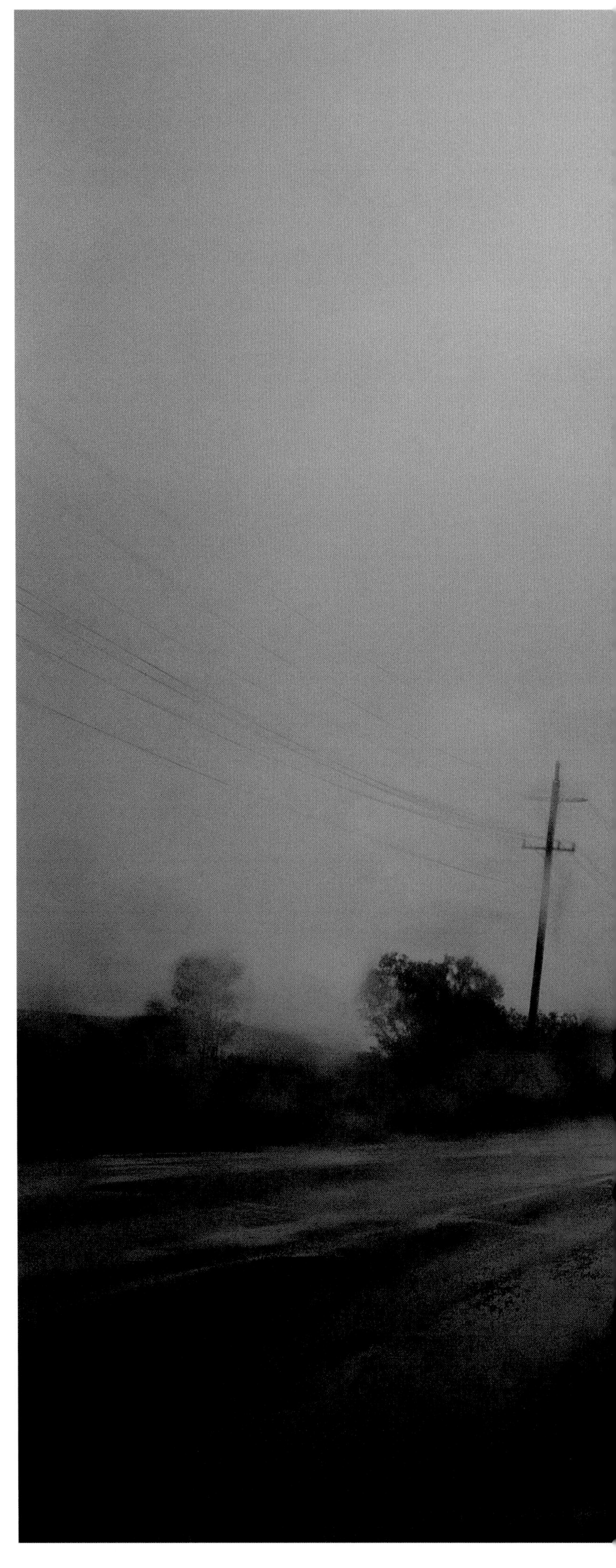

#7557 / Martinez, CA / *A Road Divided, Nymph Daughters*

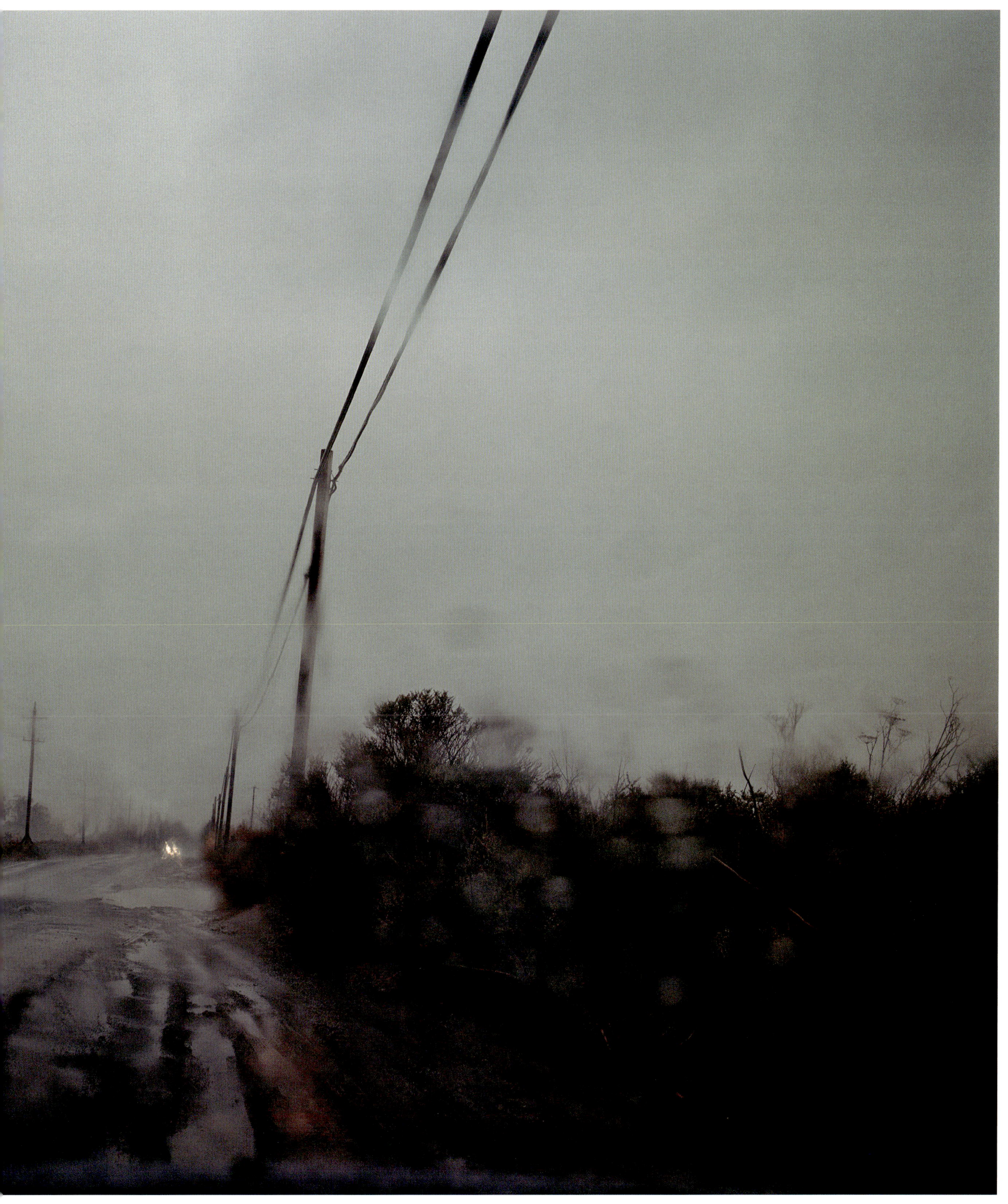

#7900-a / Denair, CA / *Nymph Daughters, Excerpts from Silver Meadows* #7987-a / Oakland, CA #8227-a / Streetsboro, OH

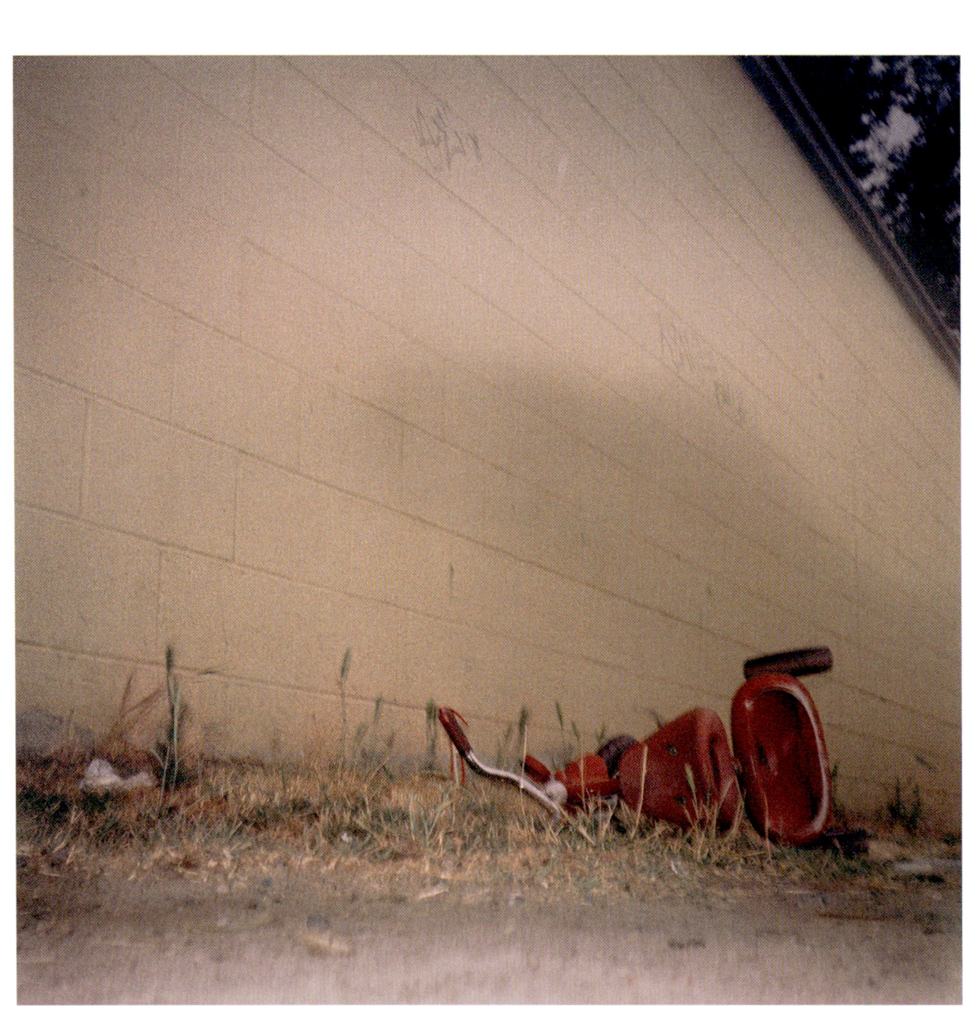

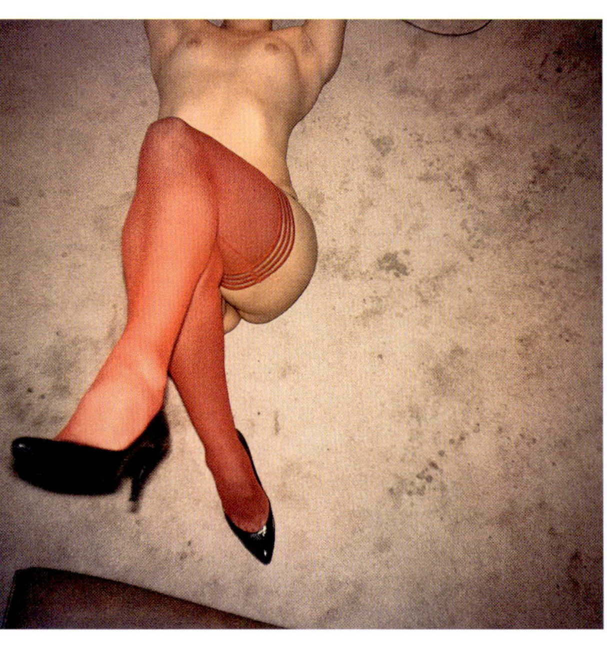

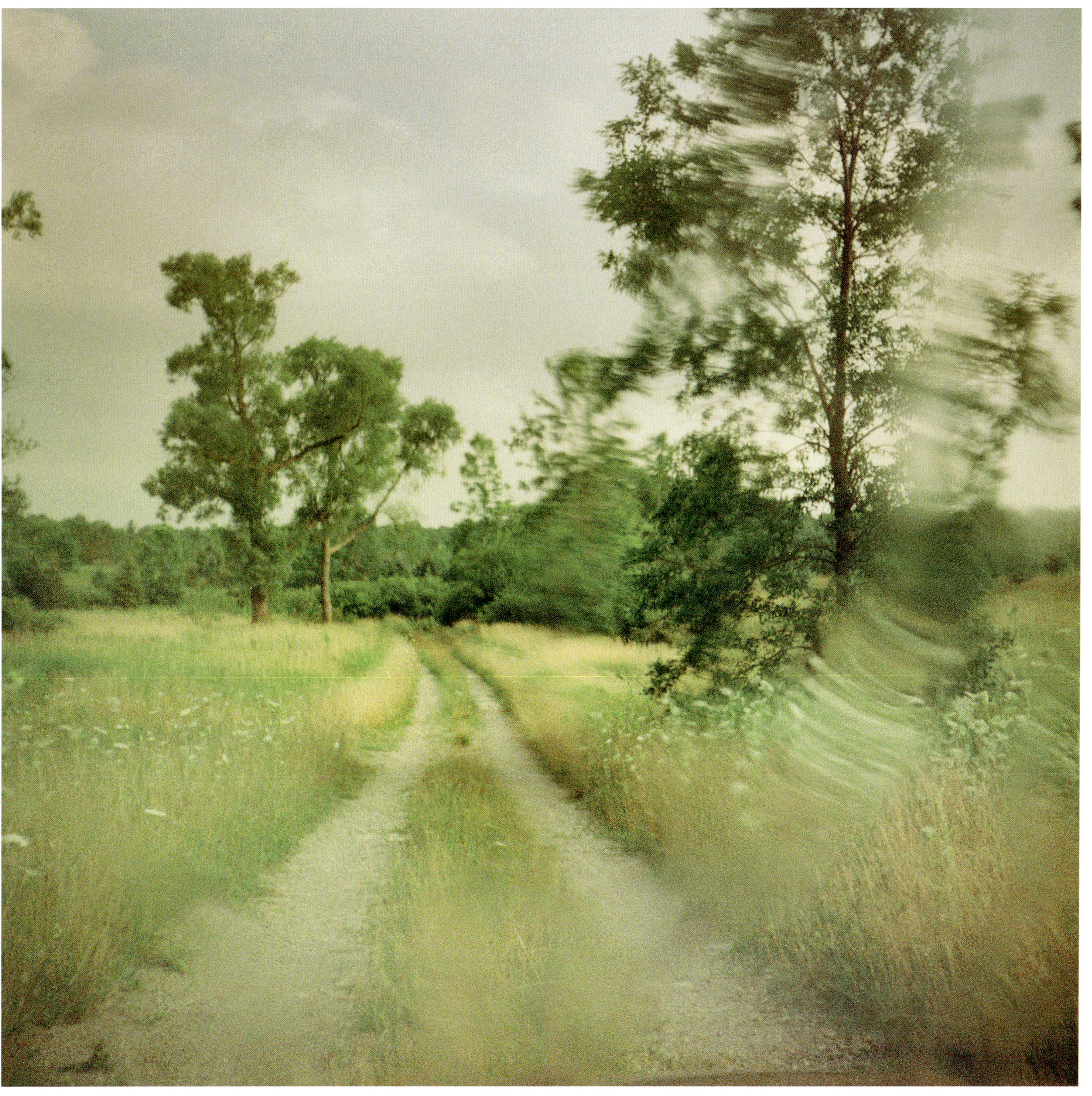

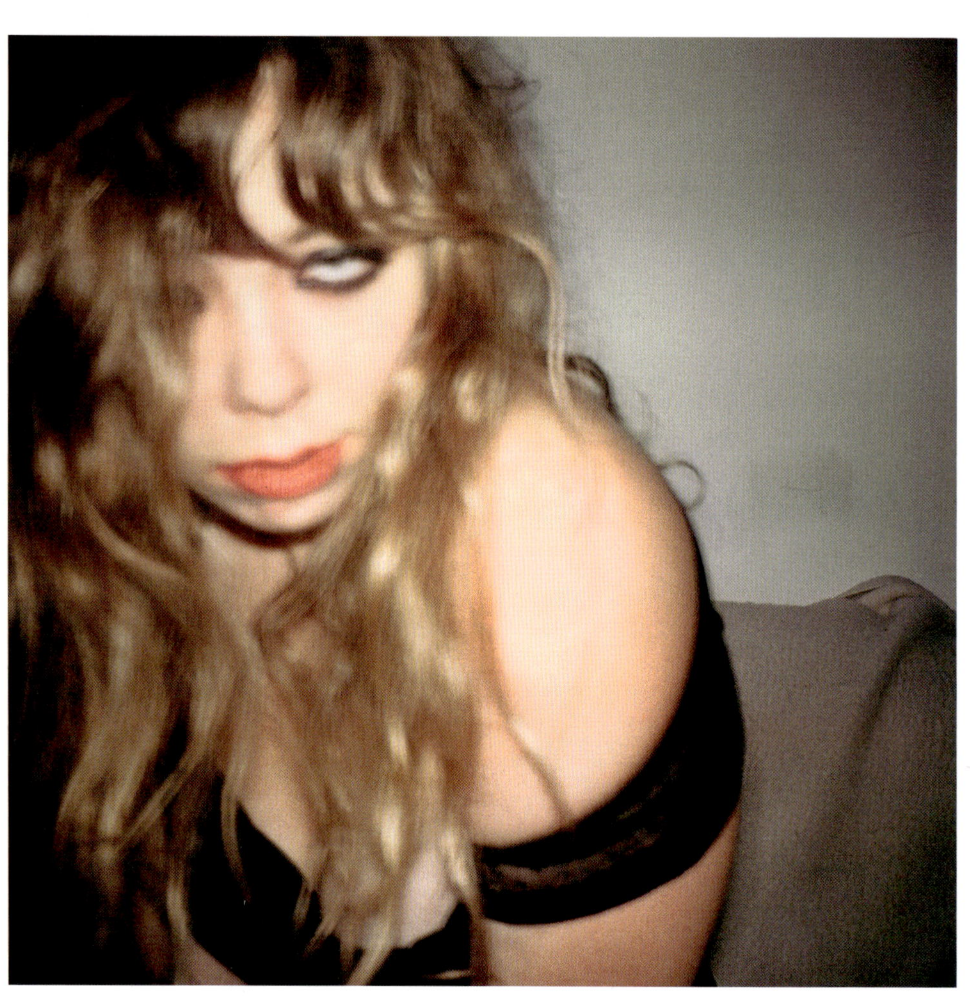

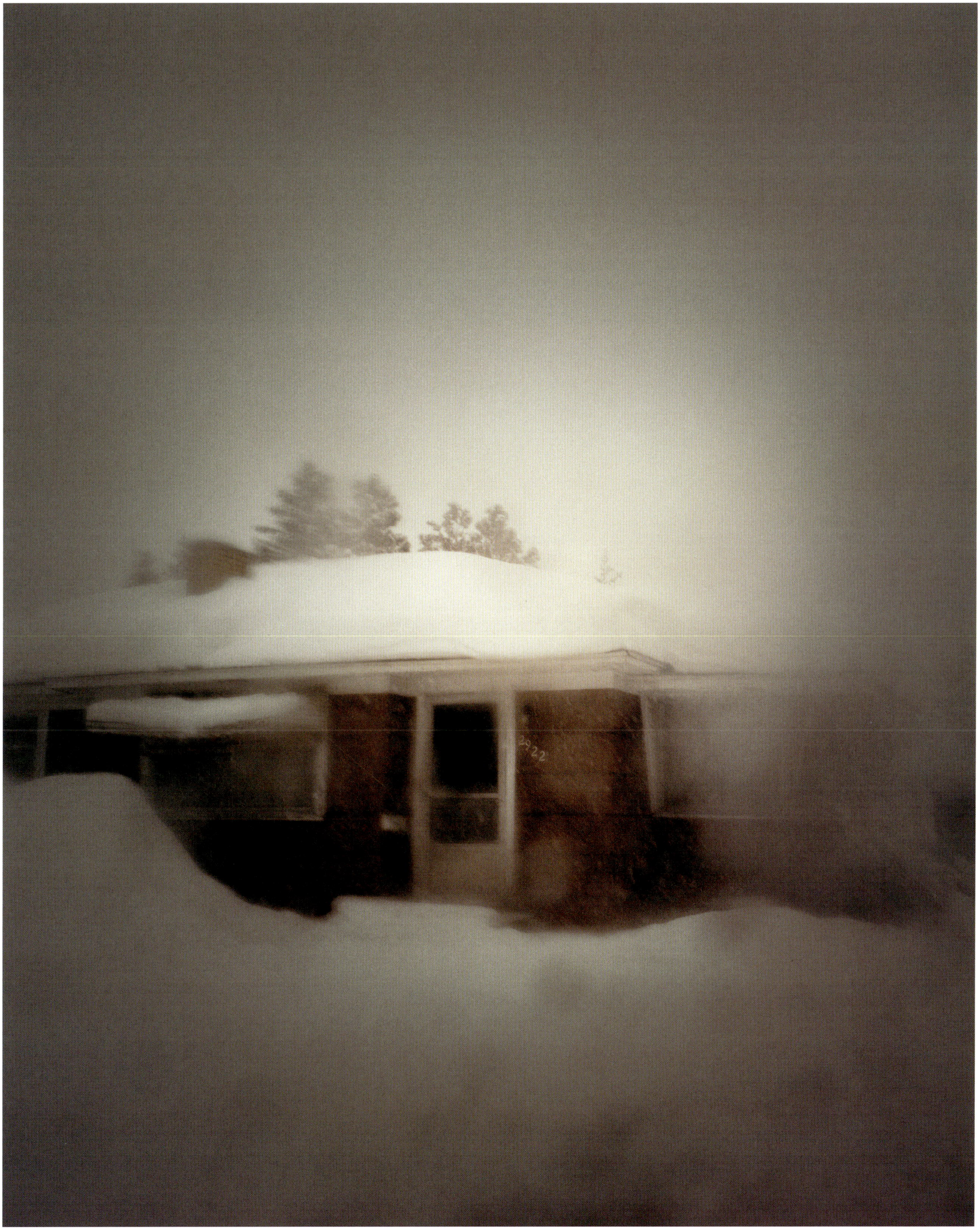

#8496-b / Oakland, CA / *Nymph Daughters, Excerpts from Silver Meadows* **#8610** / Post Falls, ID / *Excerpts from Silver Meadows*

A ROAD DIVIDED 2010

Hido says that *A Road Divided*, published in 2010, "snuck up" on him. "I had been photographing landscapes for a couple of years, but had no intention of making anything of them. I had no other purpose of making them other than responding to the beauty that I saw." The result is this book, which Hido thinks of as a "more mature" collection of landscapes, propelled by the obsessive need to create, and untethered from the need to "prove" anything—such as (as he says, laughing) "I'm not just that guy who photographs houses at night."

A Road Divided expresses the unconventional beauty particular to Hido's work: the open road on a rainy day, seductive in its promise of freedom, but reined in by fences and traffic signs—order and containment despite a perceived desire to break out. Persistent in Hido's work is the idea of coming back to an emotion, if not a place, after leaving, but this time with the weight of experience, maybe even a sort of resignation to the cyclical nature of the mind.

When he's on the road for a show or a lecture, Hido can't settle in his hotel room at night. "I want to be out in the world," he says, so he goes out driving in the late hours, parks somewhere, and—using his dashboard as a desk—works on a new book, or reviews his photographs, turns up the music, and immerses himself in the questions of a still night in a small town. Hido's photographs may work as a hypothetical look into the lives of others, but they are necessarily a reflection of the artist as well.

Hido says he's the type of photographer who works on multiple projects at once, most often taking photographs to satisfy some sort of magnetism toward a specific image rather than to "storyboard" a future collection. "I don't just work for my projects," he says, "I work because I need to take a picture when I see it in front of me."

A book or show often comes together much later in his process, sometimes years later, as he sifts through various photographs on his desk or dash and finds the startling connections between them. This course of editing and combing through his own work is one way that Hido "constructs maps from large bodies of photographs."

A Road Divided is a strong example of this process: the book is a collection of magnetic images that form a relationship when they meet. Individually, these images might point in various directions, but together, they form a narrative and a path forward. "Without the bookmaking process," says Hido. "I wouldn't know where to start."

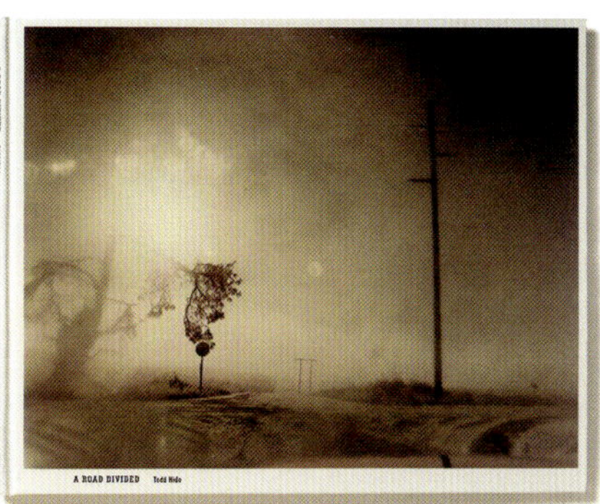

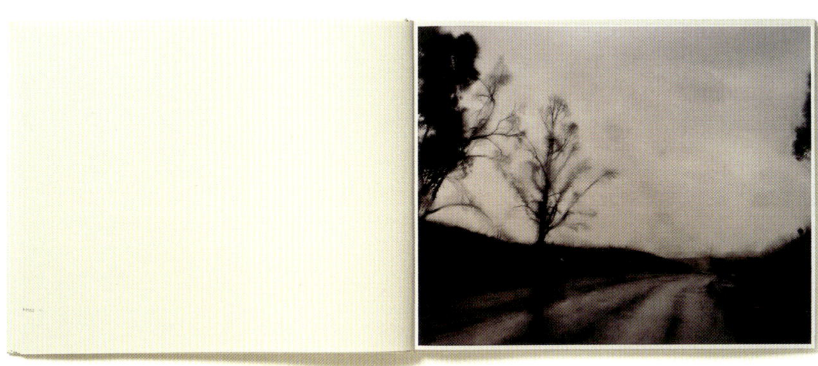

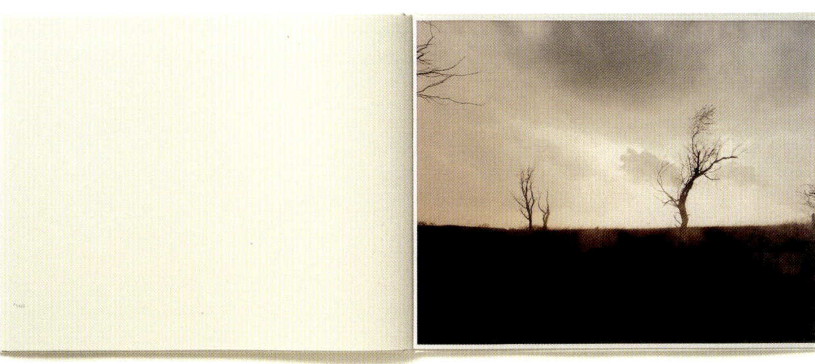

A Road Divided
Published 2010 by Nazraeli Press
16½×13½ inches
64 pages

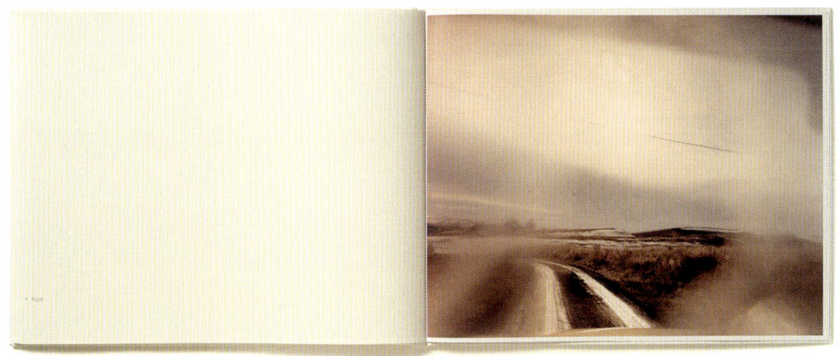

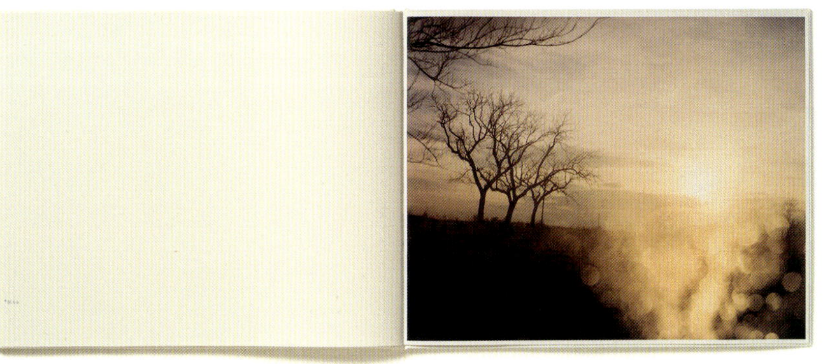

CHRONOLOGY
2010–2013

2010 Super Labo publishes *Nymph Daughters*

2010 Kehrer Verlag publishes *One Day*, a compilation of ten photographers' monographs

2010 Nazraeli Press publishes *Motel Club*, *Cracked Trees*, and *Crooked Cracked Tree in Fog*

2011 The Fred and Laura Bidwell Foundation commissions a work about Ohio for inaugural exhibition at Transformer Station, Cleveland

2011 Makes first extra-large-scale print, at 60 by 76 inches

2011 Group exhibition: *Here*, Pier 24 Photography, San Francisco. Includes forty-five-image grid from *House Hunting*

2011 Group exhibition: *American Psyche: A Generation in Contemporary Photography*, Religare Arts, New Delhi, India

2012 Begins photographing with digital camera

2013 Group exhibition: *At the Window: The Photographer's View*, Getty Center, Los Angeles

2013 Solo exhibition: *Excerpts from Silver Meadows*, Transformer Station, Cleveland

2013 Nazraeli Press publishes *Excerpts from Silver Meadows*

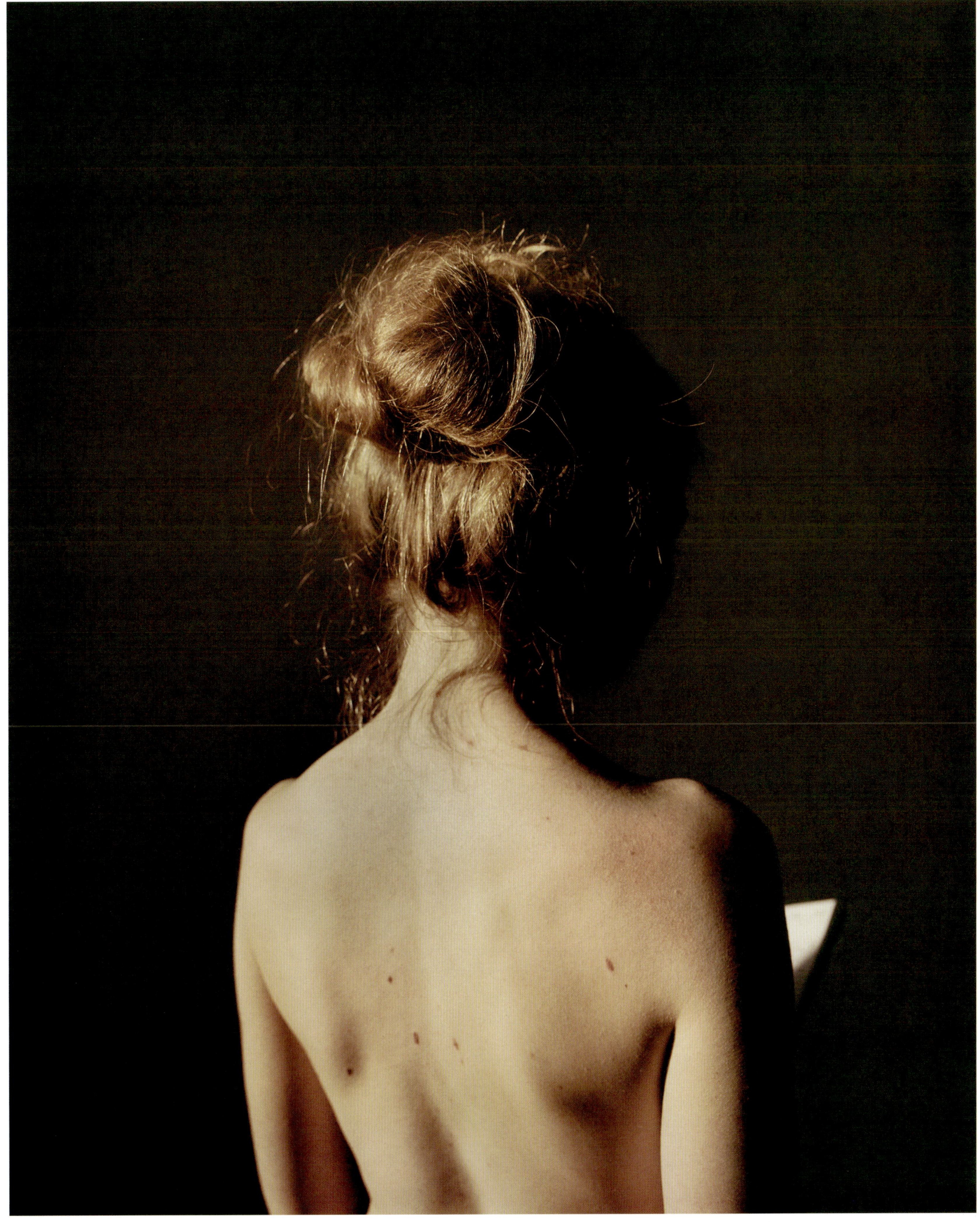

#8869 / Oakland, CA

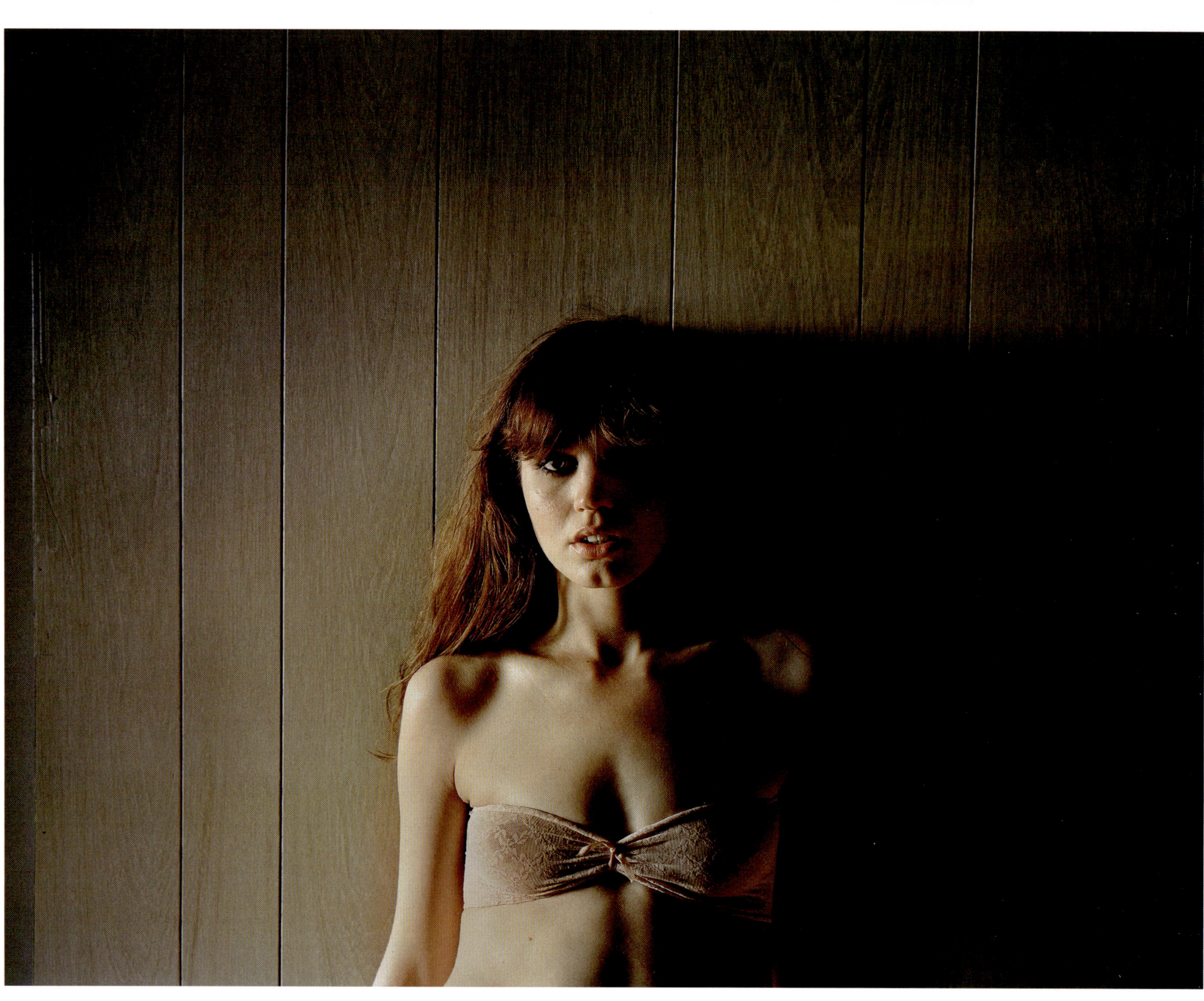

#8906 / Oakland, CA / *Excerpts from Silver Meadows*

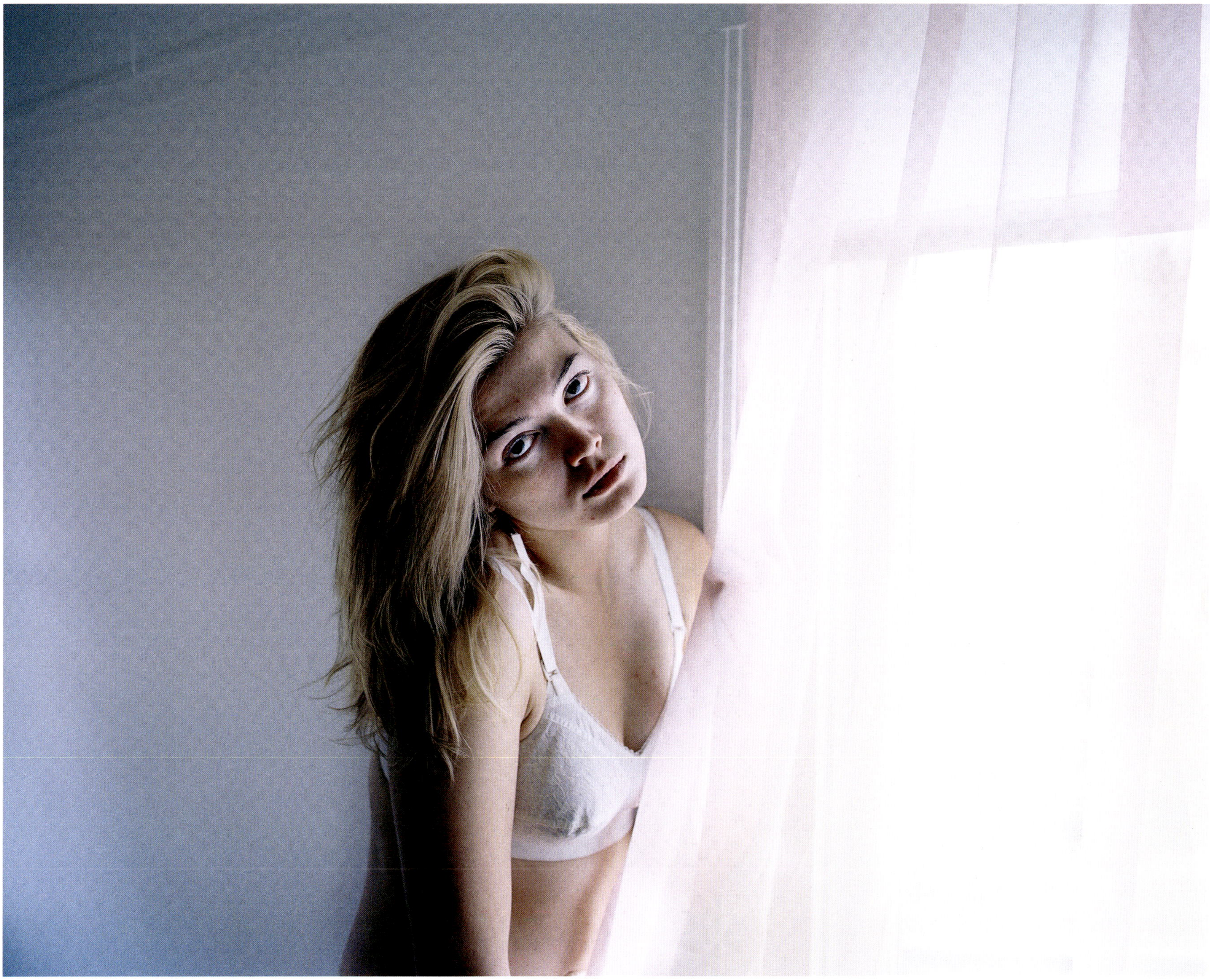

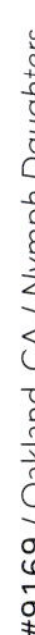

#9169 / Oakland, CA / *Nymph Daughters*

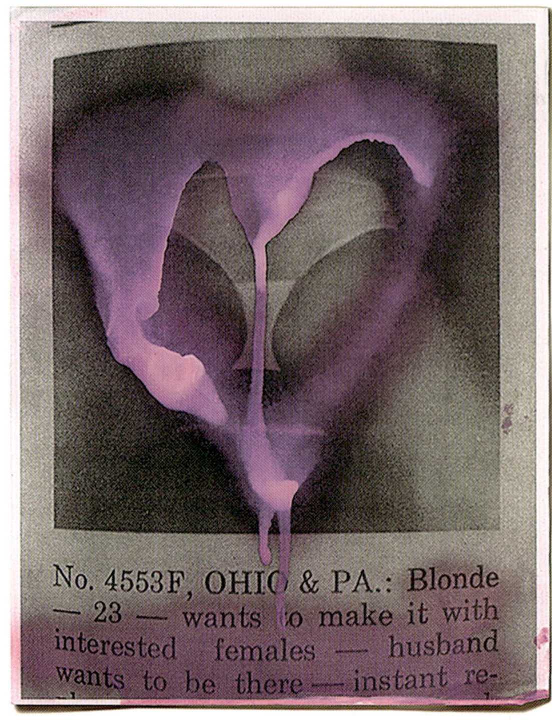

No. 4553F, OHIO & PA.: Blonde — 23 — wants to make it with interested females — husband wants to be there — instant re-

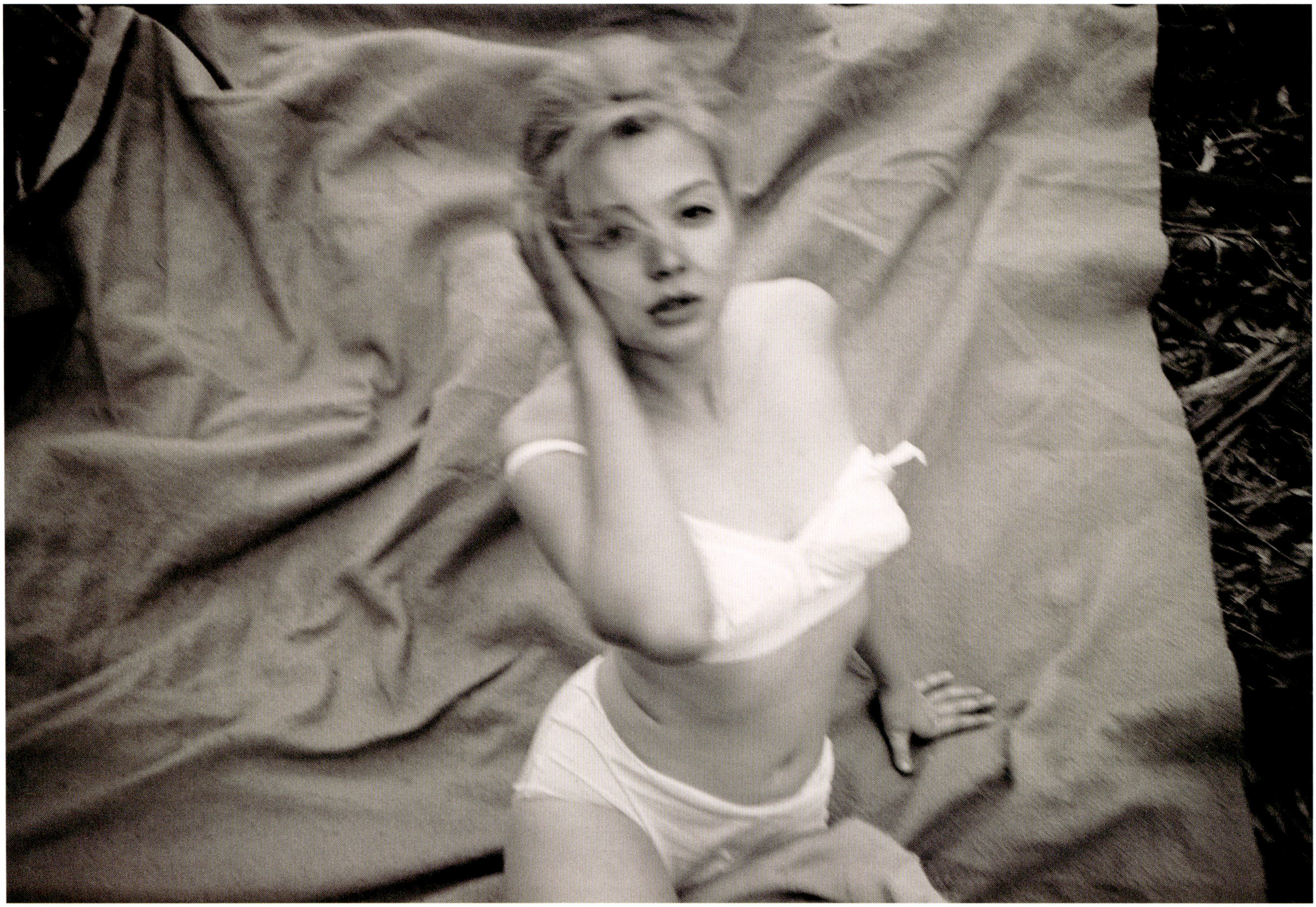

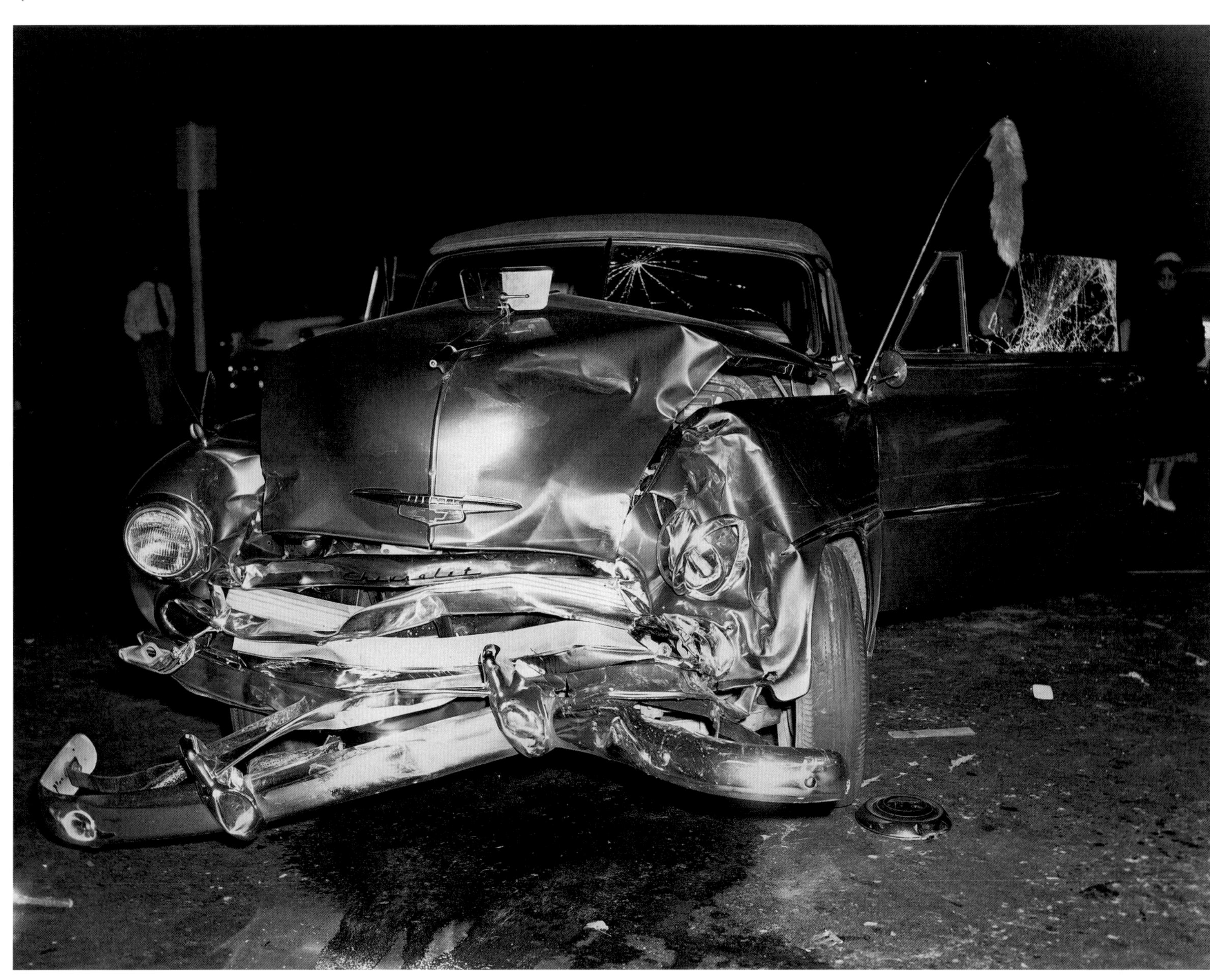

#9176 / Berkeley, CA / *Nymph Daughters* **#9314-ad-heart-panties** / found and altered / *Nymph Daughters, Excerpts from Silver Meadows* **#9185-fd** / found / *Nymph Daughters, Excerpts from Silver Meadows*

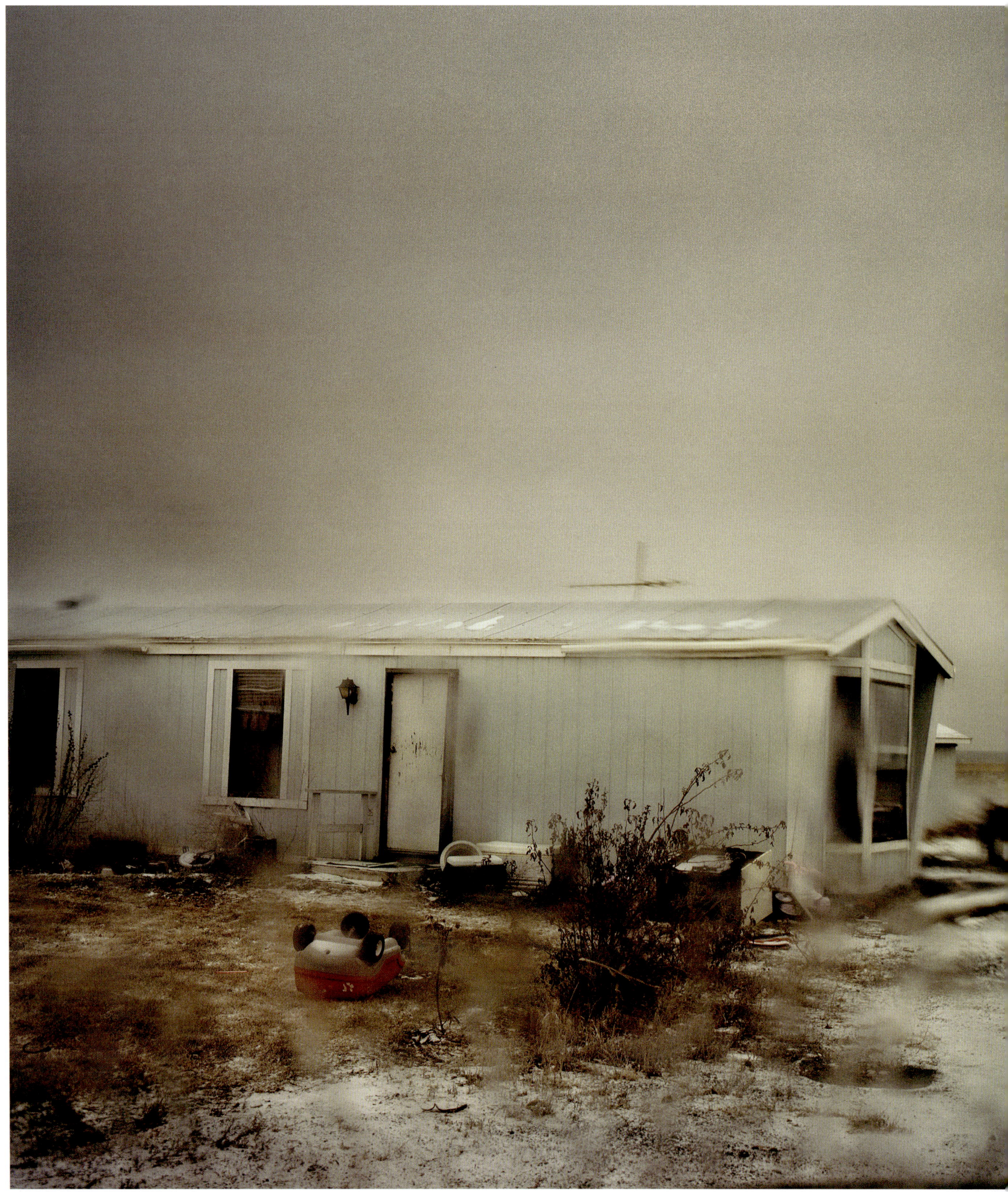

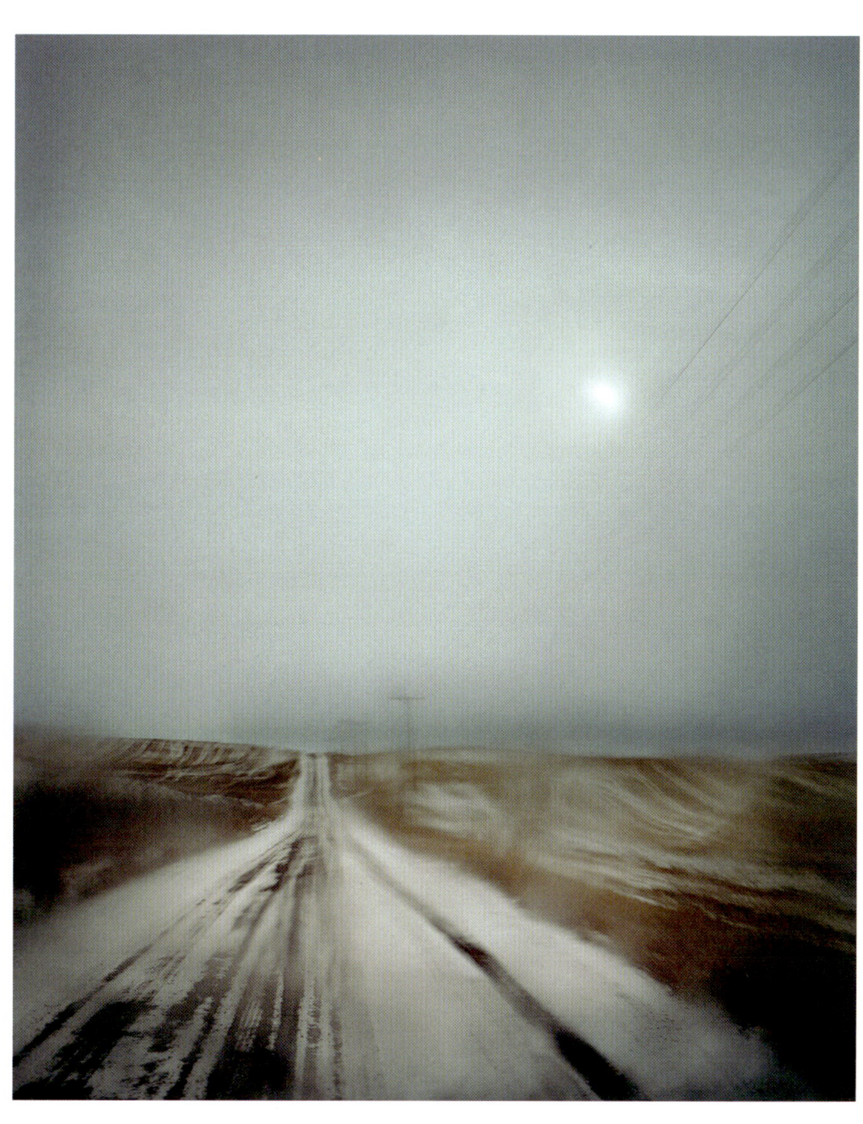

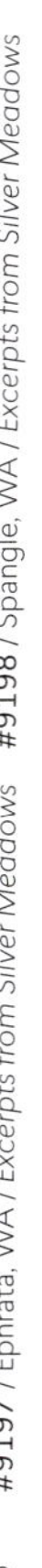

#9197 / Ephrata, WA / *Excerpts from Silver Meadows*   **#9198** / Spangle, WA / *Excerpts from Silver Meadows*

#9202 / Pullman, WA / *Excerpts from Silver Meadows*

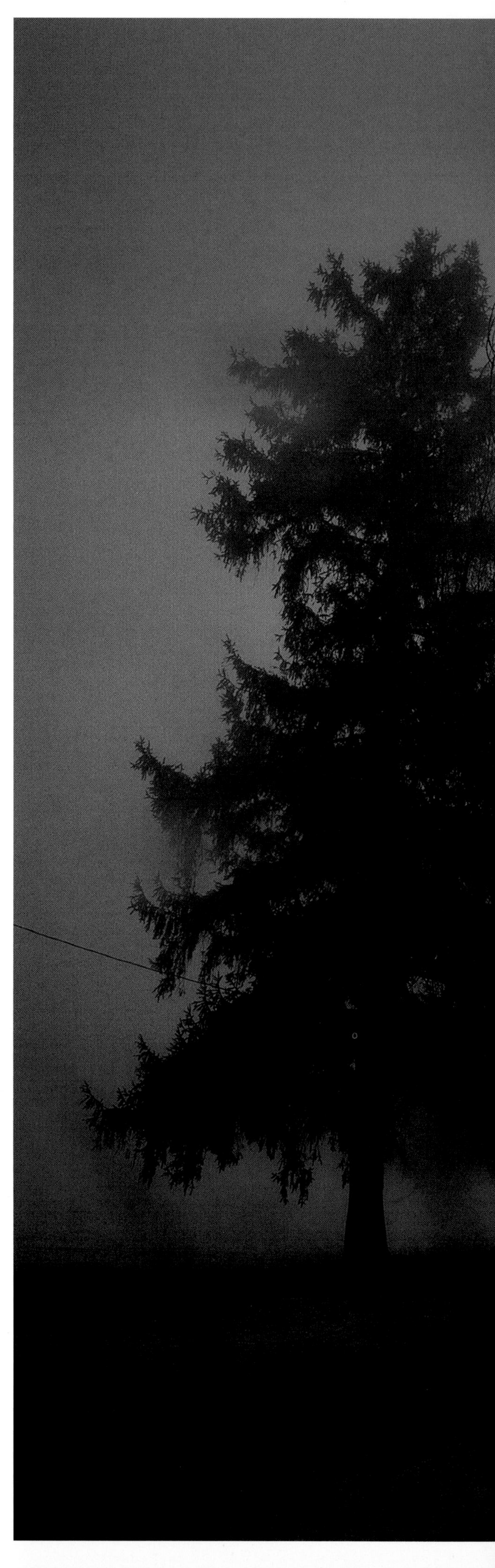

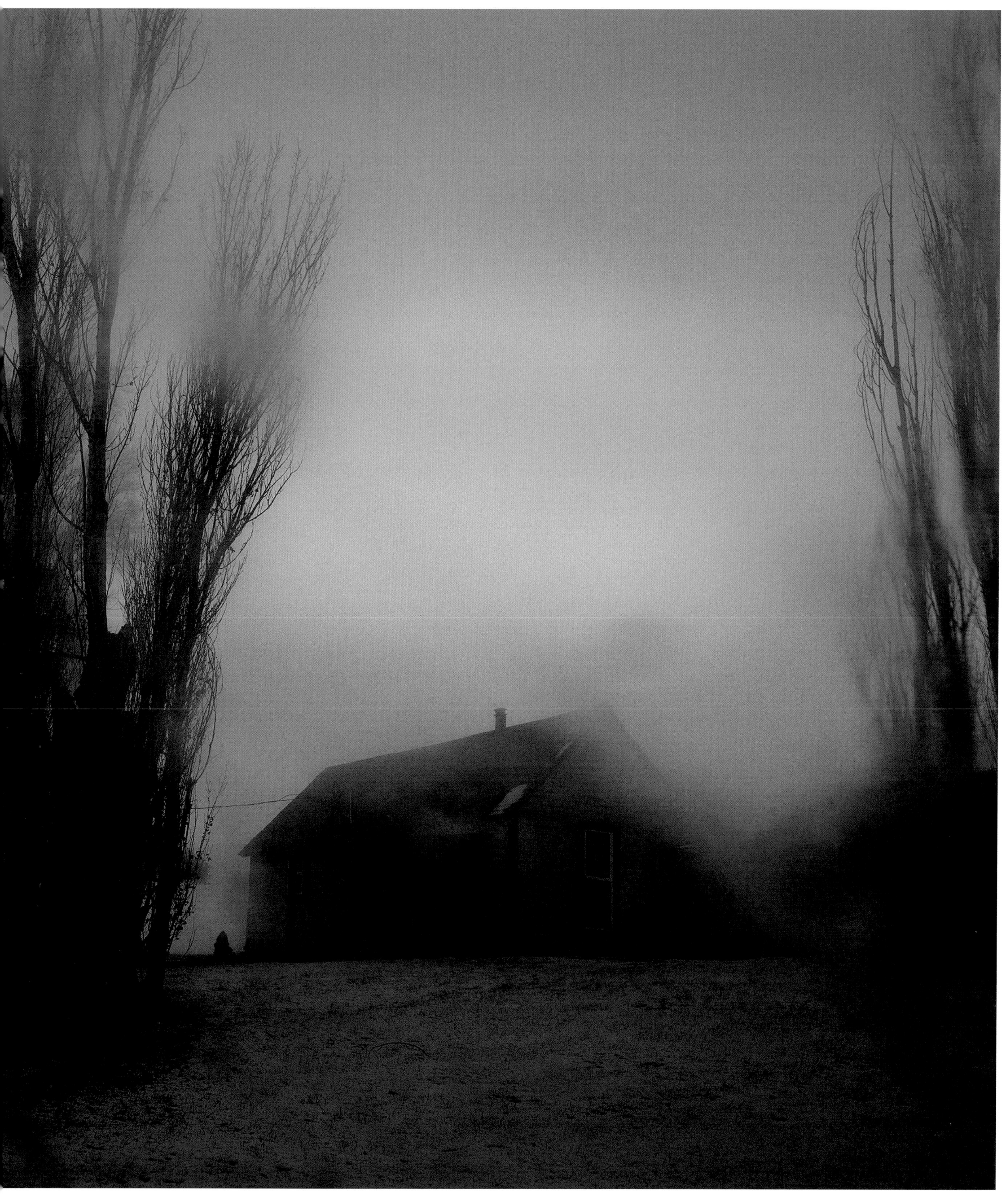

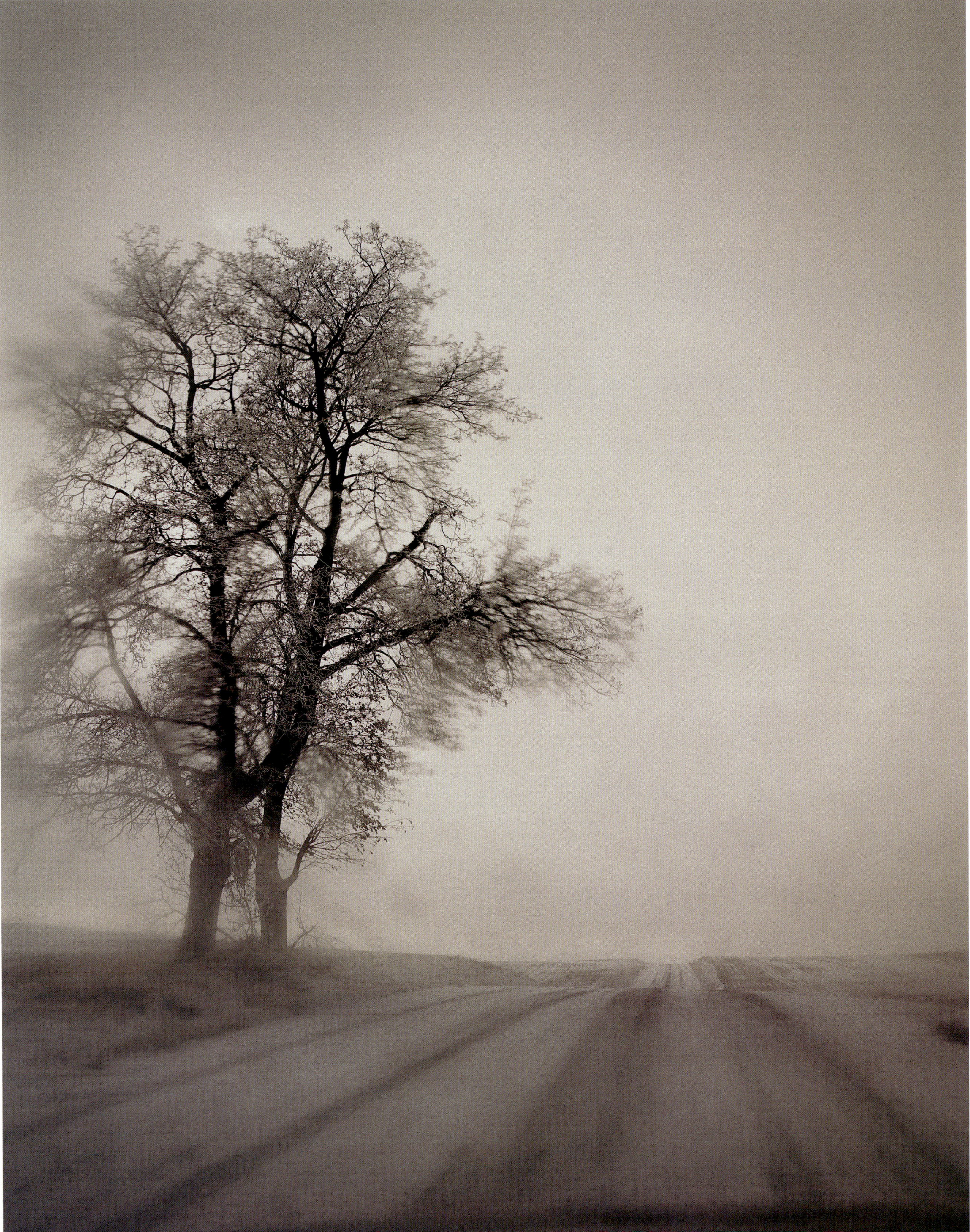

#9238-a / Chardon, OH / *Excerpts from Silver Meadows*

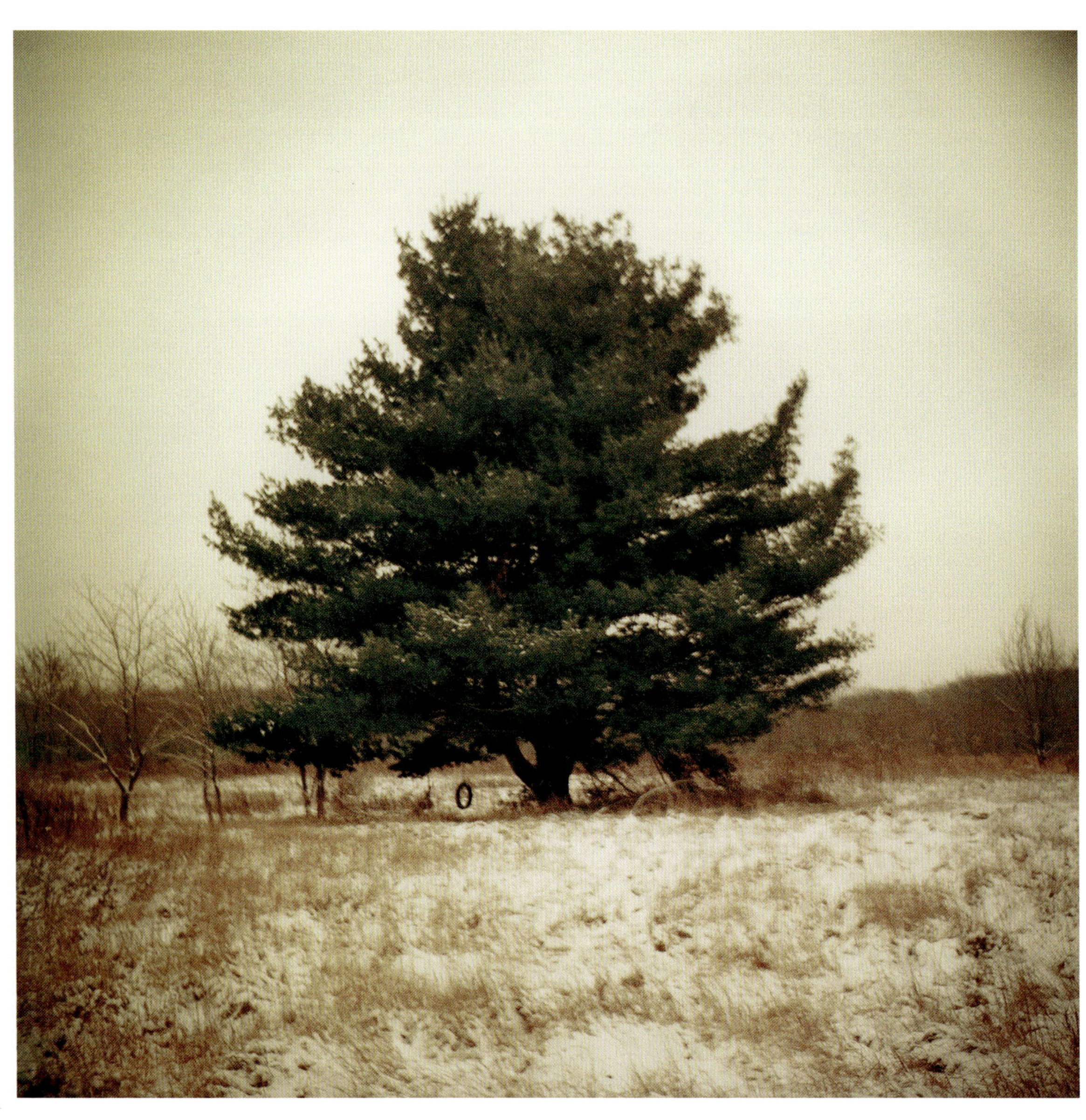

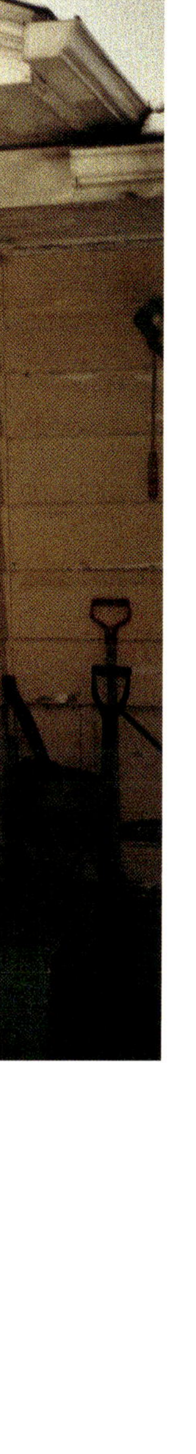

#9238-d / Peninsula, OH / *Excerpts from Silver Meadows*

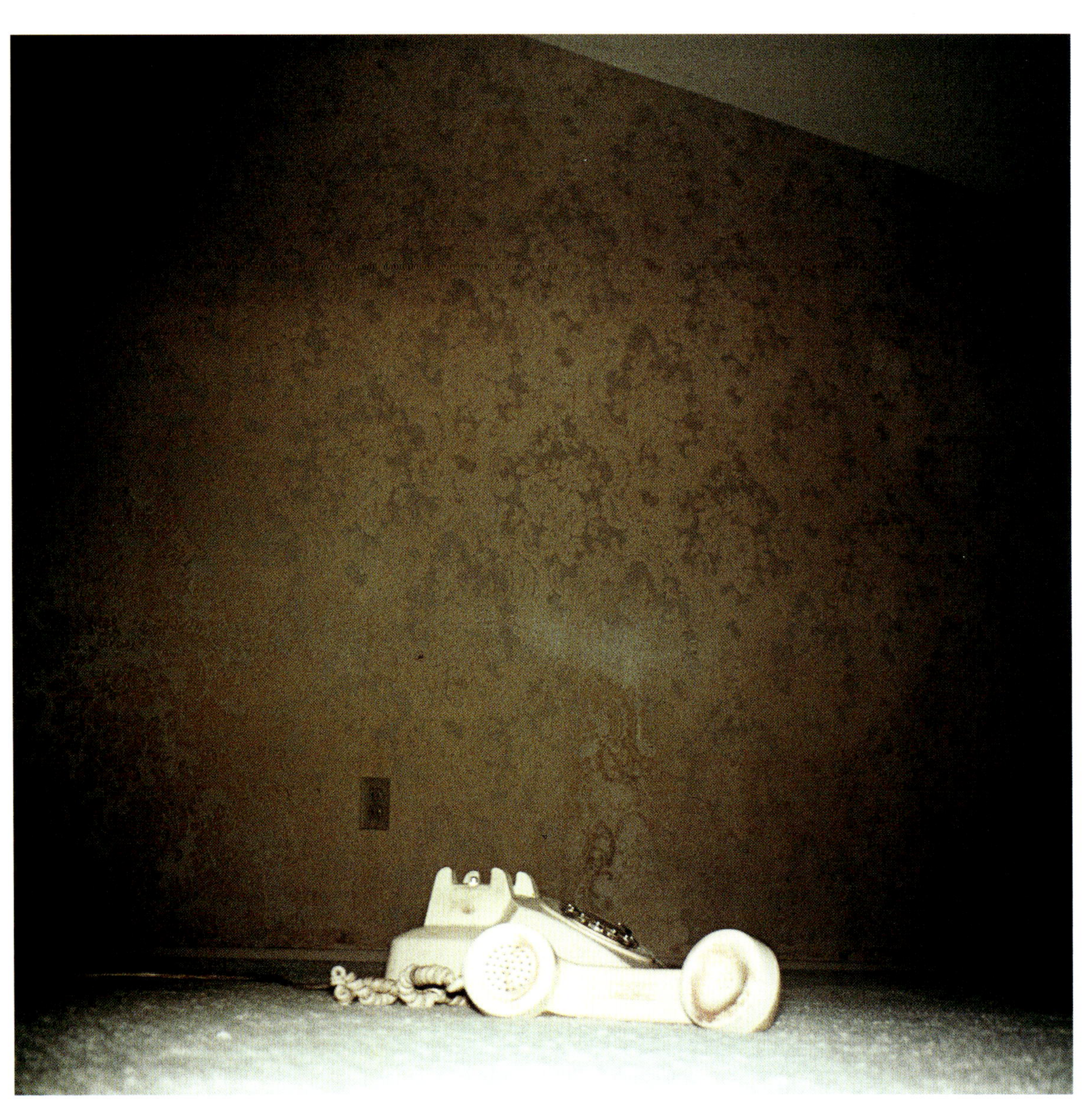

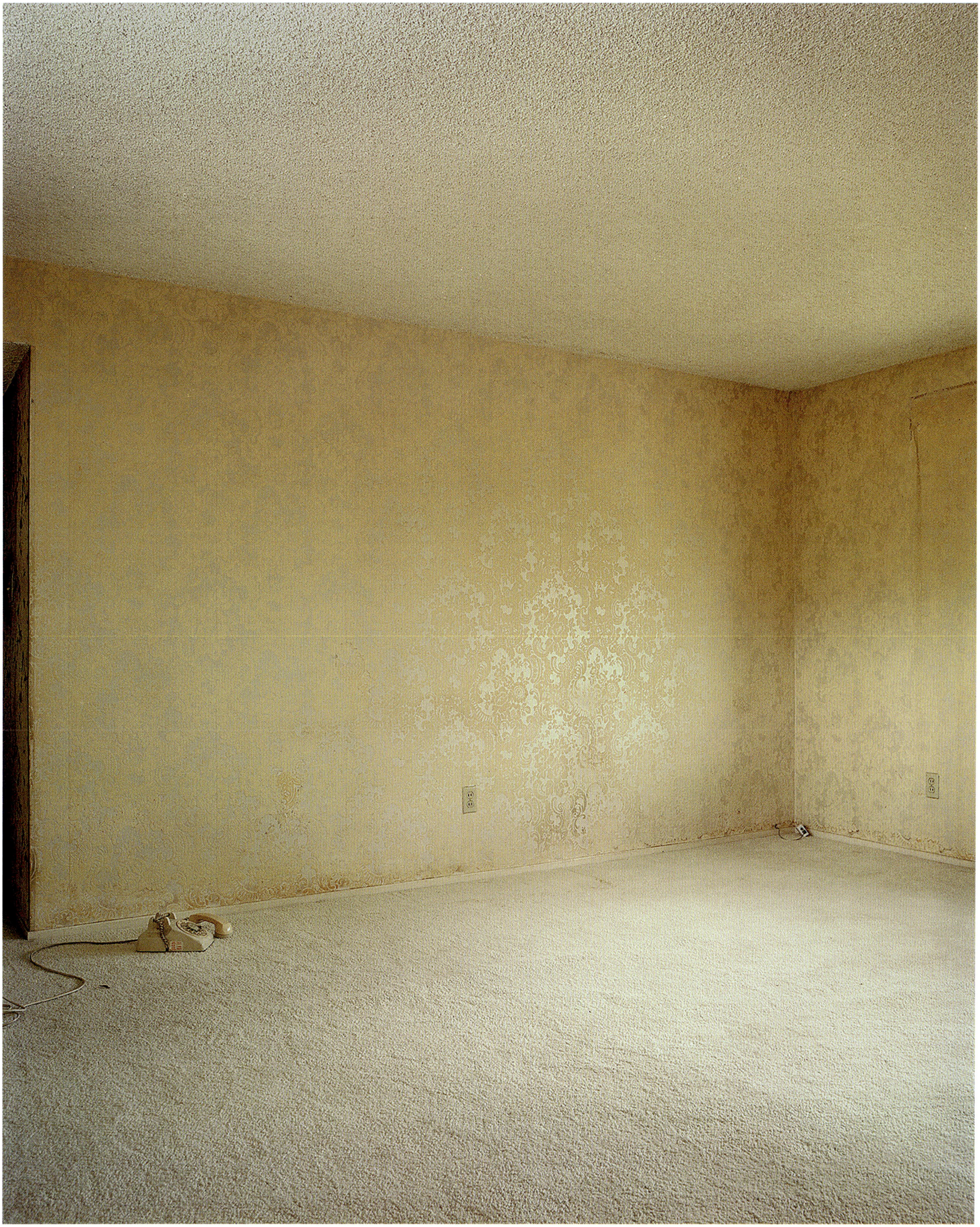

#9248-a / Roseville, CA / *Excerpts from Silver Meadows*   **#9243** / Roseville, CA / *Excerpts from Silver Meadows*

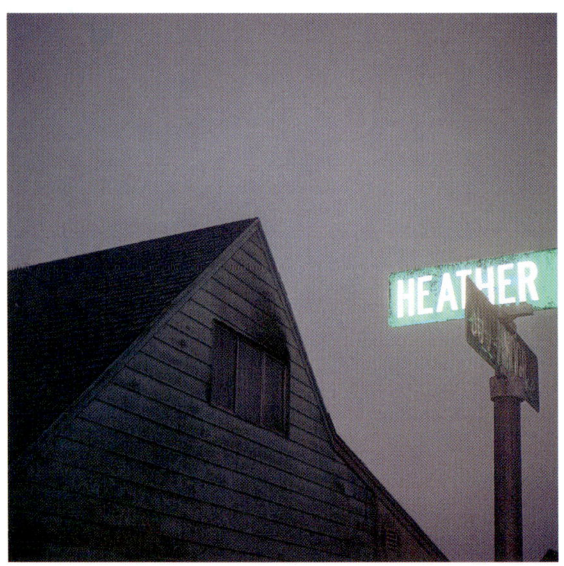
HEATHER

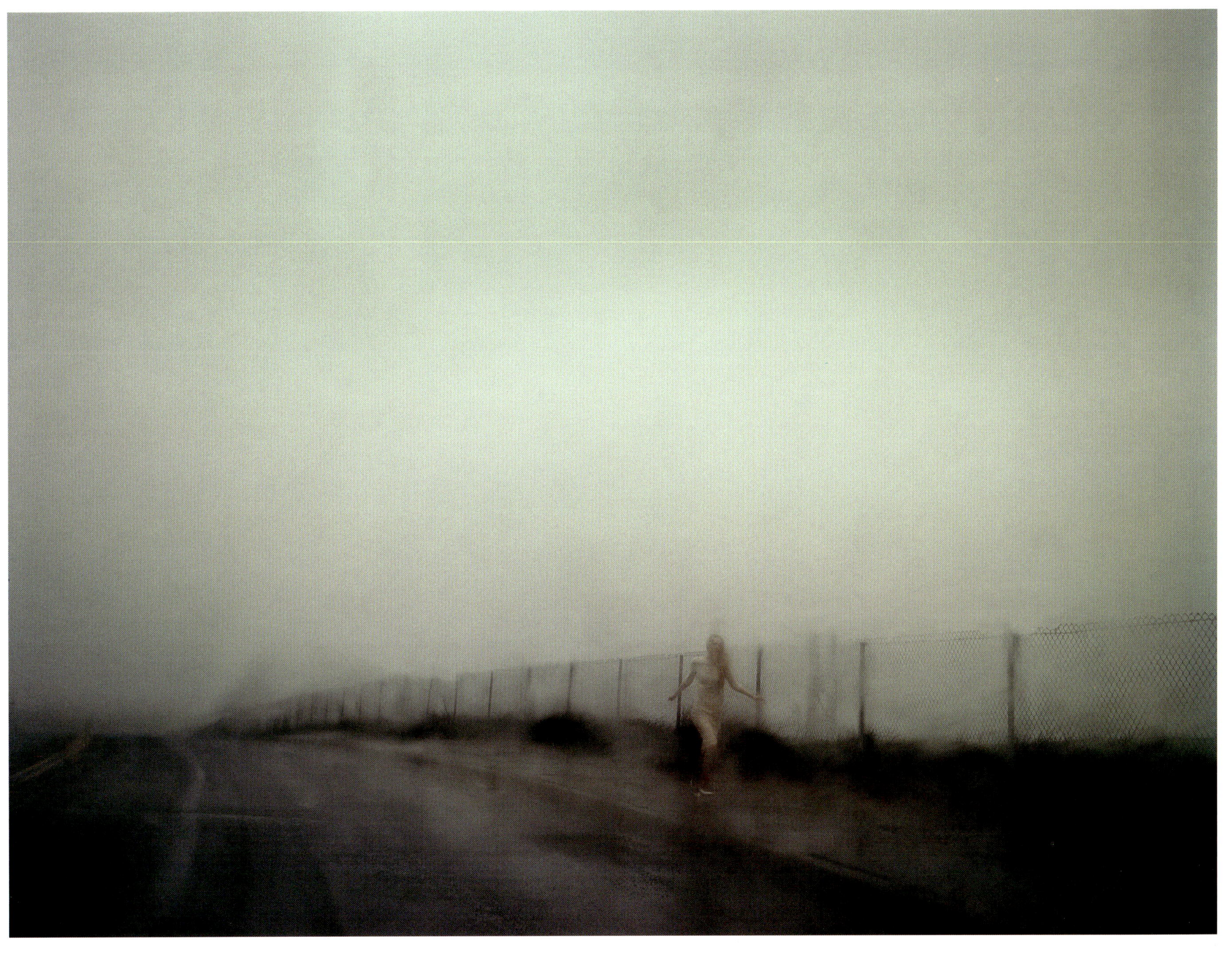

#9270-a / Pacifica, CA / *Excerpts from Silver Meadows* **#9297** / Concord, CA

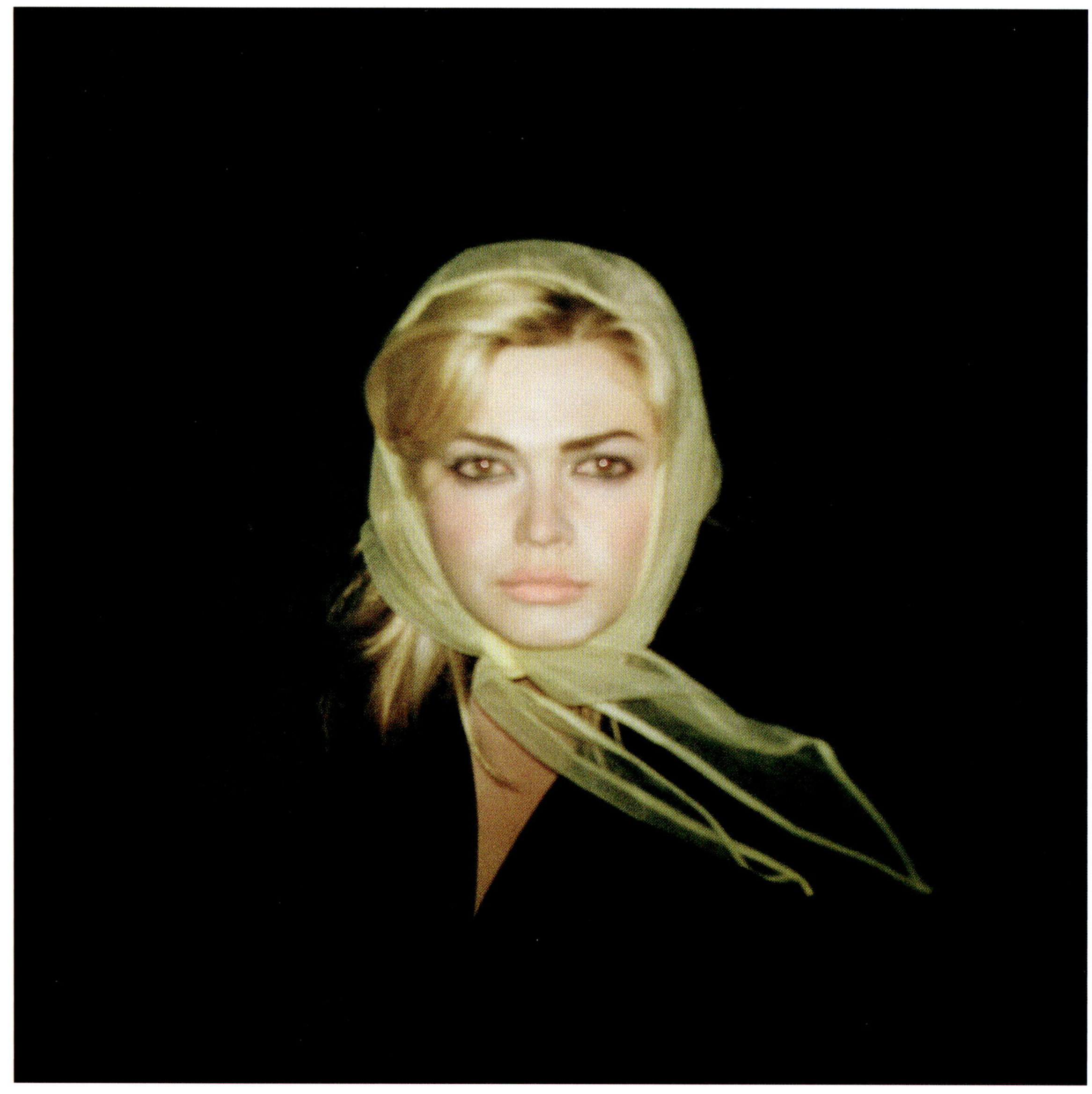

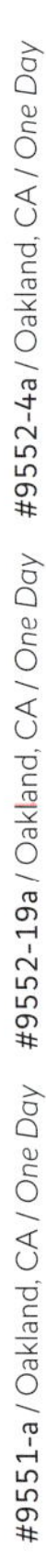

#9551-a / Oakland, CA / *One Day*

#9552-19a / Oakland, CA / *One Day*

#9552-4a / Oakland, CA / *One Day*

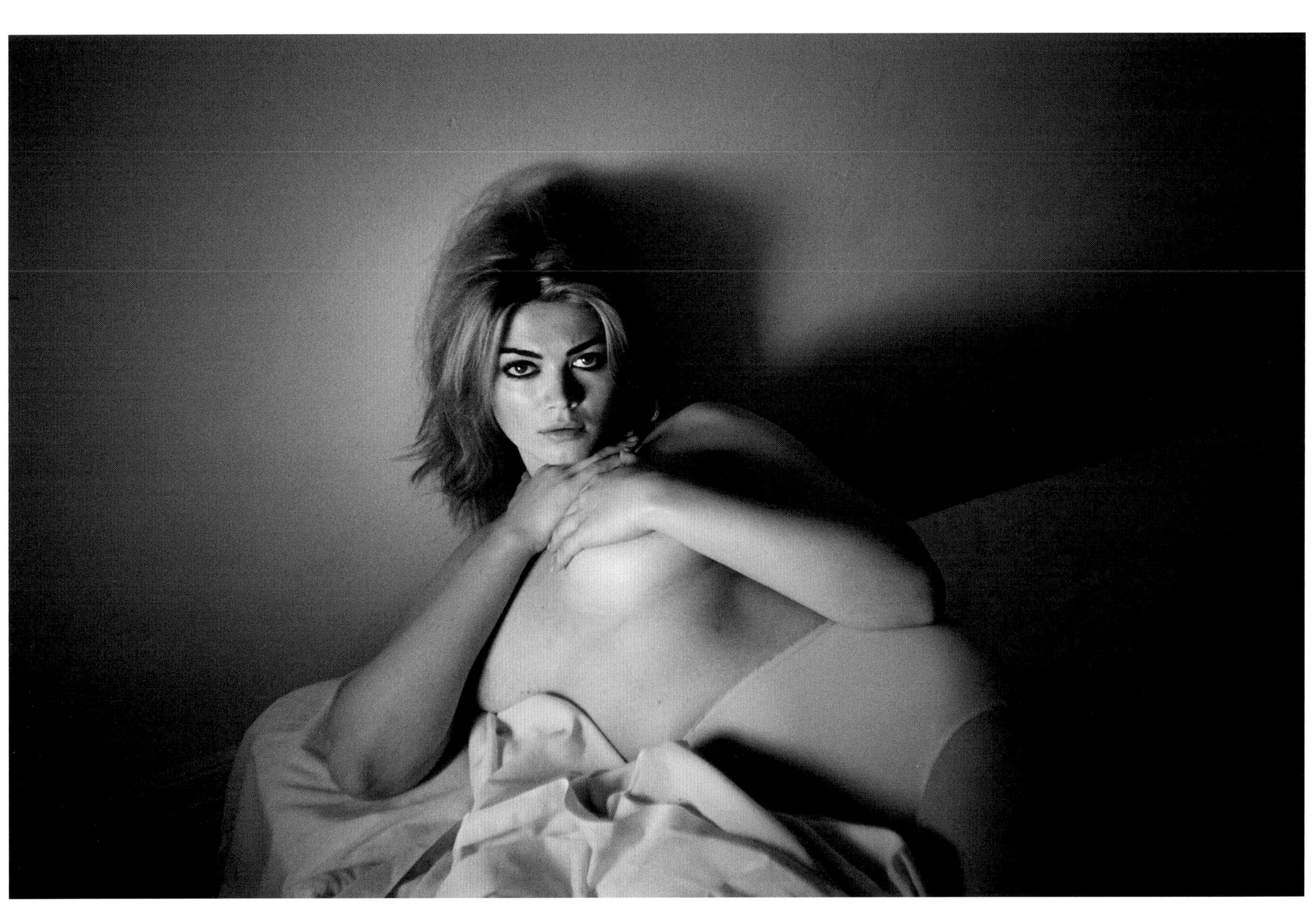

LIMITED-EDITION AND EXPERIMENTAL BOOKS 2009–2010

Ohio
Published 2009 by TBW Books
6×8 inches
42 pages

Nymph Daughters
Published 2010 by Super Labo
7×10 inches
32 pages

One Day
Published 2010 by Kehrer Verlag
6½×8⅝ inches
32 pages

Motel Club
Published 2010 by Nazraeli Press
11¼×14¼ inches
32 pages

Since 2009, Hido has complemented his tightly edited "big" books with experimental, limited-edition booklets and zines that have allowed him to try new ways of organizing imagery and building narrative. What have begun as nascent investigations in these publications have often developed into the strongest arcs for Hido's subsequent work.

Ohio, published in 2009, was the first of Hido's small-run publications. It was an opportunity for him to introduce images from his personal family archives into a collection of his own photographs. In Hido's vision, *Ohio* was a "container for what I was imagining inside the houses I was shooting at night." He found new ways for scraps of his own biography to reinforce the fictions he was building.

Immediately following *Ohio*, in 2010, Hido felt he could take even fuller advantage of the elasticity of fiction with *Nymph Daughters*, a small-format softcover that ran at five hundred copies, distributed exclusively in Japan. For this book, Hido worked archival images into sequencing experiments—like those he had done in a graduate school class taught by Larry Sultan, whom Hido reveres as both an important influence and a good friend.

In the creation of *Nymph Daughters*, Hido set out to "bridge the gap" between two 1950s found photographs: a studio portrait of a woman who he says "seemed to be a mother," and a newspaper photograph of the immediate aftermath of an automobile accident. Hido connected these two images with a sequence of 126 mm snapshot photographs that he had recently taken of homes and women, and in so doing created a coherent tragedy from two seemingly unrelated possibilities.

Motel Club, also published in 2010, is composed of Instamatic 126 mm photographs—"some of the edgiest images I had ever made to that point," says Hido. And *One Day*, published later that year, gave him the opportunity to sculpt a very singular narrative using the same model, Khrystyna Kasakova, who now appears regularly in his work.

Within the loose framework of unconventional publications, Hido has been able to expand on unconventional ideas, which eventually progress into larger-scale book projects. Most notably, his book *Excerpts from Silver Meadows* draws upon the riskier compositions of the small publications that preceded it. In *Excerpts*, Hido wanted a widely distributed monograph that nevertheless had the "experimental sense" of a zine. "I thought about how to Velcro the spirit of all of these little books into a single package," he says. This led to the idea of using double gatefolds, "with layouts of up to twenty images, that actually ended up exceeding the risks I was taking in smaller publications."

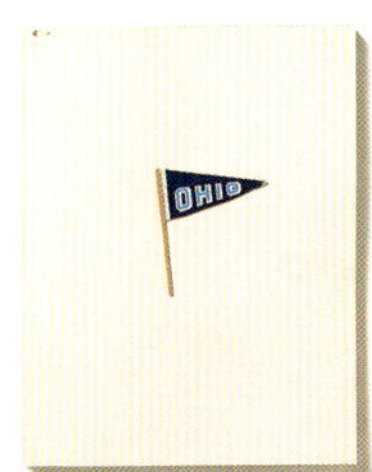
OHIO

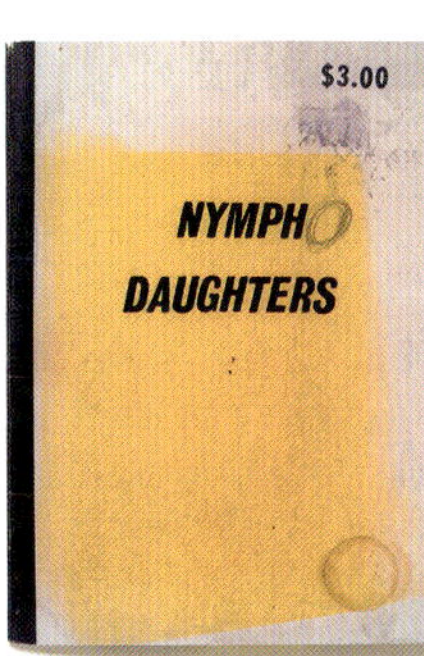
$3.00
NYMPHO
DAUGHTERS

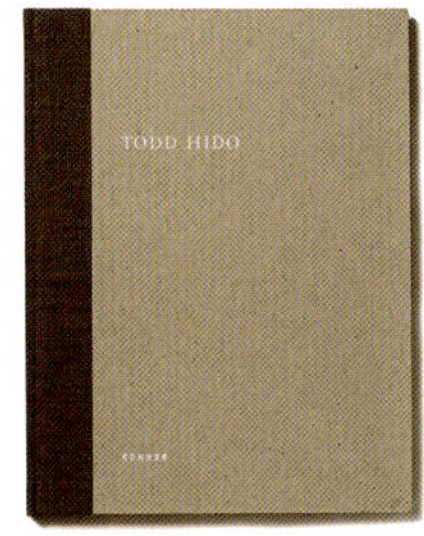
TODD HIDO

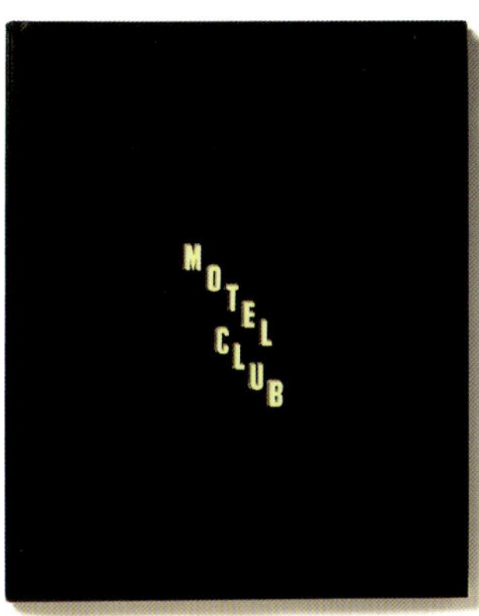
MOTEL
CLUB

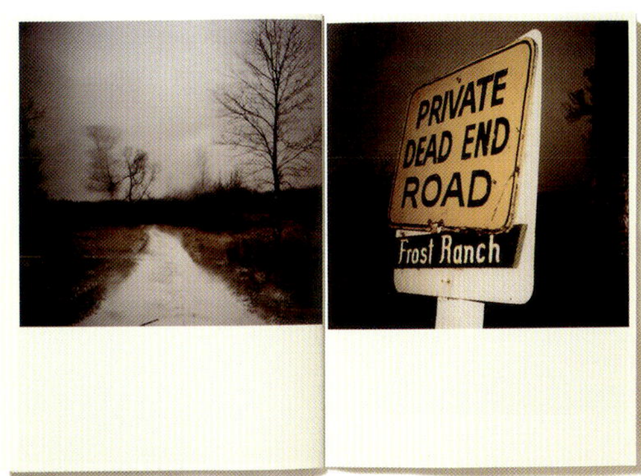
PRIVATE
DEAD END
ROAD
Frost Ranch

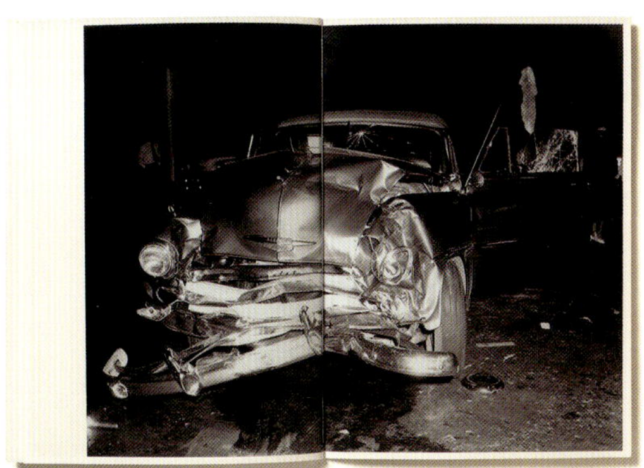

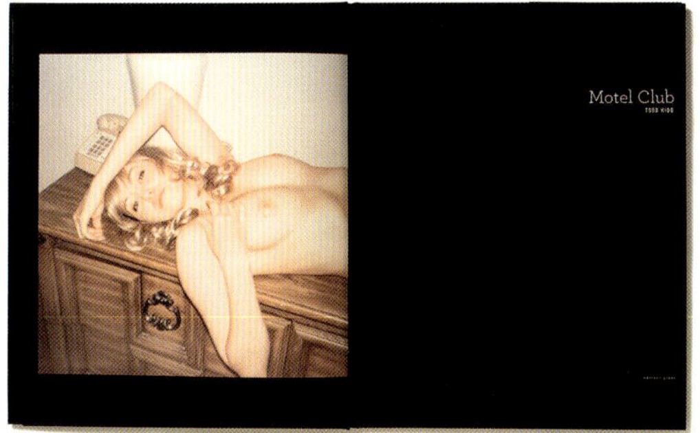
Motel Club

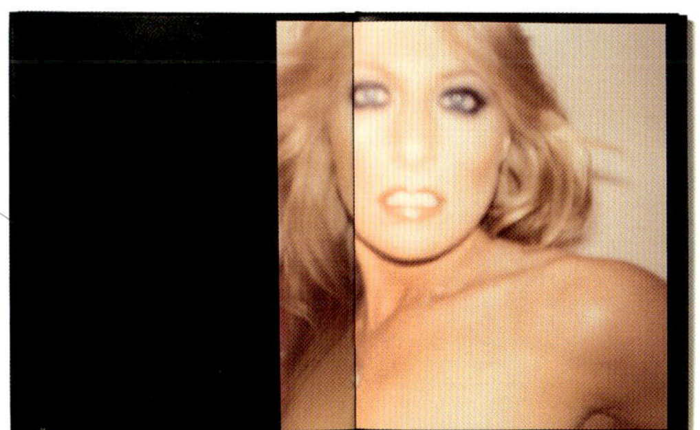

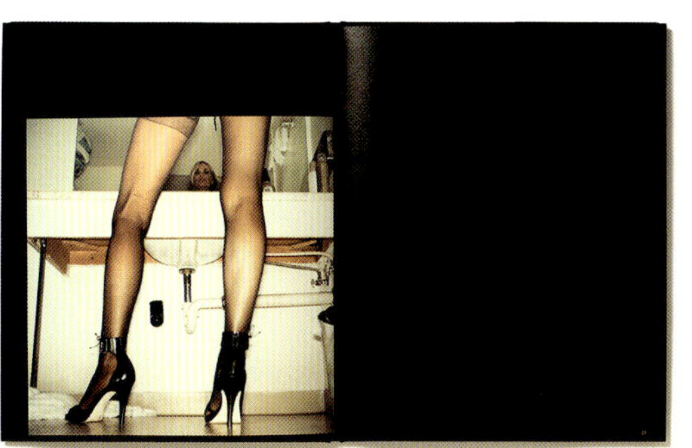

#10096 / Oakesdale, WA / *Excerpts from Silver Meadows*

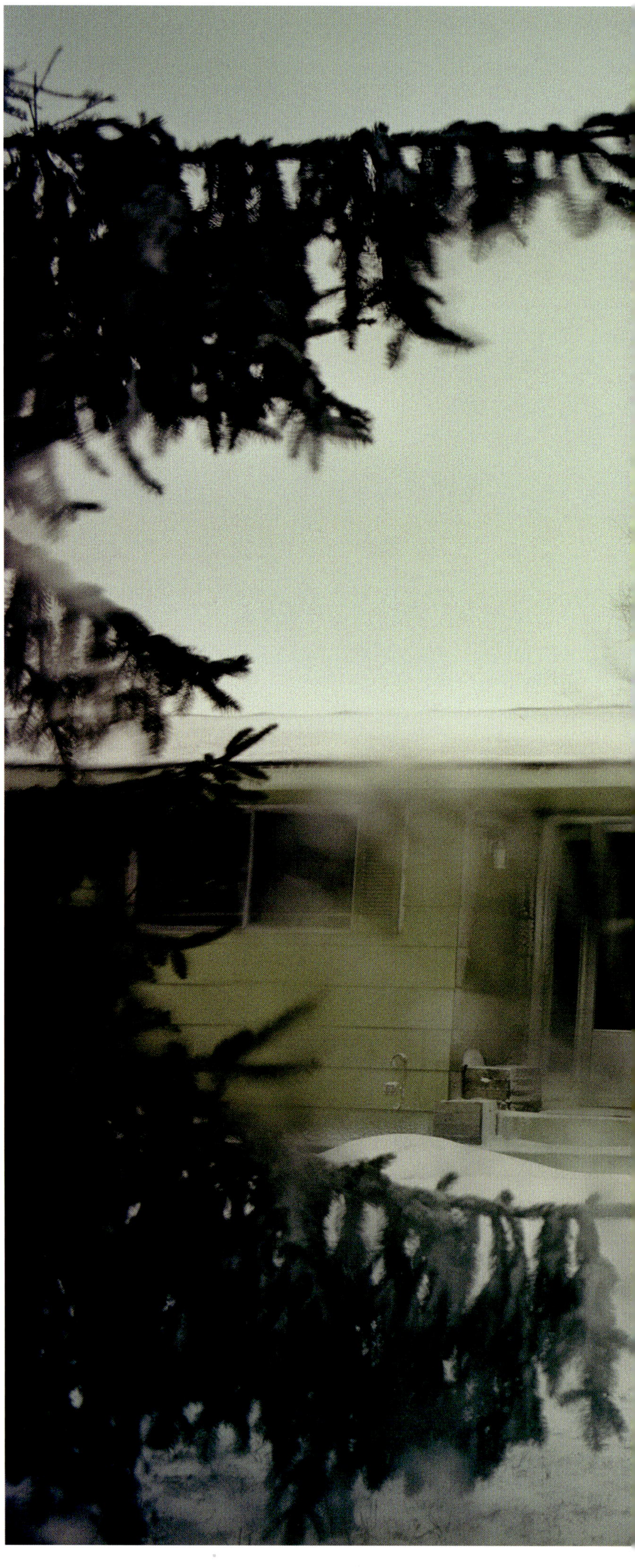

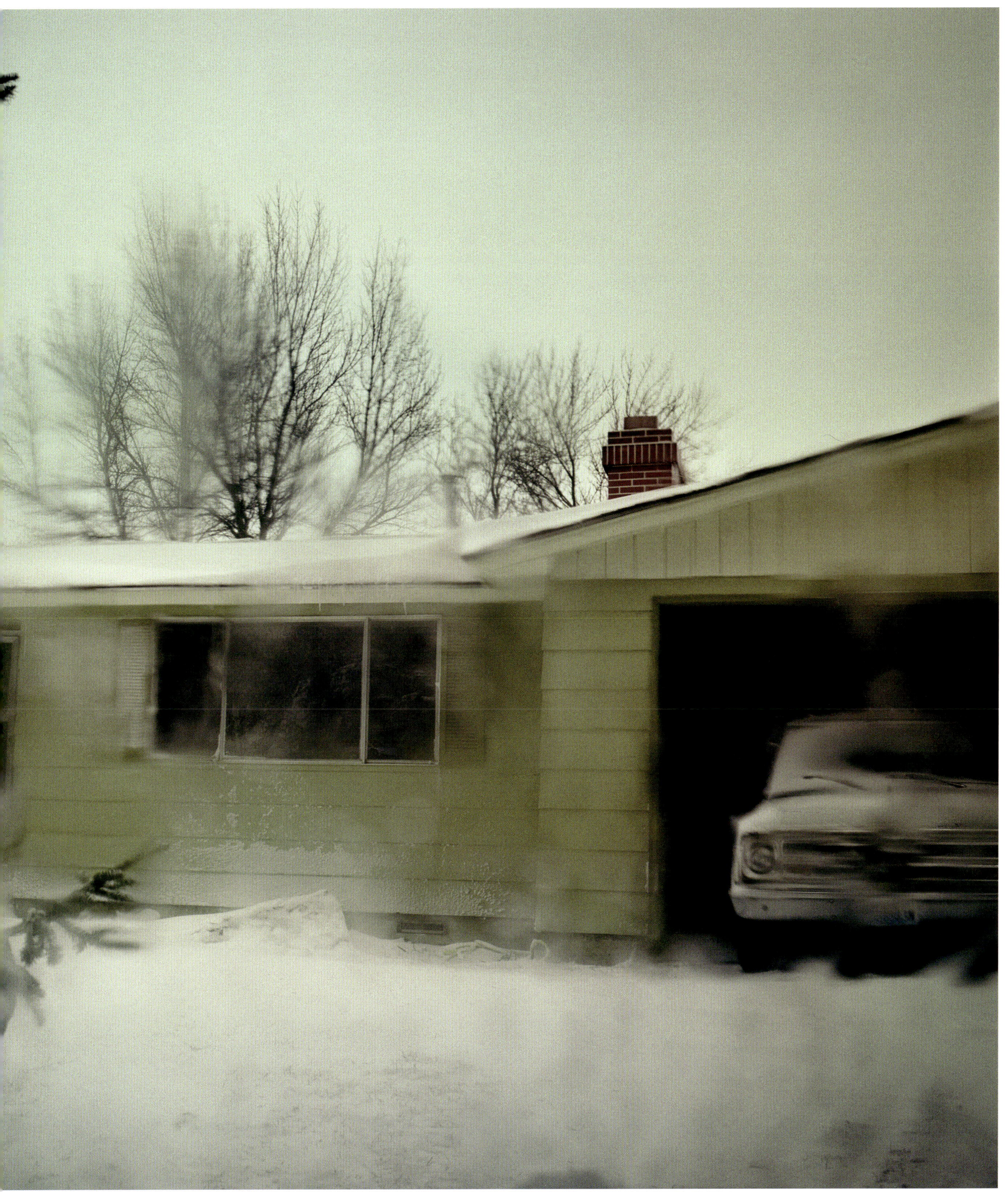

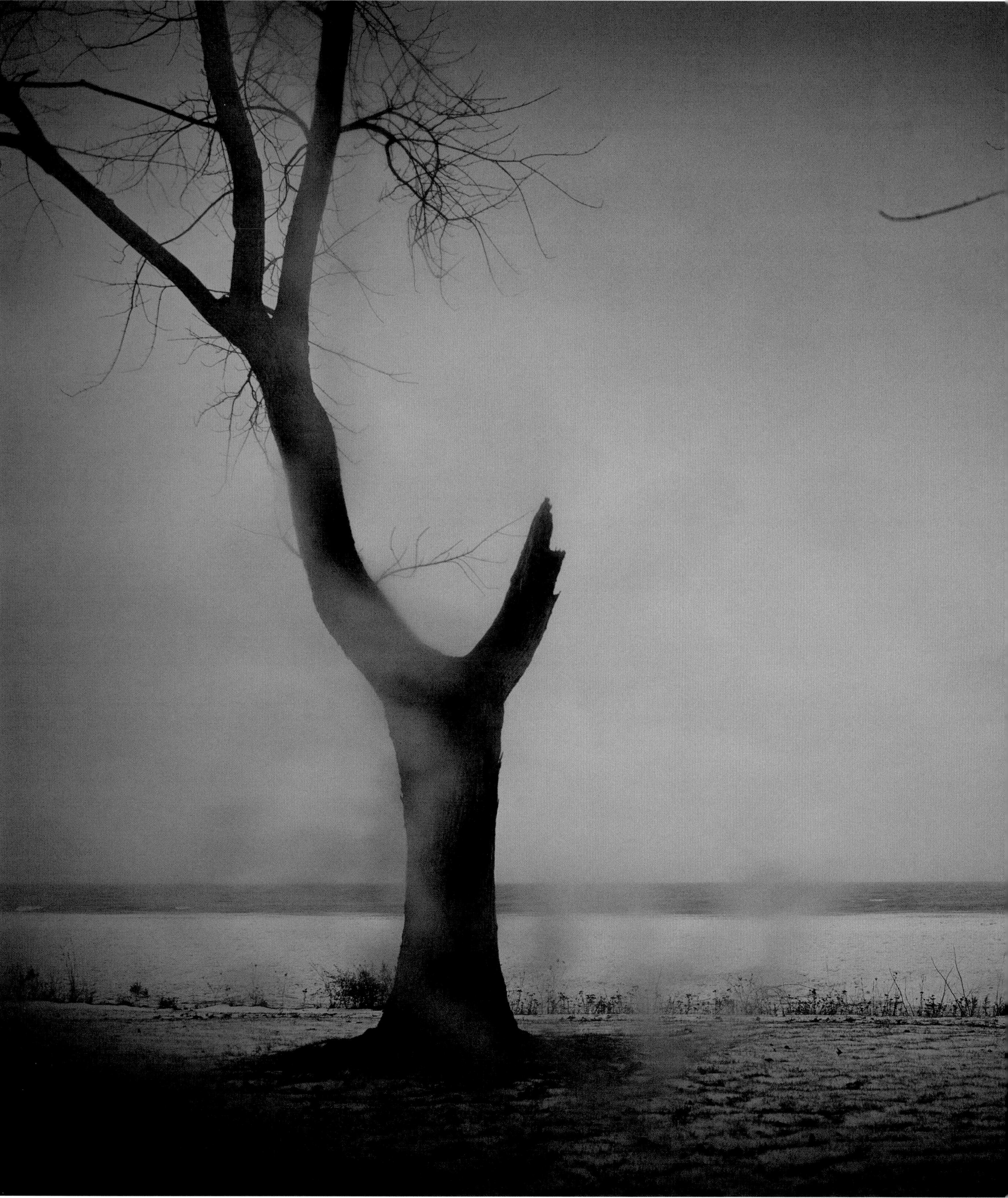

#10101 / Geneva on the Lake, OH / *Excerpts from Silver Meadows*

#10106 / *Geneva on the Lake, OH* / *Excerpts from Silver Meadows*

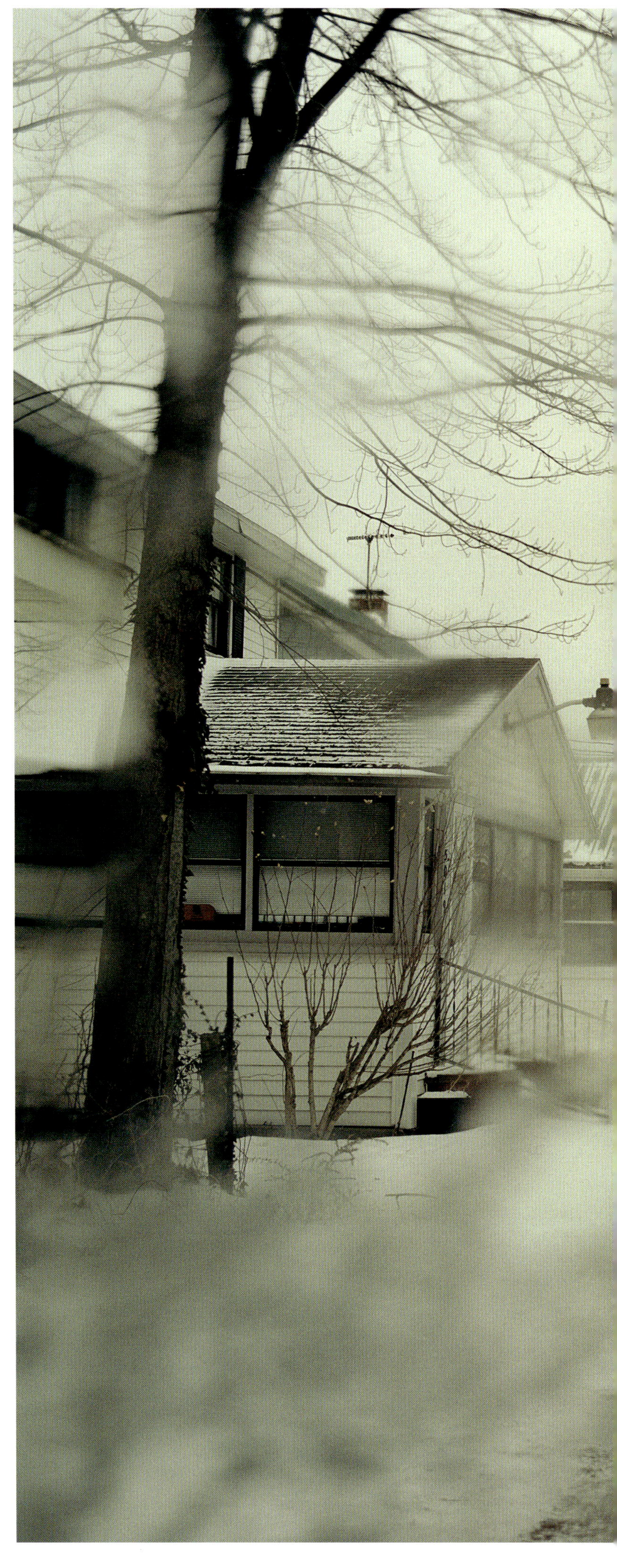

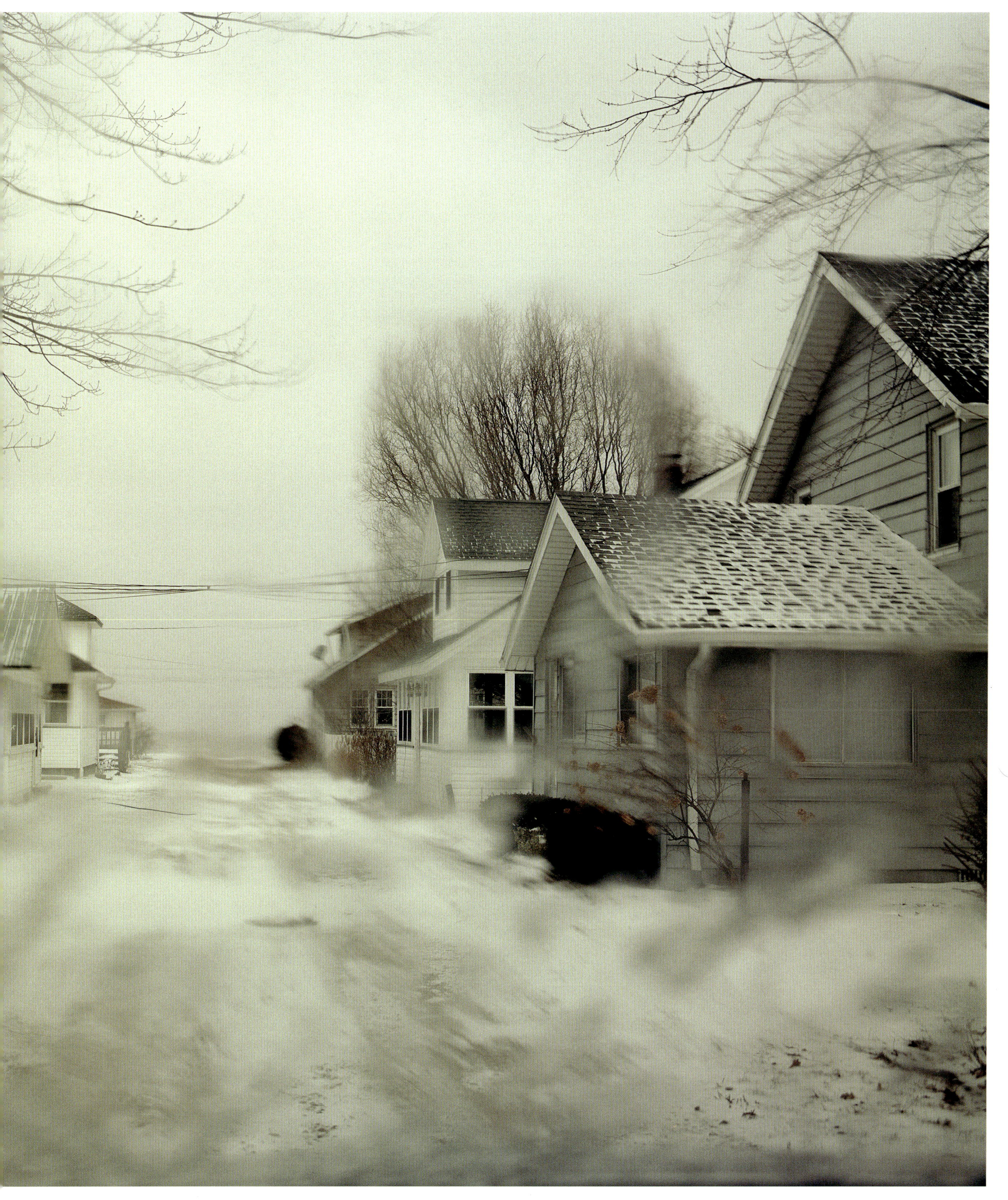

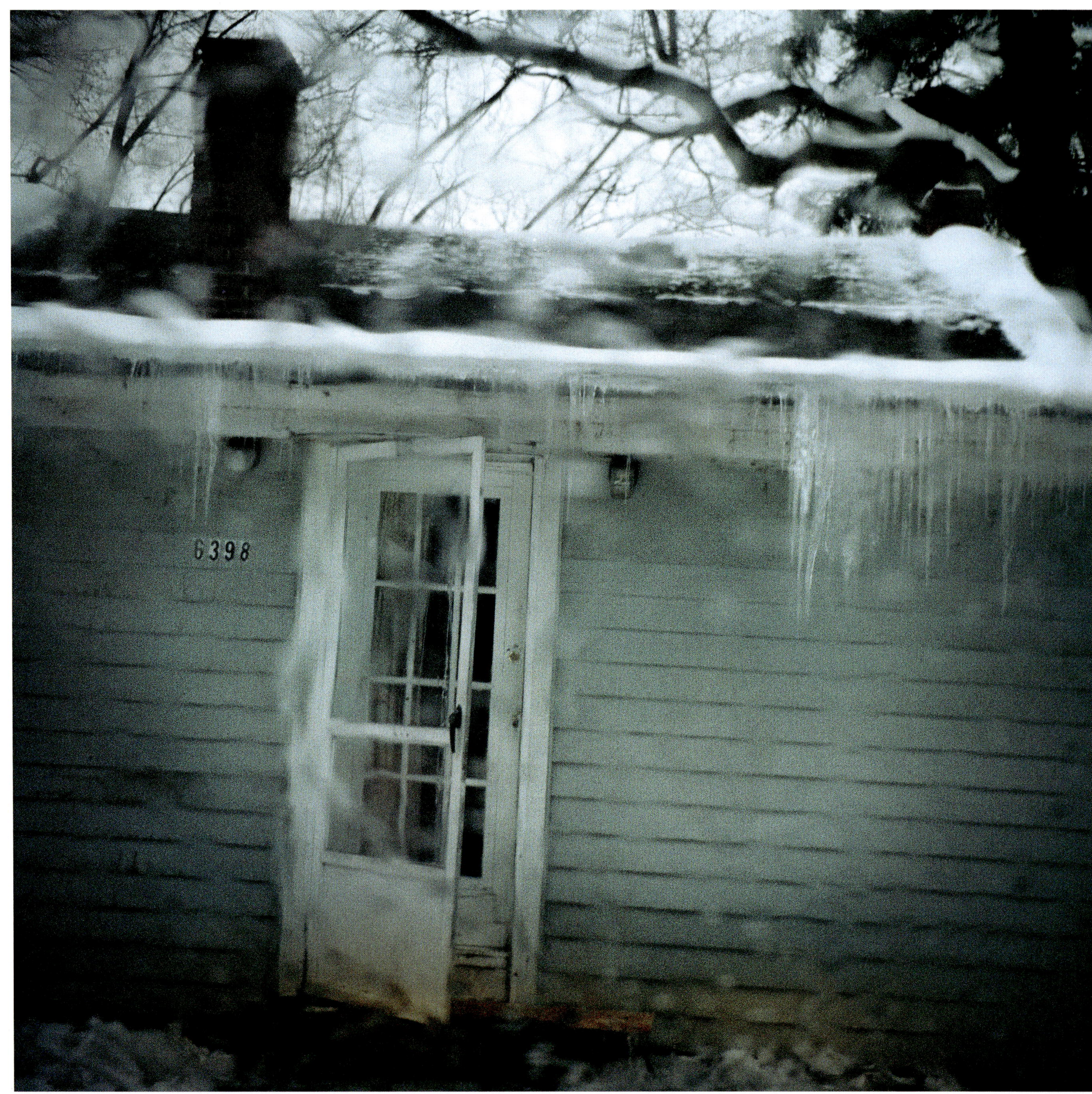
6398

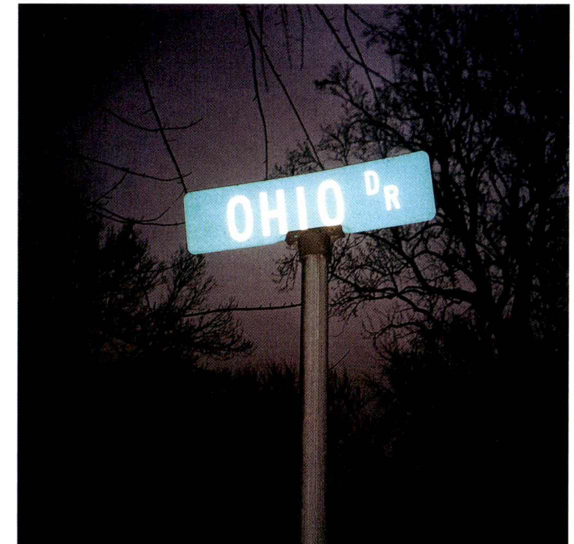

#10116-a / Brady Lake, OH / *Excerpts from Silver Meadows*   **#10121-a** / Conneaut, OH / *Excerpts from Silver Meadows*

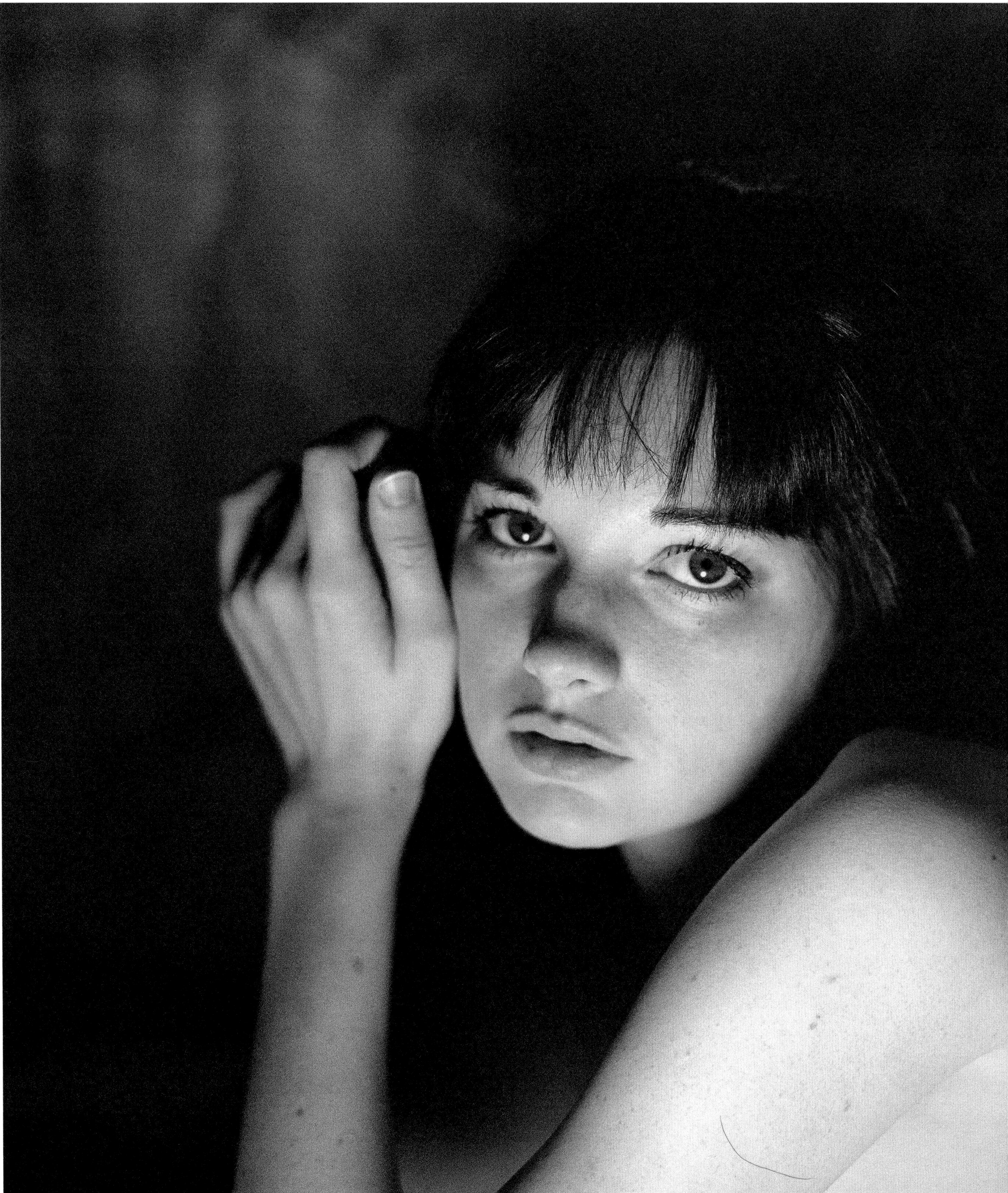

#10230 / Oakland, CA / *Excerpts from Silver Meadows* #10213 / Oakland, CA

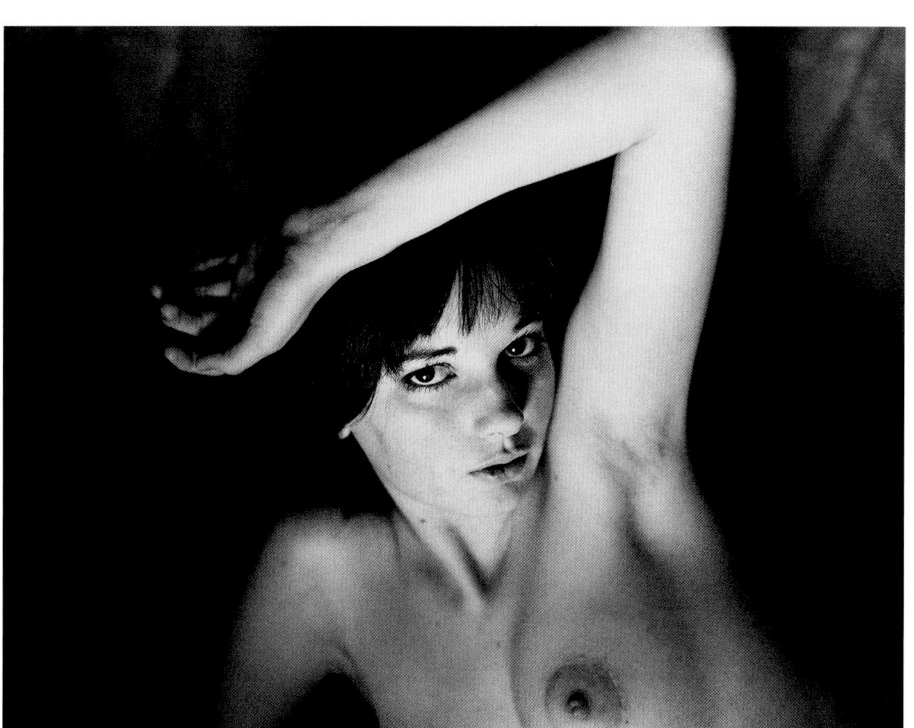

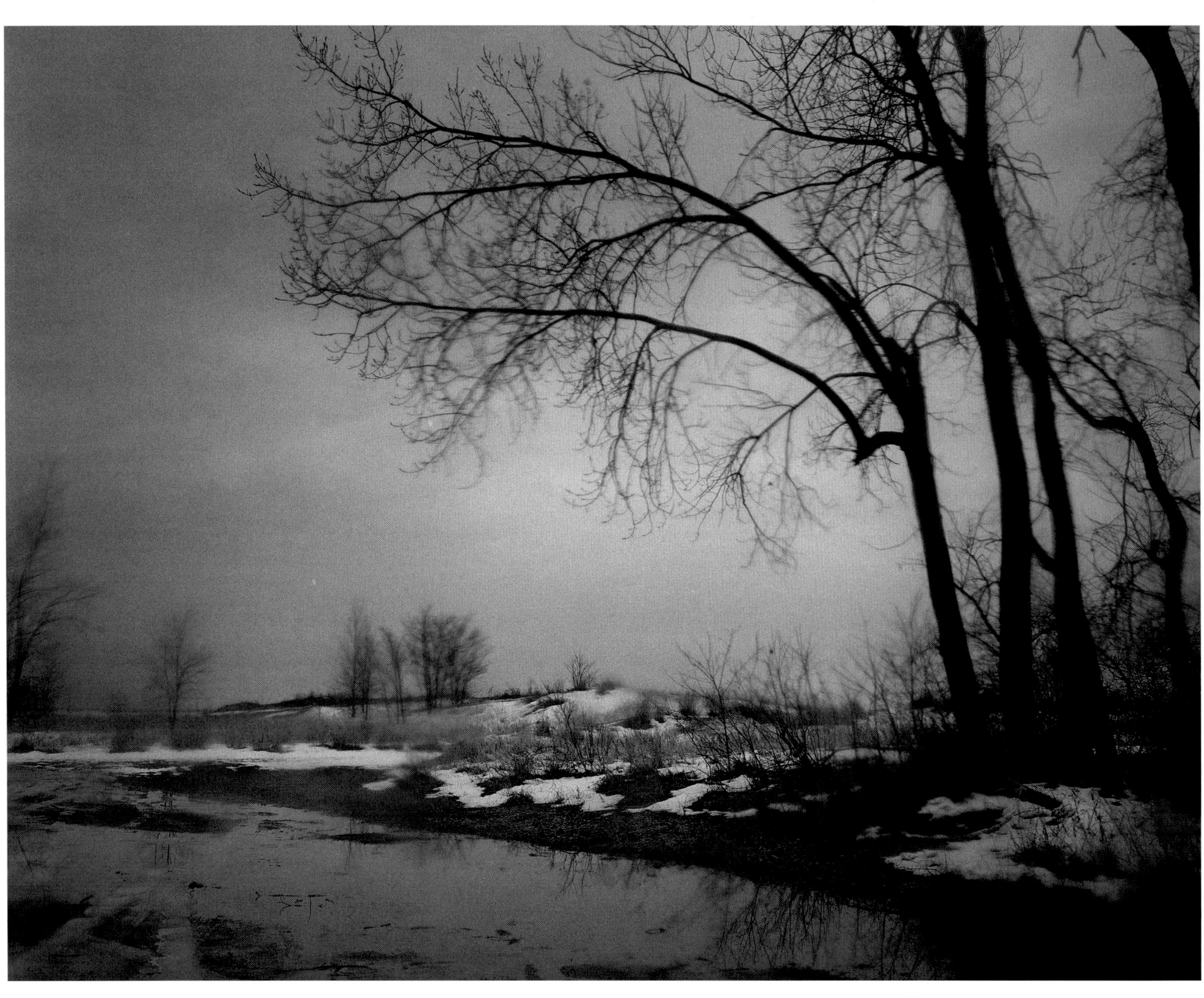

#10245-8 / Erie, PA / *Excerpts from Silver Meadows*

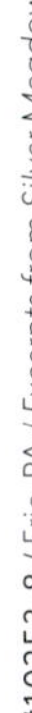

#10253-8 / Erie, PA / *Excerpts from Silver Meadows*

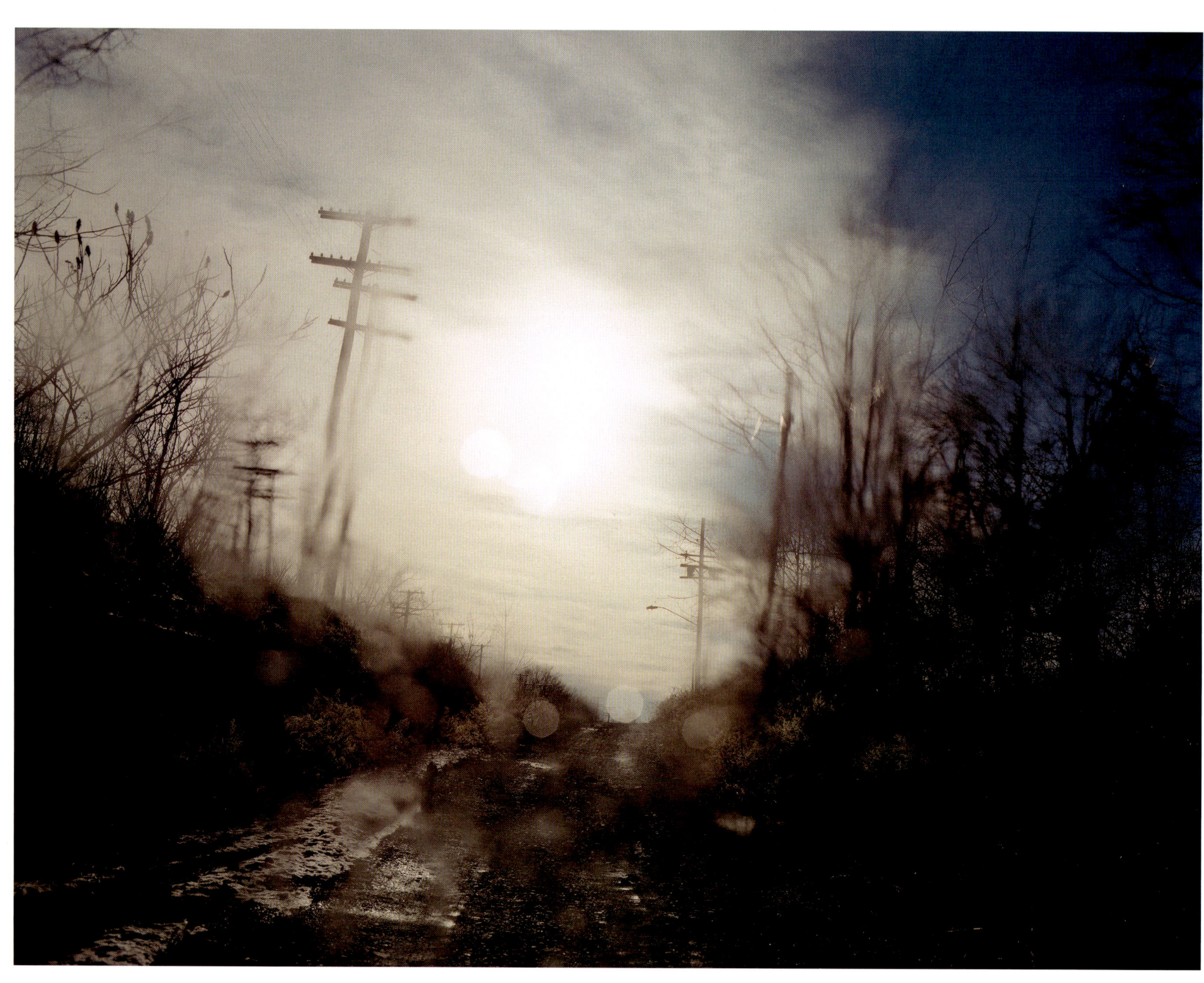

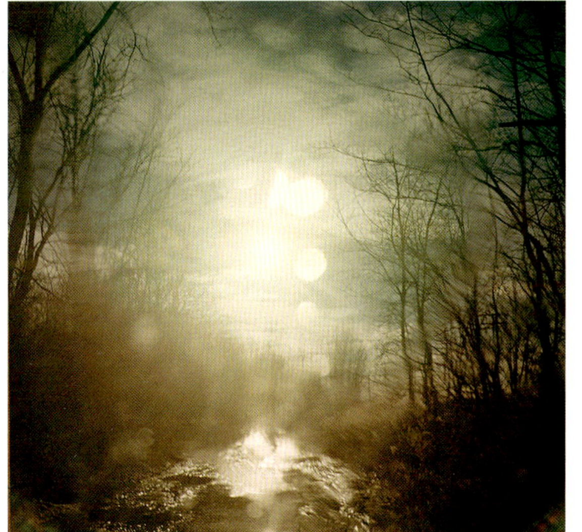

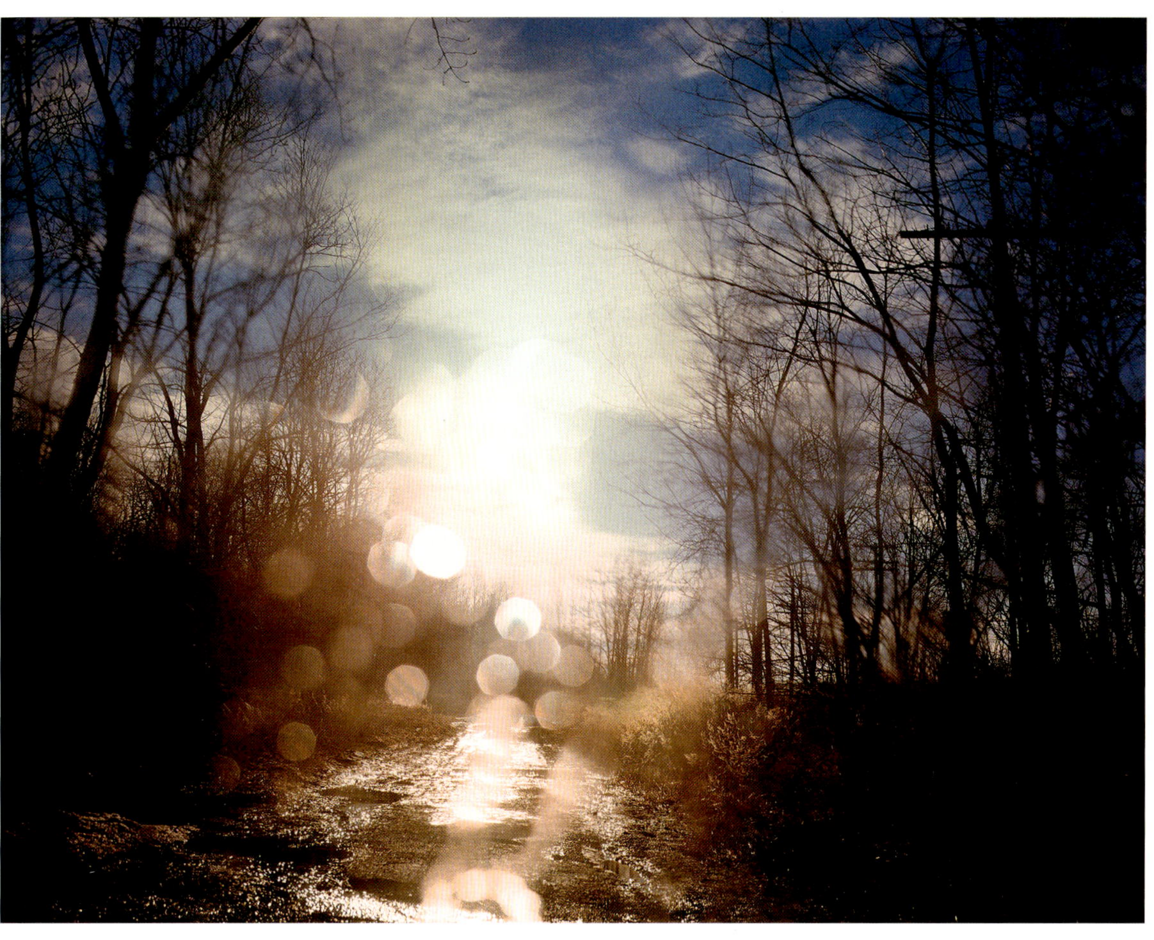

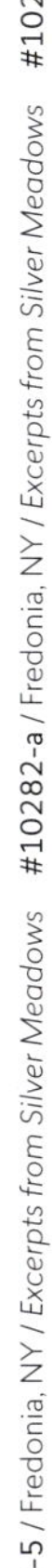

#10275-5 / Fredonia, NY / *Excerpts from Silver Meadows* **#10282-a** / Fredonia, NY / *Excerpts from Silver Meadows* **#10276** / Fredonia, NY

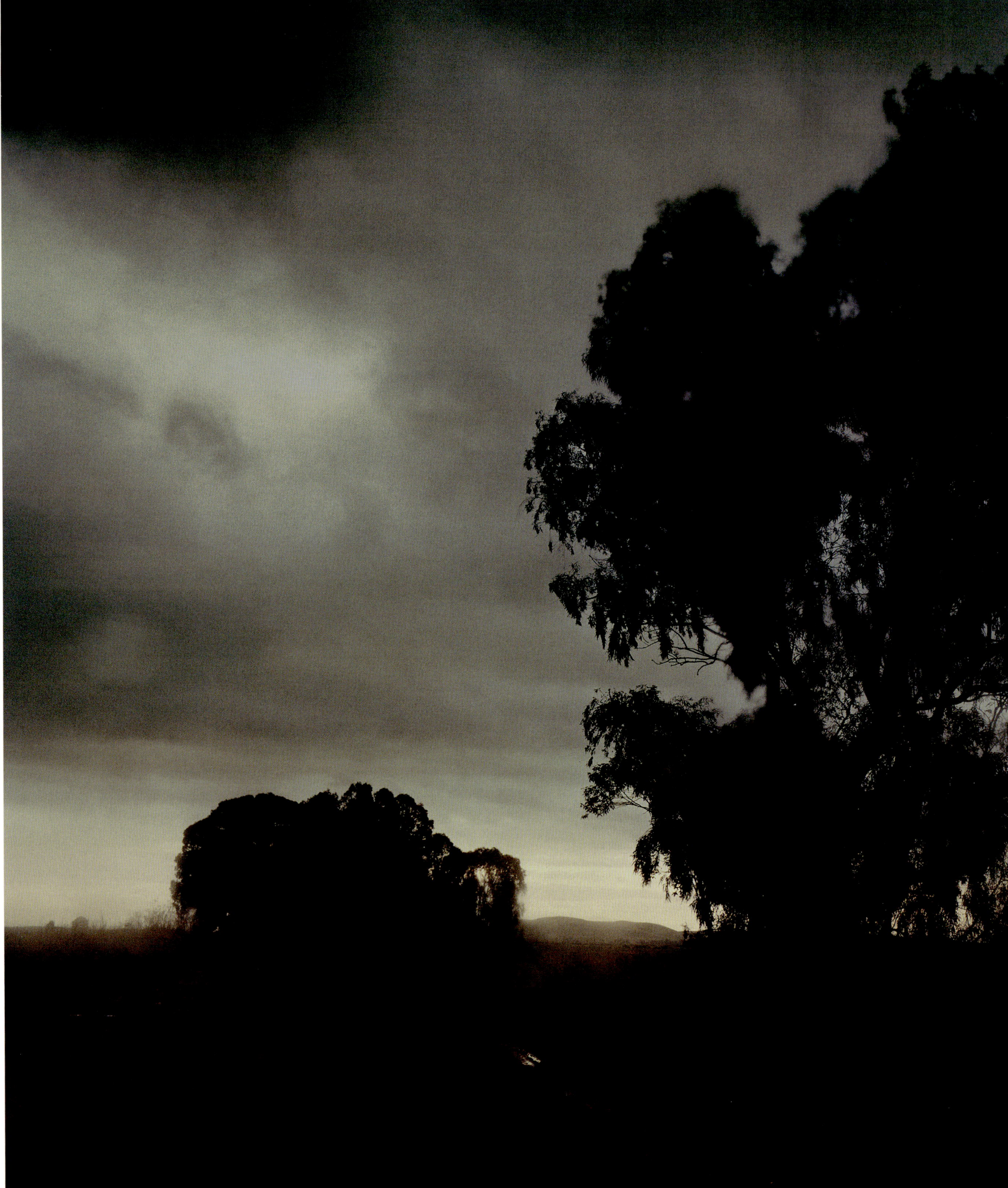

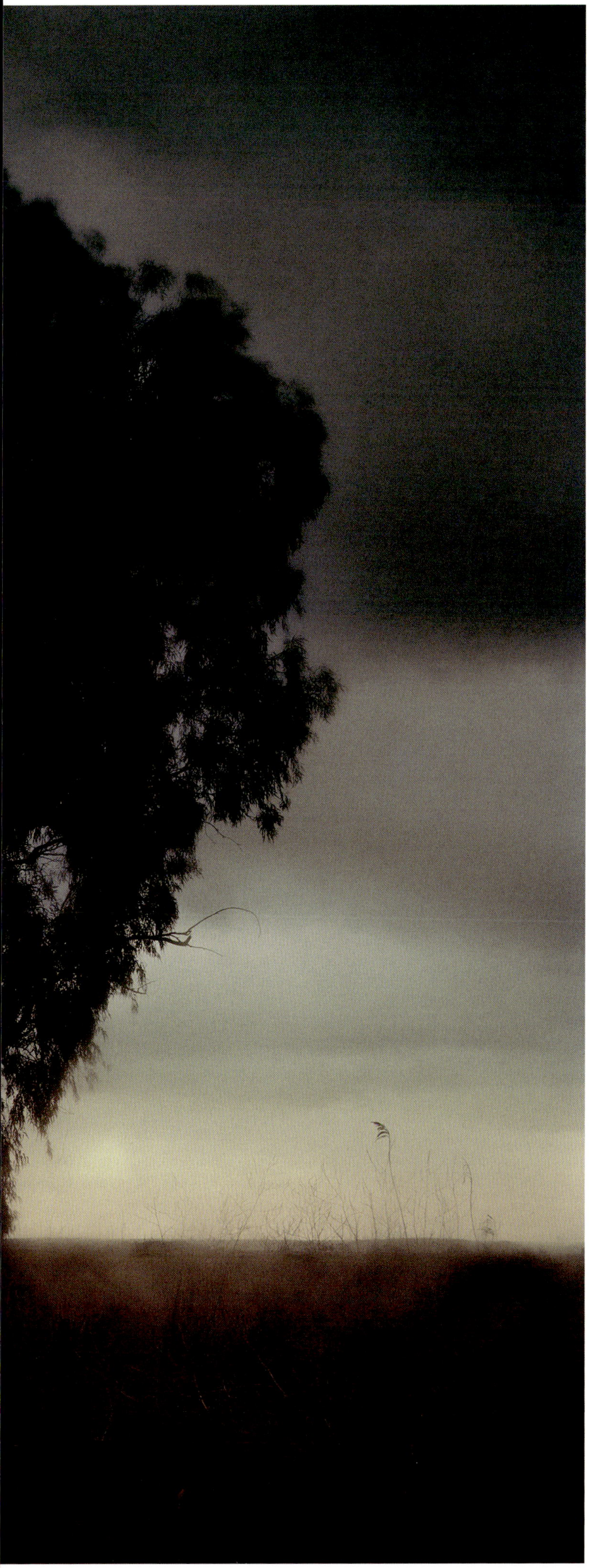

#10320 / Bird's Landing, CA #10472-barry-self-edit / family album

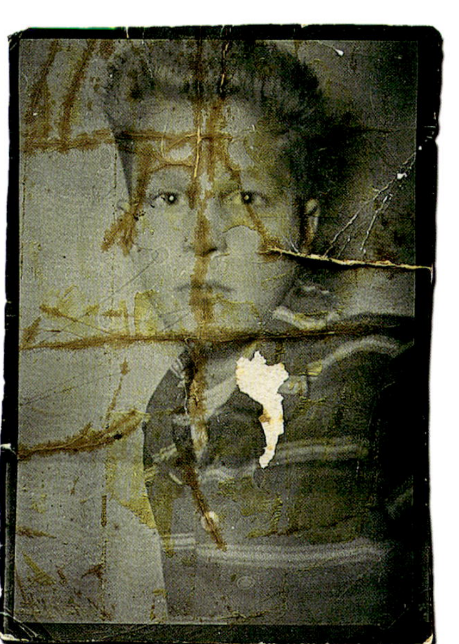

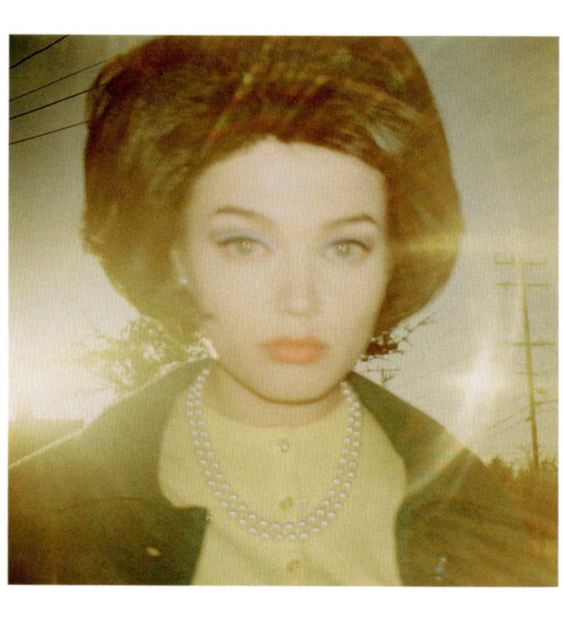

#10474-c / Alameda, CA / *Excerpts from Silver Meadows*   #10477-11 / Alameda, CA / *Excerpts from Silver Meadows*

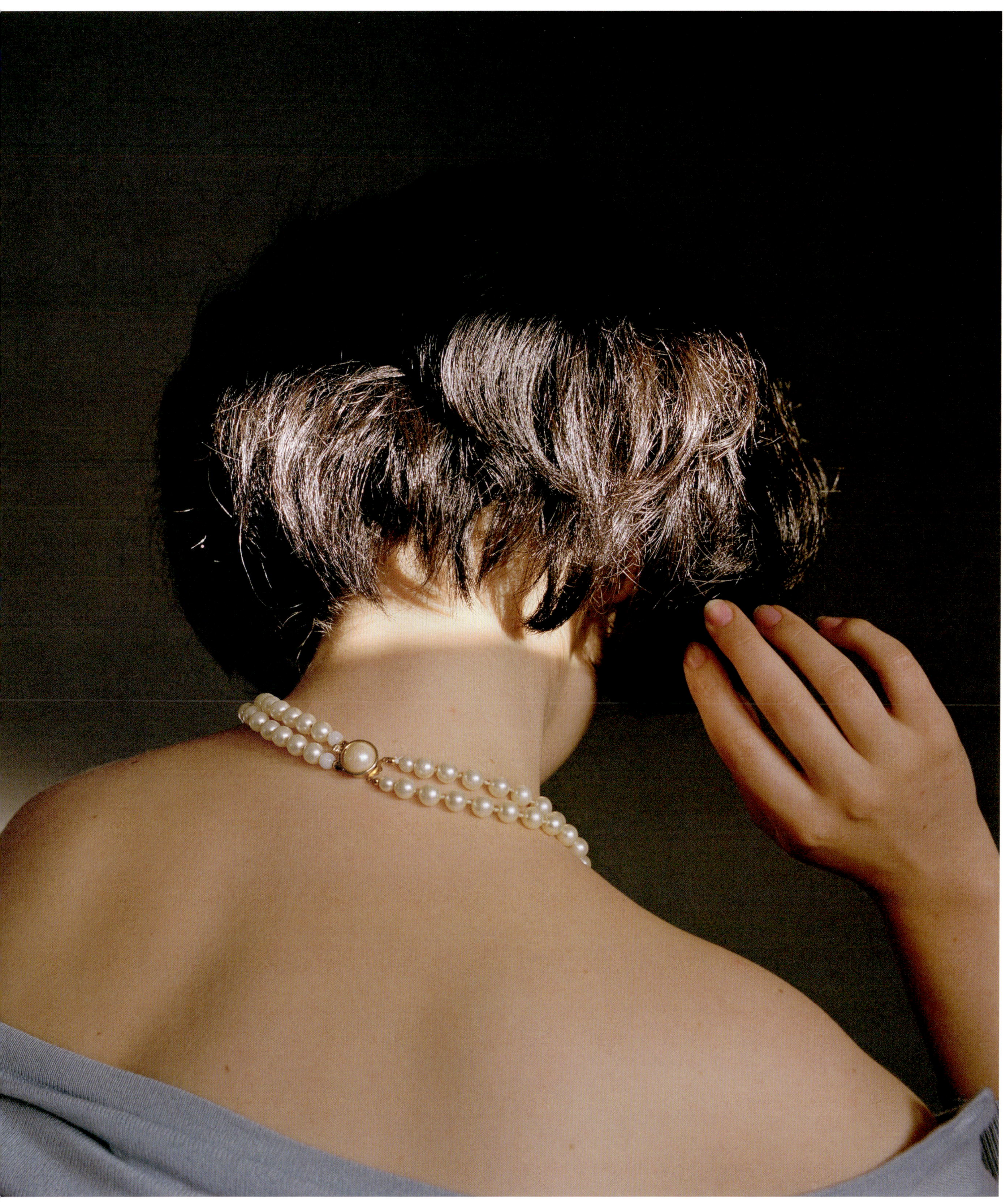

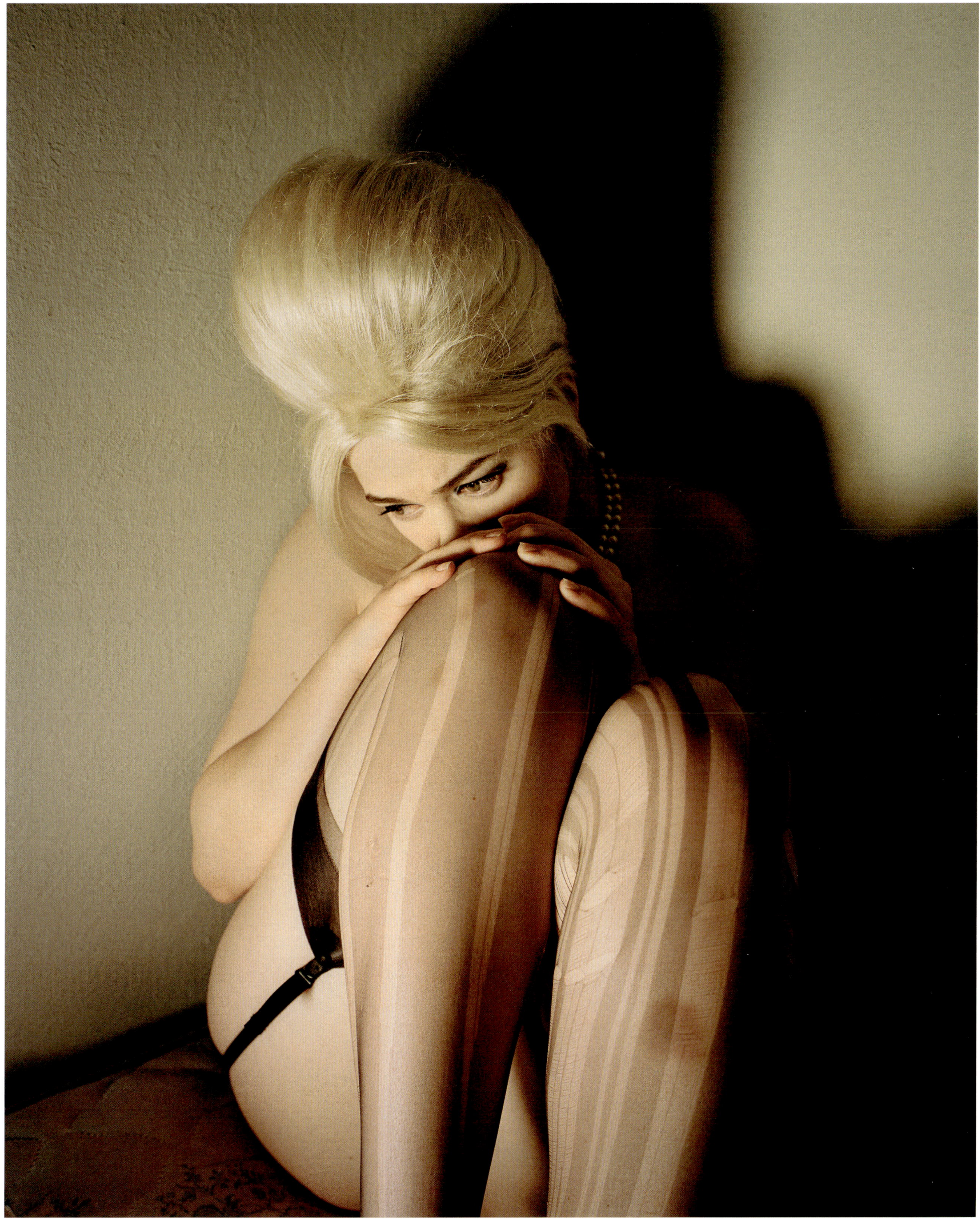

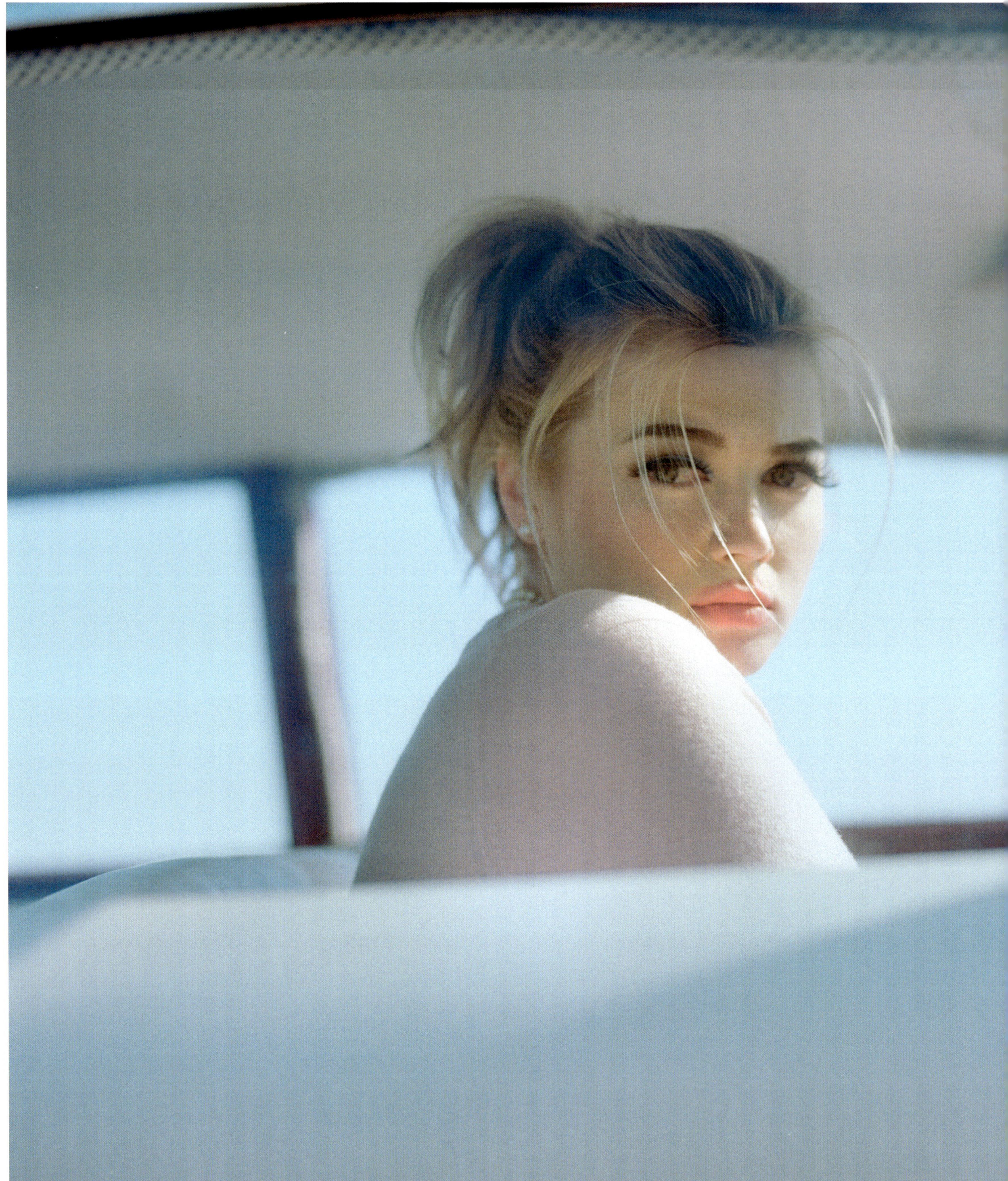

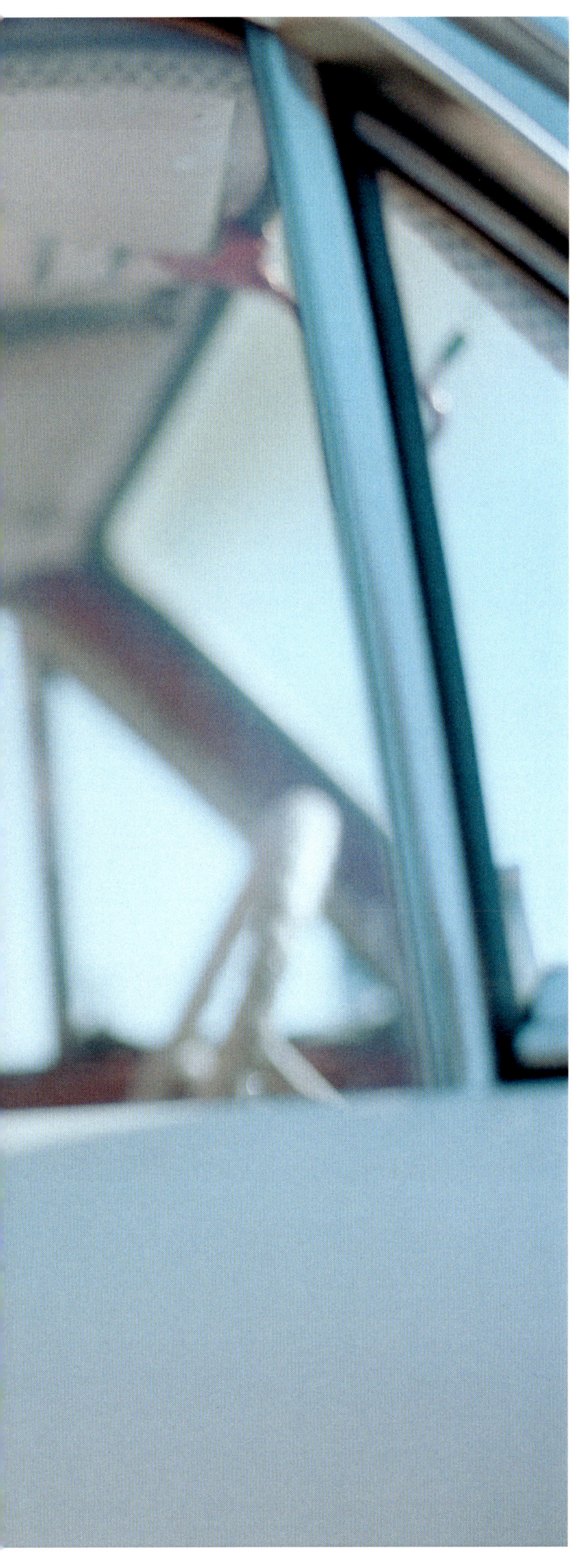

#10504-9 / Alameda, CA

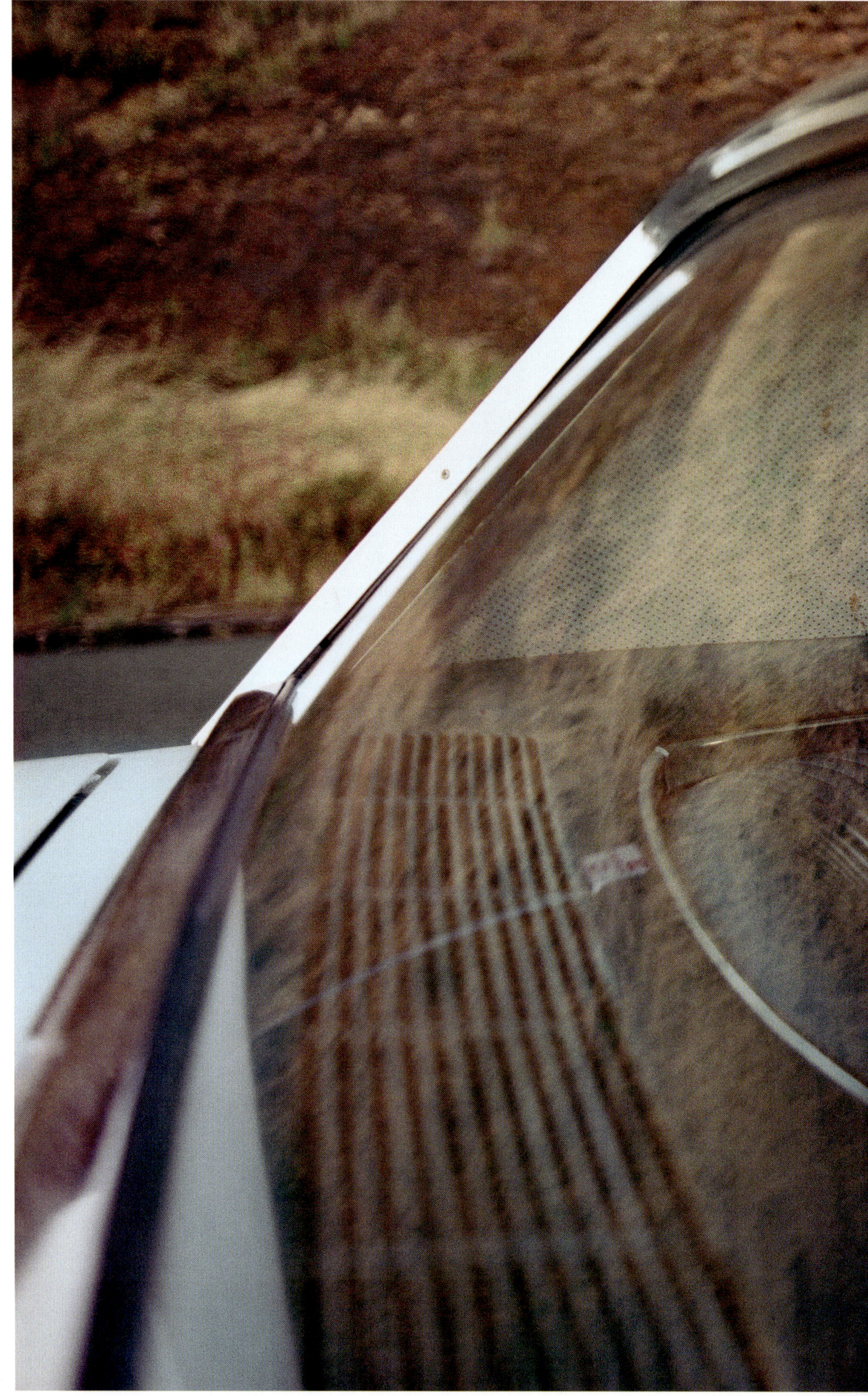

#10552-c / San Francisco, CA

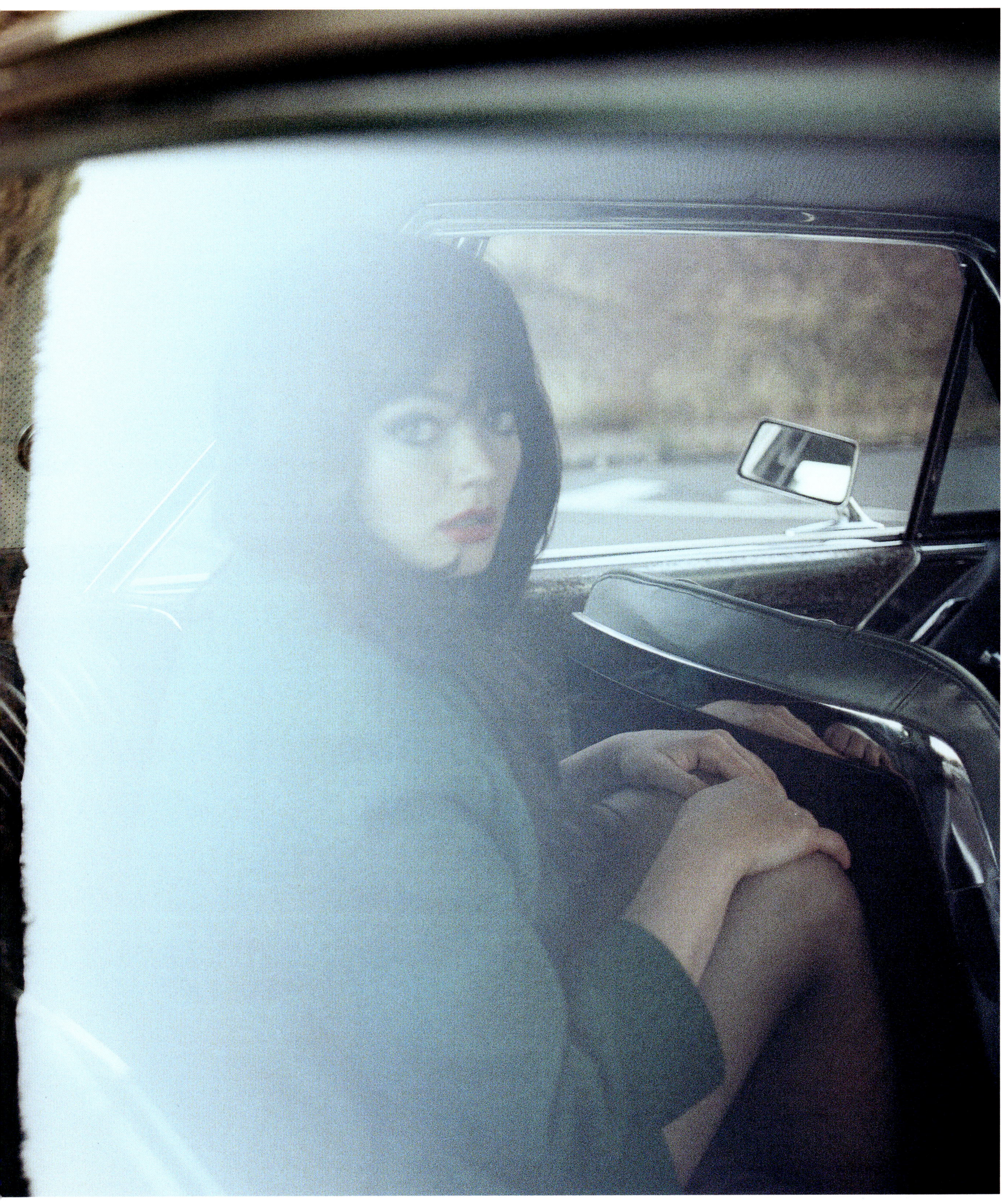

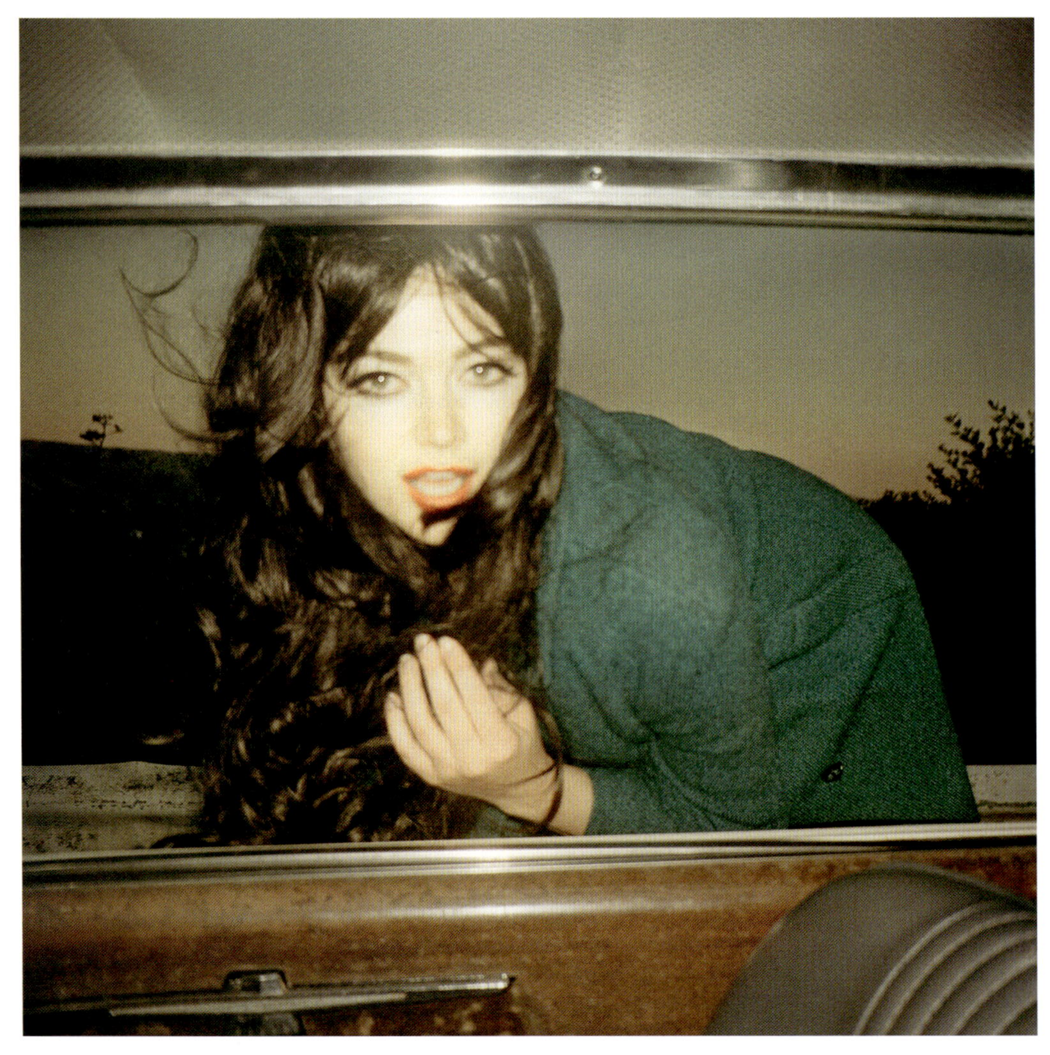

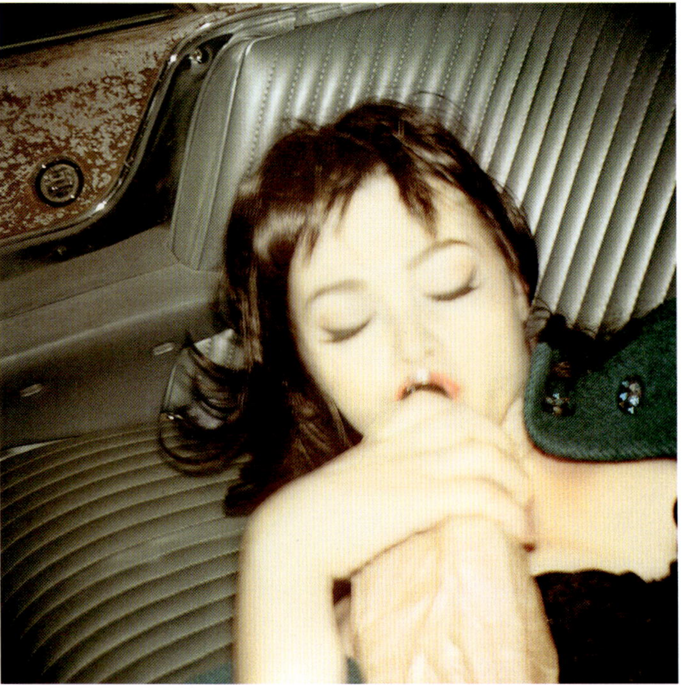

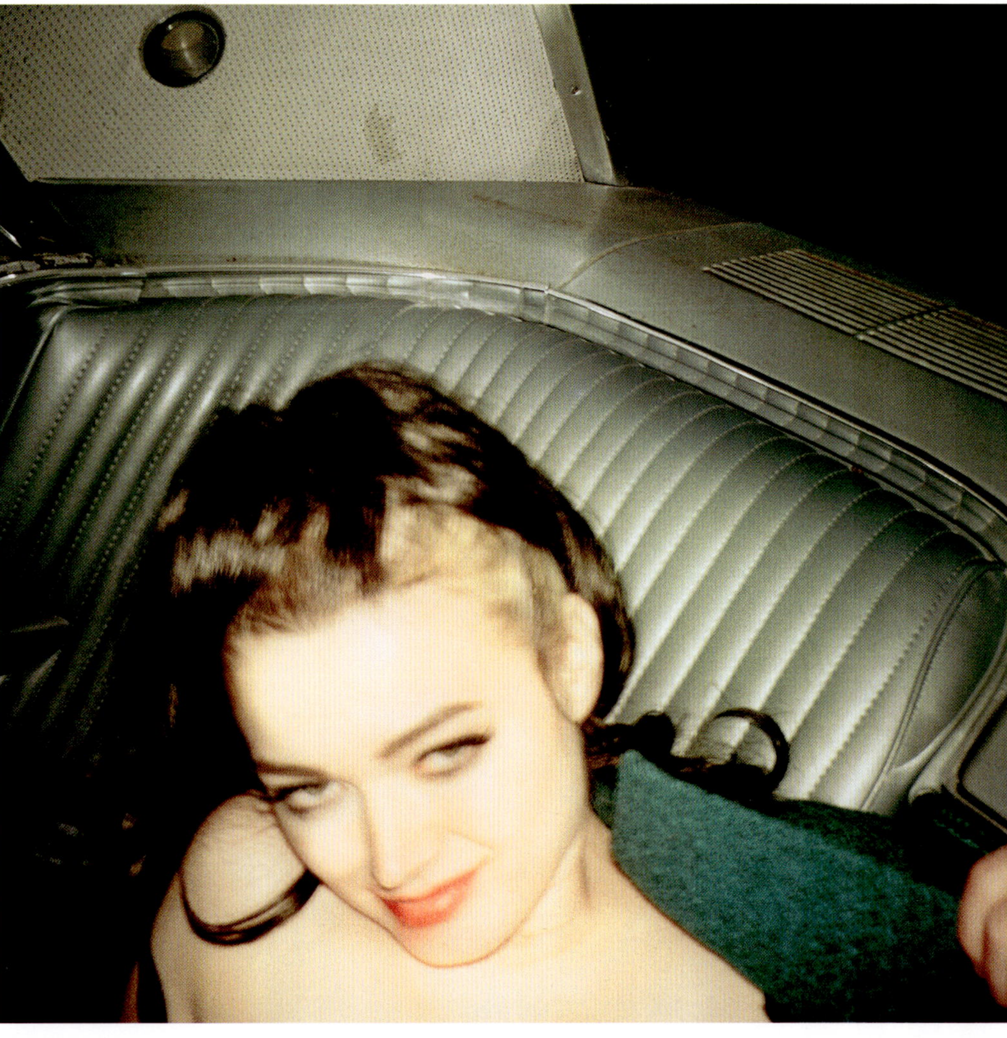

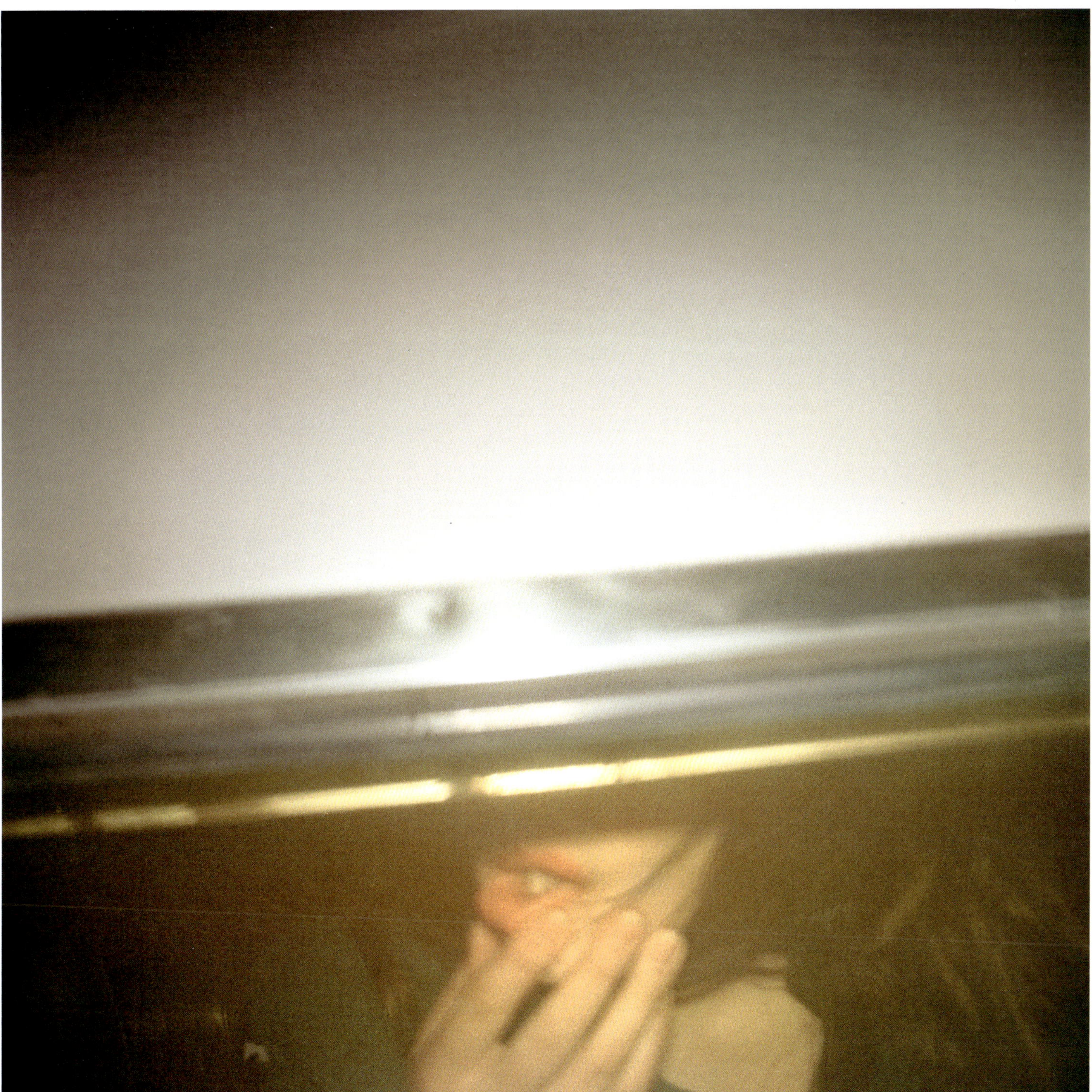

#10574-a / San Francisco, CA / *Excerpts from Silver Meadows*   **#10573-a** / San Francisco, CA / *Excerpts from Silver Meadows*   **#10573-b** / San Francisco, CA / *Excerpts from Silver Meadows*   **#10578-d** / San Francisco, CA / *Excerpts from Silver Meadows*

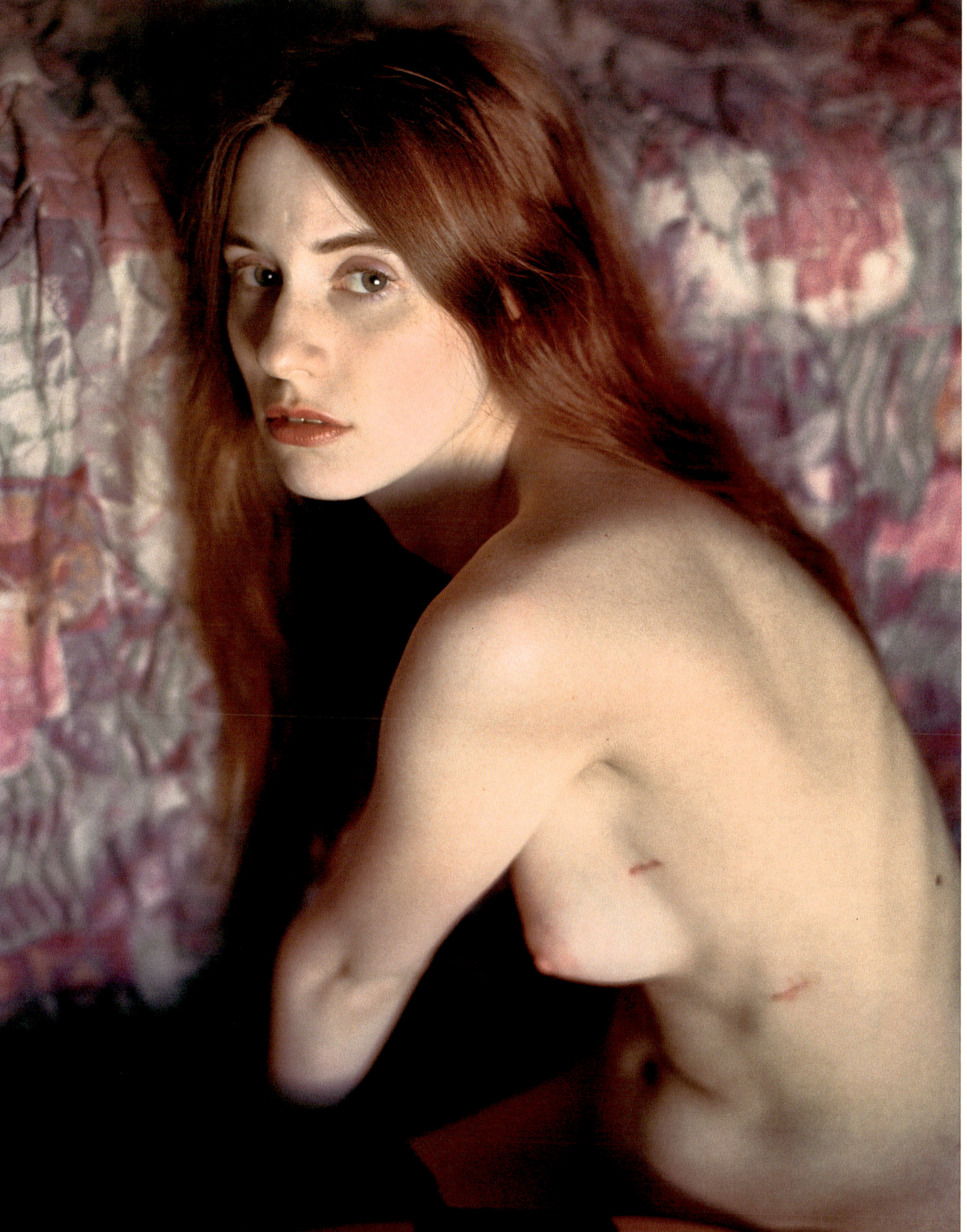

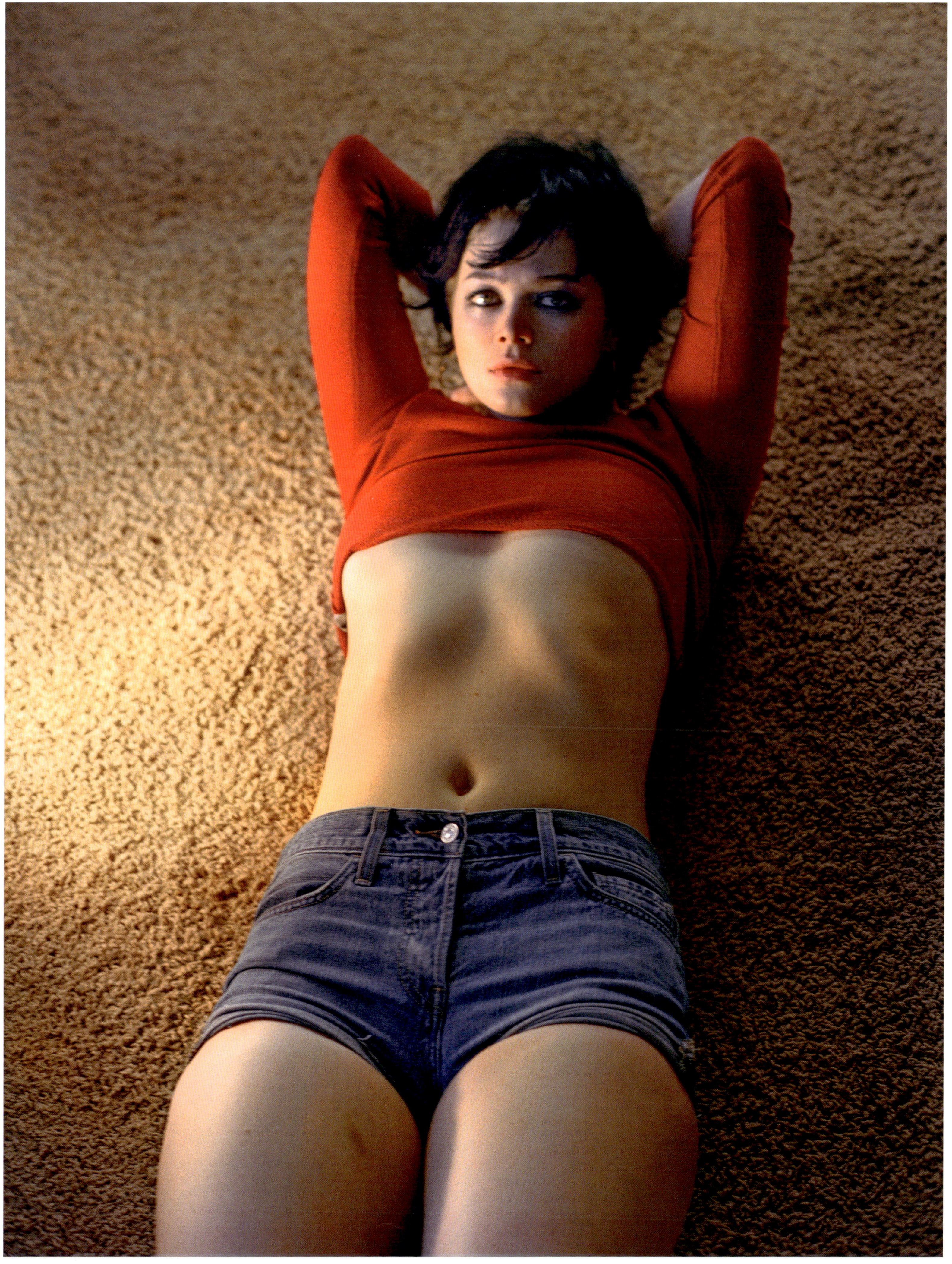

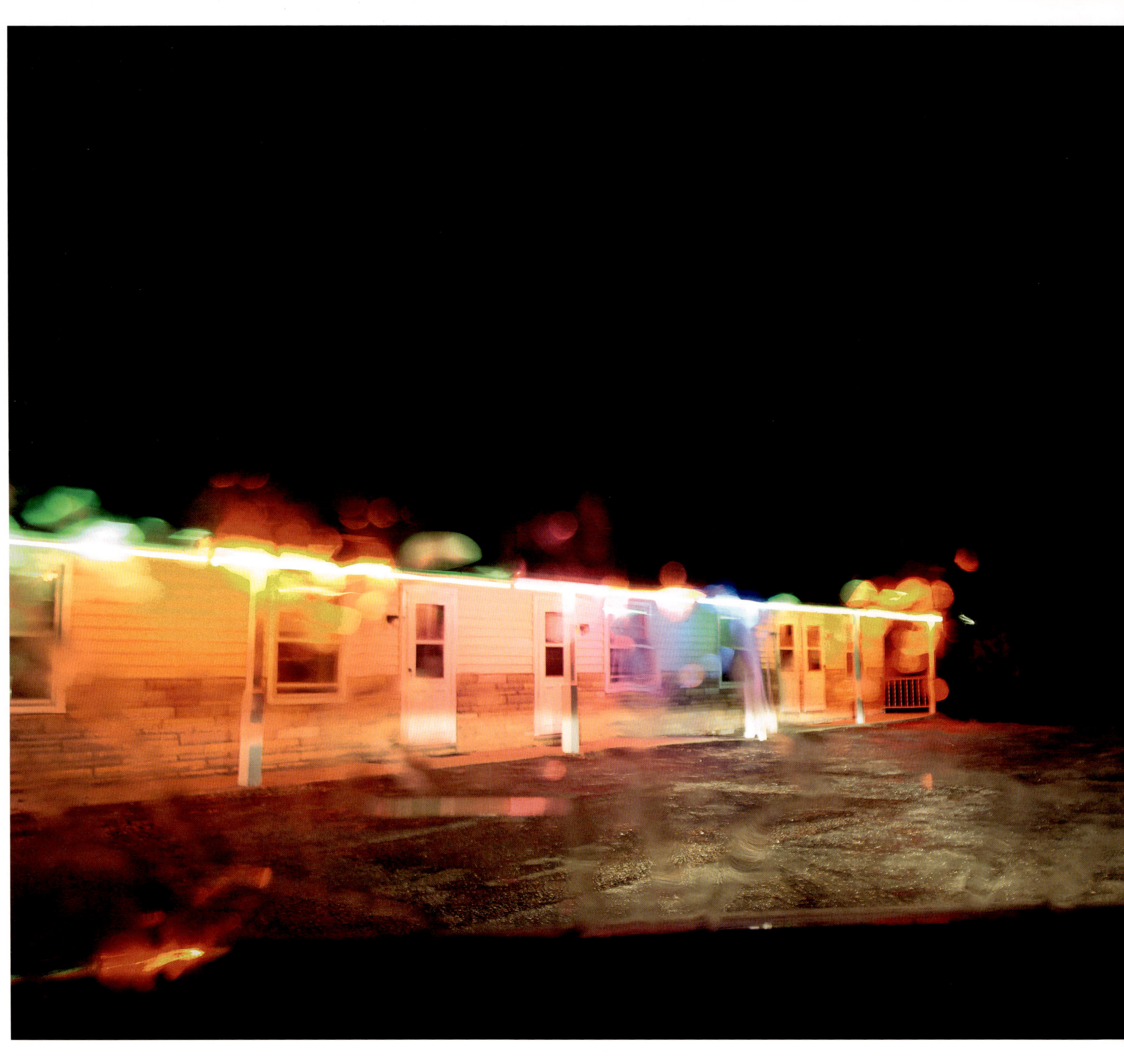

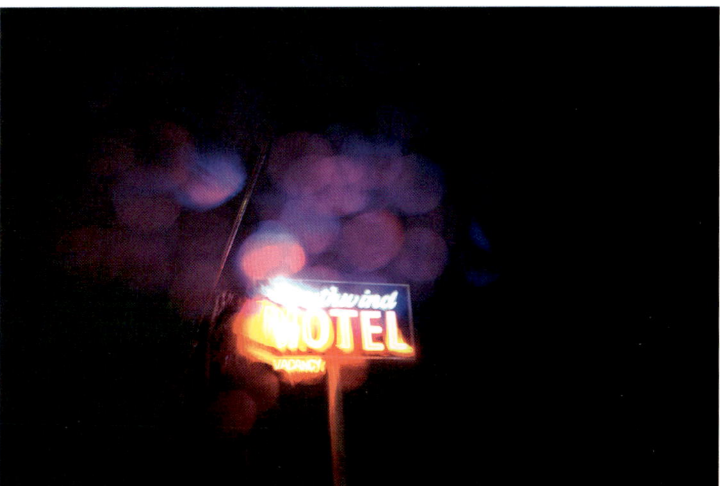

#10789-2109 / Erie, PA / *Excerpts from Silver Meadows*   **#10759-1221** / Houston, TX / *Excerpts from Silver Meadows*

#10690-1 / Oakland, CA / *Excerpts from Silver Meadows*

#10827-12 / Streetsboro, OH

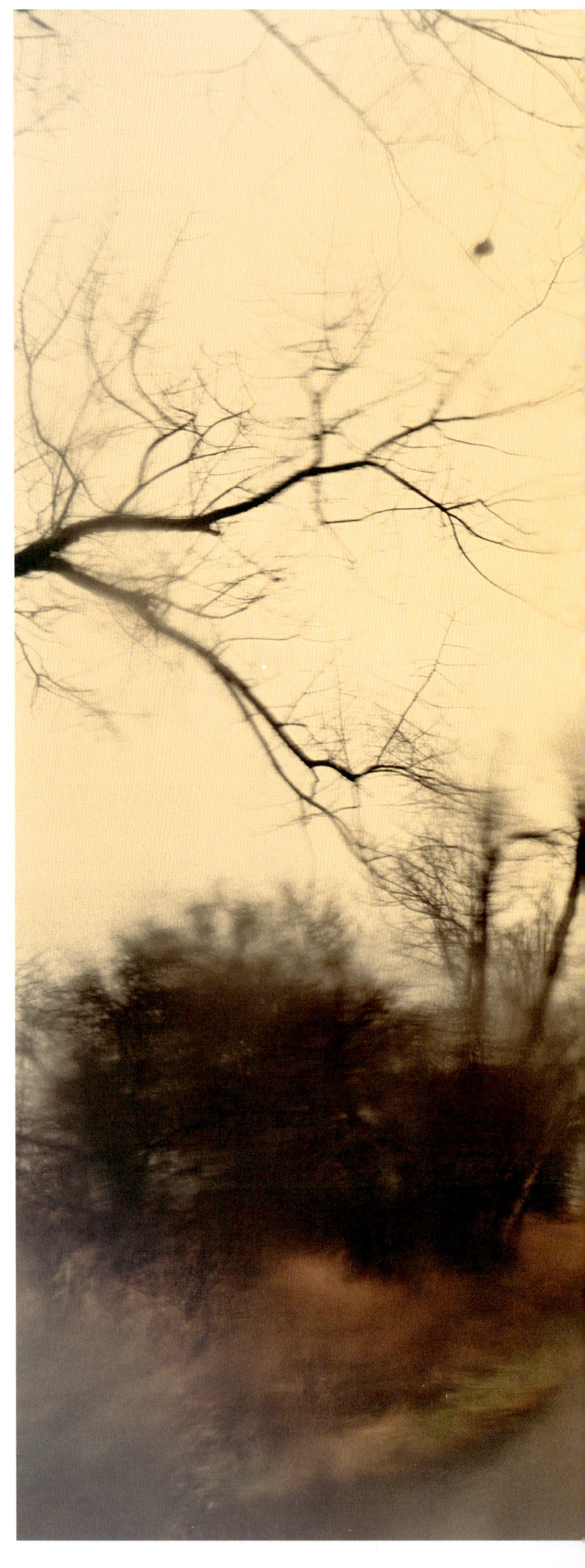

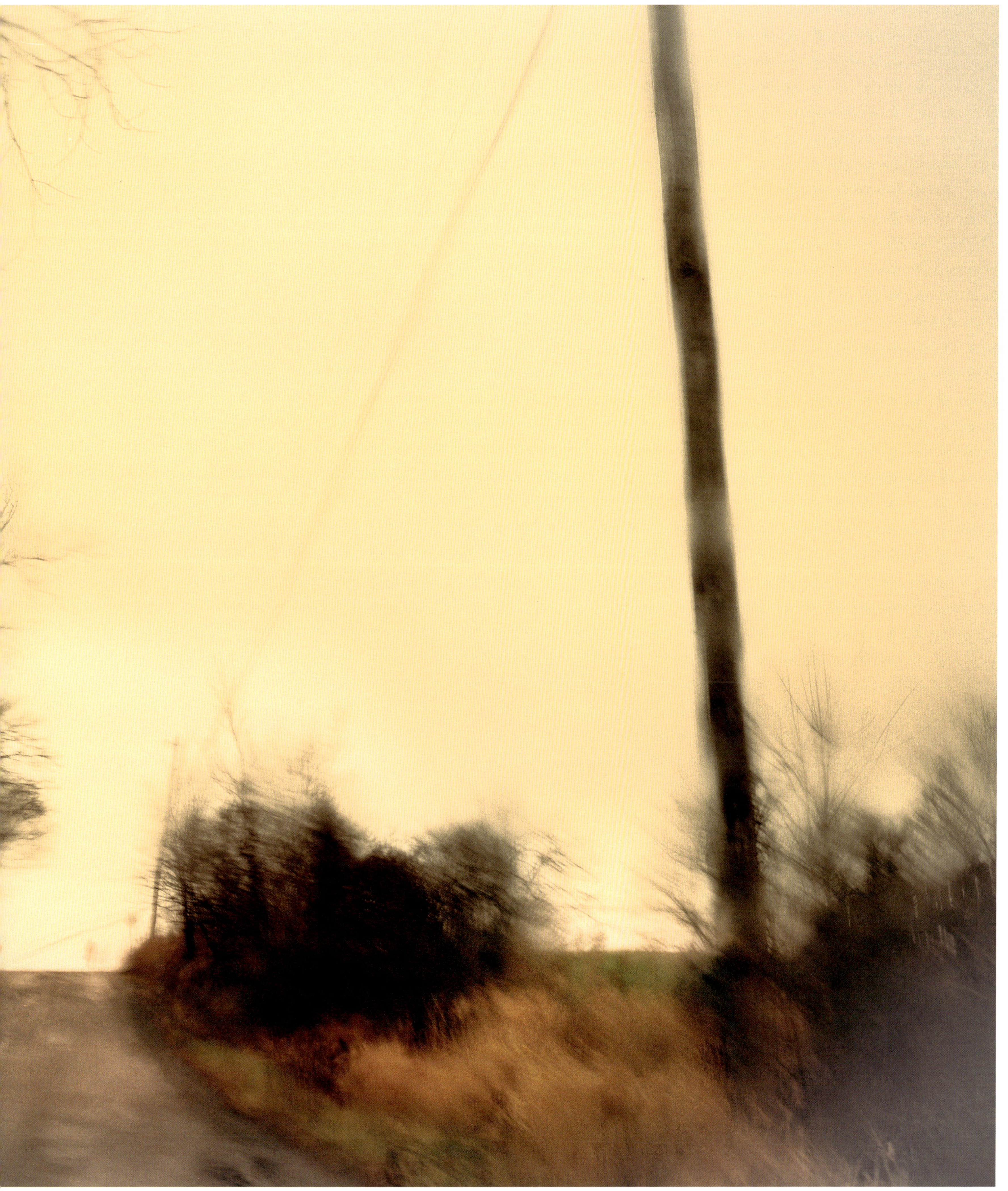

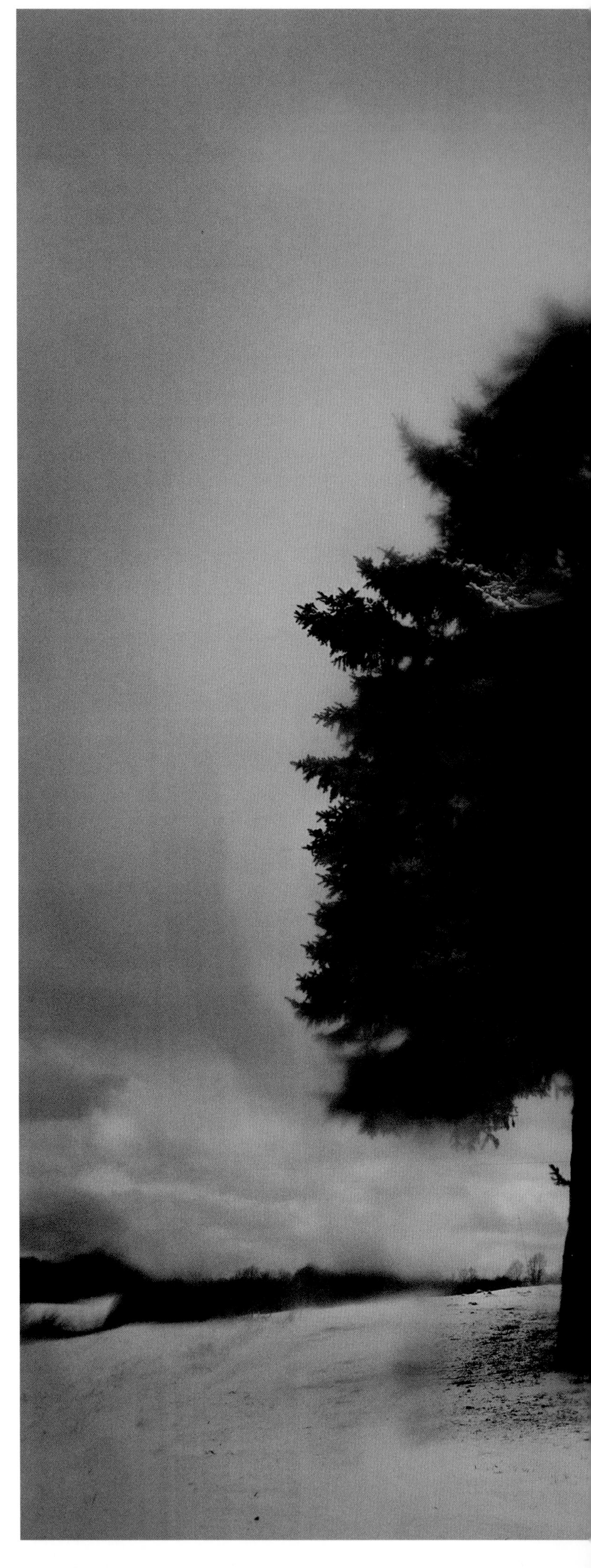

#10845-7 / Streetsboro, OH / *Excerpts from Silver Meadows*

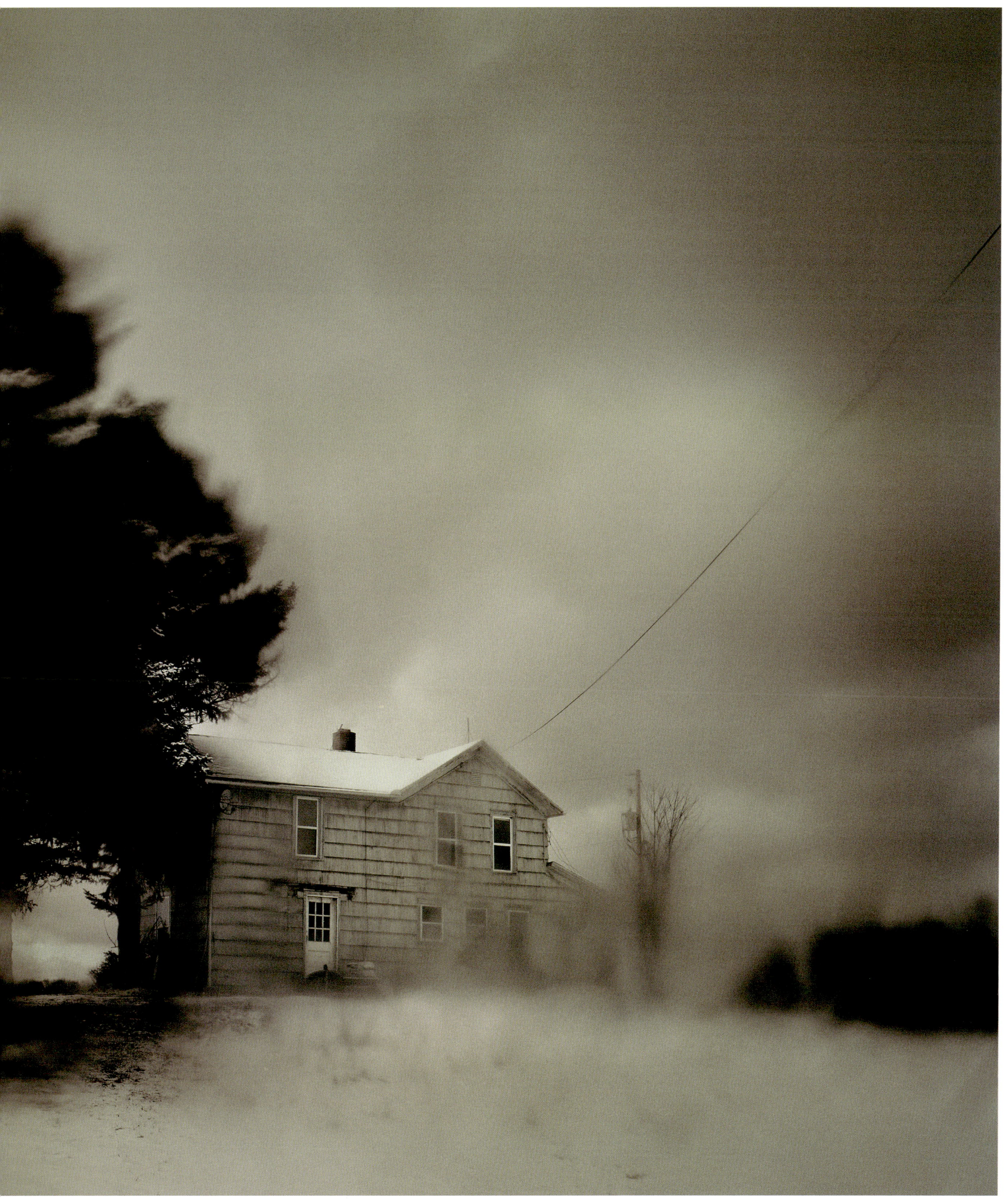

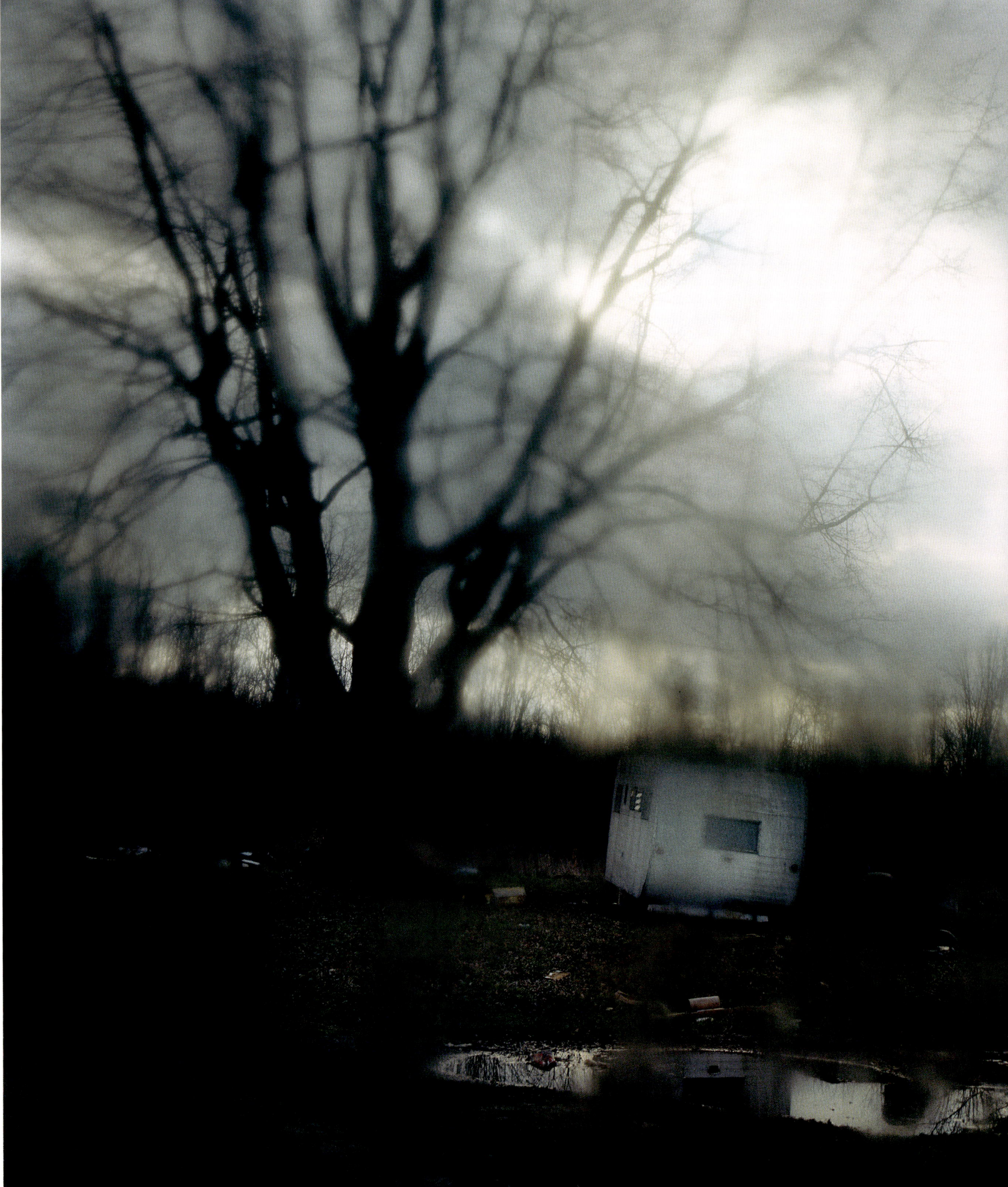

#10854-7 / West Springfield, PA / *Excerpts from Silver Meadows*

#10845-fd-panties-off / found and altered / *Excerpts from Silver Meadows*

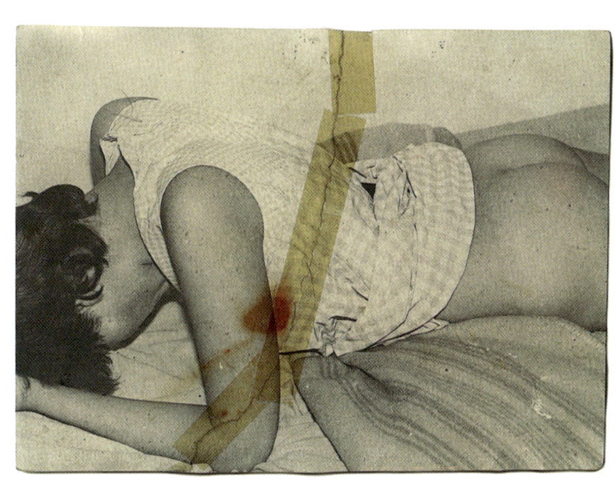

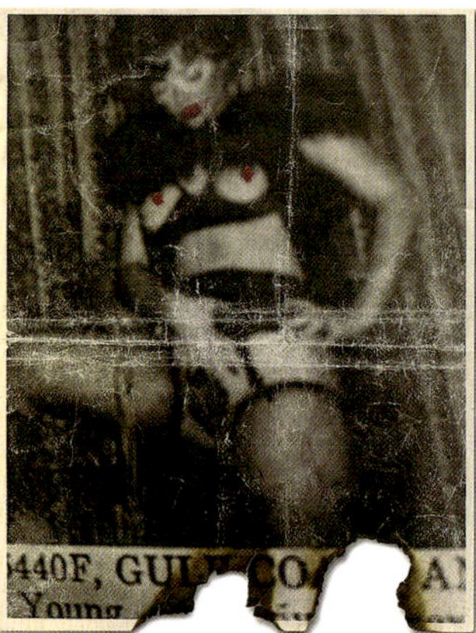

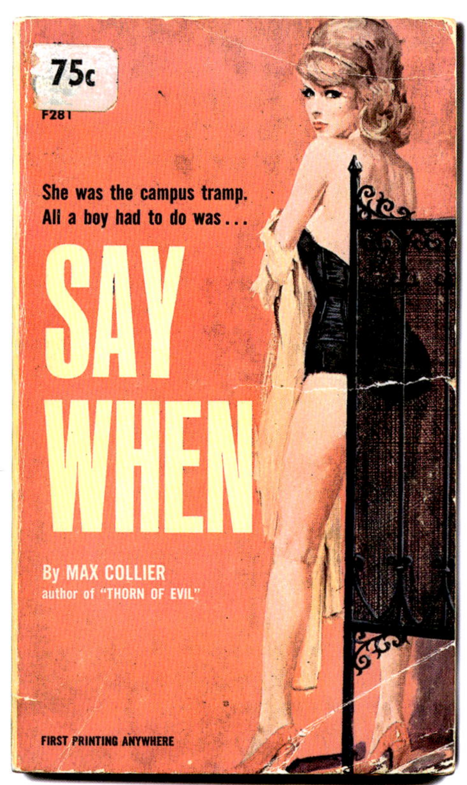

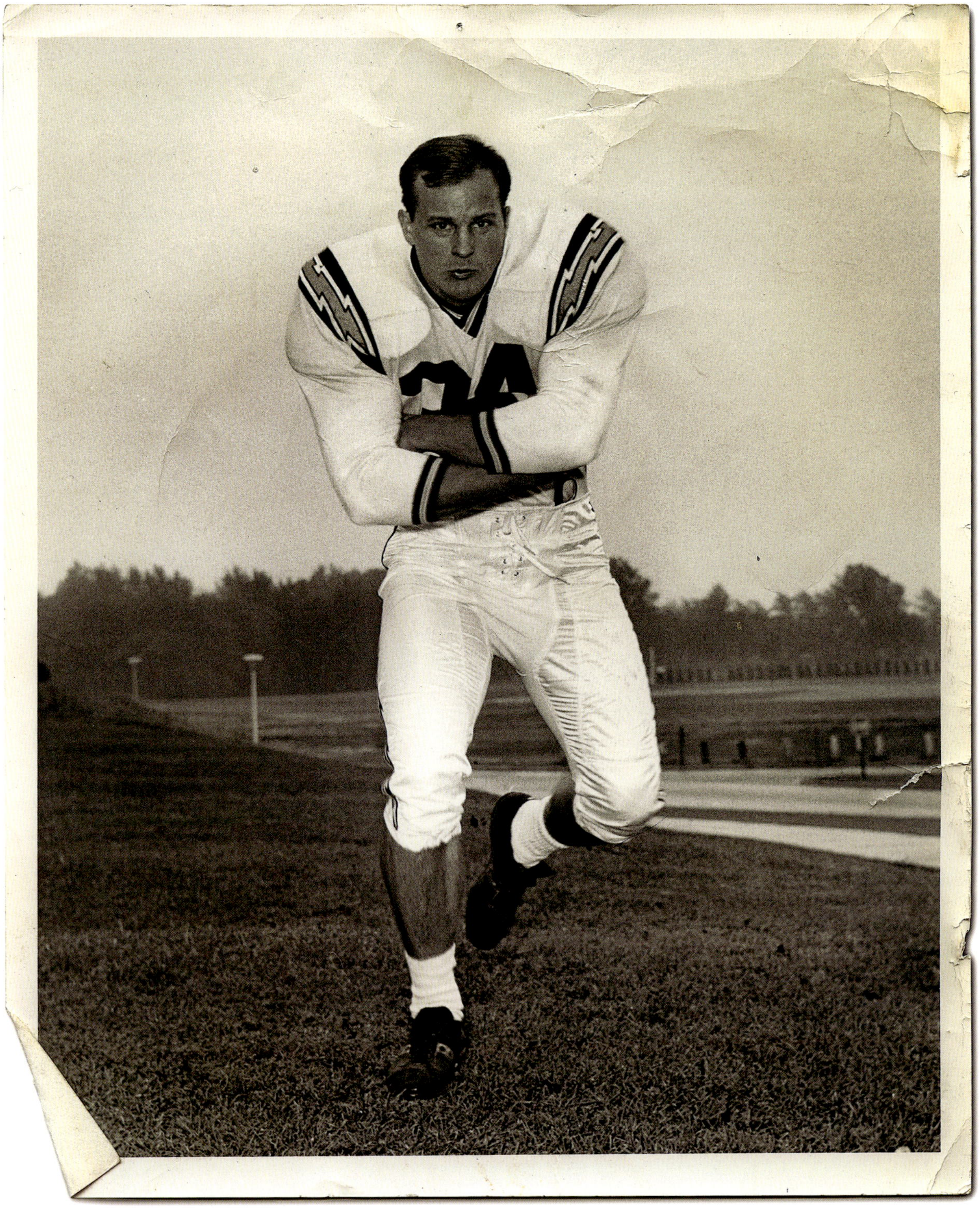

All images from *Excerpts from Silver Meadows* / **#10981-say-when** / found **#10982-ad-gulf-coast** / found and altered **#10955-barry-hido-football** / family album **#10955-hido-action** / family album **#10975-handshake** / family album

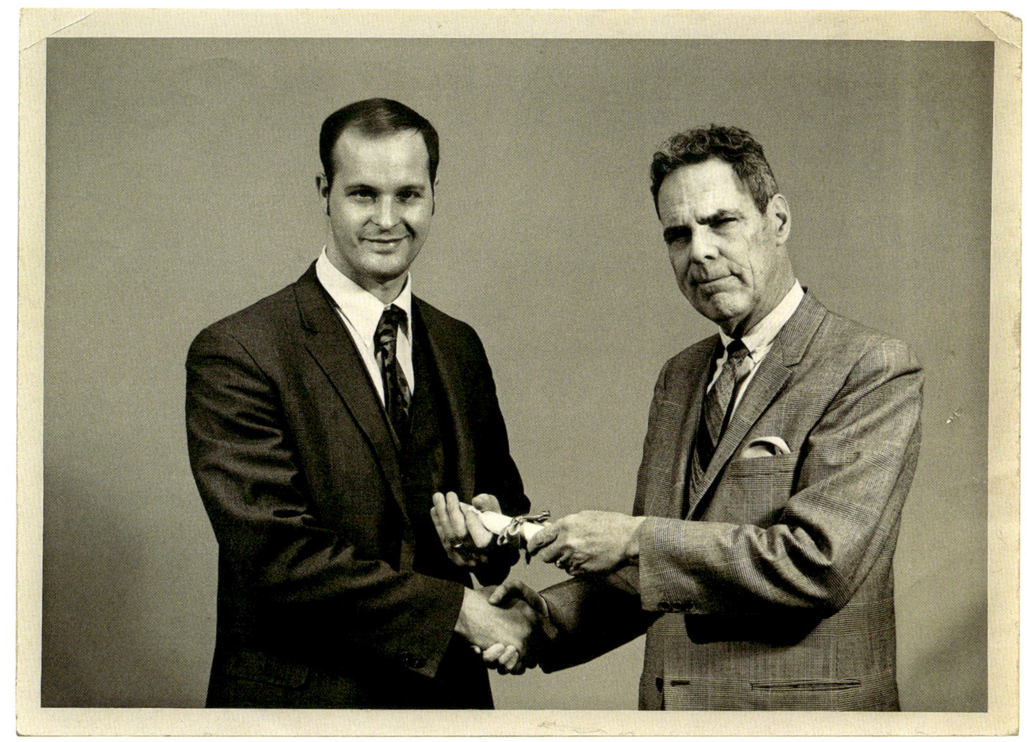

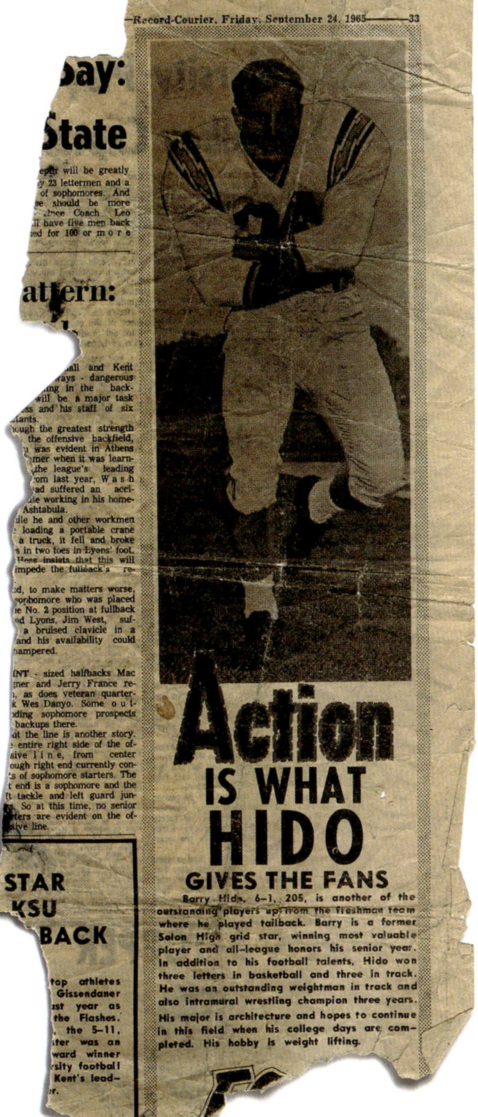

Record-Courier, Friday, September 24, 1965 — 33

Day:

State

epth will be greatly
y 23 lettermen and a
of sophomores. And
se should be more
since Coach Leo
ll have five men back
ed for 100 or more

attern:

all and Kent
ways - dangerous
ing in the back-
will be a major task
ss and his staff of six
stants.
ough the greatest strength
the offensive backfield,
was evident in Athens
mer when it was learn-
the league's leading
om last year, Wash
ad suffered an acci-
le working in his home-
Ashtabula.
ile he and other workmen
loading a portable crane
a truck, it fell and broke
s in two toes in Lyons' foot.
Hess insists that this will
impede the fullback's re-

d, to make matters worse,
sophomore who was placed
e No. 2 position at fullback
d Lyons, Jim West, suf-
a bruised clavicle in a
and his availability could
hampered.

INT - sized halfbacks Mac
ner and Jerry France re-
, as does veteran quarter-
k Wes Danyo. Some out-
ding sophomore prospects
backups there.
t the line is another story.
entire right side of the of-
sive line, from center
ough right end currently con-
s of sophomore starters. The
t end is a sophomore and the
t tackle and left guard jun-
s. So at this time, no senior
ters are evident on the of-
sive line.

STAR
KSU
BACK

top athletes
Gissendaner
st year as
the Flashes.
, the 5-11,
ster was an
ward winner
sity football
Kent's lead-
r.

Action IS WHAT HIDO GIVES THE FANS

Barry Hido, 6-1, 205, is another of the outstanding players up from the freshman team where he played tailback. Barry is a former Solon High grid star, winning most valuable player and all-league honors his senior year. In addition to his football talents, Hido won three letters in basketball and three in track. He was an outstanding weightman in track and also intramural wrestling champion three years. His major is architecture and hopes to continue in this field when his college days are completed. His hobby is weight lifting.

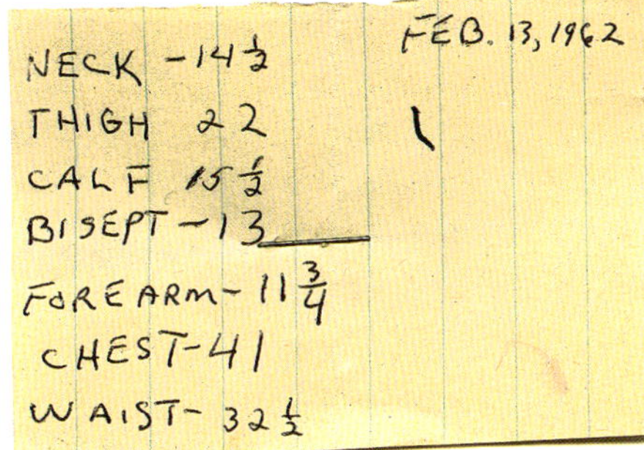

FEB. 13, 1962

NECK - 14 ½
THIGH 22
CALF 15 ½
BISEPT - 13
FOREARM - 11 ¾
CHEST - 41
WAIST - 32 ½

NOV. 27, 1962

BICEPS - 13 ¾"
FOREARM - 11 ⅞"
CHEST - 42
WAIST - ~~32~~ ½
THEI - 22 ½
CALF - 15 ½
NECK - 15 ½
RIST 7 ½

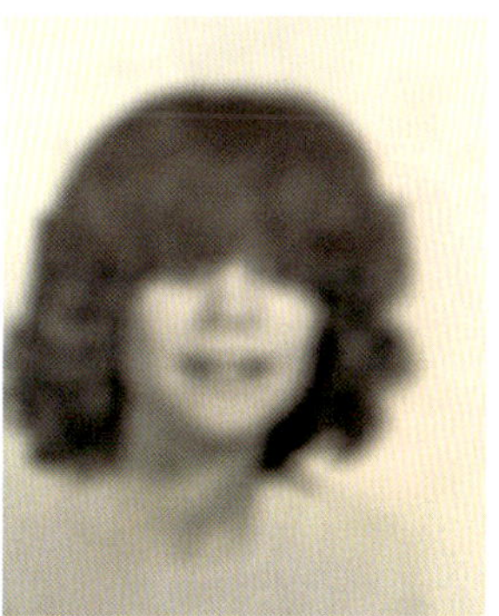

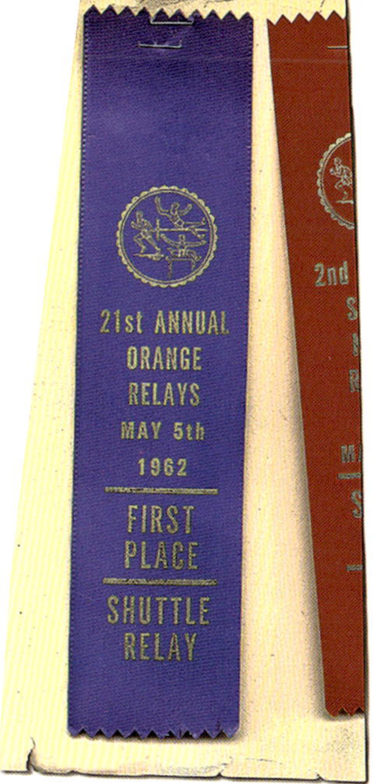

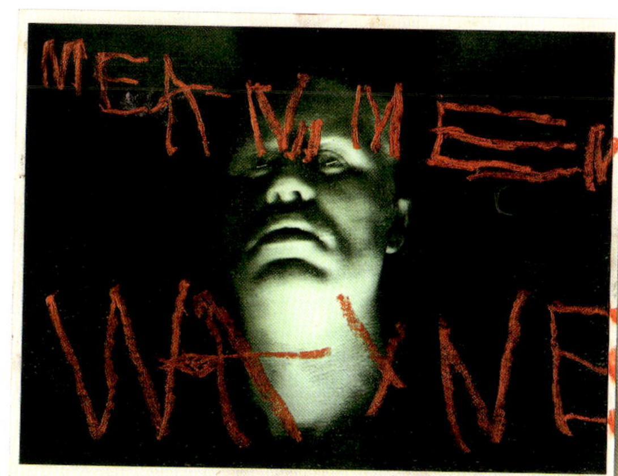

#10975-2-13-62 / family album #10975-11-27-62 / family album #10981-0528 / found and altered #10975-ribbons / family album #10980-mean-mean-wayne

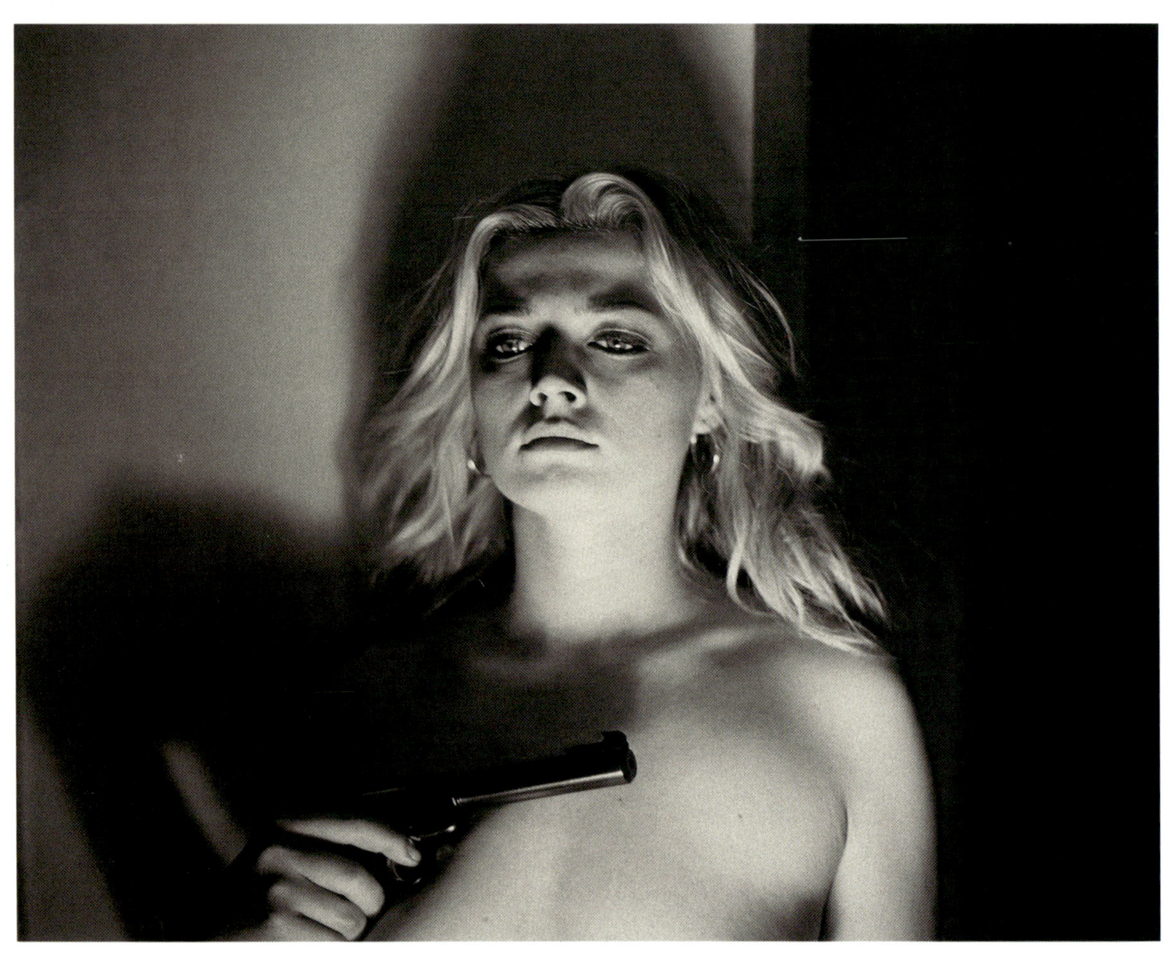

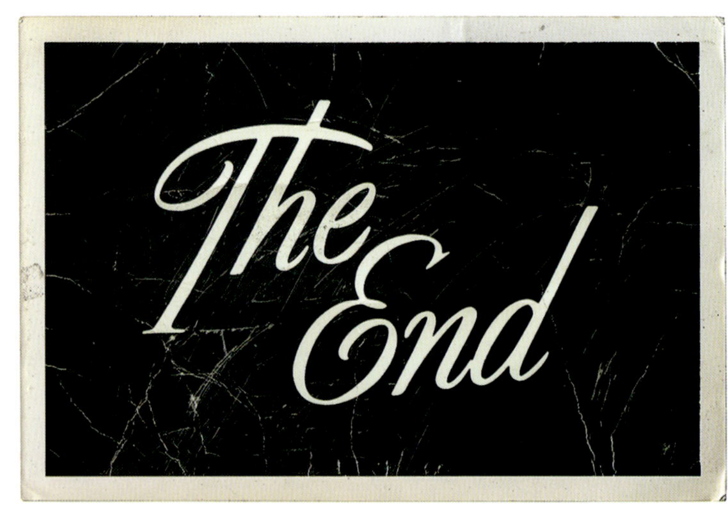
The End

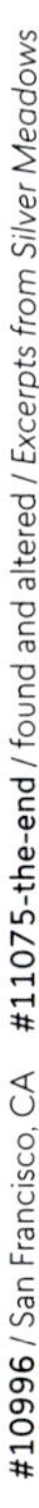

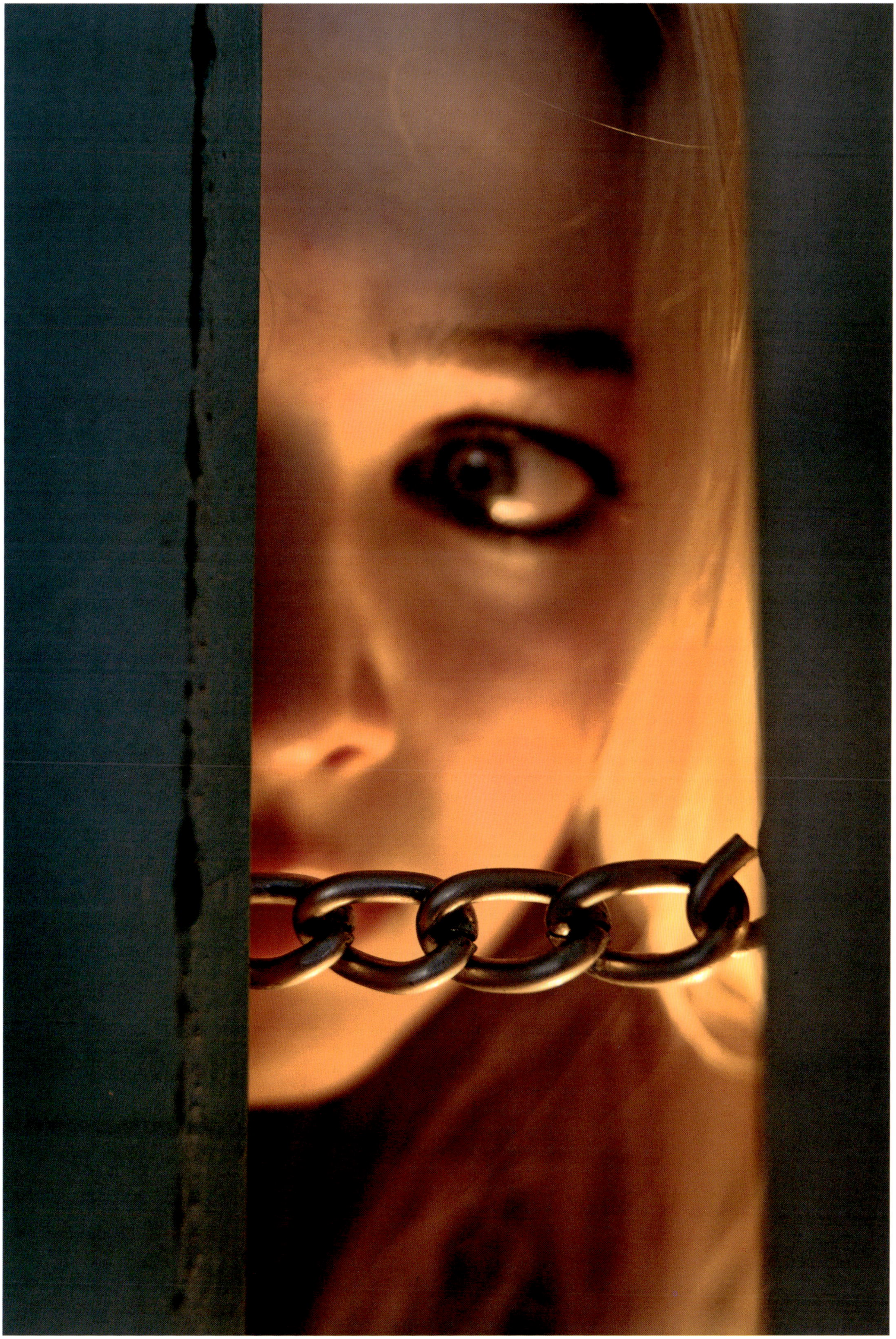

#10996 / San Francisco, CA **#11075-the-end** / found and altered / *Excerpts from Silver Meadows* **#10983-4622** / San Francisco, CA

EXCERPTS FROM SILVER MEADOWS 2013

Hido considers *Excerpts from Silver Meadows*, published in 2013, the "culmination" of everything he put into his previous books. And it came together at the "perfect moment," he says. At a point when he kept hearing that the future of publication was e-books, when photography was becoming widely understood as a form of rapid and feathery documentation—a vehicle for selfies—Hido wanted to create a book that "could only be a physical, tangible experience."

Of note are the four gatefolds in *Excerpts from Silver Meadows*, which Hido says are "intended to further the notion of having to peel back the layers of what can exist inside the pages of a book." The other result of having "super-size gatefolds," he adds, is that "viewers have to sit their asses down and get off of their phones to look through each page." This is a book created as the result of considerable time and thought. It is meant to be experienced with considerable time and thought, as well.

Excerpts from Silver Meadows is a challenging composition of portraits, landscapes, and personal and vintage photographs and documents that tell a number of stories—or one story, in different ways. As always in Hido's work, these stories reveal themselves through shadows, and never under direct light. On the other hand, this is perhaps Hido's most openly "personal" work, crossing a previous border of apparent privacy.

Perhaps more than his previous books, *Excerpts* is specific to the Ohio streets where Hido grew up. In fact, Silver Meadows was the name of the main drag that bisected his neighborhood. The photographs in this book may have been taken elsewhere, but poetically, Hido returns to 1970s suburban Ohio with these compositions—in part because he cannot return to that Ohio otherwise. It no longer exists, though Hido still finds it in "pockets of undeveloped land in eastern Washington," in the Sacramento–San Joaquin Delta during the winter months, or in stretches of California's Central Valley on a rainy day. "Those places are surrogates," he says, for environments that are resigned to live on only in his memory and old family albums.

"Much of the Ohio I grew up in has been plowed over by strip malls," Hido explains, but it nevertheless informs the backdrop of his works, and, whether or not viewers know it, is the origin of what the photographer calls his "cast of characters"—open spaces, empty living rooms, and anonymous expressions among them. That said, Hido's works are free of any indications of time or, worse yet, times gone by. These photographs are not nostalgic. They have the immediacy of unexpected and sometimes totally unwelcomed flashbacks, happening in real time. And despite the multiple characters in *Excerpts*, it is a work of solitude. "I don't have assistants setting up lights for the perfect shot," says Hido. "I'm usually just outside or in my car, alone."

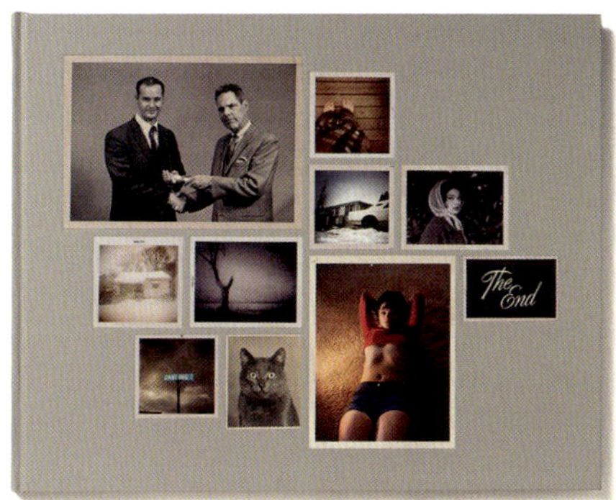

Excerpts from Silver Meadows
Published 2013 by Nazraeli Press
16½×13½ inches
108 pages

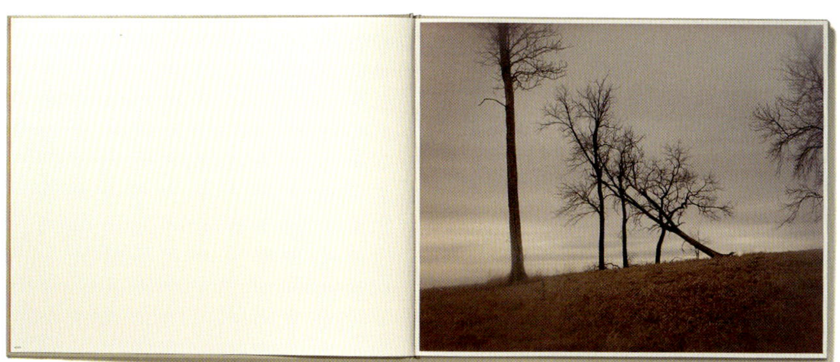

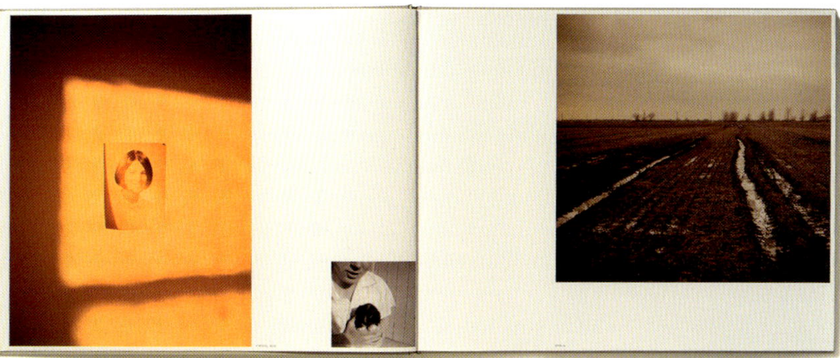

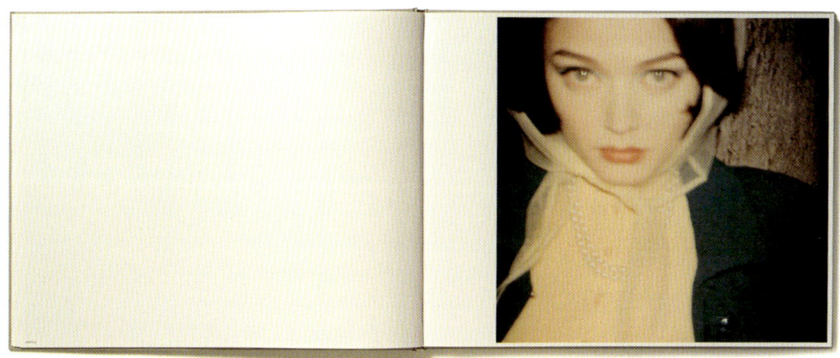

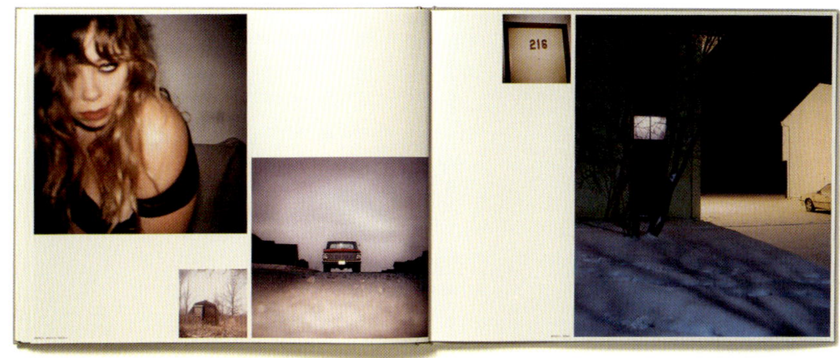

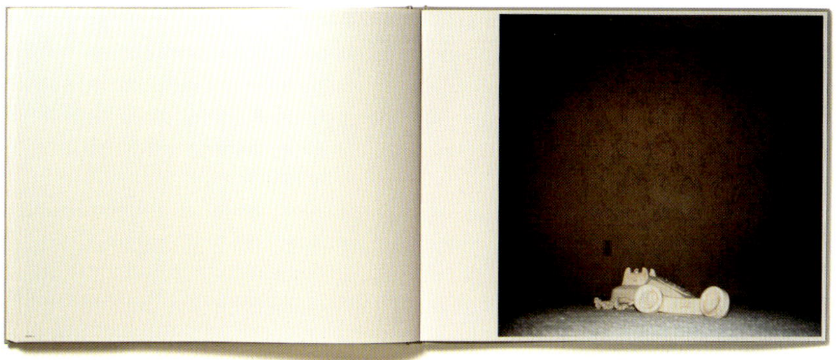

2014 Aperture publishes *Todd Hido on Landscapes, Interiors, and the Nude* as part of The Photography Workshop Series

2014 Group exhibition: *Edward Hopper and Photography*, Whitney Museum of American Art, New York

2015 Reflex Amsterdam publishes *Khrystyna's World*

2015 Hotshoe publishes *Crude Metaphors*

2015 Begins experimenting with risograph printing and solvent-transfer techniques

2015 Pier 24 Photography acquires complete archive of published works (ongoing as new work is published)

2015 Finishes construction on new studio in Oakland, California

2016 Deadbeat Club Press publishes *Collage Number Three*

2016 Group exhibition: *The Open Road: Photography and the American Road Trip* (traveling exhibition produced by Aperture)

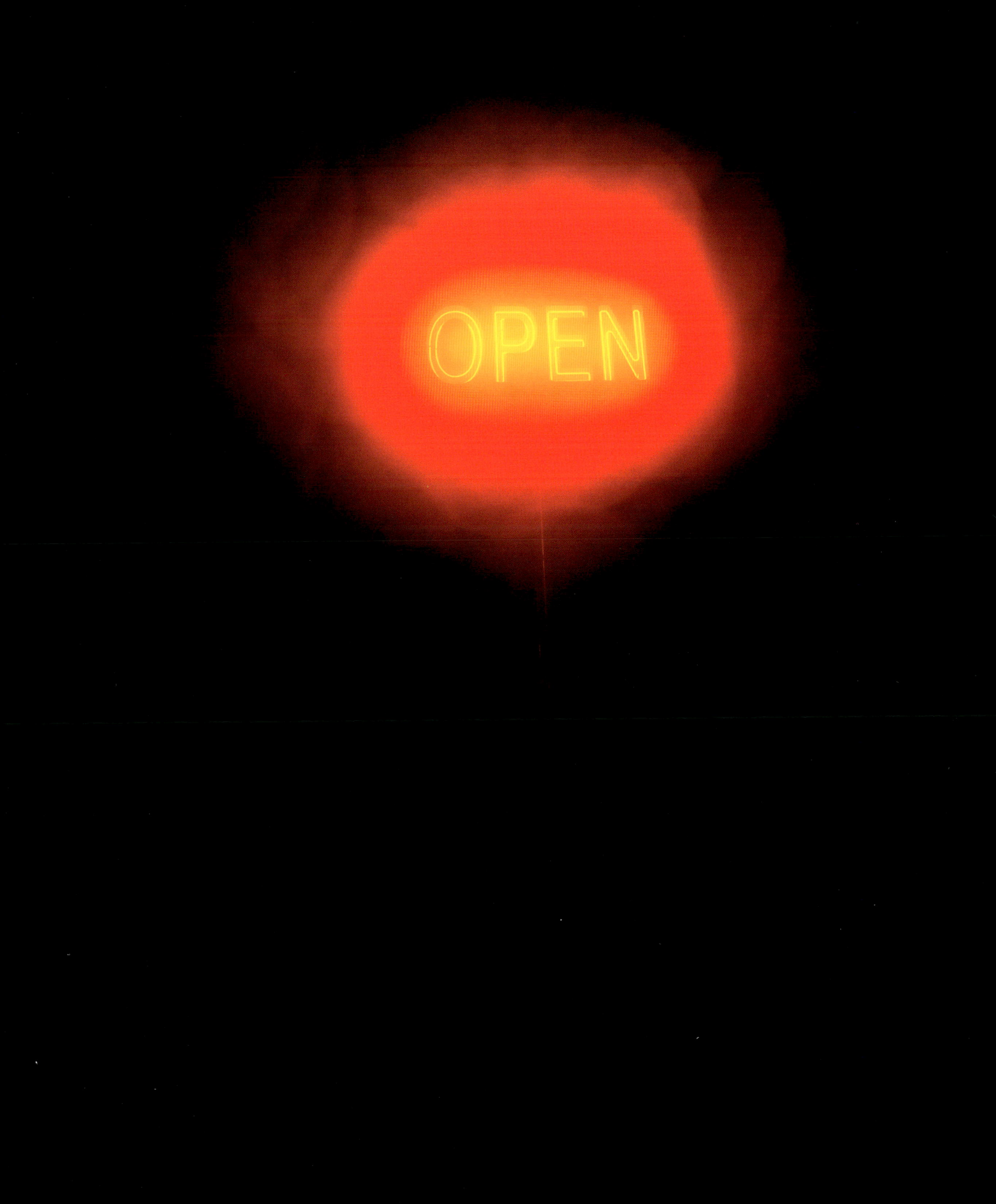

#11174-7345 / Conneaut, OH

#11171-6868 / Ravenna, OH

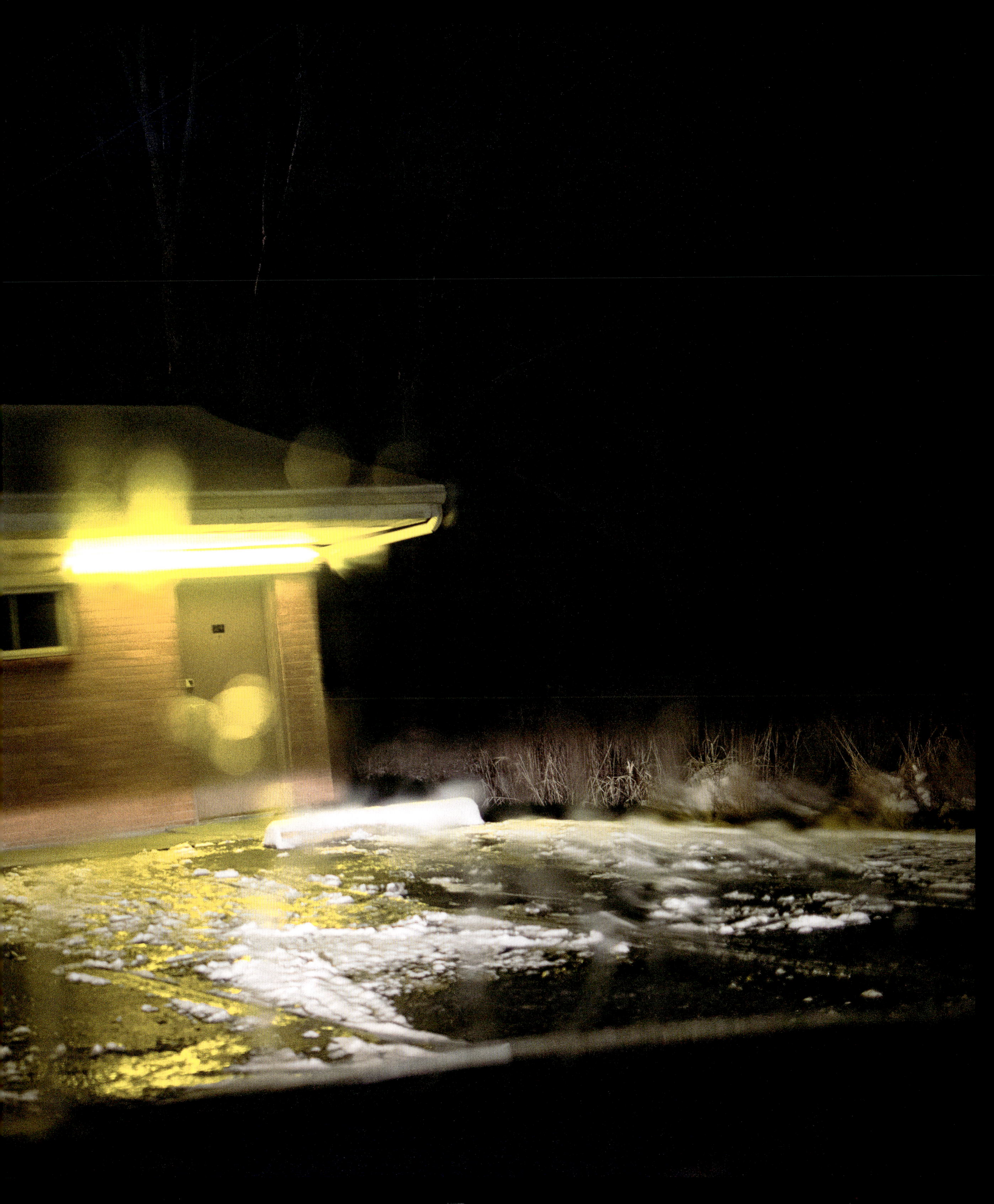

#11234-6207 / Vallejo, CA

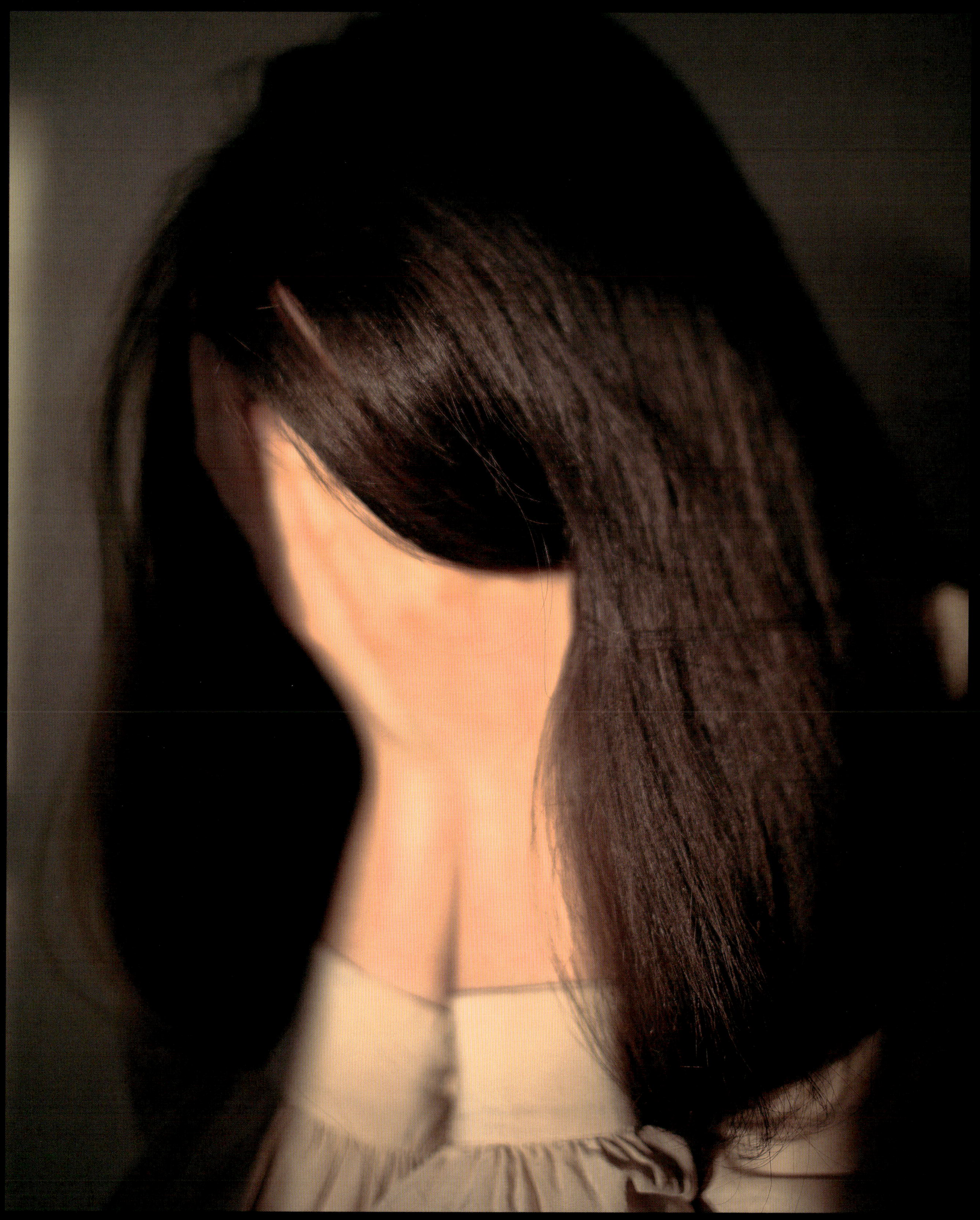

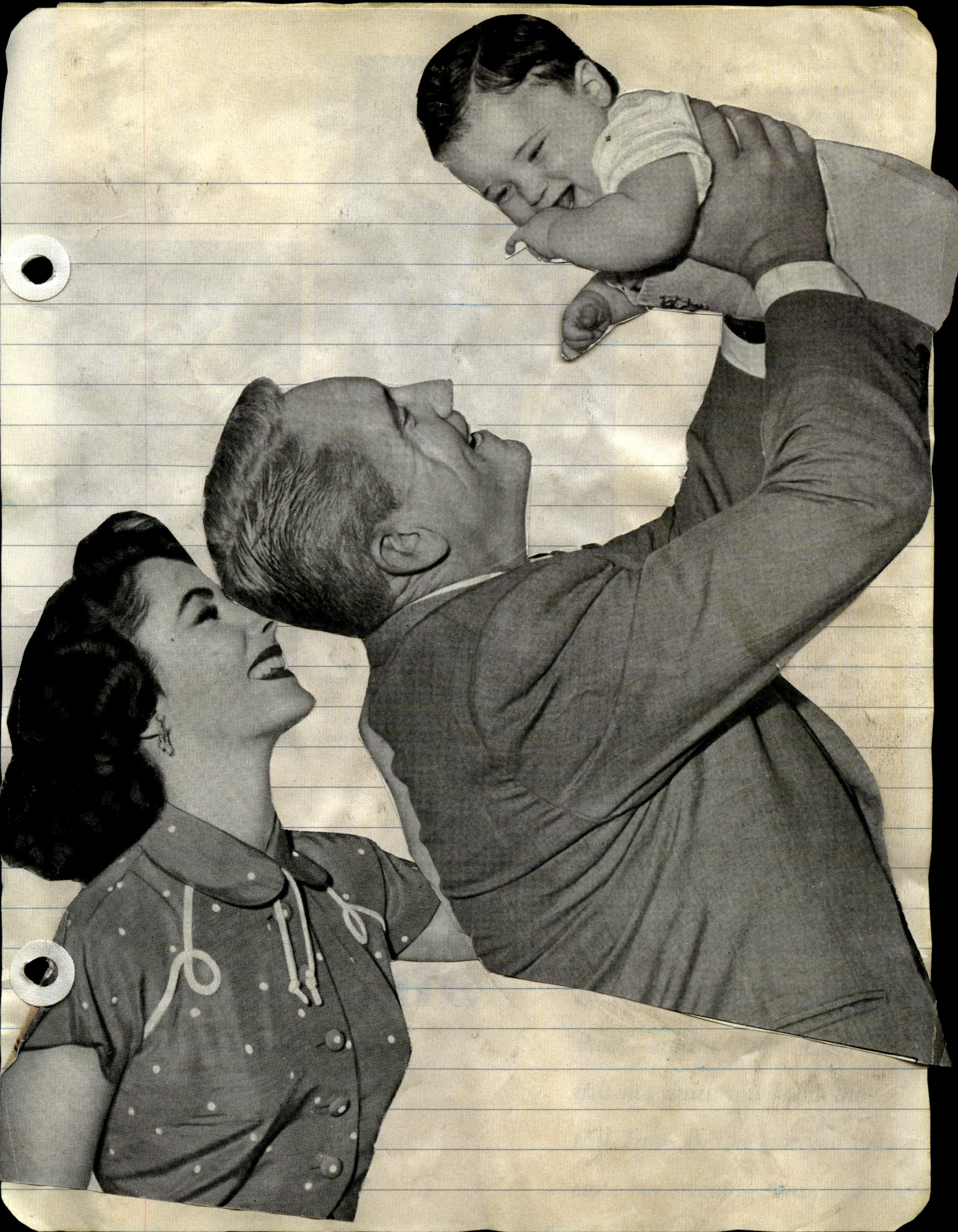

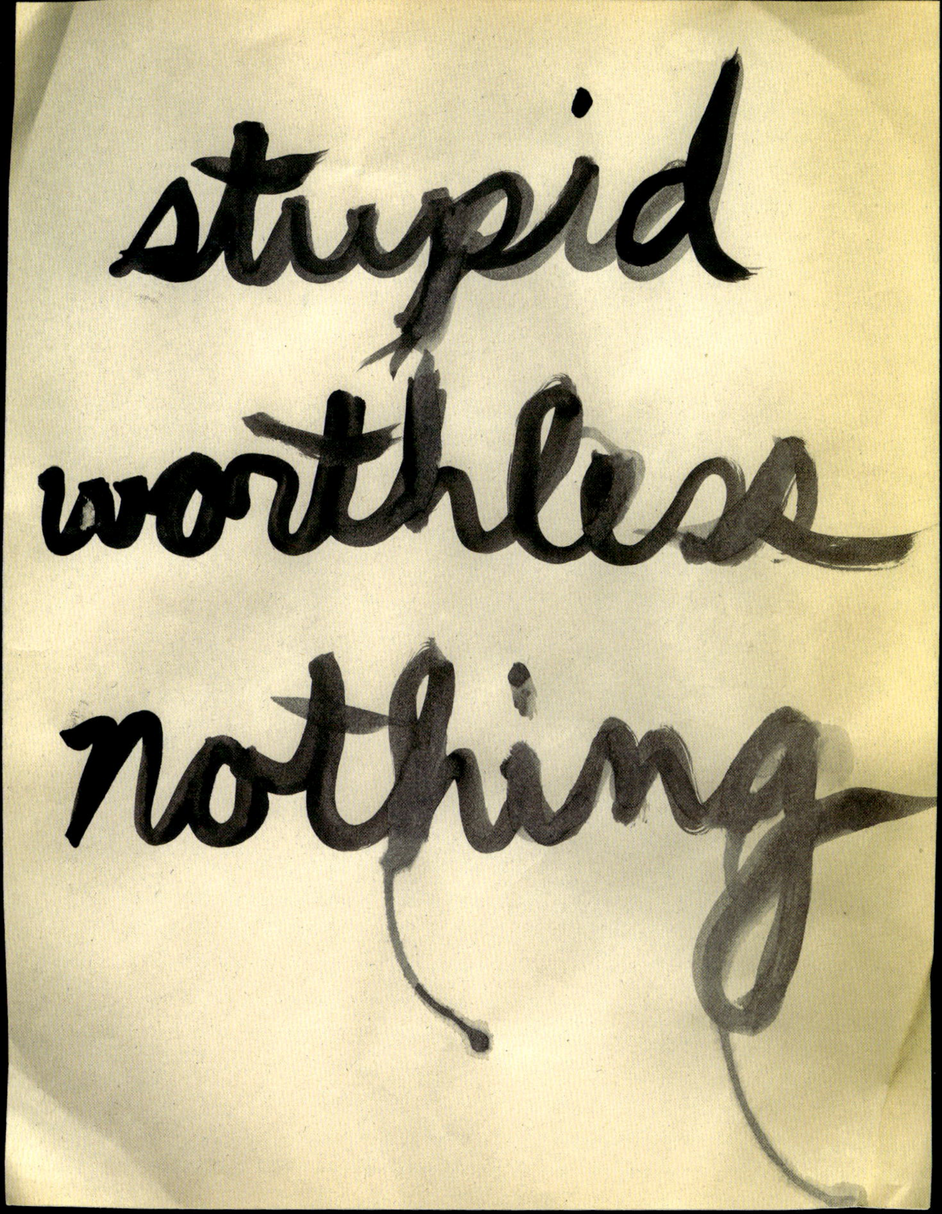

stupid
worthless
nothing

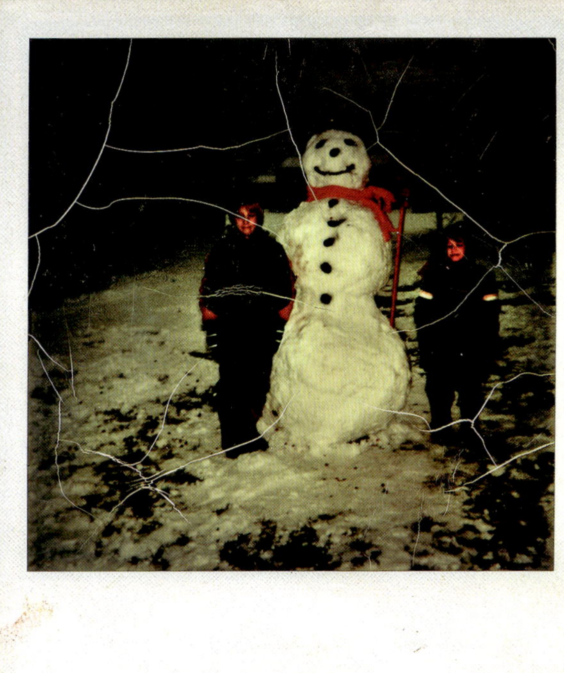

#11350-stupidworthless / Oakland, CA #11360-snowmanpola / family album

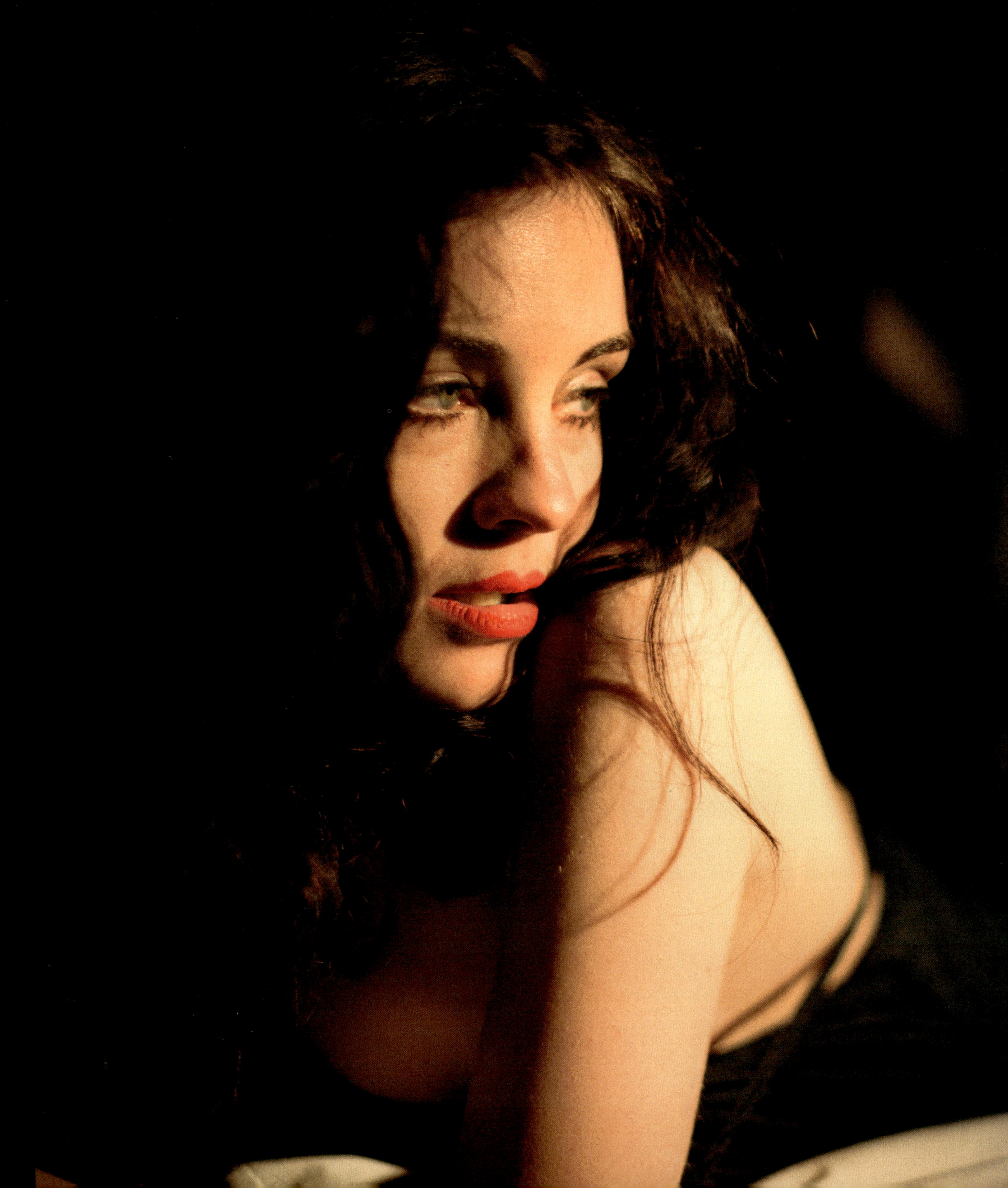

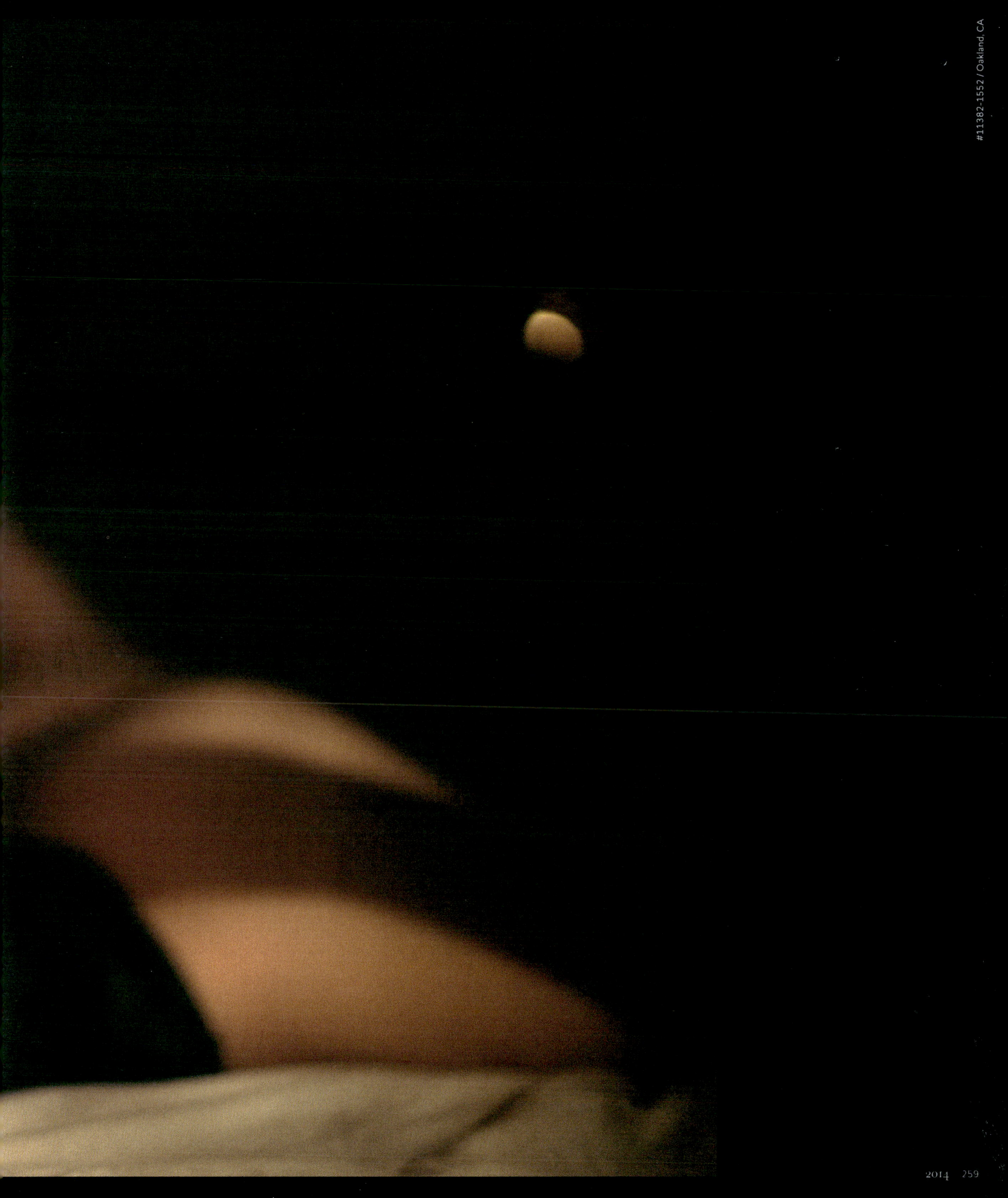

#11382-1552 / Oakland, CA

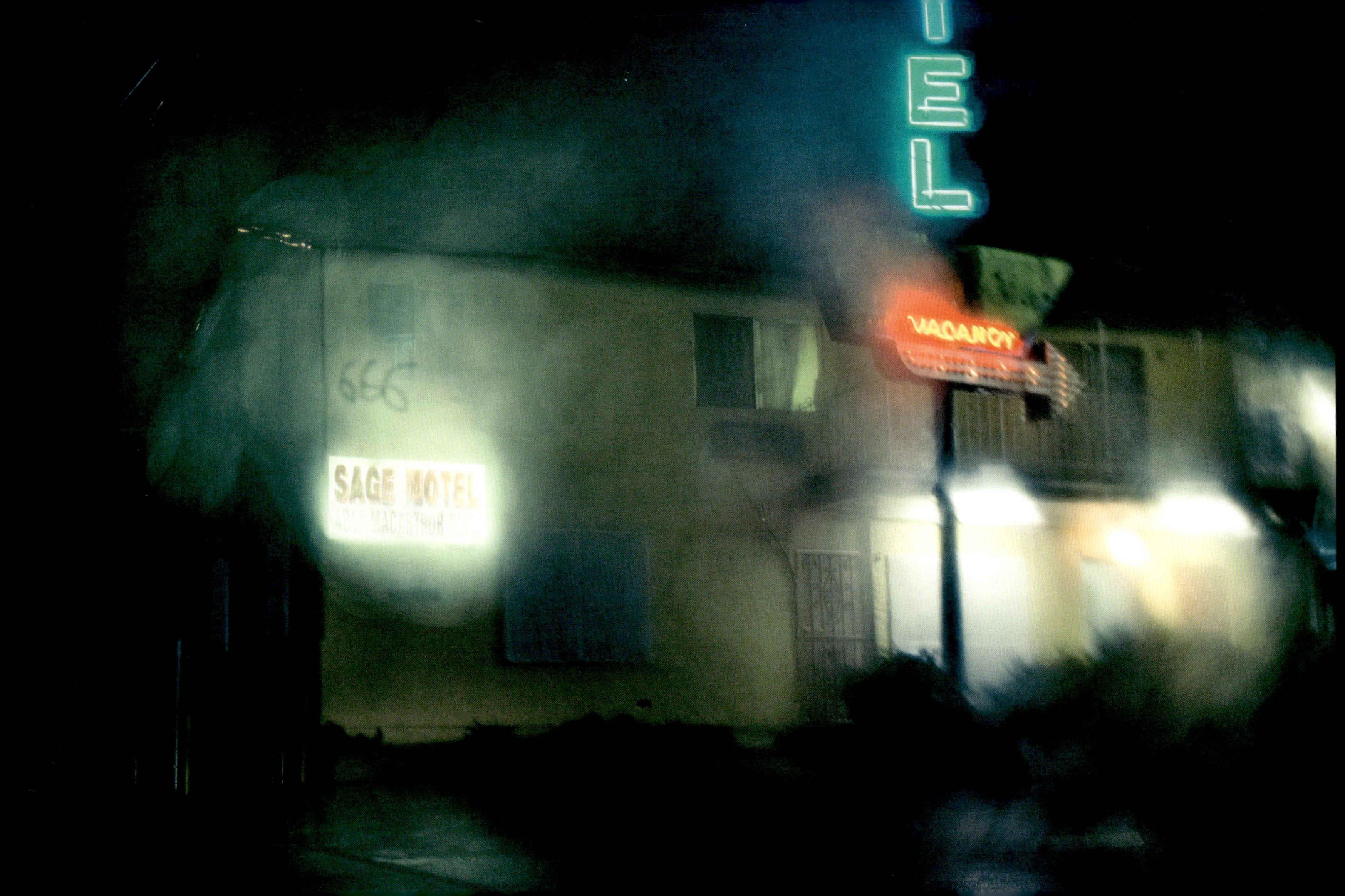
VACANCY
SAGE MOTEL

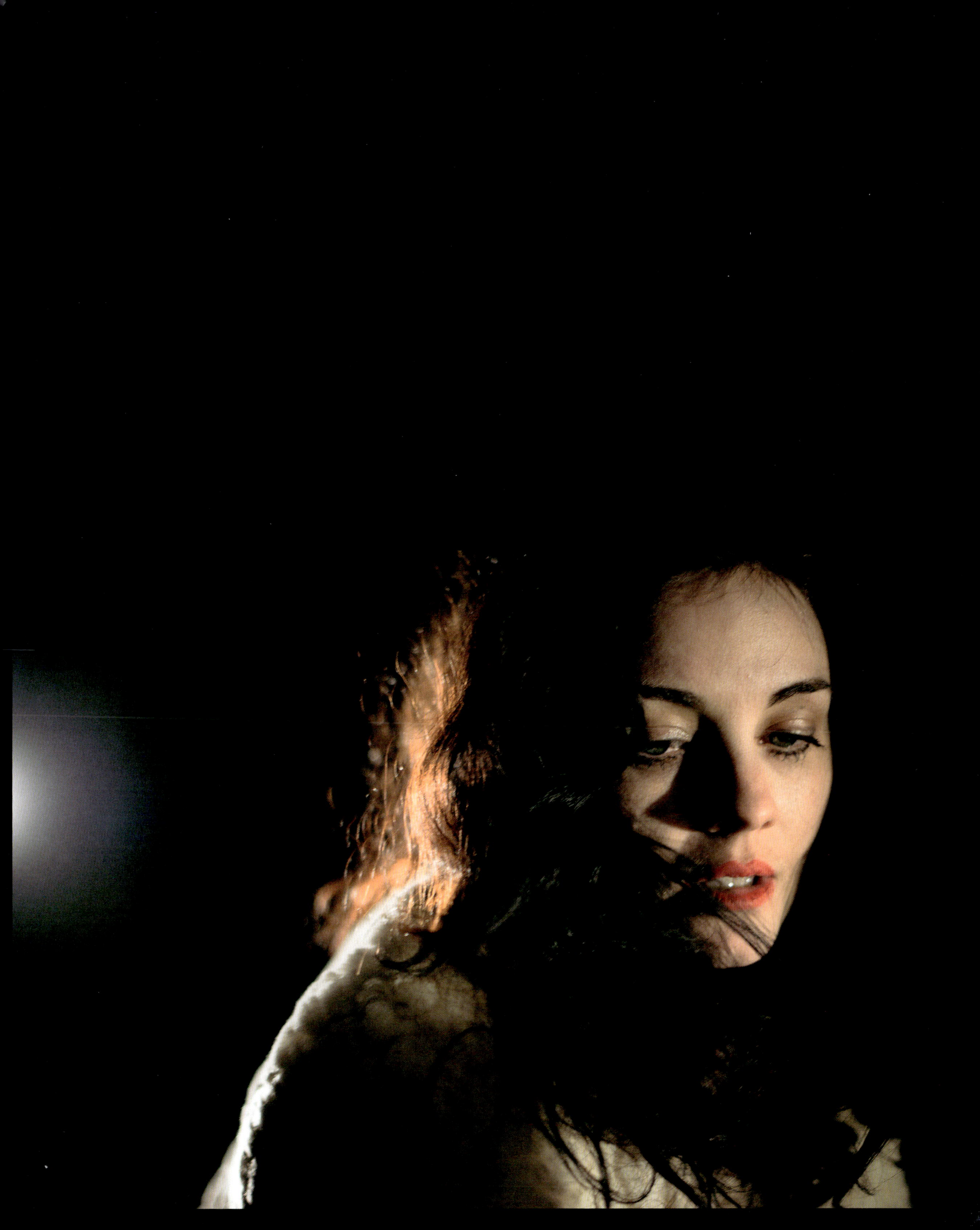

#11374-8145 / Oakland, CA #11382-1611 / Oakland, CA

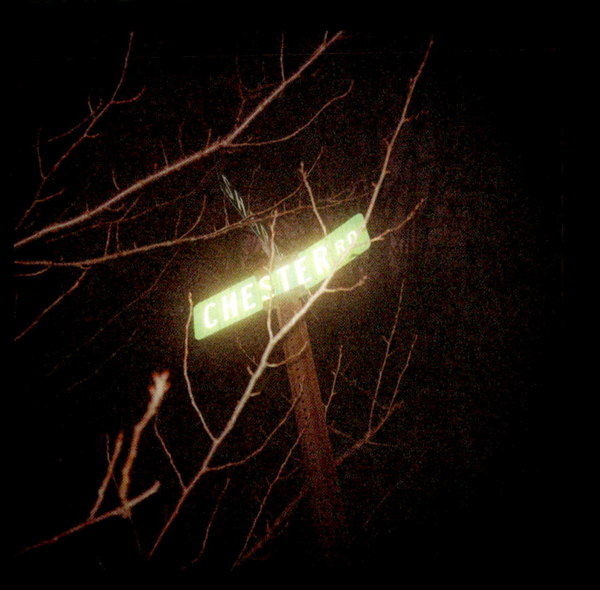

 2014

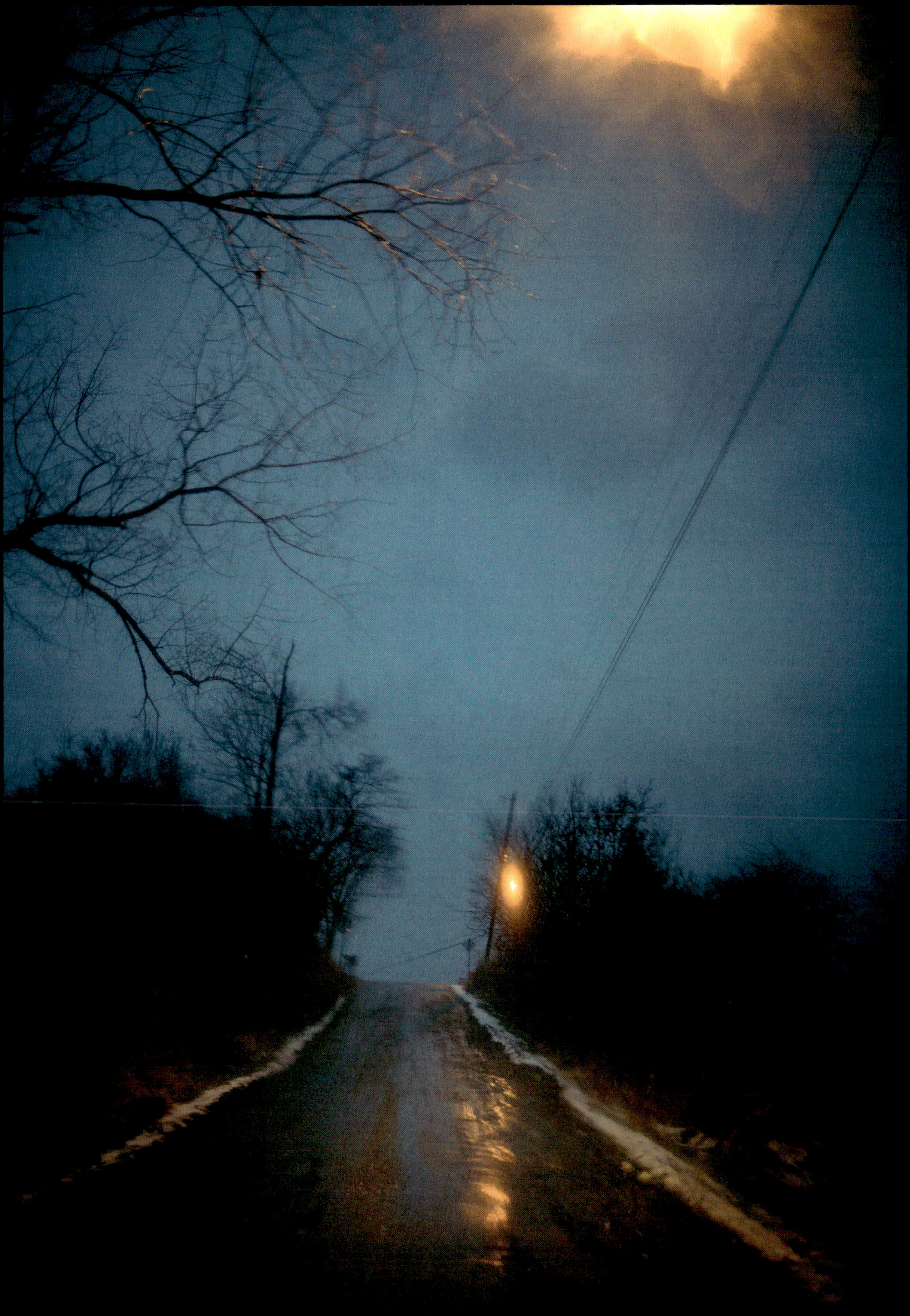

#11406-G / Columbus, OH #11385-1746 / Streetsboro, OH

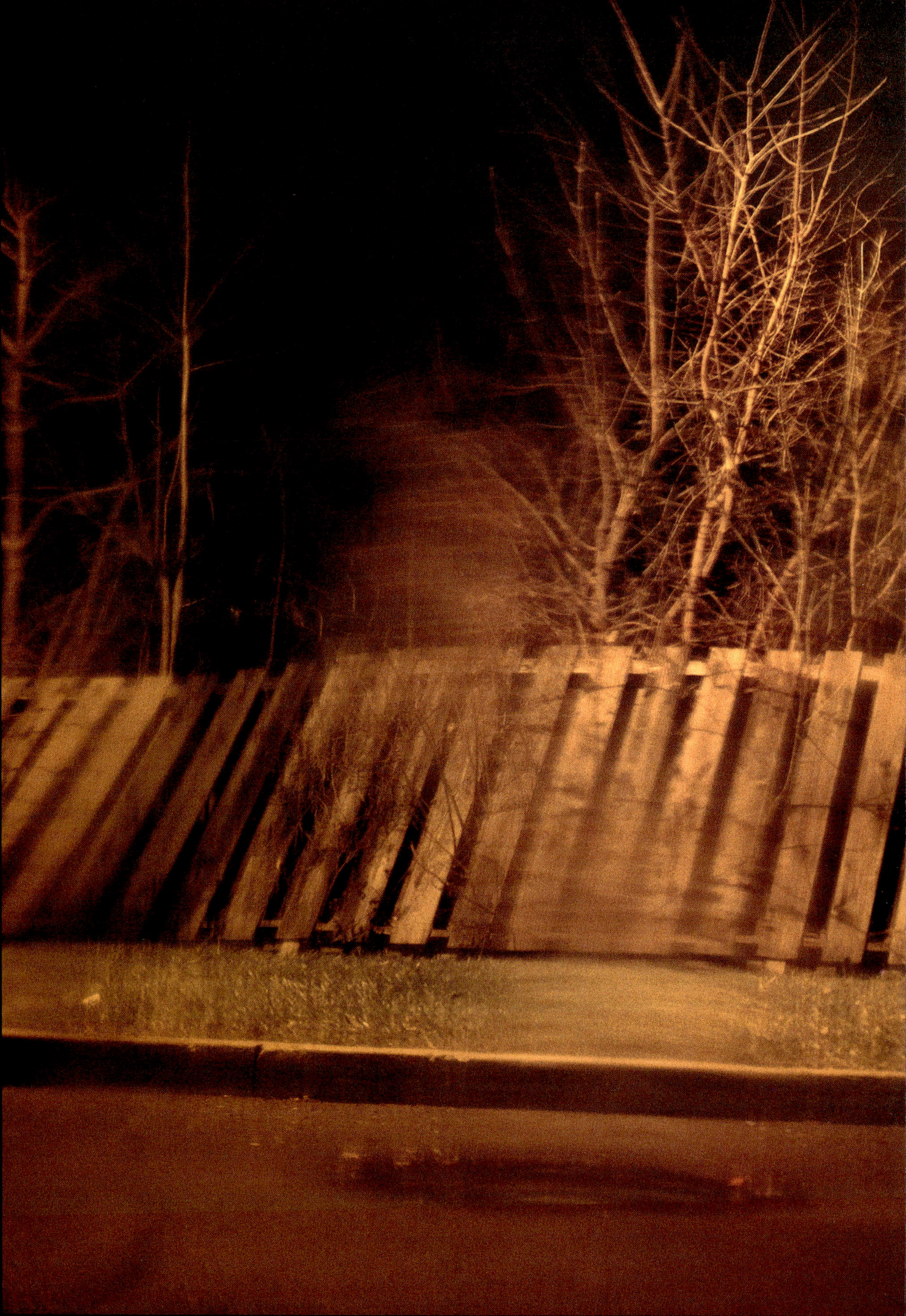

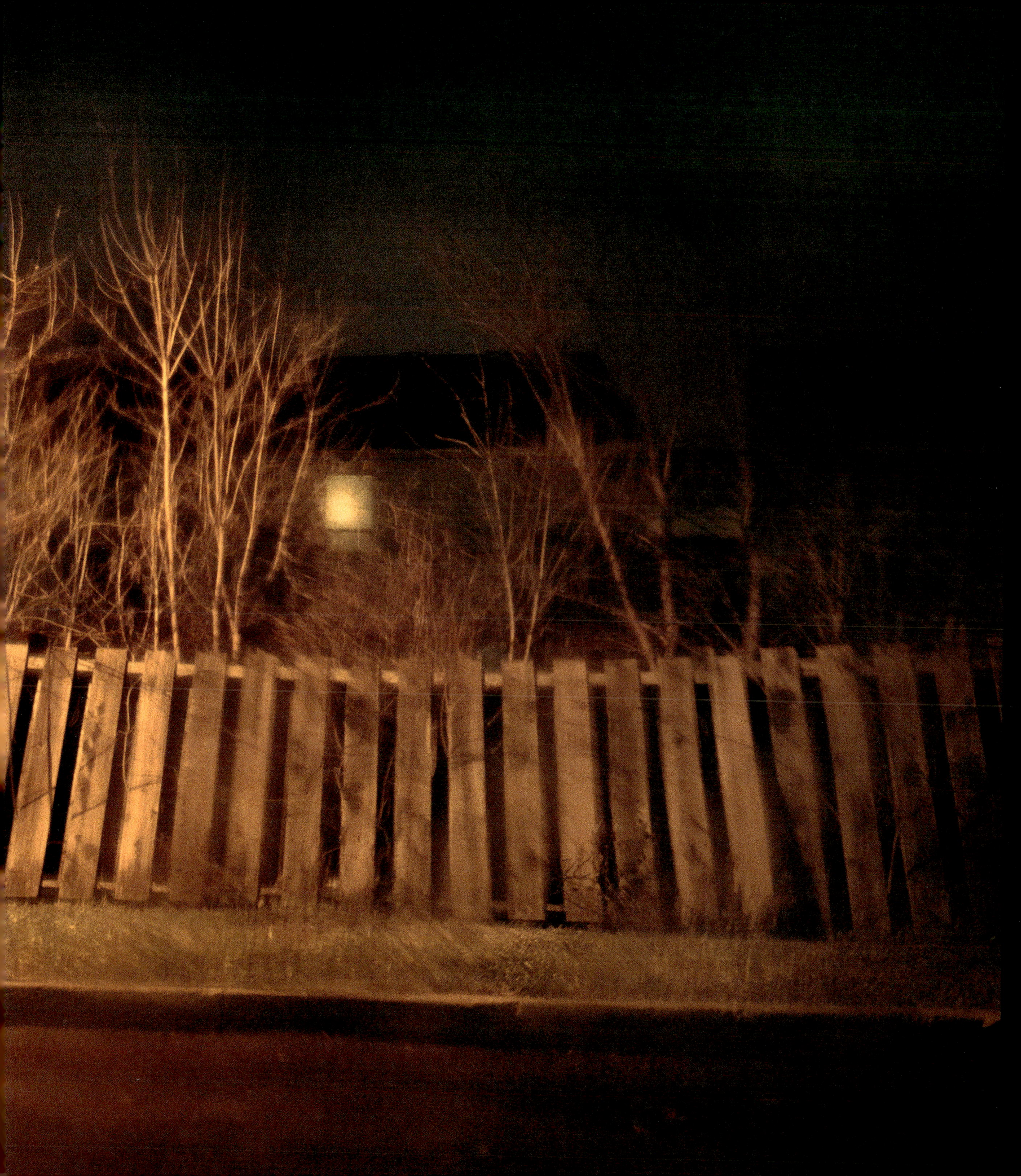

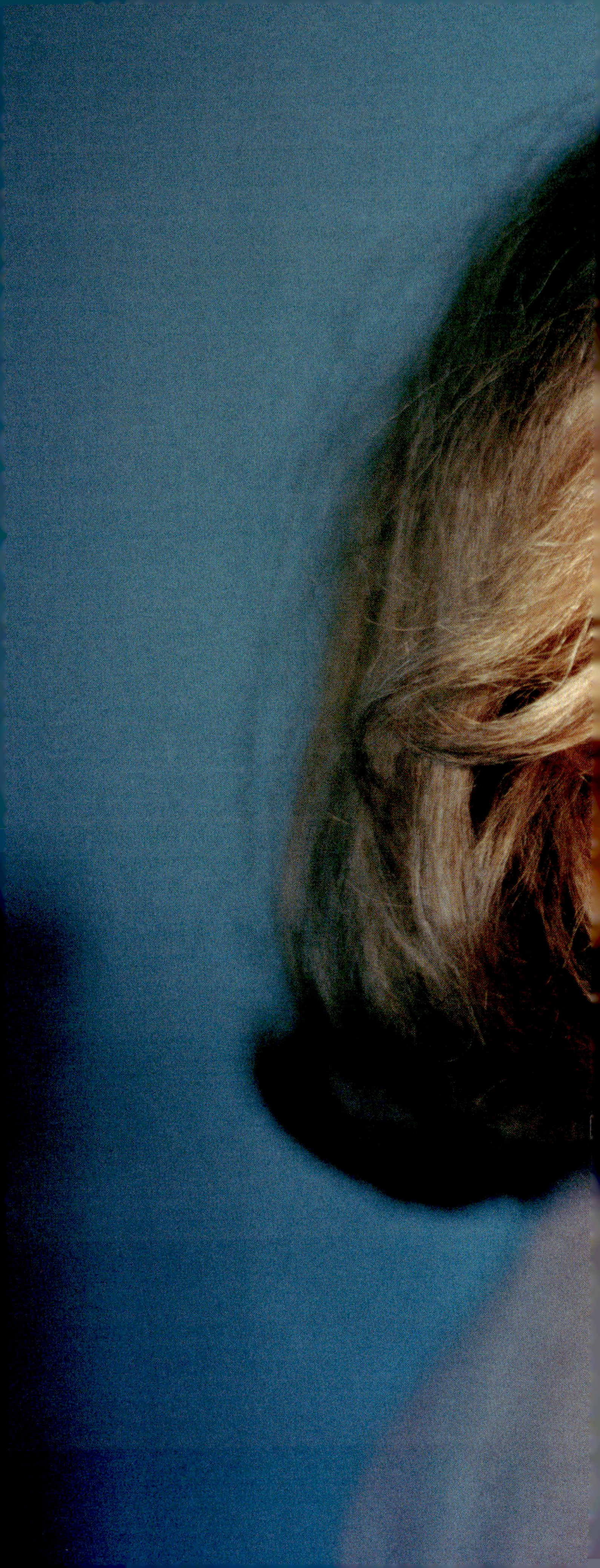

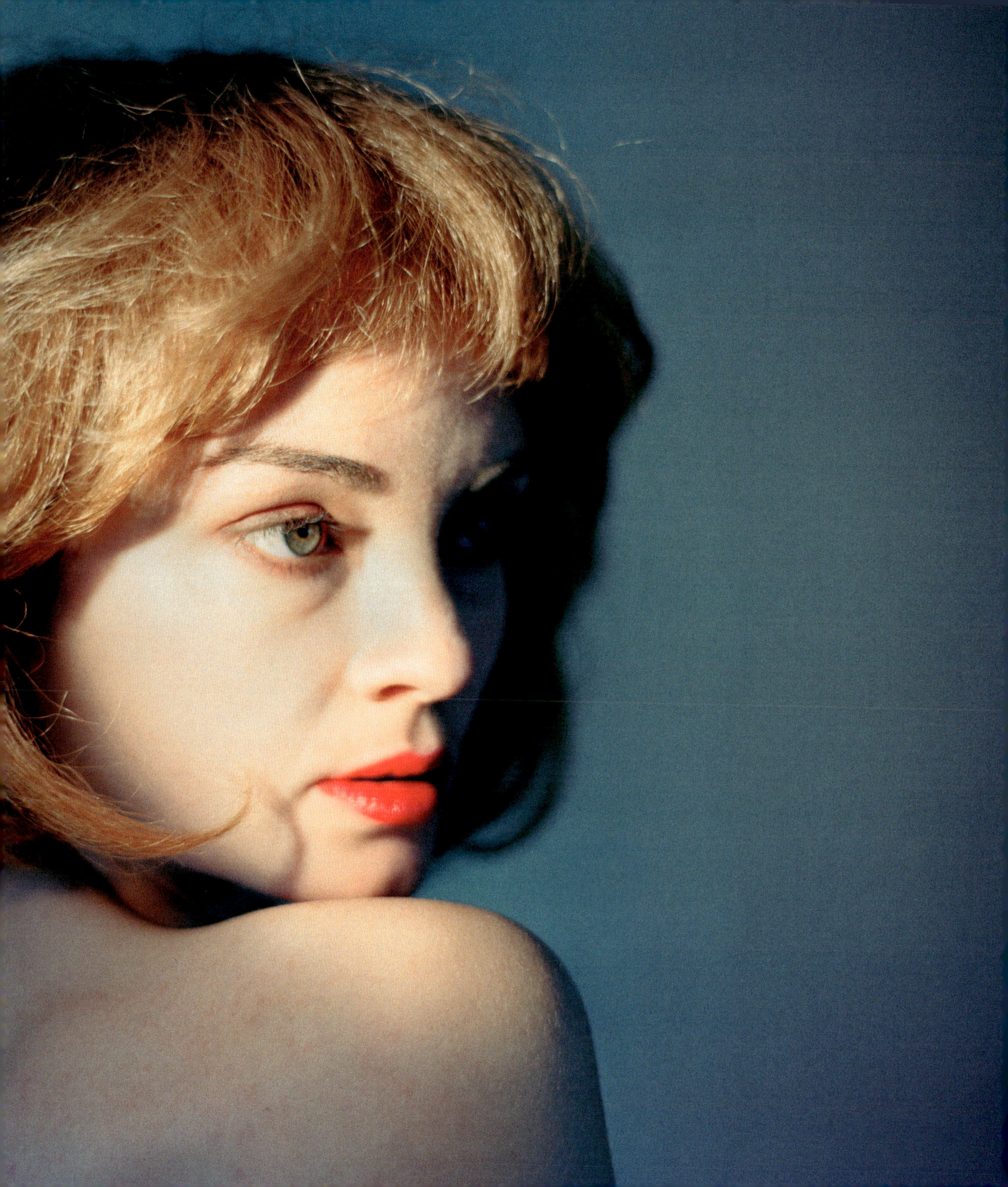

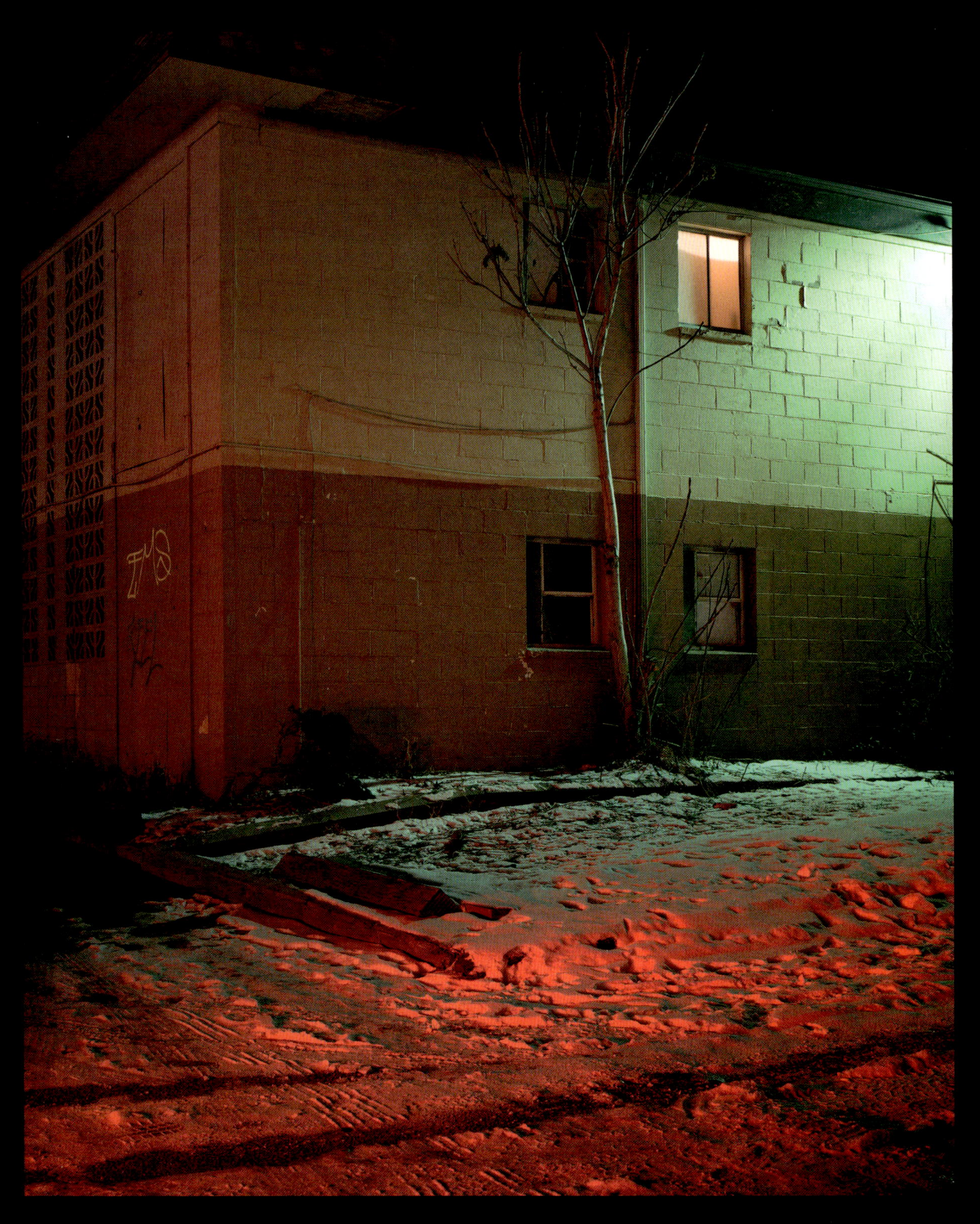

Oakland, CA

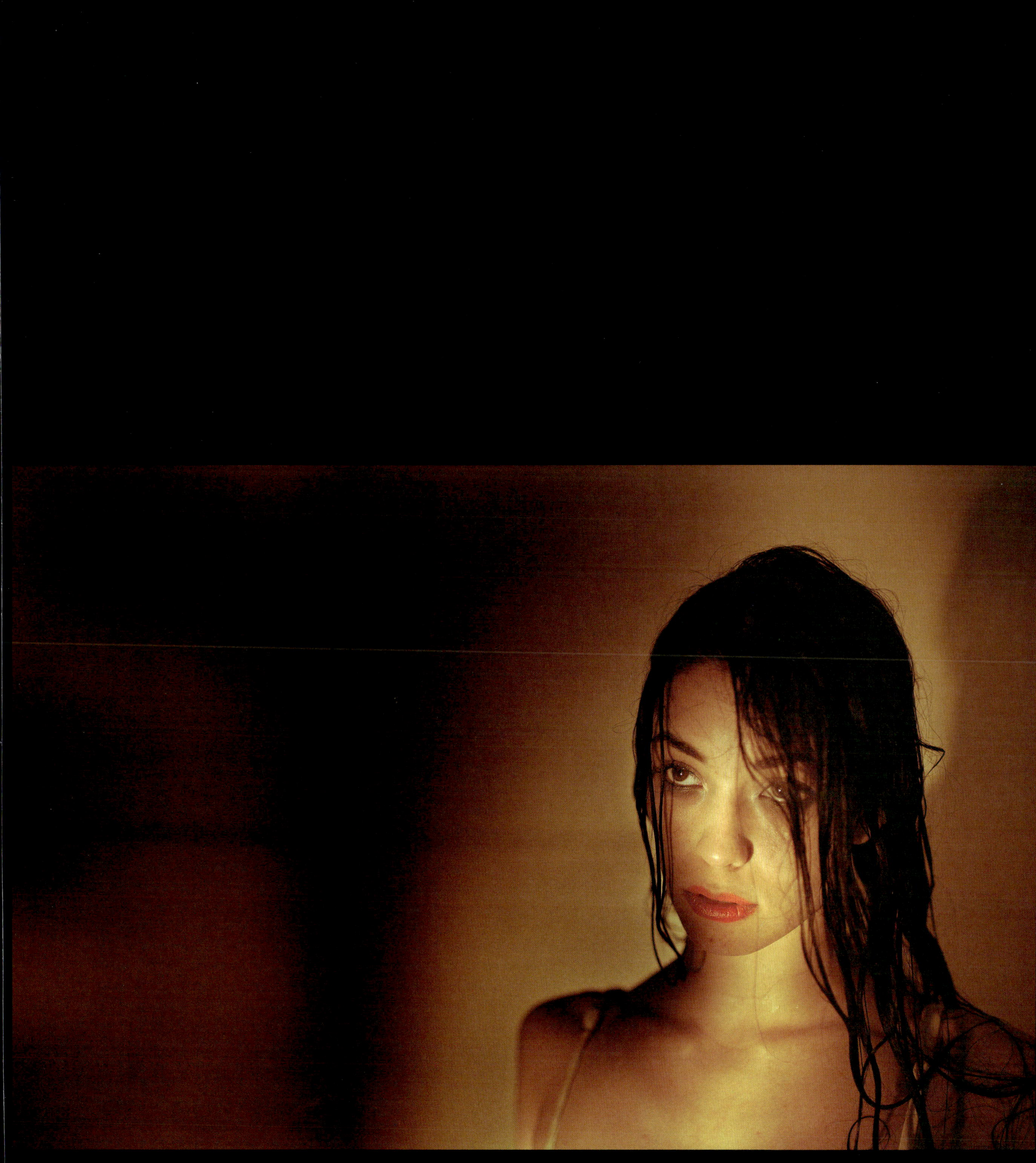

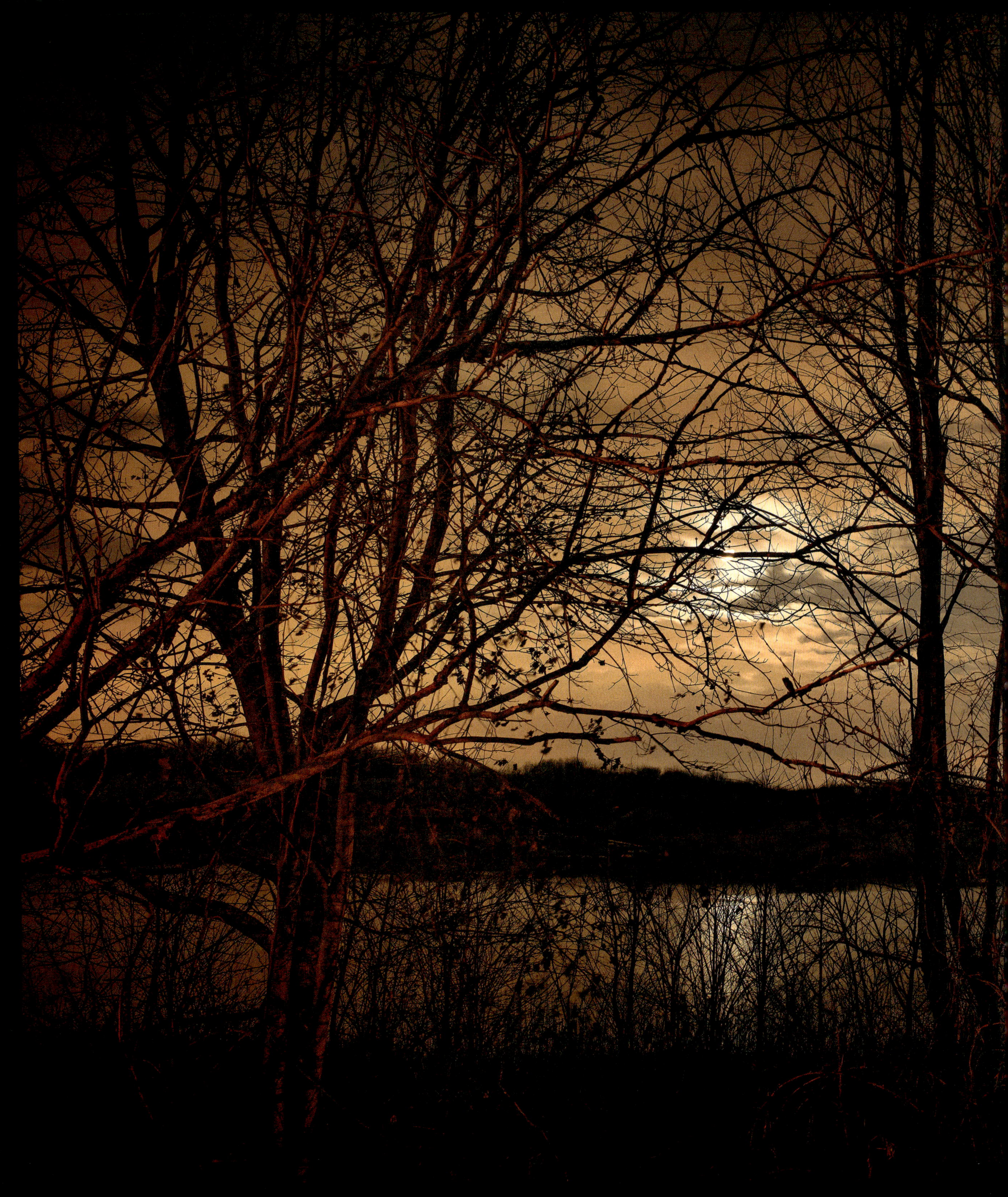

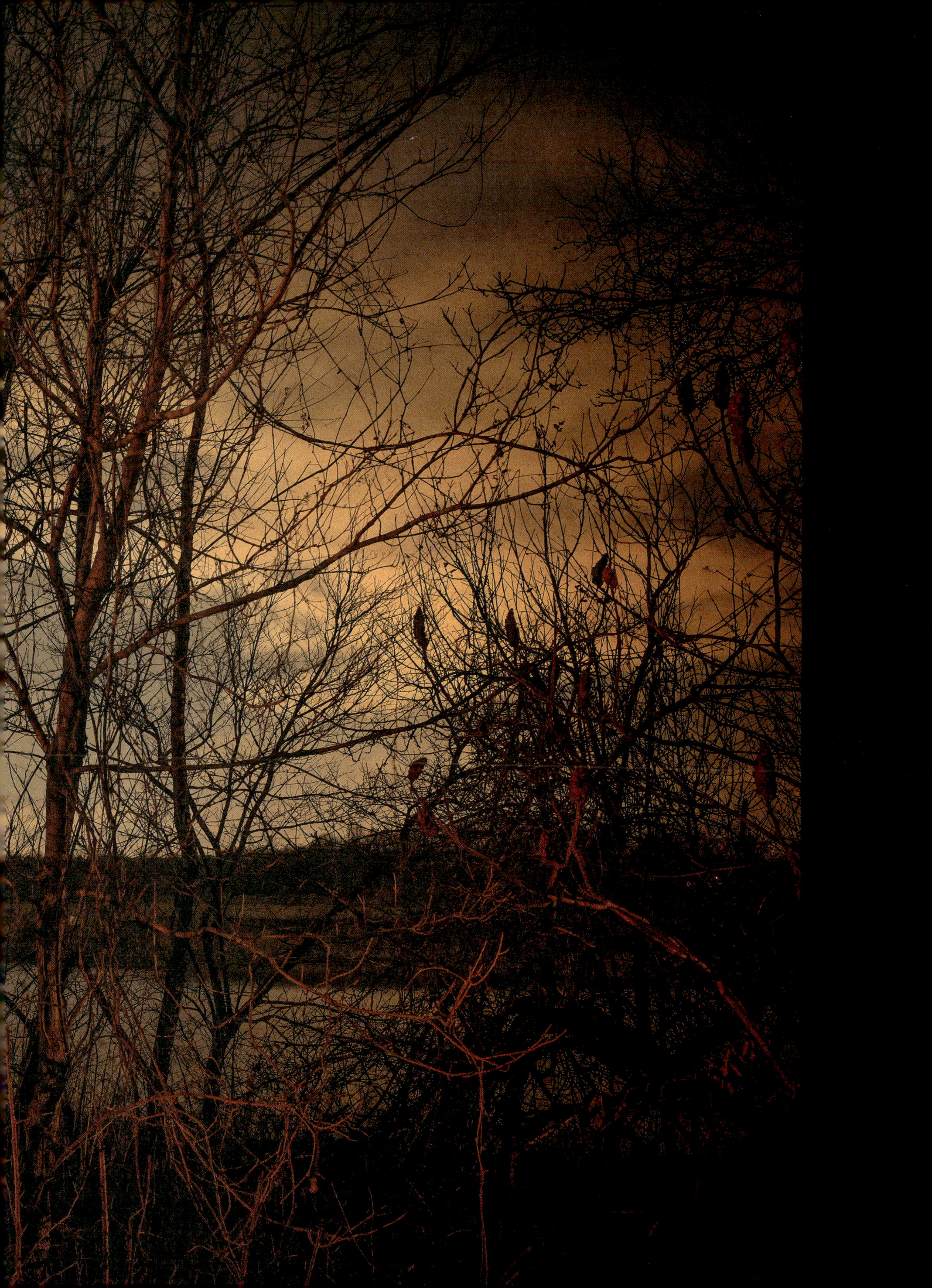

#11599-5811 / Kent, O

Intimate Distance: Twenty-Five Years of Photographs, A Chronological Album
Photographs by Todd Hido
Essay by David Campany
Texts by Katya Tylevich

Editor: Denise Wolff
Designer: Bob Aufuldish, Aufuldish & Warinner
Production Director: Nicole Moulaison
Production Manager: Thomas Bollier
Copy Editor: Madeline Coleman
Proofreader: Sally Knapp
Senior Text Editor: Susan Ciccotti
Work Scholars: David Arkin and Melissa Welikson

Additional staff of the Aperture book program includes:
Chris Boot, Executive Director; Sarah McNear, Deputy Director; Lesley A. Martin, Creative Director; Amelia Lang, Managing Editor; Kellie McLaughlin, Director of Sales and Marketing; Richard Gregg, Sales Director, Books; Angie Chen, Sales and Rights Associate; Samantha Marlow, Assistant Editor; Katie Clifford, Associate Editor; Taia Kwinter, Assistant to the Managing Editor

The images in this publication are sequenced in the chronological order in which they were made with the exception of the following: *#1741-pussy-cat, #3101-a, #3511, #3972-d, #5114, #5407, #9314-ad-heart-panties, #10690-1, #11174-7345, #11374-8145, #11406-G, #11669-1778.*

First edition, 2016
Printed in China
10 9 8 7 6 5 4 3

Library of Congress Control Number: 2016905668
ISBN 978-1-59711-360-1

To order Aperture books, contact:
+1 212.946.7154
orders@aperture.org

For information about Aperture trade distribution worldwide, visit:
aperture.org/distribution

aperture
Aperture Foundation
547 West 27th Street, 4th Floor
New York, N.Y. 10001
aperture.org

Aperture, a not-for-profit foundation, connects the photo community and its audiences with the most inspiring work, the sharpest ideas, and with each other—in print, in person, and online.

ACKNOWLEDGMENTS

This book was made possible, in part, by a generous contribution in 2014 from Pier 24 Photography toward the scanning and mastering of my entire archive of published works. I am humbled by their ongoing commitment to my work.

I want to thank Jamie Lunder for being an unending source of positive encouragement and incredible support for my work. With remarkable grace, you have always come through at exactly the times I needed it the most. In addition, my appreciation for your help in placing my work in multiple public and private collections is unbounded.

I also wish to express my gratitude to my friends, advisors, collaborators, and supporters:

Fred and Laura Bidwell, Darius Himes, Markus Schaden, Ed and Deanna Templeton, Bob Aufuldish, Chris Pichler, Maya Ishiwata, Alison Crosby, Connie and Stephen Wirtz; Pier 24 Photography: Christopher McCall, Seth Curcio, and Allie Haeusslein; Casemore Kirkeby: Julie Casemore, Stefan Kirkeby, and Jennifer O'Keeffe; La Galerie Particulière: Guillaume Foucher, Frédéric Biousse, and Audrey Bazin; Reflex Amsterdam: Alex Daniels and Viola Winokan; Rose Gallery: Rose Shoshana, Molly Toberer, and Mark Giorgione; Bruce Silverstein Gallery: Bruce Silverstein, Liam Van Loenen, and Meredith Rockwell; Baldwin Gallery: Richard Edwards and Kiki Jai Raj; Edge Reps: Rob Magnotta, Kacy Strand, and Madeline Park.

Aperture Foundation: Chris Boot, Denise Wolff, Nicole Moulaison, Thomas Bollier, Madeline Coleman, and David Arkin. Les éditions Textuel: Marianne Théry and Manon Lenoir. David Campany and Katya Tylevich.

Candela Fine Art: Brad Boca; Hahnemuhle Paper: Veronica Cotter; General Graphics Exhibits: Brenda Sharp and Wing Law; Smith Anderson North: Rebecca Lukens; Mark Rutherford; Connect Art International: Andrew Bigler.

Aaron Hido, Barry Hido, Mary Hido, Robin Hido, Rebecca Jurado, Alexandra and Kevin Wong, Andrew and Ashley Hadzopoulos, Paul Palacios, Katie Baum, and Esneda Merced.

Thank you to all of the models and actors that I have worked with over the last twenty years, who are listed here in the order of appearance: Emily Hallowell, Laura Lawee, Jill Dreskin, Kendra Stanifer, Katie Kniestedt, Astrid Klein, Liliane Machado, Tobi Grover, Kumi, Sasha Monet, Thea Kinyon, Sita Edwards, Claudia Galata, Cynthia Gralla, Sarah Krebs, Lily Baldwin, Naomi Austin, Sandi Leeper, Vika Ivanova, Jennifer Hotz, Natasha Strange, Angela Butler, Melissa Dillard, Osula Freeman, Rebecca Cohen, Jessica Brown, Rachael Maier, Amanda Batz, Khrystyna Kazakova, Amanda Boe, Lindsay Gardner, Andrea Margaret, Tara Niami, Brittany Markert, and Rachel Sutton.

France Pierson, Aubri Balk, Pirjo Visser, Brynn Doering, Suzanne Rubin, Look Model Agency, Jeffery Hasseler, and Meaganne McCandess.

My assistants and interns: Shy Adelman, Amanda Boe, Hannah Braue, Lance Brewer, Norma Cordova, Pippa Drummond, Oscar Edwards, Julia Haas, Whitney Hubbs, Melissa Kaseman, Yoni Klein, Rosey Lakos, Brittany Luby, Phillip Maisel, Lauren Malechek, Misaki Matsui, Chris Nickel, Jena Shellito, Kelsey Shell, Minami Takashima, and Ashlei Quinones.

Very special thanks to Dianne Weinthal, who has brought an unmatched level of professionalism to the other side of my desk.

To Audrey and Owen: it's been a pleasure to watch you grow into the kind and thoughtful people you are. I am proud of you every single day. The organization of my work has always been for your future.

And finally to Marina Luz: you bring a sense of gravity, inspiration, joy, and rejuvenation into my life. I look forward to floating freely upon the waters of vulnerability in order to find that elusive, but not impossible, shore of certainty.

—T. H.